DEFINING DOCUMENTS
IN AMERICAN HISTORY

United States Involvement in the Middle East

DEFINING DOCUMENTS
IN AMERICAN HISTORY

United States Involvement in the Middle East

Editor

Michael Shally-Jensen, PhD

Volume 1

SALEM PRESS
A Division of EBSCO Information Services, Inc.
Ipswich, Massachusetts

GREY HOUSE PUBLISHING

Cover: (Photo) A desert scene in the United Arab Emirates. Image by ali suliman, via iStock. (Law) Public Law 107–40 107th Congress Joint Resolution *To authorize the use of United States Armed Forces against those responsible for the recent attacks launched against the United States.*

Copyright © 2020 by EBSCO Information Services, Inc., and Grey House Publishing, Inc.

Defining Documents in American History: United States Involvement in the Middle East, published by Grey House Publishing, Inc., Amenia, NY, under exclusive license from EBSCO Information Services, Inc.

All rights reserved. No part of this work may be used or reproduced in any manner whatsoever or transmitted in any form or by any means, electronic or mechanical, including photocopy, recording, or any information storage and retrieval system, without written permission from the copyright owner. For information, contact Grey House Publishing/Salem Press, 4919 Route 22, PO Box 56, Amenia, NY 12501.

∞ The paper used in these volumes conforms to the American National Standard for Permanence of Paper for Printed Library Materials, Z39.48 1992 (R2009).

Publisher's Cataloging-In-Publication Data
(Prepared by The Donohue Group, Inc.)

Names: Shally-Jensen, Michael, editor.
Title: United States involvement in the Middle East / editor, Michael Shally-Jensen, PhD.
Other Titles: Defining documents in American history (Salem Press)
Description: [First edition]. | Ipswich, Massachusetts: Salem Press, a division of EBSCO Information Services; Amenia, NY: Grey House Publishing, [2020] | Includes bibliographical references and index.
Identifiers: ISBN 9781642653977 (set) | ISBN 9781642653991 (v. 1) | ISBN 9781642654004 (v. 2)
Subjects: LCSH: United States–Foreign relations–Middle East–Sources. | Middle East–Foreign relations–United States–Sources. | United States–Military relations–Middle East–Sources. | Middle East–Military relations–United States–Sources. | United States–Armed Forces–Middle East–History–Sources. | Terrorism–United States–Sources. | Arab-Israeli conflict–Sources.
Classification: LCC DS63.2.U5 U55 2020 | DDC 327.73056–dc23

FIRST PRINTING
PRINTED IN THE UNITED STATES OF AMERICA

Table of Contents

Publisher's Note vii
Editor's Introduction ix
Contributors xii
Full Table of Contents xiii

Volume 1

COLONIALISM AND THE TRANSITION TO US INFLUENCE

On the Jewish State 3
The D'Arcy Oil Concession 11
Hussein-McMahon Correspondence 23
Sykes-Picot Agreement 44
Balfour Declaration 51
Palestine Mandate 57
White Paper of 1939 71
Truman Statement on Immigration into Palestine 86
Declaration of the Establishment of the State of Israel 93
CIA Summary of the Overthrow of Premier Mossadeq of Iran 100
Baghdad Pact 109
The Nationalization of the Suez Canal 115
The Eisenhower Doctrine 123

ARAB VOICES IN OPPOSITION

Charter of the Arab League 136
Palestinian National Charter 148
Islam and Universal Peace 157
Islam: The Misunderstood Religion 161
Saudi Arabia: A Country Study 165

Late Twentieth-Century Wars and Peace Accords

U.N. Security Council Resolution 242 on the Arab-Israeli Conflict. 173
Camp David Accords 179
Egypt-Israel Peace Treaty 190
"Crisis of Confidence". 202
"The Great Satan" 213
Documents Relating to the Soviet Invasion of Afghanistan 223
Remarks on the Attack in Beirut. 232
Memos Concerning a Meeting between Donald Rumsfeld and Saddam Hussein. 243
The Iran-Contra Affair. 249
The Cessation of the Persian Gulf War 257
The 1993 World Trade Center Bombing: Report and Analysis. 268
Oslo Accords. 276

Publisher's Note

Defining Documents in American History series, produced by Salem Press, offers a closer look at important historical documents by pairing primary source documents on a broad range of subjects with essays written especially for the series by expert writers, including historians, professors, researchers, and other authorities in the subject under examination. This established series includes thirty-seven titles that present documents selected to illuminate specific eras in American history—including *The Vietnam War*, *Civil Rights*, and *Postwar 1940s*—or to explore significant themes and developments in American society—*The Free Press*, *Business Ethics*, *Prison Reform*, and *Slavery*.

This set, *Defining Documents in American History: United States Involvement in the Middle East*, offers in-depth analysis of sixty-four documents, including book excerpts, speeches, political debates, testimony, court rulings, legal texts, legislative acts, essays, newspaper and magazine articles, and interviews. These selections trace the role and complex history of US involvement in the conflicts in the Middle East in the twentieth and twenty-first century.

The material is organized into five sections, and each section begins with a brief introduction that examines the politics and policies of the United States and the Middle East through a variety of historical documents.

- **Colonialism and the Transition to US Influence** includes documents from the years 1896–1957 that track the history of conflicts in the Middle East at a time when most of the area had been under direct or indirect foreign rule, nationalist forces arose. including Theodor Herzl's call for a Jewish state; Truman's Statement on Immigration into Palestine, and Gamal Abder Nasser on the Nationalization of the Suez Canal;

- **Arab Voices in Opposition** includes documents that trace the evolution of Islam in the region (1744–1977) such as The Saud Family and Wahhabi Islam, Sayyid Qutb on Jihad, and the Palestinian National Charter;

- **Late Twentieth-Century Wars and Peace Accords** begins with UN Security Council Resolution 242 on the Arab-Israeli Conflict, and includes Camp David Accords, a report and analysis of the 1993 World Trade Center Bombing, and Muhammad Qutb on the Origins of Islam;

- **9/11, Afghanistan, and Iraq** is the most extensive section, covering a period of time from 1996–2013 and includes such pivotal documents in the relationship between the US and the Middle East such as Osama bin-Laden's Declaration of Jihad against the Americans, Colin Powell on Iraqi Weapons of Mass Destruction, "Mission to Niger" and the Valerie Plame Affair, The Zelikow Memo, and President Obama's Remarks on the Killing of Osama bin Laden; and

- **Arab Spring, ISIS, and After**, which takes us from 2011 to the present, with documents such as *Flashing Red: A Special Report on the Terrorist Attack at Benghazi;* Donald Trump's "Muslim Ban" Speech"; and "US Gov't Misled Public about Afghan War."

These documents provide an overview of the turbulent history and current state of US relations with the Middle East.

Essay Format

Each Historical Document is supported by a critical essay, written by historians and teachers, that includes a Summary Overview, Defining Moment, About the Author, Document

Analysis, and Essential Themes. An important feature of each essay is a close reading of the primary source that develops broader themes, such as the author's rhetorical purpose, social or class position, point of view, and other relevant issues. Each essay also includes section entitled Bibliography and Further Reading that provides suggestions for additional readings and research.

Appendixes

- **Chronological List** arranges all documents by year.
- **Web Resources** is an annotated list of websites that offer valuable supplemental resources.
- **Bibliography** lists helpful articles and books for further study.

Contributors

Salem Press would like to extend its appreciation to all involved in the development and production of this work. The essays have been written and signed by scholars of history, humanities, and other disciplines related to the essays' topics. Without these expert contributions, a project of this nature would not be possible. A full list of the contributors to this set with their affiliations appears following the Editor's Introduction.

Editor's Introduction

Since the First Barbary War, during which the United States under the leadership of Thomas Jefferson, fought with Sweden against the Barbary states (Tripoli, Algiers, Tunis, and Morocco), the Middle East and the United States have had a complex relationship, especially as it relates to the conflicts and wars that the region has experienced in the twentieth and twenty-first centuries. The United States has engaged in military and covert operations with various groups and nations throughout the Middle East in an effort to protect its own strategic interests, maintain access to oil resources, settle rivalries, and prevent the spread of terrorism and weapons of mass destruction. Shifting alliances and humanitarian crises have led presidents from Eisenhower to Obama to develop specific doctrines to uphold some regimes, dampen the influence of other world powers (especially the Soviet Union/Russia), and to wipe out the cells that have spawned some of the world's most terrifying extremist groups, including the Taliban and the Islamic State.

The Middle East, of course, is a central region linking three different continents: Asia, Europe, and Africa. It has been an area of strategic importance throughout history and continues to be so today, particularly in light of its economic importance, which mainly centers on oil resources. Ongoing hostilities between Islamist extremist groups in the region and various Middle Eastern and Western governments add to the political importance of the area. For the past three-quarters of a century there has been enough turmoil in the region to, more than once, threaten the peace of the world.

The Middle East is well known for having given birth, in ancient times, to Judaism and Christianity, and, in the early medieval era, to Islam. It is equally well known for the tensions that have arisen between these religions at times, not to mention the tensions between sects *within* these religions (Eastern and Western forms of Christianity; Sunni and Shiite Islam; moderate and ultra-orthodox forms of Judaism). Under Islamic rule, Jews and Christians traditionally were granted protected status, primarily on the basis of the monotheistic beliefs (Abrahamic religion) which they share with Islam. But conflict came, often enough, from one side or the other. Today, Christians and Jews remain a small but significant minority: around 5 percent of Middle Easterners identify as Christian and about 1 percent as Jewish—even as Israel, of course, stands as a majority Jewish state.

Modern History Prior to Major US Involvement

There is a long history of European colonialism in the region. The French gained a protectorate over most of Lebanon in 1860, the British over Cyprus and Egypt in 1878 and 1882, respectively. Nationalist uprisings also have occurred—in the past and more recently. The absolute power of the Ottoman sultan Abdul-Hamid II (reigned 1876–1909) was sharply limited in 1908 as a result of a nationalist-constitutionalist revolt headed by the Young Turks, as they were known. A similar change occurred in Iran around the same time, affecting the shah's power. By that time the first major oil concession had already begun delivering most of Iran's oil wealth to Britain.

With the advent of World War I, the Young Turks hoped to reestablish Turkish power in the region, joining with Germany and Austria-Hungary in the fight against the Allied Powers. Their military efforts were valiant at times but unsustainable over the course of the war. Other entanglements with the West also created problems. British armies occupied large areas of Iraq and elsewhere, and sought to project British power into the Arabian Peninsula. In exchange for British guarantees for a new Arab kingdom there after the war, Hussein ibn Ali (also known as Sharif of Mecca) promised to lead an Arab revolt against the Ottoman overlords. The revolt began in early 1916, led by Hussein's son Faisal; but within a month the British headed in a different direction diplomatically. Under the Sykes-Picot Agreement (1916), the French and the British agreed to divide the lands of eastern Arabia between them: the French would gain control of Syria, Lebanon, and parts of Anatolia while the British would obtain most of Iraq and areas surrounding the Persian Gulf. Russia, too, would acquire lands around the Bosporus and the Black Sea. Sharif Hussein and his Arab revolt were left in the lurch.

Around this time, too, in November 1917, the British issued the Balfour Declaration, which supported the idea of a Jewish homeland in Palestine. This helped bolster the actions of leaders of a growing Zionist movement that aimed to repatriate European Jews in the Holy Land. By 1922 a Palestinian Mandate—essentially a colony sanctioned by the League of Nations—was in place under British administration. It would last, not without conflict, until the declaration of the state of Israel in 1948.

At this low point in Middle Eastern history, with most of the area under direct or indirect foreign rule, nationalist forces once again arose. In Iran, the Persians refused to accept British oversight. General Reza Khan (later Reza Shah Pahlavi) led a military coup and established a nationalistic, modernizing government (1921). In 1925 he removed the last of the Qajar royals and became shah. Meanwhile, in Turkey, General Mustafa Kemal Atatürk rallied his fellow countrymen. Within a few years he had put down opposition, both inside and outside of Turkey; angled to get a fair peace settlement from the Allies; and created a secular, nationalist republic (1923). This marked the end of the Ottoman Empire. In later years, the Turkish leader Recep Tayyip Erdoğon (ruled 2003-present) would seek to recapture the glory of Atatürk's political muscularity while turning away from secularism and toward Islamic conservatism.

On the Arabian Peninsula, a long string of post–World War I tribal wars continued into the 1920s. By 1926, however, the powerful Al Saud family had gained the upper hand, putting down Sharif Hussein and other opponents. In 1932 the peninsula was united as a kingdom under Abdul al-Aziz ibn Saud (reigned 1932–53). Oil was discovered in the kingdom in the mid-1930s, and through the consortium known as Aramco (made up of American and British oil companies), vast sums of money were transferred to the Saudi rulers. The House of Saud, not known for its liberal outlook but nevertheless a transactional, global player, would remain ascendant well into the twenty-first century.

By the end of World War II, most of the Middle Eastern nations had attained independence; the French gave up their mandates in Syria and Lebanon, for example, but fought to maintain control in Algeria in a long, ugly war (1954–62). The British continued to maintain significant economic and political influence in a number of states, backed by a military presence. It was only with the start of native military coups led by populist figures like Gamal Abdel Nasser of Egypt (ruled 1956–70) that some of the older constitutional monarchies were overthrown and British influence in the region was weakened. An attempt to arrange a peaceful transfer of power in Palestine in 1948 did not work out; instead, war erupted between the newly proclaimed Israeli government and the Palestinian Arabs backed by Jordan and Egypt. Lebanon, Jordan, and Syria each absorbed significant populations of Palestinian refugees after the 1948–49 war.

—*Michael Shally-Jensen, PhD*

Bibliography and Additional Reading

Badie, Dina. *AFTER SADDAM: American Foreign Policy and the Destruction of Secularism in the Middle East*. S.L., Lexington Books, 2019.

Burk, James. *How 9/11 Changed Our Ways of War*. Stanford, Calif., Stanford Univ. Press, 2013.

Dorani, Sharifullah. *America in Afghanistan: Foreign Policy and Decision Making from Bush to Obama to Trump*. London ; New York, Ny, I.B. Tauris, 2019.

Dower, John W. *The Violent American Century: War and Terror since World War II*. Chicago, Illinois, Haymarket Books, 2017.

Dunford, David J. *From Sadat to Saddam: The Decline of American Diplomacy in the Middle East*. Lincoln, Nebraska Potomac Books, An Imprint Of The University Of Nebraska Press, 2019.

Lust, Ellen. *The Middle East*. Thousand Oaks, California, Cq Press, An Imprint Of Sage Publications, 2020.

Prifti, Bledar. *US Foreign Policy in the Middle East: The Case for Continuity*. Cham, Switzerland, Palgrave Macmillan, 2017.

Wright, Lawrence. *The Looming Tower: Al-Qaeda and the Road to 9*. Thorndike Press, New York, 2007.

Contributors

Anna Accettola, MA
University of California, Los Angeles

Michael P. Auerbach, MA
Marblehead, Massachusetts

Jakub Basista, PhD, DLitt
Jagiellonian University

Steven L. Danver, PhD
Walden University

Amber R. Dickinson, PhD
Washburn University

Bethany Groff Dorau, MA
Historic New England

Ashleigh Fata, MA
University of California, Los Angeles

Aaron Gulyas, MA
Mott Community College

Michael Shally-Jensen, PhD
Amherst, Massachusetts

Mark S. Joy, PhD
Jamestown University

Scott A. Merriman, PhD
Troy University

Scott C. Monje, PhD
Tarrytown, New York

Hannah Rich, MA
Philadelphia, Pennsylvania

David Simonelli, PhD
Youngstown State University

Michele McBride Simonelli, JD
Poland, Ohio

Robert Surbrug, PhD
Bay Path University

Anthony Vivian, MA
University of California, Los Angeles

Donald A. Watt, PhD
Middleton, ID

Full Table of Contents

Publisher's Note vii
Editor's Introduction ix
Contributors xii

Volume 1

COLONIALISM AND THE TRANSITION TO US INFLUENCE

On the Jewish State 3
The D'Arcy Oil Concession 11
Hussein-McMahon Correspondence 23
Sykes-Picot Agreement 44
Balfour Declaration 51
Palestine Mandate 57
White Paper of 1939 71
Truman Statement on Immigration into Palestine 86
Declaration of the Establishment of the State of Israel 93
CIA Summary of the Overthrow of Premier Mossadeq of Iran 100
Baghdad Pact 109
The Nationalization of the Suez Canal 115
The Eisenhower Doctrine 123

ARAB VOICES IN OPPOSITION

Charter of the Arab League 136
Palestinian National Charter 148
Islam and Universal Peace 157
Islam: The Misunderstood Religion 161
Saudi Arabia: A Country Study 165

Late Twentieth-Century Wars and Peace Accords

U.N. Security Council Resolution 242 on the Arab-Israeli Conflict. 173
Camp David Accords 179
Egypt-Israel Peace Treaty 190
"Crisis of Confidence". 202
"The Great Satan". 213
Documents Relating to the Soviet Invasion of Afghanistan 223
Remarks on the Attack in Beirut. 232
Memos Concerning a Meeting between Donald Rumsfeld and Saddam Hussein. 243
The Iran-Contra Affair. 249
The Cessation of the Persian Gulf War 257
The 1993 World Trade Center Bombing: Report and Analysis. 268
Oslo Accords. 276

Volume 2

9/11, Afghanistan, and Iraq

From *The Clash of Civilizations* 294
Declaration of Jihad against the Americans 303
News Account of the USS *Cole* Bombing 323
The Urgent Need to Address the al-Qaeda Threat. 328
Destruction of the Buddhist Statues at Bamiyan 334
Bin-Laden's Video Statement of October 2001 339
Excerpts from *Knights under the Prophet's Banner* 344
NATO Press Conference with Donald Rumsfeld 354
Iraq's Programs for Weapons of Mass Destruction. 363
Address on Iraqi Weapons of Mass Destruction 370
U.N. Weapons Inspection Efforts in Iraq 398
Address to the Nation on Military Operations in Iraq 407
From *The Crisis of Islam* 414
"The Military's Media". 425
Order Dissolving Iraqi Military and Security Organizations 435
"Mission to Niger" and the Valerie Plame Affair. 444
On Counterterrorism and US Foreign Policy 449

Declaration of al-Zarqawi at the Execution of Nicholas Berg 465
Public Statement on the Release of the *9/11 Commission Report* 473
Fay Report on the Abu Ghraib Prisoner Abuse Scandal 482
Halliburton Overcharges Report. 490
The Zelikow Memo regarding Torture 496
"Obama to 'Surge' 30,000 Troops to Afghanistan" 505
Manning-Lamo Chat Logs. 511
Remarks on the Killing of Osama Bin Laden 518
Snowden Email 524

Arab Spring, ISIS, and After

U.N. Security Council Resolution 1973 on Libya 533
Flashing Red: A Special Report on the Terrorist Attack at Benghazi 546
Address at the U.N. "Youth Takeover Event" 555
Alleged Use of Chemical Weapons in the Ghouta Area of Damascus 562
Proclamation of the Caliphate. 574
Remarks by Abdullah II of Jordan before the U.N. General Assembly. 581
Hassan Rouhani's Address before the U.N. General Assembly 589
Benjamin Netanyahu's Speech before the U.N. General Assembly 599
Donald Trump's "Muslim Ban" Speech 612
Gaza—Ten Years Later. 619
Statement by President Donald Trump on Jerusalem 625
The Saudi Crown Prince and the Killing of Journalist Jamal Khashoggi. 634
President Trump and President El-Sisi of Egypt before Bilateral Meeting 639
President Trump on the Situation in Northern Syria 645
Al-Baghdadi Killed. 654
"US Public Misled about Afghanistan War" 660
US-Iran Conflict and Implications for US Policy 678

Appendixes

Chronological List 689
Web Resources 691
Bibliography. 692
Index. 705

COLONIALISM AND THE TRANSITION TO US INFLUENCE

Throughout the nineteenth and early twentieth centuries, the Great Powers of Europe—principally Britain, France, and Russia but also Germany and, in the later years, Italy—competed for influence and domination in the lands abandoned by the Ottomans (who had maintained an empire in the region for centuries). Britain had interests in Egypt, the Arabian Peninsula, southern Iran, southern Iraq, Afghanistan, Palestine, and elsewhere. The French had a presence in Lebanon, parts of Syria, and North Africa. The Russians had interests in northern Iran and Syria, among other areas.

With the advent of World War I, the entire region was thrown into disarray. British armies occupied parts of Iraq and sought to gain a firmer foothold in the Arabian Peninsula. The British promised a kingdom in that region to the Sharif of Mecca in exchange for his expelling the last remnants of Ottoman control. In the end, however, the British reneged. Under the Sykes-Picot Agreement (1916), the French and the British agreed to divide the lands of eastern Arabia between them: the French would gain control of Syria, Lebanon, and parts of Anatolia while the British would obtain most of Iraq and areas surrounding the Persian Gulf. Russia, too, would acquire lands around the Bosporus and the Black Sea.

Around this time, too, in November 1917, the British issued the Balfour Declaration, which supported the idea of a Jewish homeland in Palestine. This helped bolster the actions of the leaders of a growing Zionist movement which aimed to repatriate European Jews in the Holy Land. By 1922 a Palestinian Mandate—essentially a colony sanctioned by the League of Nations—was in place under British administration. It would last, not without conflict, until the declaration of the state of Israel in 1948.

At this point in Middle Eastern history, with most of the area under direct or indirect foreign rule, nationalist forces arose. In Iran, the Persians refused to accept British oversight. General Reza Khan (later Reza Shah Pahlavi) led a military coup and established a nationalistic, modernizing government (1921). In 1925 he removed the last of the Qajar royals and became shah. Meanwhile, in Turkey, General Mustafa Kemal Ataturk rallied his fellow countrymen. Within a few years he had put down opposition both inside and outside of Turkey, angled to get a fair peace settlement from the Allies, and created a secular, nationalist republic (1923). This marked the final end of the Ottoman Empire.

On the Arabian Peninsula, a long string of post–World War I tribal wars continued into the 1920s. By 1926, however, the powerful Al Saud family had gained the upper hand, putting down Sharif Hussein and other opponents. In 1932, the peninsula was united as a kingdom under Abdul al-Aziz ibn Saud (reigned 1932–53). Oil was discovered in the kingdom in the mid-1930s, and through the consortium known as Aramco (made up of American and British oil companies), vast sums of money were transferred to the Saudi rulers. Both the British and, increasingly, the United States coveted these resources.

Following World War II, the United States began to emerge as the major outside power in the Middle East. The European powers had either been pushed out in the course of the war (as in the case of Italy and Germany) or pressured to exit due to domestic events or new developments in the region. France hung on to its colony in Algeria, but after a long, dirty war there (1954–62) it lost control and left the country, which became independent. As additional nationalistic movements took root and swept through the region, Britain, too, exited under pressure from Egypt's Gamal Abdel Nasser (ruled 1956–70).

The United States viewed these nationalist movements as being aligned with the Soviet Union and communism, which was only partially true. Washington's intervention in Iran, where a US and British-backed coup ousted Prime Minister Mohammad Mossadegh in 1953, added to mistrust of the United States in the Middle East. (The action would come back to roost when, in 1979, Iran ousted the US-backed shah Mohammed Reza Pahlavi [ruled 1941–79] and declared an Islamic republic there.) In the case of the United States, the three main interests in the region were Persian Gulf oil, support and protection of the new state of Israel (from 1948), and containment of the Soviet Union. These goals proved difficult to manage, especially with the rise of Arab nationalism.

The United States was among the first nations to recognize Israel in 1948. That same year war erupted between the new Israeli government and the Palestinian Arabs backed by Jordan and Egypt. Lebanon, Jordan, and Syria each absorbed significant populations of Palestinian refugees after the 1948–49 war.

On the Jewish State

Date: 1896
Author: Theodor Herzl
Geographic region: Jewish homeland
Genre: Political pamphlet

Summary Overview

Der Judenstaat, or *On the Jewish State*, was written by Theodor Herzl, one of the founding members of the modern Zionist movement. The text reproduced here represents segments of a pamphlet that Herzl circulated in 1896. Herzl's pamphlet was discussed thoroughly at the first Zionist Congress in 1897, which he largely organized. Herzl was arguing for the creation of Jewish state, preferably in the ancient Jewish homeland (in what was then Palestine). Realizing, however, that people already inhabited that region, Herzl was willing to point to a new homeland for his fellow Jews in part of modern-day Uganda. The Jewish people had lived much of their history in dispersed communities in different part of the globe, he noted, although they were originally situated mainly in one area of the ancient Near East, the kingdom of Judea. Over time, that kingdom grew and shrank, was conquered and retaken, and was finally decimated by the Romans. In the decades and centuries after the fall, most Jews ended up scattering and relocating to areas that were nominally tolerant of their religion and historical background. Those belonging to the Zionist movement, which was beginning to gain ground at the time of Herzl's pamphlet, sought to bring together all Jews in a province or country of their own.

Defining Moment

When this pamphlet originally came out, the Jewish people had been expelled from their homeland for 1,761 years. After the Bar Kokhba rebellion against Rome and its Emperor Hadrian, Hadrian commanded that all Jews must leave their homeland and never return. This forced the population, already spread out over the Roman Empire, to move even farther away from their ancestral territory. Many relocated to parts of Europe, north Africa, and other areas where they could make a new home for themselves. Every Jew was now part of a diaspora, or an exile community. This was not an entirely novel concept for the Jewish people, as they had been expelled for the first time in the eighth century BCE, but the Roman banishment was the most lasting. As of the late nineteenth century, there were only glimmerings of hope about possibly reuniting the Jews in their ancient homeland or somewhere else.

As is usual when a group has been marginalized, a few souls stand out as leaders seeking to improve the prospects of their people. Theodor Herzl was one such person, and he found many other like-minded activists when he formed the First Zionist Congress in 1897. The Jewish communities throughout the world had faced hardship and degradation for hundreds of years, but most of them had found ways to function and even thrive within the borders of the German, Polish, Italian, or other states in which they were situated. Overall, while many people in the

DER JUDENSTAAT.

VERSUCH

EINER

MODERNEN LÖSUNG DER JUDENFRAGE

VON

THEODOR HERZL

DOCTOR DER RECHTE.

LEIPZIG und WIEN 1896.
M. BREITENSTEIN'S VERLAGS-BUCHHANDLUNG
WIEN, IX., WÄHRINGERSTRASSE 5.

The book Der Judenstaat (The Jewish State, 1896) *by Theodor Herzl.*

Jewish diaspora were enthusiastic about coming together once again as a single community, few were quite ready to abandon the lives they had built for themselves in their adopted countries, where, oftentimes, they and their ancestors had lived for ages. Some people feared, too, that they might be treated worse by non-Jewish populations if they distinguished themselves as Jews first and foremost and expressed their wish to leave.

The Zionist push for Jewish recognition and independence gained momentum in the last decades of the nineteenth century and the early years of the twentieth, in part because of Herzl and the Zionist Congress but also because of the work of other activists and a growing interest among the populace at large. The idea to create a new homeland for the Jews in Palestine, first formally proposed at the 1897 congress, was called the Basel (Basle) Program, after the Swiss city in which the congress was held.

Author Biography

Theodor Herzl was born on May 2, 1860, in Pest (modern Budapest), in the former Kingdom of Hungary. His father was a businessman and his mother stayed at home to take care of him and his older sister (who tragically died as a child from typhus). While identifying as ethnic Jews, the family was largely secular. During his studies at school Herzl became entranced by German culture and believed that the Germans were the most civilized of the European peoples. That belief caused him to think that through intense study of European classical literature, he and his fellow Jews might separate themselves from an ethnicity that some among them considered unfortunate or even shameful. The self-directed anti-Semitism of such thoughts did not fade in Herzl until he enrolled in the University of Vienna.

After studying law at university, Herzl had a short legal career and then directed his attention to journalism. He eventually became the editor of *Neue Freie Presse* (New Free Press), a Parisian publication. Through his experiences in Paris and other parts of Europe, Herzl became disillusioned by the anti-Semitism that seemed to be everywhere. He came to believe that it could never be changed, but only avoided. It was at this point that he wrote *On the Jewish State*.

For the last eight years of his life, Herzl worked with political leaders, religious leaders, and even Pope Pius X to try to find a suitable home for the Jewish diaspora to settle in. Herzl proposed forming a colony in Uganda, but that idea died with him. He passed away on July 3, 1904, from a heart condition.

HISTORICAL DOCUMENT: From *On the Jewish State*

The idea which I have developed in this pamphlet is a very old one: it is the restoration of the Jewish State.
   The world resounds with outcries against the Jews, and these outcries have awakened the slumbering idea.

...

We are a people—one people.
   We have honestly endeavored everywhere to merge ourselves in the social life of surrounding communities and to preserve the faith of our fathers. We are not permitted to do so. In vain are we loyal patriots, our loyalty in some places running to extremes; in vain do we make the same sacrifices of life and property as our fellow

continued from page 5

citizens; in vain do we strive to increase the fame of our native land in science and art, or her wealth by trade and commerce. In countries where we have lived for centuries we are still cried down as strangers, and often by those whose ancestors were not yet domiciled in the land where Jews had already had experience of suffering. The majority may decide which are the strangers; for this, as indeed every point which arises in the relations between nations, is a question of might. I do not here surrender any portion of our prescriptive right, when I make this statement merely in my own name as an individual. In the world as it now is and for an indefinite period will probably remain, might precedes right. It is useless, therefore, for us to be loyal patriots, as were the Huguenots who were forced to emigrate. If we could only be left in peace....

...

[However,] oppression and persecution cannot exterminate us. No nation on earth has survived such struggles and sufferings as we have gone through. Jew-baiting has merely stripped off our weaklings; the strong among us were invariably true to their race when persecution broke out against them....

However much I may worship personality—powerful individual personality in statesmen, inventors, artists, philosophers, or leaders, as well as the collective personality of a historic group of human beings, which we call a nation—however much I may worship personality, I do not regret its disappearance. Whoever can, will, and must perish, let him perish. But the distinctive nationality of Jews neither can, will, nor must be destroyed. It cannot be destroyed, because external enemies consolidate it. It will not be destroyed; this is shown during two thousand years of appalling suffering. It must not be destroyed. . . . Whole branches of Judaism may wither and fall, but the trunk will remain.

> *The idea which I have developed in this pamphlet is a very old one: it is the restoration of the Jewish State.*

...

The Jewish Question

No one can deny the gravity of the situation of the Jews. Wherever they live in perceptible numbers, they are more or less persecuted. Their equality before the law, granted by statute, has become practically a dead letter. They are debarred from filling even moderately high positions, either in the army, or in any public or private capacity. And attempts are made to thrust them out of business also: "Don't buy from Jews!"

Attacks in Parliaments, in assemblies, in the press, in the pulpit, in the street, on journeys—for example, their exclusion from certain hotels—even in places of recreation, become daily more numerous. The forms of persecutions varying according to the countries and social circles in which they occur....

...

The Plan

Let the sovereignty be granted us over a portion of the globe large enough to satisfy the rightful requirements of a nation; the rest we shall manage for ourselves.

The creation of a new State is neither ridiculous nor impossible. We have in our day witnessed the process in connection with nations which were not largely members of the middle class, but poorer, less educated, and consequently weaker than ourselves. The Governments of all countries scourged by Anti-Semitism will be keenly interested in assisting us to obtain the sovereignty we want.

The plan, simple in design, but complicated in execution, will be carried out by two agencies: The Society of Jews and the Jewish Company.

The Society of Jews will do the preparatory work in the domains of science and politics, which the Jewish Company will afterwards apply practically.

The Jewish Company will be the liquidating agent of the business interests of departing Jews, and will organize commerce and trade in the new country.

We must not imagine the departure of the Jews to be a sudden one. It will be gradual, continuous, and will cover many decades. The poorest will go first to cultivate the soil. In accordance with a preconceived plan, they will construct roads, bridges, railways and telegraph installations; regulate rivers; and build their own dwellings; their labor will create trade, trade will create markets and markets will attract new settlers, for every man will go voluntarily, at his own expense and his own risk. The labor expended on the land will enhance its value, and the Jews will soon perceive that a new and permanent sphere of operation is opening here for that spirit of enterprise which has heretofore met only with hatred and obloquy.

GLOSSARY

domiciled: established in a domicile (a place of residence, house or home)

prescriptive right: depending on or arising from effective legal prescription or direction, as a right or title established by a long unchallenged tenure

Huguenots: French Protestants forced to leave France during the 1680s because of their religion

8 • COLONIALISM AND THE TRANSITION TO US INFLUENCE

> **Jew-baiting:** active anti-Semitism; active persecution or harassment of Jews
>
> **liquidate:** to convert (inventory, securities, property, or other assets) into cash
>
> **obloquy:** censure, blame, disgrace, or abusive language aimed at a person or thing, especially by numerous persons or by the general public

Document Analysis

This text includes several themes, illustrating the way that Herzl thinks about his Zionist dream, but also reflecting the times in which he lived and the changes to national borders he had seen or experienced. The proposal is not one that sees a future, solely, of endless possibility, for it recognizes, too, a variety of built-in problems. While Herzl wishes for the betterment of the Jewish people, he is limited by the types of government and social systems available to him at the time. His idealism is tempered with pragmatism.

The overall tone of the piece is one of disillusion or even hopelessness regarding the

The "Basel program" approved at the 1897 First Zionist Congress. The first line states: "Zionism seeks to establish a home (Heimstätte) for the Jewish people in Palestine secured under public law."

present condition of the Jews and their fate in the near future. Can the Jewish people ever find a real and welcoming home outside of a Jewish state? In one of the opening paragraphs Herzl lists a series of actions that the Jews have taken "in vain." For example, "in vain do we strive to increase the fame of our native land in science and art, or her wealth by trade and commerce." There is a tension here in Herzl's words—one that is most intentional. As he sees it, the Jewish people work to better their "native lands" "in vain." Even though Herzl recognizes that various communities have long made their homes in European countries, he uses the term "native" somewhat ironically. Despite the fact the Jewish diaspora should now be embedded in their respective lands, they continue to be singled out by their religion and their ethnicity. They are not allowed to *be* "native," even when they work as hard as any other citizen to improve their lives and their country.

Herzl explains that his dream could be a practical reality. "The creation of a new State is neither ridiculous nor impossible. We have in our day witnessed the process…" While today it may seem to be fairly far-fetched to create a state out of nothing, the creation of new independent nations was not unknown at the time in which Herzl and his compatriots were advocating for it. Practically next door, for example, Luxembourg gained its independence in 1890, while, farther away, the Greater Republic of Central America (modern-day Honduras and Nicaragua) freed itself from colonial rule the same year as Herzl's pamphlet. Nation building and the throwing off of colonial restraints to create independent and self-governing lands were viable ideas near the end of the nineteenth century.

However well-intentioned, though, Herzl's plan came with a few inherent drawbacks. Among other things, the plan implies the creation of a social hierarchy. When Herzl states, "The poorest will go first to cultivate the land…," he likely has the best of intentions.

The poorest parts of society always suffer the most, lacking in basic necessities; sending them to a new land first would seem to hold promise. However, it also makes them into laborers. And as other members of society come, Herzl seems to say that they will pick up their trades and grow the economy. Nowhere within the outline is there a way for those who are first admitted into the new land to take advantage of later opportunities. Traditionally, hierarchies of labor reproduce themselves without much upward mobility—blacksmiths remain blacksmiths, coal miners mine, businessmen stay in business, and farmers farm. Since "the poorest" are not given a choice in their profession, it seems likely that the hierarchies that Herzl so rails against in Europe may, unintentionally, reproduced themselves in the Jewish State, albeit on a class basis rather than on religious or ethnic grounds.

Essential Themes

As noted, Herzl did not live to see his dream of the Jewish State. It did, of course, become a reality nearly a half century after his death with the establishment, in 1948, of the state of Israel. While, in the wake of World War II, the Jewish Agency for Palestine (which was created at the 16th Zionist Conference) approved the United Nations' plan to split Palestine into two nations, most of the leaders of the Arab world (along with Great Britain) did not do so. This led immediately to the 1948 Arab-Israeli War, which broke out the day after the declaration of Israeli Independence. The war lasted ten months and tensions between Israel and the surrounding Arab nations have been tense ever since, with frequent violent outbursts.

In the seventy years since the founding of Israel, the controversy over its creation and its place in the region has never ceased. Proponents of Zionism see Israel as the saving grace for a persecuted people who are finally able to live a normal life in the land from which they were forcibly exiled. Critics, on the other hand, think that the establishment of Israel represents an imperialistic, exclusionary, even racist act that gives little consideration to the people who already lived in the region and in some cases have done so for millennia.

Today, Israeli's view Theodor Herzl as the founding father of their nation, celebrating Herzl Day (in April or June of each year) as a national holiday. On this holiday, Israeli children learn about Herzl's life and vision. A 2004 law requires a public council to convene on that day and discuss aspects of Herzl's vision for Israel and its implementation. Herzl's remains were moved from Vienna to Jerusalem's national cemetery—Mount Herzl—in 1949.

—Anna Accettola

Bibliography and Additional Reading

Avineri, Shlomo. *Herzl's Vision: Theodor Herzl and the Foundation of the Jewish State*. BlueBridge, 2014.

Berkowitz, Michael. *Zionist Culture and West European Jewry before the First World War*. Cambridge University Press, 1993.

Cohn, Henry J. "Theodor Herzl's Conversion to Zionism." *Jewish Social Studies* (1970): 101–110.

"Herzl Law." *World Zionist Organization*. knesset.gov.il/vip/herzl/eng/Herz_Law_eng.html.

Sachar, Howard M. *A history of Israel: From the rise of Zionism to our time*. Knopf, 2013.

Wistrich, Robert S. "Theodor Herzl: Zionist icon, myth-maker and social utopian." *Israel Affairs* 1.3 (1995): 1–37.

The D'Arcy Oil Concession

Date: May 28, 1901
Authors: Alfred Marriott and George Grahame
Geographic region: Persia (modern-day Iran)
Genre: Government grant treaty

Summary Overview

Persia—modern-day Iran—has a history of political-military power and empire dating back to the sixth century BCE. In the 1800s, however, the advance of European imperialism threatened to subject Persia to foreign dominance, whether through economic control by the British Empire or diplomatic bullying by the Russian Empire. By the end of the century, a combination of popular unrest, religious protest and political aspiration seemed to promise a more modern and representative twentieth century, in which Persia might reassert itself as one of the world's most influential countries.

As it turned out, Persia sat atop the single most important commodity—petroleum—that would determine power relationships in the twentieth century. In 1901, a British financial speculator named William Knox D'Arcy had his representative attorneys negotiate a grant of opportunity to search for petroleum deposits throughout the Persian countryside, referred to as a concession. The D'Arcy concession would become a model for other corporate agreements with governments over mineral rights in the non-western world. It opened up the exploitation of petroleum deposits in southwestern Asia that continues today, and its terms were copied and modified by other corporations and companies in the region. However, the concession also inadvertently but permanently shut down any opportunity for Persia to exploit its own resources or establish a constitutional, democratic regime, a tragedy which has still not been reversed in the early twenty-first century.

Defining Moment

In 1794, the new Qajar dynasty became established in Tehran as the next shahs, or rulers, of Persia. To the north of their empire lay the expanding Russian Empire, soon to war with Persia and capture Azerbaijan, to their east was India, a conglomeration of principalities at war with each other (and Persia) but whose most powerful entity was the British East India Company. Without many western weapons or diplomatic connections, Persia therefore was destined to be a pawn in the "Great Game" between these two empires over the next hundred years. Thrown into the mix was the Qajar family's seemingly genetic predisposition toward greed, and the result was a long period in which Persians saw their proud civilized traditions buried in great power rivalry and indirect economic control. In essence, over a hundred years, the Qajars sold control of the nation's economy over to the Russians and the British. Wealthy Persian aristocratic families sent their sons to Europe to get educated, and it occurred to more than one of them that the Europeans who had schooled them in values of self-government, equal justice before the law and capitalism were the same people who undermined their ability to bring those values home to their own people.

By the 1880s, Nasir al-Din Shah vacationed in Switzerland and made improvements to his imperial palace by granting concessions to British companies to run Persian banks, factories and mines, and allowing the Russians to maintain agricultural combines, run the Persian mint and maintain a profitable lottery. The shah sold control over different sectors of the economy to either British or Russian concerns, collecting payments that supplemented the national treasury's contribution to his income while inviting the two empires' squabbling over influence on the Persian economy. Often, the concessions were so brazenly exploitative and the competition to attain them so fierce that they could backfire on the shah. For example, by 1890, at a time when railroads crisscrossed the entire globe, there were five miles of track total in all Persia because British and Russian diplomats threatened reprisals if Nasir al-Din chose the other power to get the concession to build more track.

A breaking point came in 1891, when the shah granted the British Imperial Tobacco Company the exclusive right to grow tobacco and sell cigarettes in Persia. Persians had been growing tobacco for two centuries, and smoking was considered integral to Persian culture, yet the profits from this habit would be entirely controlled by British businessmen. A famous Persian intellectual, Jamal ad Din al-Afghani, called on the beloved Shi'ite Muslim mullah Hasan Shirazi to mobilize the Persian people in defense of their economy and culture. Shirazi decided to issue a fatwah, or religious ruling, calling on Persian Shi'ites (Shias) to give up smoking, and amazingly, within days, no one in Persia bought or smoked cigarettes. Terrified, the shah cancelled the concession, and his last years on the throne were marked by depleted funds, corruption, and disorder in the rural areas of Persia. Nasir ad-Din was assassinated in 1896; Persia was at a crossroads in its history.

In 1872, Nasir ad-Din had granted a concession to Baron Julius de Reuter, a British subject, to build roads, telegraphs, mills, factories, and other public works—in essence, to develop the Persian economy and its infrastructure. Amongst the rights granted to Reuter was the exploitation of all the mineral resources in Persia, which were delineated as coal, iron, copper, lead, and petroleum. The Russian government and many Persian elites strenuously objected to their economy being beholden to one man, and the concession was cancelled. Reuter was compensated with the right to run a bank and search for the minerals, but his Persian Mining Corporation had its concession annulled when he ran out of money.

During the era of the Reuter concession, petroleum was perhaps the least useful of Persia's minerals to be mined, as its major uses were for the extraction of kerosene and the greasing of moveable parts. The waste product from this process, called gasoline, was simply thrown away. By the time Reuter's concession came to an end in 1899, the combustion engine had been invented, and now gasoline was the best use of petroleum available. Though automobiles were still rare, world navies were investing in more efficient oil burning engines, in 1903, the invention of the airplane would prove that the potential of petroleum as an energy source was limitless.

Thus, lots of speculators had an interest in replacing Reuter as the master of Persia's mineral rights, since geologists knew that the country sat atop massive petroleum deposits. One of the world's largest petroleum deposits sat just to Persia's north outside the city of Baku on the Caspian Sea, in Azerbaijan; Baku had once been a Persian city until the Russians had captured it in a war in 1806. In Persia itself, there was so much petroleum available that small pockets of it bubbled to the earth's surface, to be pooled by peasants and used as a water repellent, heating fuel or a protective tar for roofs or boats. The new shah, Mozaffar al-Din, shared his father's proclivity for high living on a small tax base extracted from a poor population. Like his father, then, petroleum represented a fabulous opportunity to secure a new source of revenue for his coffers, and he encouraged speculators to consider gambling on the profits promised by extracting Persia's petroleum reserves.

The most daring of these speculators was William Knox D'Arcy. D'Arcy was a lawyer who, upon moving to Australia, had partnered in a mining company that found gold outside Queensland in 1886, making him substantially wealthy. He moved back to his native England in 1889, inclined to gamble on mining investments to add to his fortune. D'Arcy's potential as an investor was suggested to an agent of the shah's government named Antoine Kitabci, and when Kitabci approached him, D'Arcy offered to foot £20,000 to open a sixty-year concession to explore for petroleum. The shah agreed, and in April 1901, D'Arcy's lawyer, Arthur Marriott, arrived in Tehran to negotiate the deal. The limits of D'Arcy's involvement in oil exploration ended there—despite his name being attached to the concession, William Knox D'Arcy would never set foot in Persia. Instead, it was his company and the engineers they hired, later merged with Burmah Oil, who would find vast reserves of petroleum in the Persian desert and change the course of the nation's history from then onward.

Author Biographies

William Knox D'Arcy provided £20,000 in cash for the concession, £650 in annual rent, and bribe money to distribute to the shah's local government officials and other important people in Persia, but from there, his authorship of the agreement ends—his role was entirely as the initial investor. Eventually, he was not even the primary investor; as the £20,000 metastasized into an even larger outlay, he faced the same problem as Reuter, and had to merge his company with Burmah Oil in 1905 in order to keep the search for petroleum reserves going.

The real authors of the concession were the many figures surrounding D'Arcy and the Persian shah who were interested in extracting oil from Persia. D'Arcy's primary envoy was Alfred Marriott, an attorney who was appointed based on his relationship as a first cousin of D'Arcy's secretary. Edouard Cotte was a French diplomat who knew Persian culture and the Persian state well enough to advise both sides on the fairness of the contract. Antoine Kitabci was, of course, the shah's emissary who had sought D'Arcy out as the major investor in the petroleum extraction scheme; the British agent who had given him D'Arcy's name, Sir Henry Drummond Wolfe, himself received shares in the company's profits. Marriott and Cotte consulted in Tehran with the shah's grand vizier, Atabake Azzam, with few hiccups in the negotiations. The British ambassador, Sir Arthur Hardinge, and one of his vice-consuls, George Grahame, shadowed the discussions and gave official assent to whatever shape the concession took.

Once the concession was written up as a draft, the Russian embassy protested, and Marriott and Hardinge handed over half of D'Arcy's £20,000 before the signing in order to hurry Mozaffar al-Din's approval. The concession was finally written up in English, French (the language of international diplomacy at the time), and Farsi and signed by Marriott and the shah on May 28, 1901.

HISTORICAL DOCUMENT: *The D'Arcy Oil Concession*

Between the Government of His Imperial Majesty the Shah of Persia of the one part and William Knox D'Arcy of independent means residing in London at No. 42 Grosvenor Square (hereinafter called "the Concessionaire") of the other part. The following has by these presents been agreed on and arranged, viz.:

Article I
The Government of His Imperial Majesty the Shah grants to the Concessionaire by these presents a special and exclusive privilege to search for, obtain, exploit, develop, render suitable for trade, carry away and sell natural gas, petroleum, asphalt and ozokerite throughout the whole extent of the Persian Empire for a term of 60 years as from the date of these presents.

Article II
This privilege shall comprise the exclusive right of laying the pipelines necessary from the deposits where there may be found one or several of the said products up to the Persian Gulf, as also the necessary distributing branches. It shall also comprise the right of constructing and maintaining all and any wells, reservoirs, stations and pump services, accumulation services and distribution services, factories and other works and arrangements that may be deemed necessary.

Article III
The Imperial Persian Government grants gratuitously to the Concessionaire all uncultivated lands belonging to the State, which the Concessionaire's engineers may deem necessary for the construction of the whole or any part of the above-mentioned works. As for cultivated lands belonging to the State, the Concessionaire must purchase them at the fair and current price of the Province. The Government also grants to the Concessionaire the right of acquiring all and any other lands or buildings necessary for the said purpose, with the consent of the proprietors, on such conditions as may be arranged between him and them without their being allowed to make demands of a nature to surcharge the prices ordinarily current for lands situate in their respective localities. Holy places with all their dependencies within a radius of 200 Persian archines are formally excluded.

Article IV
As three petroleum mines situate at Schouster Kassre-Chirine in the Province of Kermanschahan and Daleki near Bouchir are at present let to private persons and produce an annual revenue of two thousand tomans for the benefit of the Government, it has been agreed that the three aforesaid mines shall be comprised in the Deed of Concession in conformity with Article I, on condition that over and above the 16 per

cent mentioned in Article 10 the Concessionaire shall pay every year the fixed sum of 2,000 (two thousand) tomans to the Imperial Government.

Article V
The course of the pipelines shall be fixed by the Concessionaire and his engineers.

Article VI
Notwithstanding what is above set forth, the privilege granted by these presents shall not extend to the Provinces of Azerbadjan, Ghilan, Mazendaran, Asdrabad and Khorassan, but on the express condition that the Persian Imperial Government shall not grant to any other person the right of constructing a pipeline to the southern rivers or to the south coast of Persia.

Article VII
All lands granted by these presents to the Concessionaire or that may be acquired by him in the manner provided for in Articles 3 and 4 of these presents, as also all products exported shall be free of all imposts and taxes during the term of the present concession. All material and apparatuses necessary for the exploration, working and development of the pipeline shall enter Persia free of all taxes and custom-house duties.

The Government of His Imperial Majesty the Shah grants to the Concessionaire by these presents a special and exclusive privilege to search for, obtain, exploit, develop, render suitable for trade, carry away and sell natural gas, petroleum, asphalt and ozokerite throughout the whole extent of the Persian Empire for a term of 60 years as from the date of these presents.

Article VIII
The concessionaire shall immediately send out to Persia and at his own cost one or several experts with a view to their exploring the region in which there exist, as he believes, the said products, and in the event of a satisfactory nature, the latter shall immediately send to Persia and at his own cost all the technical staff necessary with the working plant and machinery required for boring and sinking wells and ascertaining the value of the property.

Article IX
The Imperial Persian Government authorizes the Concessionaire to found one or several companies for the working of the Concession. The names, "statutes" and capital of the said companies shall be fixed by the concessionaire, and the directors

continues on page 16

continued from page 15

shall be chosen by him on the express condition that on the formation of each company the Concessionaire shall give official notice of such formation to the Imperial Government through the medium of the commissioner and shall forward the "statutes" with information as to the places at which such company is to operate. Such company or companies shall enjoy all the rights and privileges granted to the Concessionaire, but they must assume all his engagements and responsibilities.

Article X
It shall be stipulated in the contract between the Concessionaire of the one part and the company of the other part that the latter is within the term of one month as from the date of the formation of the first exploitation company to pay the Imperial Persian Government the sum of £20,000 sterling in cash and an additional sum of £20,000 sterling in paid-up shares of the first company founded by virtue of the foregoing Article. It shall also pay the said Government annually a sum equal to 16 per cent of the annual net profits of any company or companies that may be formed in accordance with the said Article.

Article XI
The said Government shall be free to appoint [an] Imperial Commissioner who shall be consulted by the concessionaire and the directors of the companies to be formed. He shall supply all and any useful information at his disposal and he shall inform them of the best course to be adopted in the interest of the undertaking. He shall establish by agreement with the Concessionaire such supervision as he may deem expedient to safeguard the interests of the Imperial Government. The aforesaid powers of the Imperial Commissioner shall be set forth in the "statutes" of the companies to be created. The Concessionaire shall pay the Commissioner thus appointed an annual sum of £1,000 sterling for his services as from the date of the formation of the first company.

Article XII
The workmen employed in the service of the Company shall be subjects of His Imperial Majesty the Shah, except the technical staff such as the managers, engineers, borers and foremen.

Article XIII
At any place in which it may be proved that the inhabitants of the country now obtain petroleum for their own use, the Company must supply them gratuitously with the quantity of petroleum that they themselves got previously. Such quantity

shall be fixed according to their own declarations, subject to the supervision of the local authority.

Article XIV
The Imperial Government binds itself to take all and any necessary measures to secure the safety and the carrying out of the object of this Concession, of the plant and of the apparatuses of which mention is made for the purpose of the undertaking of the Company and to protect the representatives, agents and servants of the Company. The Imperial Government having thus fulfilled its engagements, the Concessionaire and the companies created by him shall not have power under any pretext whatever to claim damages from the Persian Government.

Article XV
On the expiration of the term of the present Concession, all materials, buildings and apparatuses then used by the Company for the exploitation of its industry shall become the property of the said Government, and the Company shall have no right to any indemnity in this connection.

Article XVI
If within the term of two years as from the present date the Concessionaire shall not have established the first of the said companies authorized by Article 9 of the present Agreement, the present Concession shall become null and void.

Article XVII
In the event of there arising between the parties to the present concession any dispute or difference in respect of its interpretation or the rights of responsibilities of one or the other of the parties therefore resulting, such dispute or difference shall be submitted to two arbitrators at Teheran, one of whom shall be named by each of the parties, and to an Umpire who shall be appointed by the arbitrators before they proceed to arbitrate. The decision of the arbitrators or, in the event of the latter disagreeing that of the umpire, shall be final.

Article XVIII
This Act of Concession made in duplicate is written in the French language and translated into Persian with the same meaning. But in the event of there being any dispute in relation to such meaning, the French text shall alone prevail.

Teheran
Sefer 1319 of the Hegine, that is to say May 1901.

continues on page 18

continued from page 17

> (Signed) William Knox D'Arcy, By his Attorney,
> (Signed) Alfred L. Marriott.
> (Signed) George Grahame, Vice-Consul.
> Dated at Gulaket near Teheran this 6 day of June 1901.
> (Signed) George Grahame, Vice-Consul.

GLOSSARY

ozokerite: a black wax produced in petroleum deposits

tomans: an Iranian supercurrency; at the time, two thousand tomans would equal about $40,000 in today's money

Document Themes and Analysis

The agreement between Mozaffar al-Din Shah and William D'Arcy was remarkable for its time in that it was an agreement between a government and an individual expecting to form a company, versus a government and the company itself or another government. Furthermore, governments usually made concessions to companies in order to exploit resources. In this agreement, the Persian government indeed determined the terms of the concession for D'Arcy's company, but since no one knew where to find the petroleum reserves, the company essentially defined the terms—it told the shah what parameters it needed to search for mineral wealth across approximately 85 percent of Persia's territory. Accordingly, in the agreement, the "Concessionaire," as it is termed in French, is D'Arcy as opposed to the shah. In the future, the body of this agreement would become the model for other concessions written between companies and governments across the petroleum-producing Arab states through the early twentieth century.

The first article states that the shah's government granted the "privilege"—an important term to use, as opposed to a "right," which had implications for which an aggrieved party could sue in international law—to D'Arcy's company to mine for petroleum and prepare it to trade outside the country. This privilege would last for sixty years, and cover "the whole extent of the Persian Empire," an area that would be modified later in Article VI. In the second article, the company was granted the "right" to build pipelines and maintain wells to exploit whatever petroleum was found. In other words, the "privilege" of searching for petroleum and its derivatives could be taken away if D'Arcy displeased the shah somehow, but he had the "right" to build and control the property his company needed to exploit the privilege. The third article allowed the company to look for oil on any public land, and to negotiate terms with land owned by individual Persians, exclusive of "[h]oly places with all their dependencies within a radius of 200 Persian archines." The fifth article allowed the company to determine the necessary route

Walter Hall and D'Arcy, ca. 885

over which to build the pipelines. Eventually, the first line would run a hundred and thirty miles through the Persian desert to a petroleum refinery built at the base of the Euphrates River at Abadan; it would be the largest refinery in the world by 1950.

Article IV was written in light of all the shah's previous economic agreements made in Persia—D'Arcy's company was given control over three already-producing petroleum sites, so it would have a full monopoly on production. In Article 10, it was agreed that the shah's treasury would collect 16 percent of the yearly profits taken in by D'Arcy's company; for these three sites, they would pay an added two thousand tomans—about $40,000 a piece—for the right to continue drilling there. This may have seemed like a lot of money in 1901. Within fifteen years, however, the spread of the automobile and the airplane, and the needs of militaries during the First World War to maintain submarines, destroyers and tanks, plus the sheer amounts of petroleum gushing out of the earth in Persia would make $40,000 a pittance, likely less than a half day's worth of production at Abadan.

The sixth article modified the first article. Five Persian provinces were excluded from the D'Arcy company's exploration—Azerbadjan, Ghilan, Mazendaran, Asdrabad and Khorassan, all provinces bordering the Russian Empire. The idea was to avoid teasing the Russians into protesting the concession by drilling oil right over the border from Baku, "on the express condition that the Persian Imperial Government shall not grant to any other person the right of constructing a pipeline to the southern rivers or to the south coast of Persia." In other words, D'Arcy's British government backers wanted to avoid harassing the Russians, but they were not about to let them mine themselves or build a pipeline across Persia either.

Article VII made D'Arcy's concession tax-free, a stunning grant considering how much British geologists, engineers, dredgers and other employees of the company would rely on Persian infrastructure to accomplish their goals. In essence, the seventh article meant that the Persian populace would pay for all of the roads, housing, land and other facilities necessary to dig up the petroleum. Such an article would never clear a concession today; like Article IV, it was a relic of the shah's nineteenth century economic agreements with the Russians and the British.

In the eighth article, D'Arcy was required to declare his intentions, to name where his company would dig and provide the means to get his people and supplies to the site. In other words, all the costs and all the risks for the actual petroleum exploration would be borne by D'Arcy. Once the digging sites were determined, the ninth article required the company to provide its people's names, company rules, and accounting books for the perusal of the shah's state, for the purposes of honesty and communication as to the rules of the concession. "Such company or companies shall enjoy all the rights and privileges granted to the Concessionaire, but they must assume all his engagements and responsibilities."

The tenth article began to set the terms for what the Persian government would get out of the concession. The £20,000 sterling which D'Arcy had provided had to be handed over within a month (again, half of it was handed over immediately to avoid Russian interference in the signing). Furthermore, the company agreed to pay the shah another £20,000 per month over the coming years as the company continued its search for petroleum. Once petroleum was found, the Persian government would receive 16 percent of the annual profits of the petroleum products brought out of Persia—an amount that, as in the 2000 tomans handed over in Article IV, was pitifully small in comparison to how much the British companies would make out of their refinery at Abadan. Even then, argument over how much the Anglo-Iranian Oil Company made off Persian oil and how much 16 percent of its profits amounted to would be a constant source of friction. Article XI would seem to have dealt with these contradictions by having the Persian government appoint an "Imperial Commissioner" to keep an eye on affairs around the petroleum digs. However, it also stipulated that D'Arcy's companies would determine what his "aforesaid powers" would be, and they would supply him with his £1,000 sterling annual salary. In modern terms, then, he was to be a puppet of the company.

The next four articles protected the Persian people and the company's employees. Article XII demanded that the company provide jobs for the shah's subjects, and Article XIII protected their own petroleum finds by demanding that the company compensate them for taking over their oil fields and provide them with the oil they needed to maintain their lifestyles. In return, Article XIV promised that D'Arcy's employees and equipment would be protected by the Persian government, and in return the company could not sue the Persian government under any circumstances. Finally, once the concession was finished, all the equipment and facilities would be turned over the shah's government, according to the fifteenth article. All of this seemed comparatively fair, but in the long run, the company would keep its Persian workers in squalid poverty on site in Abadan, and as a result, the only people the Anglo-Iranian Oil Company needed protection from was the angry Persian populace themselves.

The concession had a two-year lifespan, according to Article XVI; if D'Arcy did not establish his digging companies by then, the concession was null and void. In the seventeenth article, any disputes over the concession would be settled by an independent arbitration team, one appointed by the shah's government and one appointed by D'Arcy's company, surrounding an umpire that the two arbitrators chose themselves. And finally, the agreement was to be written up in Persian and French; if there was a dispute, "the French text shall alone prevail."

The contract was the first to be concluded between a western corporation and an Asian country with petroleum resources, so it would be copied in numerous future agreements, with a few modifications. It protected D'Arcy from most of the consequences if his investment failed, but it also required him to better the economic situations of the Persian people he encountered in his explorations, employing them and assuring them of a certain value for their petroleum reserves. In the end, though, that would not prove to be much of a requirement.

Upon receiving his concession, D'Arcy put together a mining company run by George Reynolds, an engineer out of India who had previously drilled for oil in the Dutch East Indies (today's Indonesia). Reynolds explored and drilled for three years, but beyond those sites where petroleum was already known to exist, D'Arcy's company found nothing. The British military were concerned not to lose D'Arcy's concession to the Russians, Admiral John Fisher of the Royal Navy wanted to convert the Royal Navy's battleships to oil-consuming combustion engines, and the airplane held some small promise as a wartime weapon as well. So the British government helped negotiate a partner for D'Arcy before his company went bankrupt.

In 1905, Burmah Oil merged with D'Arcy's company to form the roots of a new company, with D'Arcy as its director.

Seven years after the concession, even this merger was on the verge of financial collapse. D'Arcy himself began to consider the end of his efforts to drill in the Persian desert. Then, mere days before giving up, in May 1908, a gusher of petroleum blew fifty feet over the top of a drilling rig at Majid-i-Suleiman in the Zagros Mountains. Reynolds had a pipeline built out to Abadan, and D'Arcy's company went public in 1909, renaming itself the Anglo-Persian Oil Company—the roots of what would become BP, or British Petroleum. When the Abadan refinery broke down in 1913, the British Admiralty, led by Winston Churchill, convinced the British government to buy 51 percent of Anglo-Persian stock to maintain the concession in Britain's favor; the sale was completed five days after Britain had declared war on Germany, beginning the First World War. Persian oil would power the Royal Navy and the Royal Air Force throughout both world wars.

Persia—renamed Iran in 1935—became a pawn in the hands of Britain and its allies. In 1907, the Persian people demanded and received from the shah a constitution, establishing for themselves a parliament, the Majlis, and elections for representatives to sit in it. In the same year, Britain and Russia settled their differences in Persia in the Anglo-Russian Entente, granting spheres of influence to each other, the Russians in the north and the British in the south. The petroleum strike at Majid-i-Suleiman a year later mean that the Majlis would never have anything but the most cursory control over the Persian economy ever after—the British military's demand for oil precluded it. In 1925, British intelligence paid an army colonel, Mohammed Reza, to overthrow the Qajar shah in 1925 and establish a pro-British and anti-Soviet regime with the Majlis firmly subordinated to his rule. Twenty-eight years later, in 1953, the Anglo-Iranian Oil Company, Churchill, the CIA and Reza's son, the Shah Muhammad Reza Pahlavi, conspired to overthrow the Majlis' prime minister and establish Pahlavi as a dictator, all in the interests of keeping the oil flowing. Another quarter century later, in 1978, Ayatollah Ruhollah Khomeini's Islamic Revolution would throw out all of Iran's foreign influences; in return, Iran's oil was sanctioned and its sales limited on the international market, led by a boycott imposed by the United States and Britain. Iran's oil sanctions last in limited form all the way to the present day. Truly, the D'Arcy concession conceded more of Iran's future than was obvious in 1901.

—David Simonelli

Bibliography and Additional Reading

Books

Axworthy, Michael. *A History of Iran: Empire of the Mind*. New York: Basic Books, 2010.

Bamberg, James. *British Petroleum and Global Oil, 1950–1975: The Challenge of Nationalism*. New York: Cambridge University Press, 2000.

Parra, Francisco R. *Oil Politics: A Modern History of Petroleum*. London: I.B. Tauris, 2004.

Yergin, Daniel. *The Prize: The Epic Quest for Oil, Money & Power*. New York: Free Press, 1991.

Websites

Mina, Parviz. "Oil Agreements in Iran". *Encyclopaedia Iranica* (July 20, 2004) [accessed March 17, 2018].

Smith, Robert R., Hassaan S. Vahidy and Fereidun Fesharaki. "OPEC's Evolving Role: D'Arcy Concession Centennial and OPEC Today—An Historical Perspective". *Oil & Gas Journal* (July 9, 2001) [accessed March 17, 2018].

Boghoziyan, Albert. "One for Us, Six for Britons!: William Knox D'Arcy in History of Iran". *Iran Review* (May 25, 2016) http://www.iranreview.org/content/Documents/One-for-Us-Six-for-Britons-.htm [accessed March 17, 2018].

■ Hussein-McMahon Correspondence

Date: October 24, 1915
Authors: Sir Henry McMahon; Hussein bin Ali
Geographic region: Middle East
Genre: Correspondence

Summary Overview

The correspondence examined here is significant as it sets forth, in the minds of many Arabs, what was promised to them after World War I. They were promised to be both considered in the area and given control of most of it in return for their support of the British, French and Russian side (called the Triple Entente at the beginning of the war). The Arabs moved to confront the Ottoman Empire and so did their part, but they feel that the British did not ever intend to carry out their side of the bargain. The two authors, Hussein bin Ali and Henry McMahon, were the leaders, respectively, of the Arab forces (and the man in control of Mecca, the most holy site of Islam) and the British High Commissioner for Egypt (and thus the British official in charge of the region). The British, after making this promise to the Arabs, also promised to establish part of the same region as a Jewish homeland and divided up the region a third time with the French. Thus, rightfully so, the Arabs felt betrayed. The situation needs to be looked at in terms of so-called Great Power diplomacy, as Great Britain (along with France, the US and other powers) drew and re-drew lines of countries and colonies all over the world and did not pay any attention to the desires or needs of the people of those places.

Defining Moment

This series of letters (collectively called the correspondence) was a Defining Moment in history, as in them the British promised the Arabs control over most of the Middle East in return for Arab assistance in fighting the Ottoman Empire. The British wanted this because they were desperate for help in that area. However, the British were also promising the Jewish world population a homeland in Palestine at this time. The Sykes-Picot Agreement, written at about the same time, divided up the Middle East between Britain and France. The British, then, were promising the same land to two different groups. The British later tried to play it three ways, claiming that the three agreements could all be read with the same intent. The Arabs, not surprisingly, felt betrayed. This experience poisoned the chance for good relations between the Arabs and the British (and French), which had ramifications after World War I.

The situation also plays into the long-term history of the Middle East. Many Arabs feel that their wishes have not been taken into account for the last century (or more) and that Israel was thrust upon them. While the Hussein-McMahon correspondence seems to take the Arab view into account (and would have had it been enacted), it cannot be viewed in a vacuum. As noted, the area was promised to three parties. Thus, when in later years the Arabs claimed they were not given what they were promised, they were correct. Had this been the only slight, it might not have been an issue. However, 25 years later, the Europeans still controlled the area and after World War II, Israel was created without much consideration of what the people in the area wanted.

Author Biographies

The two main authors were Sir Henry McMahon and Hussein bin Ali, the Sharif of Mecca. Hussein was a descendant of Mohammed and his family line had ruled Mecca since the thirteenth century. Hussein came to power in 1908 and remained loyal to the Ottoman Empire. In 1915, during World War I, Hussein began to think it was better to separate from the Ottomans (and his son advised this). He began corresponding with Lord Kitchener (Secretary of State for War of England) and then with Henry McMahon. After the war, Hussein refused to sign the treaties proposed by the European powers as they gave all power to the British and French; Hussein was eventually deposed. The British did appoint his two sons as kings of Iraq and Jordan (called Transjordan at the time; with king of Jordan starting the royal line that still rules Jordan today).

Sir Henry McMahon's father and grandfather both served in the English East India Company and McMahon was born in India. McMahon served in the British Administration in India and was awarded several titles for his service. He knew several languages and during World War I was appointed British High Commissioner for Egypt, arriving in 1915. McMahon then conducted the correspondence with Hussein. It should be noted that McMahon was fluent in Arabic but that someone else prepared the translation, which led to some difficulties. He became Sir Henry McMahon in 1906.

HISTORICAL DOCUMENT: *Hussein-McMahon Correspondence*

No. 1

Translation of a letter from Sharif Husayn of Mecca to Sir Henry McMahon, His Majesty's High Commissioner at Cairo, July 14, 1915

Whereas the whole of the Arab nation without any exception have decided in these last years to accomplish their freedom, and grasp the reins of their administration both in theory and practice; and whereas they have found and felt that it is in the interest of the Government of Great Britain to support them and aid them in the attainment of their firm and lawful intentions (which are based upon the maintenance of the honor and dignity of their life) without any ulterior motives whatsoever unconnected with this object;

And whereas it is to their (the Arabs') interest also to prefer the assistance of the Government of Great Britain in consideration of their geographic position and economic interests, and also of the attitude of the above-mentioned Government, which is known to both nations and therefore need not be emphasized;

For these reasons the Arab nation sees fit to limit themselves, as time is short, to asking the Government of Great Britain, if it should think fit, for the approval, through her deputy or representative, of the following fundamental propositions, leaving out all things considered secondary in comparison with these, so that it may prepare all means necessary for attaining this noble purpose, until such time as it finds occasion for making the actual negotiations:-

Firstly.—England will acknowledge the independence of the Arab countries, bounded on the north by Mersina and Adana up to the 37th degree of latitude, on which degree fall Birijik, Urfa, Mardin, Midiat, Jezirat (Ibn 'Umar), Amadia, up to the border of Persia; on the east by the borders of Persia up to the Gulf of Basra; on the south by the Indian Ocean, with the exception of the position of Aden to remain as it is; on the west by the Red Sea, the Mediterranean Sea up to Mersina. England to approve the proclamation of an Arab Khalifate of Islam.

Secondly.—The Arab Government of the Sherif will acknowledge that England shall have the preference in all economic enterprises in the Arab countries whenever conditions of enterprises are otherwise equal.

Thirdly.—For the security of this Arab independence and the certainty of such preference of economic enterprises, both high contracting parties will offer mutual assistance, to the best ability of their military and naval forces, to face any foreign Power which may attack either party. Peace not to be decided without agreement of both parties.

Fourthly.—If one of the parties enters into an aggressive conflict, the other party will assume a neutral attitude, and in case of such party wishing the other to join forces, both to meet and discuss the conditions.

Fifthly.—England will acknowledge the abolition of foreign privileges in the Arab countries, and will assist the Government of the Sherif in an International Convention for confirming such abolition.

Sixthly.—Articles 3 and 4 of this treaty will remain in vigor for fifteen years, and, if either wishes it to be renewed, one year's notice before lapse of treaty is to be given.

Consequently, and as the whole of the Arab nation have (praise be to God) agreed and united for the attainment, at all costs and finally, of this noble object, they beg

> *For these reasons the Arab nation sees fit to limit themselves, as time is short, to asking the Government of Great Britain… for the … following fundamental propositions…so that it may prepare all means necessary for attaining this noble purpose, until such time as it finds occasion for making the actual negotiations*

continues on page 26

continued from page 25

the Government of Great Britain to answer them positively or negatively in a period of thirty days after receiving this intimation; and if this period should lapse before they receive an answer, they reserve to themselves complete freedom of action. Moreover, we (the Sherif's family) will consider ourselves free in work and deed from the bonds of our previous declaration which we made through Ali Effendi.

No. 2

Translation of a letter from McMahon to Husayn, August 30, 1915

To his Highness the Sherif Hussein.

(After compliments and salutations.)

WE have the honour to thank you for your frank expressions of the sincerity of your feeling towards England. We rejoice, moreover, that your Highness and your people are of one opinion—that Arab interests are English interests and English Arab. To this intent 'we confirm to you the terms of Lord Kitchener's message, which reached you by the hand of Ali Effendi, and in which was stated clearly our desire for the independence of Arabia and its inhabitants, together with our approval of the Arab Khalifate when it should be proclaimed. We declare once more that His Majesty's Government would welcome the resumption of the Khalifate by an Arab of true race. With regard to the questions of limits and boundaries, it would appear to be premature to consume our time in discussing such details in the heat of war, and while, in many portions of them, the Turk is up to now in effective occupation; especially as we have learned, with surprise and regret, that some of the Arabs in those very parts, far from assisting us, are neglecting this their supreme opportunity and are lending their arms to the German and the Turk, to the new despoiler and the old oppressor.

Nevertheless, we are ready to send your Highness for the Holy Cities and the noble Arabs the charitable offerings of Egypt so soon as your Highness shall inform us how and where they should be delivered. We are, moreover, arranging for this your messenger to be admitted and helped on any journey he may make to ourselves. Friendly reassurances. Salutations!

(Signed) A. H. McMAHON.

No. 3

Translation of a letter from Husayn to McMahon, September 9, 1915

To his Excellency the Most Exalted, the Most Eminent-the British High Commissioner in Egypt; may God grant him Success.

WITH great cheerfulness and delight I received your letter dated the 19th Shawal, 1333 (the 30th August, 1915), and have given it great consideration and regard, in spite of the impression I received from it of ambiguity and its tone of coldness and hesitation with regard to our essential point.

It is necessary to make clear to your Excellency our sincerity towards the illustrious British Empire and our confession of preference for it in all cases and matters and under all forms and circumstances. The real interests of the followers of our religion necessitate this.

Nevertheless, your Excellency will pardon me and permit me to say clearly that the coolness and hesitation which you have displayed in the question of the limits and boundaries by saying that the discussion of these at present is of no use and is a loss of time, and that they are still in the hands of the Government which is ruling them, &c., might be taken to infer an estrangement or something of the sort.

As the limits and boundaries demanded are not those of one person whom we should satisfy and with whom we should discuss them after the war is over, but our peoples have seen that the life of their new proposal is bound at least by these limits and their word is united on this.

Therefore, they have found it necessary first to discuss this point with the Power in whom they now have their confidence and trust as a final appeal, viz., the illustrious British Empire.

Their reason for this union and confidence is mutual interest, the necessity of regulating territorial divisions and the feelings of their inhabitants, so that they may know how to base their future and life, so not to meet her (England?) or any of her Allies in opposition to their resolution which would produce a contrary issue, which God forbid.

For the object is, honorable Minister, the truth which is established on a basis which guarantees the essential sources of life in future.

Yet within these limits they have not included places inhabited by a foreign race. It is a vain show of words and titles.

May God have mercy on the Khalifate and comfort Moslems in it.

I am confident that your Excellency will not doubt that it is not I personally who am demanding of these limits which include only our race, but that they are all proposals of the people, who, in short, believe that they are necessary for economic life.

continues on page 28

continued from page 27

> Is this not right, your Excellency the Minister?
>
> In a word, your high Excellency, we are firm in our sincerity and declaring our preference for loyalty towards you, whether you are satisfied with us, as has been said, or angry.
>
> With reference to your remark in your letter above mentioned that some of our people are still doing their utmost in promoting the interests of Turkey, your goodness (lit. "perfectness") would not permit you to make this an excuse for the tone of coldness and hesitation with regard to our demands, demands which I cannot admit that you, as a man of sound opinion, will deny to be necessary for our existence; nay, they are the essential essence of our life, material and moral.
>
> Up to the present moment I am myself with all my might carrying out in my country all things in conformity with the Islamic law, all things which tend to benefit the rest of the Kingdom, and I shall continue to do so until it pleases God to order otherwise.
>
> In order to reassure your Excellency I can declare that the whole country, together with those who you say are submitting themselves to Turco-German orders, are all waiting the result of these negotiations, which are dependent only on your refusal or acceptance of the question of the limits and on your declaration of safeguarding their religion first and then the rest of rights from any harm or danger.
>
> Whatever the illustrious Government of Great Britain finds conformable to its policy on this subject, communicate it to us and specify to us the course we should follow.
>
> In all cases it is only God's will which shall be executed, and it is God who is the real factor in everything.
>
> With regard to our demand for grain for the natives, and the moneys ("surras") known to the Wakfs' Ministry and all other articles sent here with pilgrims' caravans, high Excellency, my intention in this matter is to confirm your proclamations to the whole world, and especially to the Moslem world, that your antagonism is confined only to the party which has usurped the rights of the Khalifate in which are included the rights of all Moslems.
>
> Moreover the said grain is from the special Wakfs and has nothing to do with politics.
>
> If you think it should be, let the grain of the two years be transported in a special steamer to Jedda in an official manner, in the name of all the natives as usual, and the captain of the steamer or the special "Mamur" detailed as usual every year to hand it over on his arrival at the port will send to the Governor of Jedda asking for the Mamur of the grain at Jedda or a responsible official to take over the grain and give the necessary receipt signed by the said Mamur, that is the Mamur of the grain

himself. He should make it a condition that he would (? not) accept any receipt but that signed by this Mamur.

Let the captain of the steamer or the "Mamur" (detailed with the grain) be instructed that if he finds anything contrary to this arrangement he should warn them that he will return home with the cargo. Thereupon the Mamur and the special committee detailed with him, which is known as the committee of the grain for the natives, will take over the grain in the proper form.

Please accept my best regards and salutations.

If you choose to send a reply to this, please send it with the bearer. 29th *Shawal*, 1333.

No. 4

Translation of a letter from McMahon to Husayn, October 24, 1915

I have received your letter of the 29th Shawal, 1333, with much pleasure and your expressions of friendliness and sincerity have given me the greatest satisfaction.

I regret that you should have received from my last letter the impression that I regarded the question of the limits and boundaries with coldness and hesitation; such was not the case, but it appeared to me that the time had not yet come when that question could be discussed in a conclusive manner.

I have realized, however, from your last letter that you regard this question as one of vital and urgent importance. I have, therefore, lost no time in informing the Government of Great Britain of the contents of your letter, and it is with great pleasure that I communicate to you on their behalf the following statement, which I am confident you will receive with satisfaction:-

The two districts of Mersina and Alexandretta and portions of Syria lying to the west of the districts of Damascus, Homs, Hama and Aleppo cannot be said to be purely Arab, and should be excluded from the limits demanded.

With the above modification, and without prejudice of our existing treaties with Arab chiefs, we accept those limits.

As for those regions lying within those frontiers wherein Great Britain is free to act without detriment to the interest of her ally, France, I am empowered in the name of the Government of Great Britain to give the following assurances and make the following reply to your letter:—

1. Subject to the above modifications, Great Britain is prepared to recognize and support the independence of the Arabs in all the regions within the limits demanded by the Sherif of Mecca.

continues on page 30

continued from page 29

2. Great Britain will guarantee the Holy Places against all external aggression and will recognize their inviolability.
3. When the situation admits, Great Britain will give to the Arabs her advice and will assist them to establish what may appear to be the most suitable forms of government in those various territories.
4. On the other hand, it is understood that the Arabs have decided to seek the advice and guidance of Great Britain only, and that such European advisers and officials as may be required for the formation of a sound form of administration will be British.
5. With regard to the vilayets of Bagdad and Basra, the Arabs will recognize that the established position and interests of Great Britain necessitate special administrative arrangements in order to secure these territories from foreign aggression, to promote the welfare of the local populations and to safeguard our mutual economic interests.

I am convinced that this declaration will assure you beyond all possible doubt of the sympathy of Great Britain towards the aspirations of her friends the Arabs and will result in a firm and lasting alliance, the immediate results of which will be the expulsion of the Turks from the Arab countries and the freeing of the Arab peoples from the Turkish yoke, which for so many years has pressed heavily upon them.

I have confined myself in this letter to the more vital and important questions, and if there are any other matters dealt with in your letter which I have omitted to mention, we may discuss them at some convenient date in the future.

It was with very great relief and satisfaction that I heard of the safe arrival of the Holy Carpet and the accompanying offerings which, thanks to the clearness of your directions and the excellence of your arrangements, were landed without trouble or mishap in spite of the dangers and difficulties occasioned by the present sad war. May God soon bring a lasting peace and freedom to all peoples!

I am sending this letter by the hand of your trusted and excellent messenger, Sheikh Mohammed Ibn Arif Ibn Uraifan, and he will inform you of the various matters of interest, but of less vital importance, which I have not mentioned in this letter.
(Compliments)
(Signed) A. H. McMAHON.

No. 5

Translation of a letter from Husayn to McMahon, November 5, 1915

(In the name of God, the Merciful, the Compassionate!)

To his Excellency the most exalted and eminent Minister who is endowed with the highest authority and soundness of opinion.

May God guide him to do His Will!

I RECEIVED with great pleasure your honored letter, dated the 15th Zil Hijja (the 24th October, 1915), to which I beg to answer as follows:

1. In order to facilitate an agreement and to render a service to Islam, and at the same time to avoid all that may cause Islam troubles and hardships-seeing moreover that we have great consideration for the distinguished qualities and dispositions of the Government of Great Britain-we renounce our insistence on the inclusion of the vilayets of Mersina and Adana in the Arab Kingdom. But the two vilayets of Aleppo and Beirut and their sea coasts are purely Arab vilayets, and there is no difference between a Moslem and a Christian Arab: they are both descendants of one forefather.

   We Moslems will follow the footsteps of the Commander of the Faithful Omar ibn Khattab, and other Khalifs succeeding him, who ordained in the laws of the Moslem Faith that Moslems should treat the Christians as they treat themselves. He, Omar, declared with reference to Christians: "They will have the same privileges and submit to the same duties as ourselves." They will thus enjoy their civic rights in as much as it accords with the general interests of the whole nation.

2. As the Iraqi vilayets are parts of the pure Arab Kingdom, and were in fact the seat of its Government in the time of Ali ibn Abu Talib, and in the time of all the Khalifs who succeeded him; and as in them began the civilization of the Arabs, and as their towns were the first towns built in Islam where the Arab power became so great; therefore they are greatly valued by all Arabs far and near, and their traditions cannot be forgotten by them. Consequently, we cannot satisfy the Arab nations or make them submit to give us such a title to nobility. But in order to render an accord easy, and taking into consideration the assurances mentioned in the fifth article of your letter to keep and guard our mutual interests in that country as they are one and the same, for all these reasons we might agree to leave under the British administration for a short time those districts now occupied by the British troops without the rights of either party being prejudiced thereby (especially those of the Arab nation; which interests are to it economic and vital), and against a suitable sum paid as compensation to the Arab Kingdom for the period of occupation, in order to meet the expenses which every new kingdom is bound to support; at the same time respecting your agreements with the Sheikhs of those districts, and especially those which are essential.

3. In your desire to hasten the movement we see not only advantages, but grounds of apprehension. The first of these grounds is the fear of the blame of the Moslems of the opposite party (as has already happened in the past), who would declare that we have revolted against Islam and ruined its forces. The second is that, standing in the face of Turkey which is supported by all the forces of Germany, we do not know what Great Britain and

continues on page 32

continued from page 31

her Allies would do if one of the Entente Powers were weakened and obliged to make peace. We fear that the Arab nation will then be left alone in the face of Turkey together with her allies, but we would not at all mind if we were to face the Turks alone. Therefore it is necessary to take these points into consideration in order to avoid a peace being concluded in which the parties concerned may decide the fate of our people as if we had taken part in the war without making good our claims to official consideration.

4. The Arab nation has a strong belief that after this war is over the Turks under German influence will direct their efforts to provoke the. Arabs and violate their rights, both material and moral, to wipe out their nobility and honor and reduce them to utter submission as they are determined to ruin them entirely. The reasons for the slowness shown in our action have already been stated.

5. When the Arabs know the Government of Great Britain is their ally who will not leave them to themselves at the conclusion of peace in the face of Turkey and Germany, and that she will support and will effectively defend them, then to enter the war at once will, no doubt, be in conformity with the general interest of the Arabs.

6. Our letter dated the 29th Shaual, 1333 (the 9th September, 1915), saves us the trouble of repeating our opinions as to articles 3 and 4 of your honored last letter regarding administration, Government advisers and officials, especially as you have declared, exalted Minister, that you will not interfere with internal affairs.

7. The arrival of a clear and definite answer as soon as possible to the above proposals is expected. We have done our utmost in making concessions in order to come to an agreement satisfying both parties. We know that our lot in this war will be either a success, which will guarantee to the Arabs a life becoming their past history, or destruction in the attempt to attain their objects. Had it not been for the determination which I see in the Arabs for the attainment of their objects, I would have preferred to seclude myself on one of the heights of a mountain, but they, the Arabs, have insisted that I should guide the movement to this end.

May God keep you safe and victorious, as we devoutly hope and desire.

27th *Zil Hijja*, 1333.

No. 6

Translation of a letter from McMahon to Husayn, December 14, 1915

(After customary greetings and acknowledgment of previous letter.)

I AM gratified to observe that you agree to the exclusion of the districts of Mersina and Adana from boundaries of the Arab territories.

I also note with great pleasure and satisfaction your assurances that the Arabs are determined to act in conformity with the precepts laid down by Omar Ibn Khattab and the early Khalifs, which secure the rights and privileges of all religions alike.

In stating that the Arabs are ready to recognize and respect all our treaties with Arab chiefs, it is, of course, understood that this will apply to all territories included in the Arab Kingdom, as the Government of Great Britain cannot repudiate engagements which already exist.

With regard to the vilayets of Aleppo and Beirut, the Government of Great Britain have fully understood and taken careful note of your observations, but, as the interests of our ally, France, are involved in them both, the question will require careful consideration and a further communication on the subject will be addressed to you in due course.

The Government of Great Britain, as I have already informed you, are ready to give all guarantees of assistance and support within their power to the Arab Kingdom, but their interests demand, as you yourself have recognized, a friendly and stable administration in the vilayet of Bagdad, and the adequate safeguarding of these interests calls for a much fuller and more detailed consideration than the present situation and the urgency of these negotiations permit.

We fully appreciate your desire for caution, and have no wish to urge you to hasty action, which might jeopardize the eventual success of your projects, but, in the meantime, it is most essential that you should spare no effort to attach all the Arab peoples to our united cause and urge them to afford no assistance to our enemies.

It is on the success of these efforts and on the more active measures which the Arabs may hereafter take in support of our cause, when the time for action comes, that the permanence and strength of our agreement must depend.

Under these circumstances I am further directed by the Government of Great Britain to inform you that you may rest assured that Great Britain has no intention of concluding any peace in terms of which the freedom of the Arab peoples from German and Turkish domination does not form an essential condition.

As an earnest of our intentions, and in order to aid you in your efforts in our joint cause, I am sending you by your trustworthy messenger a sum of twenty thousand pounds.

(*Customary ending.*)
(Signed) H. McMAHON.

No. 7

Translation of a letter from Husayn to McMahon, January 1, 1916

(In the name of God, the Merciful, the Compassionate!)

continues on page 34

continued from page 33

To his Excellency the eminent, energetic and magnanimous Minister.

WE received from the bearer your letter, dated the 9th Safar (the 14th December, 1915), with great respect and honor, and I have understood its contents, which caused me the greatest pleasure and satisfaction, as it removed that which had made me uneasy.

Your honor will have realized, after the arrival of Mohammed (Faroki) Sherif and his interview with you, that all our procedure up to the present was of no personal inclination or the like, which would have been wholly unintelligible, but that everything was the result of the decisions and desires of our peoples, and that we are but transmitters and executants of such decisions and desires in the position they (our people) have pressed upon us.

These truths are, in my opinion, very important and deserve your honor's special attention and consideration.

With regard to what had been stated in your honored communication concerning El Iraq as to the matter of compensation for the period of occupation, we, in order to strengthen the confidence of Great Britain in our attitude and in our words and actions, really and veritably, and in order to give her evidence of our certainty and assurance in trusting her glorious Government, leave the determination of the amount to the perception of her wisdom and justice.

As regards the northern parts and their coasts, we have already stated in our previous letter what were the utmost possible modifications, and all this was only done so to fulfill those aspirations whose attainment is desired by the will of the Blessed and Supreme God. It is this same feeling and desire which impelled us to avoid what may possibly injure the alliance of Great Britain and France and the agreement made between them during the present wars and calamities; yet we find it our duty that the eminent minister should be sure that, at the first opportunity after this war is finished, we shall ask you (what we avert our eyes from to-day) for what we now leave to France in Beirut and its coasts.

I do not find it necessary to draw your attention to the fact that our plan is of greater security to the interests and protection of the rights of Great Britain than it is to us, and will necessarily be so whatever may happen, so that Great Britain may finally see her friends in that contentment and advancement which she is endeavoring to establish for them now, especially as her Allies being neighbors to us will be the germ of difficulties and discussion with which there will be no peaceful conditions. In addition to which the citizens of Beirut will decidedly never accept such dismemberment, and they may oblige us to undertake new measures which may exercise Great Britain, certainly not less than her present troubles, because of our belief and certainty in the reciprocity and indeed the identity of our interests, which is the only cause that caused us never to care to negotiate with any other Power but you. Consequently, it is impossible to allow any derogation that gives France, or any other Power, a span of land in those regions.

I declare this, and I have a strong belief, which the living will inherit from the dead, in the declarations which you give in the conclusion of your honored letter. Therefore, the honorable and eminent Minister should believe and be sure, together with Great Britain, that we still remain firm to our resolution which Storrs learnt from us two years ago, for which we await the opportunity suitable to our situation, especially in view of that action the time of which has now come near and which destiny drives towards us with great haste and clearness, so that we and those who are of our opinion may have reasons for such action against any criticisms or responsibilities imposed upon us in future.

Your expression "we do not want to push you to any hasty action which might jeopardise the success of your aim" does not need any more explanation except what we may ask for, when necessary, such as arms, ammunition, &c.

I deem this sufficient, as I have occupied much of your Honour's time. I beg to offer you my great veneration and respect.

25th *Safar*, 1334.

No. 8

Translation of a letter from McMahon to Husayn, January 25, 1916

(After customary greetings.)

WE have received with great pleasure and satisfaction your letter of the 25th Safar (the 1st January) at the hands of your trusty messenger, who has also transmitted to us your verbal messages.

We fully realize and entirely appreciate the motives which guide you in this important question, and we know well that you are acting entirely in the interests of the Arab peoples and with no thought beyond their welfare.

We take note of your remarks concerning the vilayet of Baghdad, and will take the question into careful consideration when the enemy has been defeated and the time for peaceful settlement arrives.

As regards the northern parts, we note with satisfaction your desire to avoid anything which might possibly injure the alliance of Great Britain and France. It is, as you know, our fixed determination that nothing shall be permitted to interfere in the slightest degree with our united prosecution of this war to a victorious conclusion.

continues on page 36

continued from page 35

Moreover, when the victory has been won, the friendship of Great Britain and France will become yet more firm and enduring, cemented by the blood of Englishmen and Frenchmen who have died side by side fighting for the cause of right and liberty.

In this great cause Arabia is now associated, and God grant that the result of our mutual efforts and co-operation will bind us in a lasting friendship to the mutual welfare and happiness of us all.

We are greatly pleased to hear of the action you are taking to win all the Arabs over to our joint cause, and to dissuade them from giving any assistance to our enemies, and we leave it to your discretion to seize the most favorable moment for further and more decided measures.

You will doubtless inform us by the bearer of this letter of any manner in which we can assist you and your requests will always receive our immediate consideration.

You will have heard how El Sayed Ahmed el Sherif el Senussi has been beguiled by evil advice into hostile action, and it will be a great grief to you to know that he has been so far forgetful of the interests of the Arabs as to throw in his lot with our enemies. Misfortune has now overtaken him, and we trust that this will show him his error and lead him to peace for the sake of his poor misguided followers.

We are sending this letter by the hand of your good messenger, who will also bring to you all our news.

With salaams.
(Signed) H. McMAHON.

No. 9

Translation of a letter from Husayn to McMahon, February 18, 1916

(In the name of the Merciful, the Compassionate!)

To the most noble His Excellency the High Commissioner. May God protect Vim.
(After compliments and respects.)

WE received your Excellency's letter dated 25th Rabi El Awal, and its contents filled us with the utmost pleasure and satisfaction at the attainment of the required understanding and the intimacy desired. I ask God to make easy our purposes and prosper our endeavors. Your Excellency will understand the work that is being done, and the reasons for it from the following:—Firstly.-We had informed your Excellency that we had sent one of our sons to Syria to command the operations deemed necessary there. We have received a detailed report from him stating that the tyrannies of the Government there have not left of the persons upon whom they could depend, whether of the different ranks of soldiers or of others, save only a few, and those of secondary importance; and that he is awaiting the arrival of the forces announced from different places, especially from the people of the country and the surrounding Arab regions as Aleppo and the south of Mosul, whose total is calculated at not less than 100,000 by their estimate; and he intends, if the majority of the forces mentioned are Arab, to begin the movement by them; and, if otherwise, that is, of the Turks or others, he will observe their advance to the Canal, and when they begin to fight, his movements upon them will be different to what they expect.

Secondly.—We purposed sending our eldest son to Medina with sufficient forces to strengthen his brother (who is) in Syria, and with every possibility of occupying the railway line, or carrying out such operations as circumstances may admit. This is the beginning of the principal movement, and we are satisfied in its beginning with what he had levied as guards to keep the interior of the country quiet; they are of the people of Hejaz only, for many reasons, which it would take too long to set forth; chiefly the difficulties in the way of providing their necessities with secrecy and speed (although this precaution was not necessary) and to make it easy to bring reinforcements when needed; this is the summary of what you wished to understand. In my opinion it is sufficient, and it is to be taken as a foundation and a standard as to our actions in the face of all changes and unforeseen events which the sequence of events may show. It remains for us to state what we need at present:

Firstly.—The amount of £50,000 in gold for the monthly pay of the troops levied, and other things the necessity of which needs no explanation. We beg you to send it with all possible haste.

Secondly.—20,000 sacks of rice, 15,000 sacks of flour, 3,000 sacks of barley, 150 sacks of coffee, 150 sacks of sugar, 5,000 rifles of the modern pattern and the necessary ammunition, and 100 boxes of the two sample cartridges (enclosed) and of Martini-Henry cartridges and "Aza," that is those of the rifles of the factory of St. Etienne in France, for the use of those two kinds of rifles of our tribes; it would not be amiss to send 500 boxes of both kinds.

Thirdly.—We think it better that the place of deposit of all these things should be Port Sudan.

Fourthly.—As the above provisions and munitions are not needed until the beginning of the movement (of which we will inform you officially), they should remain at the above place, and when we need them we will inform the Governor there of the place to which they may be conveyed, and of the intermediaries who will carry orders for receiving them.

Fifthly.—The money required should be sent at once to the Governor of Port Sudan, and a confidential agent will be sent by us to receive it, either all at once,

continues on page 38

continued from page 37

or in two installments, according as he is able, and this (§) is the (secret) sign to be recognized for accepting the man.

Sixthly.—Our envoy who will receive the money will be sent to Port Sudan in three weeks' time, that is to say, he will be there on the 5th Jamad Awal (9th March) with a letter from us addressed to Al Khawaga Elias Effendi, saying that he (Elias) will pay him, in accordance with the letter, the rent of our properties, and the signature will be clear in our name, but we will instruct him to ask for the Governor of the place, whom you will apprise of this person's arrival. After perusal of the letter, the money should be given to him on condition that no discussion whatever is to be made with him of any question concerning us. We beg you most emphatically not to tell him anything, keeping this affair secret, and he should be treated apparently as if he were nothing out of the way.

Let it not be thought that our appointment of another man results from lack of confidence in the bearer; it is only to avoid waste of time, for we are appointing him to a task elsewhere. At the same time we beg you not to embark or send him in a steamer, or officially, the means already arranged being sufficient.

Seventhly.—Our representative, bearer of the present letter, has been definitely instructed to ensure the arrival of this, and I think that his mission this time is finished since the condition of things is known both in general and in detail, and there is no need for sending anyone else. In case of need for sending information, it will come from us; yet as our next representative will reach you after three weeks, you may prepare instructions for him to take back. Yet let him be treated simply in appearance.

Eighthly.—Let the British Government consider this military expenditure in accordance with the books which will be furnished it, explaining how the money has been spent.

To conclude, my best and numberless salutations beyond all increase.

14 *Rabi al Akhar*, 1334.

No. 10

Translation of a letter from McMahon to Husayn, March 10, 1916

(*After customary greetings.*)

We have received your letter of the 14th Rabi el Akhar (the 18th February), duly delivered by your trusted messenger.

We are grateful to note the active measures which you propose to take. We consider them the most suitable in the existing circumstances, and they have the approval of His Majesty's Government. I am pleased to be able to inform you that His Majesty's Government have approved of meeting your requests, and that which you asked to be sent with all haste is being dispatched with your messenger, who is also the bearer of this letter.

The remainder will be collected as quickly as possible and will be deposited at Port Sudan, where it will remain until we hear from you officially of the beginning of the movement and of the places to which they may be conveyed and the intermediaries who will carry out the orders for receiving them.

The necessary instructions, as set forth in your letter, have been issued to the Governor at Port Sudan, and he will arrange everything in accordance with your wishes.

Your representative who brought your last letter has been duly facilitated in his journey to Jeizan, and every assistance has been given him in his mission, which we trust will be crowned with good results.

We have arranged that, on completion, he will be brought to Port Sudan, whence he will proceed by the safest means to join you and report the results of his work.

We take the opportunity, in sending this letter, to explain to you a matter which might otherwise not have been clear to you, and which might have given rise to misunderstanding. There are various Turkish posts and small garrisons along the coasts of Arabia who are hostile to us, and who are said to be planning injury to our naval interests in the Red Sea. We may, therefore, find it necessary to take hostile measures against these posts and garrisons, but we have issued strict instructions that every care must be taken by our ships to differentiate between the hostile Turkish garrisons and the innocent Arab inhabitants, towards whom we entertain such friendly feelings.

We give you notice of this matter in case distorted and false reports may reach you of the reasons for any action which we may be obliged to take.

We have heard rumors that our mutual enemies are endeavoring to construct boats for the purpose of laying mines in the Red Sea, and of otherwise injuring our interests there, and we beg of you that you will give us early information should you receive any confirmation of such reports.

We have heard that Ibn Rashid has been selling large quantities of camels to the Turks, which are being sent up to Damascus.

We hope that you will be able to use influence with him in order that he may cease from this practice and, if he still persists, that you will be able to arrange for the Arabs who lie between him and Syria to seize the camels as they pass, a procedure which will be to our mutual advantage.

continues on page 40

40 • COLONIALISM AND THE TRANSITION TO US INFLUENCE

continued from page 39

> I am glad to be able to inform you that those misguided Arabs under Sayed Ahmed el Senussi, who have fallen victims to the wiles of Turkish and German intriguers, are now beginning to see the error of their ways, and are coming in to us in large numbers, asking for forgiveness and friendship.
>
> We have severely defeated the forces which these intriguers had collected against us, and the eyes of the Arabs are now becoming open to the deceit which has been practiced upon them.
>
> The capture of Erzerum, and the defeats sustained by the Turks in the Caucasus, are having a great effect in our favor, and are greatly helping the cause for which we are both working.
>
> We ask God to prosper your endeavors and to further the work which you have taken in hand.
>
> In conclusion, we beg you to accept our warmest salutations and expressions of friendship.
>
> *Jamad Awwal*, 1334.
> (Signed) A. H. McMAHON

GLOSSARY

Caliphate: Muslim state or nation ruled by a caliph (leader); the Sharif of Mecca claimed the title of caliph for himself and claimed to lead all Muslims

"purely Arab": the British used this term to refer to areas that were populated only by Arabs and therefore fell under Arab rule

Vilayet: a district or an area

Wakfs/Wakf: (sometimes also spelled Waqf): an endowment; in the context of these documents, it refers to a fund set up to help pilgrims reach Mecca on the haj (religious pilgrimage to Mecca) and grain that had been bought for the journey

Document Themes and Analysis

This set of letters outlines the desires of both the Arabs and the British in the first part of World War I. They also outline the fears of both sides. The position of the Arabs is that as the British want their help, they (the British) should give them control over most of the lands of the Middle East. The British, for their part, want the Arabs' help but do not want to give them any more than they must, and want to reserve a spot for the French (and possibly for other forces as well).

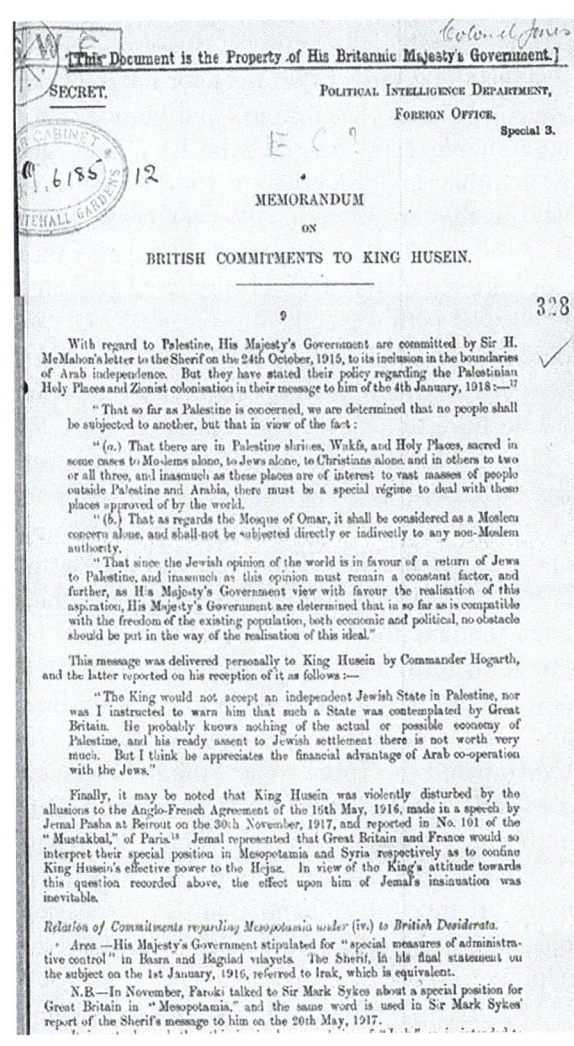

The McMahon–Hussein letter of 25 October 1915. George Antonius—the first to publish the correspondence in full—described this letter as "by far the most important in the whole correspondence, and may perhaps be regarded as the most important international document in the history of the Arab national movement... is still invoked as the main piece of evidence on which the Arabs accuse Great Britain of having broken faith with them."

In the first of these ten documents, from Hussein to McMahon, the basic agreement is laid out, presented as a formal treaty. Control of the Arabian Peninsula is requested in return for giving British help from the Arabs in the present war. In the second, representing McMahon's response, the writer supports the restoration of the Caliphate—as long as it is headed by an "Arab of true race," not a Turk—and suggests that the two sides can work together; Arabia, it is suggested, should be free. The third, from Hussein, notes that the second letter had largely ignored the issue of boundaries and that the supplies for the haj requested before needed to be delivered. It attempts to force Britain to deal with the essential issues and provide assistance.

By the time the fourth letter was exchanged, the discussion was in full force. McMahon responds by agreeing that boundaries need to be discussed and suggests some areas to be excluded, among them "the two districts of Mersina and Alexandretta and portions of Syria lying to the west of the districts of Damascus, Homs, Hama and Aleppo cannot said to be purely Arab." There is no mention of Palestine, specifically, other than a general mention of areas not wholly Arab being excluded. In the fifth letter, Hussein agrees to allow some of the areas, including Mersina, go. However, the letter does insist on some of the other areas that Britain had wanted to be excluded, including Aleppo. One difference to note here is that the Arabs were talking about specific areas, like Aleppo, while the British were focused on areas lying west of Aleppo, and the like. Part of the confusion may have been the result of translation problems, yet part of it may have been due to an effort on the part of the British to maintain ambiguity so that they might exploit it to their advantage later. Hussein points out that there is no difference, in his mind, between Christian and Muslim Arabs, perhaps aiming to prevent the British from widening their original claim to all areas not purely Arab. Hussein also does not want to grant the British the right to Baghdad; but he does agree to the grant "for a short time." In the sixth letter, McMahon tried to split the difference somewhat, noting that the Arabs had agreed to allow the British control Mersina but, when it came to Aleppo, the French had to be consulted. A complicating issue noted in both the sixth letter and in the fifth is that the Arabs are concerned about the British making a separate peace with the Turks; the British promised that they would not. The sixth letter gets to specifics, enclosing some £20,000 for the Arab military. The seventh letter, from Hussein, comes at the start of 1916 and mostly restates the previous positions; it does, however, note that the Arabs are never going to allow some areas, like what became Iraq, to be handed over.

The eighth letter, from Hussein, largely restates the desire of the Arabs for much of the area and argues that Britain's and France's success should cause them to be friendlier with each other and friendlier with the Arabs as well, as they are all in this together. It also notes that the question of Baghdad will have to wait until after the war. The letter should probably be viewed with some skepticism, as it must be doubted whether Britain (or France) by 1916 actually wanted to give up any more than they would have to, or ever had a plan to give control of Baghdad to the Arabs. The ninth letter, from Hussein, is somewhat of a status report as it announces what the Arab forces are doing and asks for supplies. The tenth and final letter is from McMahon and notes that supplies had been sent and the envoy (who had been sent by Hussein) returned. It also includes notes suggesting how the Arabs could help the war effort and a note that some Arabs might be harmed by the British if the Turks do not stop fighting (but also noted the British efforts to avoid this). This ends the correspondence. It should be noted that both sides toward the end tend to focus more on the war at hand than on discussing post-war strategy or establishing who deserves which territory.

The essential themes of this correspondence are pretty straightforward, from the Arab side. The Arabs took this set of documents to mean that they would be given a free hand in most of the Middle East. While the Arabs may have understood the area in question to be larger than what an independent analysis of the documents and their parameters might determine, they clearly were to be given autonomy in much of that area.

The theme from the British point of view is less clear. The British were clearly creating ambiguity insofar as promised the area both to themselves and to the Arabs; they also may have intended to reserve part of it for the Jews, as indicated in the subsequent Balfour Declaration

(1917). Whether or not the British were aiming at the time of this correspondence to promise a homeland for the Jews is unclear, and whether or not the same land was promised to both the Arabs and the Jews is also unclear. However, the ambiguity and seeming double-dealing produced significant distrust and forms the background for some of the problems in the Middle East today.

In terms of their legal significance, the letters and their contents had little lasting impact, as the British (and the French) repudiated them or anyway did not follow through on them in the period after World War I. Britain and France remained the main powers in the region for decades afterward.

In terms of their political significance, the correspondence had lasting impact because it came to represent a betrayal of the people of the area, particularly the Muslims. It came to underscore why Middle Easterners could not always trust the British or the French (later, this sentiment was partially extended to the Americans as well). It does however suggest that the British were at least open to the idea of negotiating directly with the Arabs, and that an agreement amenable to both parties might have worked out had the British not had competing interests. Of course, this begs the question of whether the British would have kept up their end of the deal in any case, or would instead have sought another arrangement that was to their advantage.

—*Scott A. Merriman*

Bibliography and Additional Reading

Farsoun, Samih K, and Naseer H. Aruri. *Palestine and the Palestinians: A Social and Political History*. Boulder, CO: Westview Press, 2006. Print.

Kattan, Victor. *From Coexistence to Conquest: International Law and the Origins of the Arab-Israeli Conflict, 1891–1949*. London: Pluto Press, 2009. Internet resource.

Lustick, Ian. *Arab-Israeli Relations: Historical Background and Origins of the Conflict*. New York: Garland, 1994. Print.

Neiberg, Michael S. *The World War I Reader: [primary and Secondary Sources]*. New York: New York University Press, 2007. Print.

Schneer, Jonathan. *The Balfour Declaration: The Origins of the Arab-Israeli Conflict*. New York: Random House, 2010. Print.

■ Sykes-Picot Agreement

Date: May 16, 1916 (signing date)
Authors: Mark Sykes; Francois Picot
Geographic region: Ottoman Empire (Middle East)
Genre: Treaty; agreement

Summary Overview

The Sykes-Picot Agreement is historically significant in that it represents Great Power diplomacy at its height. During World War I, the Ottoman Empire was falling apart and most observers did not expect it to survive the war. The question became, "Who would control the area?" In the nineteenth century, most everything had been controlled by the Great Powers and their desires. Would this arrangement continue in the twentieth century? In this document, France and Britain answered yes, essentially, and divided up the Middle East without taking into account the wishes of the people who lived there. These two powers, moreover, tried to hide the agreement; it had been negotiated in secret. Although called the Sykes-Picot agreement after the two men who concluded it—Mark Sykes was the British representative and Francois Georges-Picot was the main French representative—the agreement was made at the behest of the British and French governments. Those governments, particularly the British, also wanted to keep the agreement quiet. They wanted to do so, in part, to keep hidden any intentions they might have had to establish at least part of the area involved as a Jewish homeland (for Jews from Europe and elsewhere) as well as to grant control of much of the area to the Arabs in exchange for fighting the Ottomans. In fact, some areas in the region were essentially promised to three different parties—the British, the Jews, and the Arab. Such ambiguity and confusion created distrust among the Arabs vis-à-vis the British (and other westerners) after the war.

Defining Moment

In many ways, this document exemplifies the lingering force of the nineteenth-century mindset among the Great Powers in the twentieth century. All of the Great Powers considered that the only people who mattered were generally those of the upper classes in their own countries. Sometimes, that consideration extended to the middle class of their own country, and of course it included the patriotic ideal of preserving the country as a whole above all else. But as for the interests and needs of the colonized peoples, these were rarely considered—except in the sense that their colonizers sometimes claimed to be helping them to improve their civilizational standards. Such a view was common in the nineteenth century, yet it also lingered into the early decades of the twentieth century. One difference to note in this case is that the Sykes-Picot Agreement was originally secret, whereas agreements before 1900 were very often public.

Nevertheless, the region was to be divided, with the French centered mostly in the northern territories (present-day Syria, Lebanon, eastern Turkey and northern Iraq) and the British in the remaining areas—minus a small area around Jerusalem that was still to be negotiated with the Arabs there. The Russians, too, were given an area, even though they were not among the principal signatories. It is through the Russians that word of the agreement got out: after the second Russian Revolution (the October Revolution), the new Bolshevik government published the contents in *Pravda*. Thus did it become publicly known that the British were promising the Arabs control over the region even while they were secretly dividing it up—with little or no concern for the desires of the local residents.

Author Biographies

Tatton Benvenuto Mark Sykes was the 6th Baronet and was the only son of Sir Tatton Sykes. He was educated at Cambridge and joined the military, serving in the Boer Wars. He traveled in the Middle East as a youth with his father and also served in the British Embassy in Constantinople (the capital of the Ottoman Empire). He served as a justice of the peace and was elected a member of Parliament. He also married and had six children. When World War I broke out, he joined the War Office helping out with Middle Eastern Affairs. He promoted Arab Independence and designed the flag of the Arab Revolt. Sykes in 1915 was designated to make an agreement with France. After the war, he served at the Paris Peace Conference and died there of influenza in 1919.

François Marie Denis Georges-Picot was the son of a historian and about nine years older than Sykes. He was married and had three children. He was a diplomat and his posts abroad included Beijing and being Consul General in Beirut. During World War I, he had been in Cairo for a while before being recalled in order to help draft this agreement. Following the war, he was appointed high commissioner in the mandate of Syria as well as serving in other diplomatic posts. He died in 1951.

HISTORICAL DOCUMENT: *Sykes-Picot Agreement*

1. Sir Edward Grey to Paul Cambon, 15 May 1916

I shall have the honor to reply fully in a further note to your Excellency's note of the 9th instant, relative to the creation of an Arab State, but I should meanwhile be grateful if your Excellency could assure me that in those regions which, under the conditions recorded in that communication, become entirely French, or in which French interests are recognized as predominant, any existing British concessions, rights of navigation or development, and the rights and privileges of any British religious, scholastic, or medical institutions will be maintained.

His Majesty's Government are, of course, ready to give a reciprocal assurance in regard to the British area.

2. Sir Edward Grey to Paul Cambon, 16 May 1916

I have the honor to acknowledge the receipt of your Excellency's note of the 9th instant, stating that the French Government accept the limits of a future Arab State, or Confederation of States, and of those parts of Syria where French interests

continued from page 45

predominate, together with certain conditions attached thereto, such as they result from recent discussions in London and Petrograd on the subject.

I have the honor to inform your Excellency in reply that the acceptance of the whole project, as it now stands, will involve the abdication of considerable British interests, but, since His Majesty's Government recognize the advantage to the general cause of the Allies entailed in producing a more favorable internal political situation in Turkey, they are ready to accept the arrangement now arrived at, provided that the co-operation of the Arabs is secured, and that the Arabs fulfil the conditions and obtain the towns of Homs, Hama, Damascus, and Aleppo.

It is accordingly understood between the French and British Governments—

1. That France and Great Britain are prepared to recognize and protect an independent Arab State or a Confederation of Arab States in the areas (A) and (B) marked on the annexed map, under the suzerainty of an Arab chief. That in area (A) France, and in area (B) Great Britain, shall have priority of right of enterprise and local loans. That in area (A) France, and in area (B) Great Britain, shall alone supply advisers or foreign functionaries at the request of the Arab State or Confederation of Arab States.

2. That in the blue area France, and in the red area Great Britain, shall be allowed to establish such direct or indirect administration or control as they desire and as they may think fit to arrange with the Arab State or Confederation of Arab States.

3. That in the brown area there shall be established an international administration, the form of which is to be decided upon after consultation with Russia, and subsequently in consultation with the other Allies, and the representatives of the Shereef of Mecca.

4. That Great Britain be accorded (1) the ports of Haifa and Acre, (2) guarantee of a given supply of water from the Tigris and Euphrates in area (A) for area (B). His Majesty's Government, on their part, undertake that they will at no time enter into negotiations for the cession of Cyprus to any third Power without the previous consent of the French Government.

5. That Alexandretta shall be a free port as regards the trade of the British Empire, and that there shall be no discrimination in port charges or facilities as regards British shipping and British goods; that there shall be freedom of transit for British goods through Alexandretta and by railway through the blue area, whether those goods are intended for or originate in the red area, or (B) area, or area (A); and there shall be no discrimination, direct or indirect against British goods on any railway or against British goods or ships at any port serving the areas mentioned.

That Haifa shall be a free port as regards the trade of France, her dominions and protectorates, and there shall be no discrimination in port charges or facilities as regards French shipping and French goods. There shall be freedom of transit for French goods through Haifa and by the British railway through the brown area, whether those goods are intended for or originate in the blue area, area (A), or area (B), and there shall be no discrimination, direct or indirect, against French goods on any railway, or against French goods or ships at any port serving the areas mentioned.

6. That in area (A) the Baghdad Railway shall not be extended southwards beyond Mosul, and in area (B) northwards beyond Samarra, until a railway connecting Baghdad with Aleppo via the Euphrates Valley has been completed, and then only with the concurrence of the two Governments.

7. That Great Britain has the right to build, administer, and be sole owner of a railway connecting Haifa with area (B), and shall have a perpetual right to transport troops along such a line at all times.

   It is to be understood by both Governments that this railway is to facilitate the connection of Baghdad with Haifa by rail, and it is further understood that, if the engineering difficulties and expense entailed by keeping this connecting line in the brown area only make the project unfeasible, that the French Government shall be prepared to consider that the line in question may also traverse the polygon Banias-Keis Marib-Salkhab Tell Otsda-Mesmie before reaching area (B).

8. For a period of twenty years the existing Turkish customs tariff shall remain in force throughout the whole of the blue and red areas, as well as in areas (A) and (B), and no increase in the rates of duty or conversion from ad valorem to specific rates shall be made except by agreement between the two Powers.

   There shall be no interior customs barriers between any of the above-mentioned areas. The customs duties leviable on goods destined for the interior shall be collected at the port of entry and handed over to the administration of the area of destination.

9. It shall be agreed that the French Government will at no time enter into any negotiations for the cession of their rights and will not cede such rights in the blue area to any third Power, except the Arab State or Confederation of Arab States without the previous agreement of His Majesty's Government, who, on their part, will give a similar undertaking to the French Government regarding the red area.

10. The British and French Governments, as the protectors of the Arab State, shall agree that they will not themselves acquire and will not consent to a third Power acquiring territorial possessions in the Arabian peninsula, nor consent to a third Power installing a naval base either on the east coast, or on the islands, of the Red Sea. This, however, shall not prevent such adjustment of the Aden frontier as may be necessary in consequence of recent Turkish aggression.

> *I have the honor to inform your Excellency in reply that the acceptance of the whole project, as it now stands, will involve the abdication of considerable British interests...*

continues on page 48

continued from page 47

> 11. The negotiations with the Arabs as to the boundaries of the Arab State or Confederation of Arab States shall be continued through the same channel as heretofore on behalf of the two Powers.
>
> 12. It is agreed that measures to control the importation of arms into the Arab territories will be considered by the two Governments.
>
> I have further the honor to state that, in order to make the agreement complete, His Majesty's Government are proposing to the Russian Government to exchange notes analogous to those exchanged by the latter and your Excellency's Government on the 26th April last. Copies of these notes will be communicated to your Excellency as soon as exchanged.
>
> I would also venture to remind your Excellency that the conclusion of the present agreement raises, for practical consideration, the question of the claims of Italy to a share in any partition or rearrangement of Turkey in Asia, as formulated in article 9 of the agreement of the 26th April, 1915, between Italy and the Allies.
>
> His Majesty's Government further consider that the Japanese Government should be informed of the arrangement now concluded.

GLOSSARY

concession: something granted to another party; for example, a company might be granted an oil concession inside a country or territory

protectorate: a relationship of protection and control assumed by a superior power over a dependent country or territory

tariff: a surtax on trade or items of trade

Document Themes and Analysis

The major points of this agreement set out the postwar boundaries and divide up the area between France, the United Kingdom, and Russia. The agreement does not consider the grants to Russia, however, as they were handled separately. (The Russian Empire did not survive the war, but would have benefited had it survived). The main audience of the agreement was Britain and France. They each intended the agreement to remain secret, so there is no attempt in the text to dress matters up for public consumption.

An international zone was to be set up that would represent some of present-day Israel, including Haifa; while the French were given control of present-day Lebanon and Syria and areas extending into Turkey. The Russians were

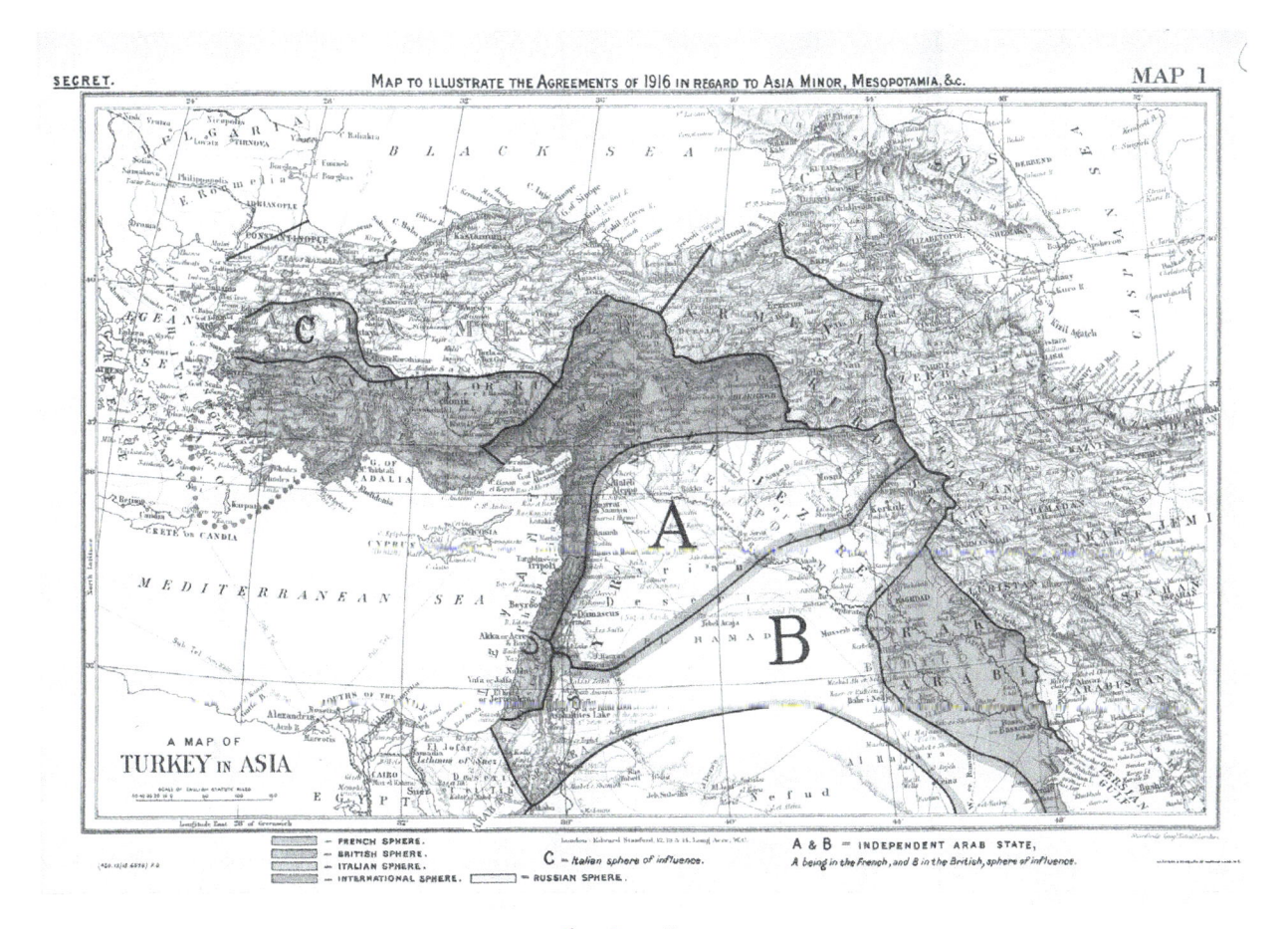

Sykes-Picot Division.

to be given areas in Turkey, which they wanted in order to reach the Mediterranean. The British were also recognized in areas that became present-day Iraq. As for the area in between, much of it was assigned to the resident Arabs, but under British (in the Middle) and French (in the North) control. The middle section, i.e., most of which makes up Saudi Arabia today, was left under Arab control as it was considered of little use to the major powers at the time.

The British and French in the agreement had multiple goals. The first was to divide up the area, which was largely accomplished. The second was to set up ground rules for how each area would interact with the others. There is a lot of language about how each empire would treat the other empire's areas, either those under direct control or those under indirect control, such as those areas that are supposed to be ruled by the Arabs under British or French influence (although one can wonder how much influence the British or French intended to allow the Arabs).

The third goal had to do with the level of economic and physical access the British and French would have to each other's zones. The British wanted to build a railroad that would reach to Baghdad (this was a version of Germany's Berlin-to-Baghdad railroad that had existed as an idea in the late nineteenth and early twentieth centuries). Thus, the agreement has a good bit of language indicating that France will allow such a railroad to go through French territory. The British were basically given sole control over whatever railway would be built connecting to the British zone in present-day Iraq. Trade was also a concern. One example of this is with the ports of Haifa (in the British zone) and Alexandretta (in the French zone). The French were given favorable treatment at Haifa and the British were given the same at Alexandretta.

Other areas in the region, some having little direct connection to the main topic, are also discussed. For instance, the British agree to not yield Cyprus to anyone without the consent of the French. The British at this point controlled Cyprus as part of their empire (Cyprus would finally become free in 1960). The British and French also promise not to give up any of their protectorates in the Middle East without gaining the agreement of the other party. The French promise to consult the British before giving up anything, and the British promise the French the same. Both nations promise to give territory to Russia, as well, and to conclude agreements with her. The only other powers considered are Italy, which was supposed to possibly gain some unnamed part of Turkey in Asia, and Japan, which is merely to be notified of such assignments.

The documents that make up the Sykes-Picot Agreement divide up the Middle East in accordance with the desires of the three major powers involved (although Russia was not an active participant in the forging of the agreement at this stage). These documents display the prevailing attitude among the Great Powers toward regions outside of Europe. The Middle East is divided between Britain and France (with some areas reserved for Russia). The negotiators involved can be seen to care little about how the arrangement might affect the people living inside the region, other than to try to keep the written agreement secret.

In many ways, the boundaries drawn in the region by Sykes-Picot to separate French and British areas foreshadow the boundaries today between Iraq, Syria, and Lebanon—boundaries that to some extent continue to cause problems. While many today might think of these countries as old, they are in many ways not as old as we think but rather represent lines on a map. The people and cultures within them may be old, but not so much the outlines of the countries themselves.

—Scott A. Merriman

Bibliography and Additional Reading

Barr, James. *A Line in the Sand: The Anglo-French Struggle for the Middle East, 1914–1948*. New York: W.W. Norton & Co, 2012. Print.

McMeekin, Sean. *The Ottoman Endgame: War, Revolution, and the Making of the Modern Middle East, 1908–1923*. New York: Penguin, 2015. Print.

Schneer, Jonathan. *The Balfour Declaration: The Origins of the Arab-Israeli Conflict*. New York: Random House, 2010. Print.

Simon, Reeva S, and Eleanor H. Tejirian. *The Creation of Iraq, 1914–1921*. New York: Columbia University Press, 2004. Internet resource.

Watson, William E. *Tricolor and Crescent: France and the Islamic World*. Westport, Conn: Praeger, 2003. Print.

■ Balfour Declaration

Date: November 2, 1917
Author: Arthur James Balfour
Geographic region: Palestine (then a province of the Ottoman Empire)
Genre: Correspondence

Summary Overview

The Balfour Declaration was a letter sent from the foreign secretary of the United Kingdom, Arthur James Balfour, to Baron Walter Rothschild, a leading figure in the British Jewish community. It was sent on November 2, 1917, at the height of World War I, and released to the press on November 9 to convey the government's support for a Jewish homeland in Palestine, then a province of the Ottoman Empire. The letter was likely intended to serve the dual purpose of bolstering Jewish support for the war effort and giving Britain a special role in the future of Palestine, a crucial territorial connection between British interests in Egypt and India. However, the latter aspiration, which hinged upon Allied victory in the war, contradicted several already conflicting previous agreements, including the Husayn-McMahon correspondence of 1915–16, which had effectively promised Arab control of Palestine and other Ottoman territory in exchange for assistance in fighting against the Ottomans, and the Sykes-Picot Agreement of 1916, which had promised international oversight of Palestine in a secret agreement between Britain and France. Despite the Balfour Declaration, the establishment of the Jewish state of Israel did not occur for another thirty-one years, but the document did establish the British role as protectors of the special Jewish right to settle in Palestine.

Defining Moment

Prior to World War I, Great Britain had long-standing trading relationships with Palestine and the other Arab provinces of the Ottoman Empire, whose vast size and tribal allegiances made for a shaky coalition of disparate interests. The Ottoman Empire had been in marked decline through most of the nineteenth century, and entered the twentieth century in serious trouble, beset with internal strife and crushed by external pressure, particularly from Russia, its powerful neighbor to the north. In the decades leading up to World War I, the Ottoman Empire attempted neutrality and also made a series of agreements with England, but when the war broke out in 1914, the empire chose the side opposed to its biggest enemy, Russia, joining Germany and Austria Hungary. Russia, France, and Great Britain saw opportunities for their own expansion and enrichment, beginning discussions about how to divide the Ottoman Empire after the war.

Great Britain's long-standing ambitions in the Middle East were focused on Egypt and Iran. Egypt was the key to control of the Suez Canal, a vital link with India, and in the decades leading up to World War I, the country had become increasingly dependent on inexpensive Iranian oil. The British Navy began upgrading its ships from coal to oil beginning in 1910, and in July 1914, the British government gained a

>
> Foreign Office,
> November 2nd, 1917.
>
> Dear Lord Rothschild,
>
> I have much pleasure in conveying to you, on behalf of His Majesty's Government, the following declaration of sympathy with Jewish Zionist aspirations which has been submitted to, and approved by, the Cabinet
>
> "His Majesty's Government view with favour the establishment in Palestine of a national home for the Jewish people, and will use their best endeavours to facilitate the achievement of this object, it being clearly understood that nothing shall be done which may prejudice the civil and religious rights of existing non-Jewish communities in Palestine, or the rights and political status enjoyed by Jews in any other country"
>
> I should be grateful if you would bring this declaration to the knowledge of the Zionist Federation.
>
> *[signature: Arthur James Balfour]*

Balfour Declaration as published in The Times, *November 9, 1917*

PALESTINE FOR THE JEWS.

OFFICIAL SYMPATHY.

Mr. Balfour has sent the following letter to Lord Rothschild in regard to the establishment of a national home in Palestine for the Jewish people:—

I have much pleasure in conveying to you, on behalf of his Majesty's Government, the following declaration of sympathy with Jewish Zionist aspirations which has been submitted to and approved by the Cabinet:—

His Majesty's Government view with favour the establishment in Palestine of a national home for the Jewish people, and will use their best endeavours to facilitate the achievement of this object, it being clearly understood that nothing shall be done which may prejudice the civil and religious rights of existing non-Jewish communities in Palestine, or the rights and political status enjoyed by Jews in any other country.

I should be grateful if you would bring this declaration to the knowledge of the Zionist Federation.

The Balfour declaration.

controlling interest in the Anglo-Persian Oil Company.

In the secret Sykes-Picot Agreement of 1916, Great Britain and France, with the knowledge of Russia, divided up areas of influence and control in the Middle East and agreed that Palestine should be under the control of an international coalition. One month after the Sykes-Picot agreement, David Lloyd George became prime minister of Great Britain, and his feelings about Palestine were markedly at odds with the Sykes-Picot agreement. Lloyd George was personally supportive of Zionism, a movement that held that the Jewish people had a God-given homeland in Palestine, and he also believed that the British needed a stronger presence in Palestine in order to protect their interests in Egypt, India, and Iran. Additionally, he felt that public support for a Jewish homeland in Palestine upon the defeat of the Ottoman Empire would bolster support for the Allies throughout the world, particularly in Russia, where the Bolsheviks had overthrown the tsar with the help and support of Russia's Jewish population.

Both the Sykes-Picot Agreement and the Balfour Declaration contradicted the Husayn-McMahon correspondence, informal letters of agreement exchanged in 1915 and 1916 between the emir of Mecca, in Saudi Arabia, and Sir Henry McMahon, the British high commissioner in Egypt. These letters had indicated to the leading Arab statesman of the time that Britain would support the establishment of an independent Arab state that included Palestine, in exchange for Arab assistance in defeating the Ottoman Empire.

Author Biography

Arthur James Balfour was born on July 25, 1848, in Whittingehame, East Lothian, Scotland. He was the nephew of three-time prime minister the Marquess of Salisbury, the formidable Robert Cecil, and was a member of one of the leading aristocratic families in Great Britain. Balfour was educated at Eton and Cambridge, and entered Parliament after graduating from university as a representative of Hertford. He developed a reputation as an intellectual Conservative and rose quickly in his uncle's administrations, becoming a member of the cabinet as secretary for Scotland and chief secretary for Ireland. In 1891, Balfour became the leader of the House of Commons and first lord of the Treasury.

After his uncle's retirement, he served as prime minister from 1902 to 1905 and was best known for his education reforms. He also supported negotiations with the French that produced the 1904 Entente Cordiale, settling outstanding conflicts over control of Egypt and Morocco and allowing for further engagement with Great Britain's traditional adversary. In 1915, he became first lord of the Admiralty, and the following year, he was made foreign secretary in the new administration of David Lloyd George. He served as lord president of the council after the war and authored 1926's Balfour Report, which settled the status of Great Britain's dominions. He died on March 19, 1930, in Woking, Surrey, Great Britain.

HISTORICAL DOCUMENT: *Balfour Declaration*

Foreign Office
November 2nd, 1917

Dear Lord Rothschild,

I have much pleasure in conveying to you, on behalf of His Majesty's Government, the following declaration of sympathy with Jewish Zionist aspirations which has been submitted to, and approved by, the Cabinet:

"His Majesty's Government view with favour the establishment in Palestine of a national home for the Jewish people, and will use their best endeavours to facilitate the achievement of this object, it being clearly understood that nothing shall be done which may prejudice the civil and religious rights of existing non-Jewish communities in Palestine, or the rights and political status enjoyed by Jews in any other country."

I should be grateful if you would bring this declaration to the knowledge of the Zionist Federation.

Yours sincerely,
Arthur James Balfour

Document Themes and Analysis

The Balfour Declaration is written in the form of a letter to Lord Rothschild and opens with an expression of pleasure in being able to report the agreement of the government to the letter's "declaration of sympathy with Jewish Zionist aspirations." The declaration itself is set off in quotation marks, clearly marking this as a statement with broad support and not just part of a letter from one man to another. The statement of support itself is short, but its language would shape international relations in the Middle East for many years to come. The letter clearly states that the British government is in favor of a national home for the Jewish people in Palestine, and will endeavor to support this establishment; however, it also includes a caveat that seeks to ensure that the non-Jewish population of Palestine maintains their "civil and religious rights," and that the declaration does not endanger the "rights and political status enjoyed by Jews in any other country." The declaration does not address the political status of non-Jewish Palestinians, closing with a wish that its contents be shared with the "Zionist Federation."

Public support of a Jewish homeland in Palestine was not enough to gain one of Great Britain's primary objectives in issuing the letter—the support of Russian Jews for the war effort. The Bolsheviks, led by Vladimir Lenin, called for an immediate armistice upon gaining control of Russia, and the ideological differences between Jewish Bolsheviks and British Zionists largely negated their influence.

The impact of the Balfour Declaration on the postwar settlement of the Middle East was considerable, however. Following the Treaty of Versailles in 1919, Great Britain was given a "mandate" to administer Palestine, though not as an official Jewish state. Still, with British support for Zionist ambitions in Palestine made clear, tens of thousands of European Jews settled in Palestine in the decade following the end of the war, despite Britain's attempts to allow only as many settlers as could be placed on available land, and tensions between Palestinian Arabs and Jews increased dramatically.

The Balfour Declaration's provisions for non-Jewish rights were ambiguous. They were assured of "civil and religious rights," which could be understood to also include territorial rights and political rights, though these were not specifically included. Many Arabs in Palestine saw the Balfour Declaration as a betrayal of promises made to them in exchange for their assistance in the defeat of the Ottoman Empire. They saw Britain's support of a Jewish homeland and their subsequent administration of Palestine as a profound betrayal of their nationalist ambitions and the promise of self-government. Instability in Palestine kept the area in limbo, with the British mandate continuing until 1948, when the State of Israel was established after World War II.

—*Bethany Groff Dorau*

Bibliography and Additional Reading

Barr, James. *A Line in the Sand: The Anglo-French Struggle for the Middle East, 1914–1948.* New York: Norton, 2012. Print.

Fromkin, David. *A Peace to End All Peace: The Fall of the Ottoman Empire and the Creation of the Modern Middle East.* New York: Holt, 2001. Print.

Rogan, Eugene. *The Fall of the Ottomans: The Great War in the Middle East.* New York: Basic, 2015. Print.

Schneer, Jonathan. *The Balfour Declaration: The Origins of the Arab-Israeli Conflict.* New York: Random, 2010. Print.

Palestine Mandate

Date: September 29, 1923 (effective date)
Geographic Region: Palestine
Genre: Legislation

Summary Overview

After World War I and the collapse of the Ottoman Empire, the League of Nations established a process to administer its former territories in the Middle East. The mandate system gave several of the victorious Allies the power to administer the government of these territories on behalf of the League of Nations until they were in a position to determine their own system of government and become independent successfully. On July 24, 1922, a British mandate for the former Ottoman territory of Palestine was approved by the Council of the League of Nations and went into effect on September 29, 1923. The mandate supported the creation of a Jewish state and laid out instructions for such issues as public health, immigration, and religious sites and rights. The British government added a statement of understanding that the provisions of the mandate dealing with the establishment of a Jewish homeland did not apply to territory east of the Jordan River, known as Transjordan. The British mandate for Palestine, known as Mandatory Palestine, was based on the public support for a Jewish state expressed by the British government in the Balfour Declaration of 1917. The League of Nations approved the British vision of Palestine as a Jewish state, failing to address rising Arab nationalism and resentment of European control of the Middle East as well as bitterness at promises made during the war that had been subsequently ignored.

Defining Moment

The British mandate for Palestine carried out the British support for a Jewish state first publicly expressed in the Balfour Declaration, a letter sent from the foreign secretary of the United Kingdom, Arthur James Balfour, to Baron Walter Rothschild, as World War I raged. The letter conveyed the British government's support for a Jewish homeland in Palestine, then a province of the Ottoman Empire. It assumed victory for Great Britain and its allies and the subsequent partitioning of Ottoman territory; the British government hoped that it would serve the dual purpose of bolstering Jewish support for the war effort and giving Great Britain a special role in the future of Palestine, a crucial bridge between British interests in Egypt and India. The Balfour Declaration contradicted several previous agreements, including the Husayn McMahon correspondence (1915–16), which had effectively promised Arab control of Palestine in exchange for assistance in fighting against the Ottoman Empire, and the Sykes-Picot Agreement (1916), which had promised international oversight in Palestine in a secret agreement between Great Britain and France. The Balfour Declaration publicly established the British role as protectors of the special Jewish right to a home state in Palestine.

The front page of the Mandate for Palestine and Transjordan memorandum, presented to UK Parliament in December 1922, prior to it coming into force in 1923.

The mandate system was established as a "sacred trust of civilisation" under Article 22 of Part I (the Covenant of the League of Nations) of the Treaty of Versailles.

Palestine was devastated by the war. Battles had raged across the landscape, and famine, disease, and punitive measures enacted by the collapsing Ottoman Empire had all taken a heavy toll. After a series of hard-fought battles, the British succeeded in occupying Palestine and setting up a military administration by the end of 1918. Occupying Palestine was not a guarantee of a role in its long term administration, however. Great Britain had been involved in several conflicting agreements regarding the future of Palestine, including promising an Arab nation, an international administration, and a Jewish state. In 1920, delegates from Palestine rejected the Balfour Declaration at a conference in Syria, voting instead to incorporate Palestine with Syria under an Arab king. One month later, however, at the San Remo Conference, the Allies put Syria and Lebanon under French control and formalized British control of Palestine. The infant kingdom of Syria, and its promise of an Arab Palestine, was over.

Even before the San Remo Conference, riots broke out in Jewish neighborhoods in Jerusalem on April 4, 1920, and raged for days, injuring more than two hundred people and killing several. The riots were attributed to Arab anger over their failure to secure an independent state, and fear of a massive influx

PEACE CONFERENCE.

PALESTINE.

Memorandum by Sir Erle Richards.

THE following memorandum has been submitted to Lord Curzon, and is now circulated, by his instructions, for the consideration of the Eastern Committee.

For convenience of reference this memorandum is arranged under the following heads :—
- I. Territories in Question.
- II. British Commitments.
- III. Military Operations.
- IV. British Proposals.
- V. Appendix.
- VI. Maps.

I.—*Territories in Question.*

Palestine, for the purposes of this memorandum, may be best described as the Palestine of the Old Testament, extending from Dan to Beersheba. There is a question as to the exact boundaries, and these will have to be settled by commissioners. For the present it is sufficient to take the northern boundary as the Litani river on the coast, and from there across to Banias, north-east of Lake Huleh, in the interior. This would give Sur (Tyre) to Palestine and Saida (Sidon) to the Lebanon. Saida is wrongly marked on the Sykes-Picot map south of the River Litani, where Sur ought to be. The western boundary is the sea. The eastern boundary is more difficult to determine. The Zionists are naturally looking eastwards to the Trans-Jordan territories, where there is good cultivation and great possibilities in the future. There is a general desire to get out of the steaming Jordan Valley and on to the uplands beyond; and we are undoubtedly face to face with a movement which is growing on the part of the Zionists that Palestine is now to include what it has not included for many centuries—if it ever did—and what would be regarded by the Arabs as part of their domain. It is assumed, however, for the purposes of this memorandum, that the Jordan and the Dead Sea will form the frontier on the east. As to the southern boundary, there are a number of different considerations. On the one hand it is contended that the cultivable areas south of Gaza ought to be part of Palestine because they are necessary to the subsistence of the people. On the other hand, this area is inhabited by Bedouins of the desert, who look really towards Sinai, and ought not to be associated with Palestine at all. It is suggested by the Foreign Office that it would be a sound principle to include in Palestine all the southern country capable of cultivation, *e.g.*, in the direction of Rafa and Beersheba; and that the remaining area, south of Gaza and the Dead Sea, to the Gulf of Akaba should be reserved to the Bedouins and attached to Egypt, since the tribes are identical with those in the Sinai peninsula, and the pre-war frontier is quite arbitrary from the tribal point of view. It is further suggested that Akaba should be left to the Arabs, but that it might be advisable to include some of the wells on the east side of the bay in Egyptian territory, so that we might be able to make a British harbour there, if it proved desirable to do so hereafter. But the definition of the southern boundary is of minor importance from the British point of view.

January 1919 Foreign Office memorandum setting out the borders of Palestine for the Eastern Committee of the British War Cabinet before the Paris Peace Conference.

of Jewish immigrants. Following the riots, the British installed a civilian administration friendly to the establishment of a Jewish state and announced that they would allow over sixteen thousand Jewish immigrants in the upcoming year.

Arab resistance continued unabated in the two years between the San Remo Conference and the Palestine Mandate. In December, representatives of the Palestinian Arabs declared that Palestine was an Arab state and that Jewish people had no special rights to settle there. In May 1921, nearly one hundred people were killed in anti-Zionist riots outside Jerusalem, and a delegation of Arab leaders visited London in the fall of 1921, demanding that the government withdraw the Balfour Declaration and allow an independent representative government. The British government, in turn, tried to allay some of their concerns by promising no more immigration than the country could handle, and by assuring Arab leaders that all of Palestine was not destined to be a Jewish homeland, only a portion of it.

Document Information

The first draft of the mandate was presented to the League of Nations council in December 1920. After further negotiations and political changes, a second draft was submitted in August 1921. The final document was approved on July 24, 1922, and the terms officially went into effect on September 29, 1923, following the addition of a September 1922 memorandum stipulating that the terms regarding the establishment of a Jewish national home were not applicable to the area known as Transjordan. The mandate is archived in the League of Nations collection, which was transferred to the United Nations in 1946 and is housed in the United Nations Archive in Geneva, Switzerland.

HISTORICAL DOCUMENT: *Palestine Mandate*

The Palestine Mandate

The Council of the League of Nations:

WHEREAS the Principal Allied Powers have agreed, for the purpose of giving effect to the provisions of Article 22 of the Covenant of the League of Nations, to entrust to a Mandatory selected by the said Powers the administration of the territory of Palestine, which formerly belonged to the Turkish Empire, within such boundaries as may be fixed by them; and

WHEREAS the Principal Allied Powers have also agreed that the Mandatory should be responsible for putting into effect the declaration originally made on November 2nd, 1917, by the Government of His Britannic Majesty, and adopted by the said Powers, in favor of the establishment in Palestine of a national home for the Jewish people, it being clearly understood that nothing should be done which might prejudice the civil and religious rights of existing non-Jewish communities in Palestine, or the rights and political status enjoyed by Jews in any other country; and

continued from page 61

WHEREAS recognition has thereby been given to the historical connection of the Jewish people with Palestine and to the grounds for reconstituting their national home in that country; and

WHEREAS the Principal Allied Powers have selected His Britannic Majesty as the Mandatory for Palestine; and

WHEREAS the mandate in respect of Palestine has been formulated in the following terms and submitted to the Council of the League for approval; and

WHEREAS His Britannic Majesty has accepted the mandate in respect of Palestine and undertaken to exercise it on behalf of the League of Nations in conformity with the following provisions; and

WHEREAS by the afore-mentioned Article 22 (paragraph 8), it is provided that the degree of authority, control or administration to be exercised by the Mandatory, not having been previously agreed upon by the Members of the League, shall be explicitly defined by the Council of the League Of Nations;

CONFIRMING the said Mandate, defines its terms as follows:

ARTICLE 1.
The Mandatory shall have full powers of legislation and of administration, save as they may be limited by the terms of this mandate.

ART. 2.
The Mandatory shall be responsible for placing the country under such political, administrative and economic conditions as will secure the establishment of the Jewish national home, as laid down in the preamble, and the development of self-governing institutions, and also for safeguarding the civil and religious rights of all the inhabitants of Palestine, irrespective of race and religion.

> *The Administration of Palestine shall be responsible for enacting a nationality law. There shall be included in this law provisions framed so as to facilitate the acquisition of Palestinian citizenship by Jews who take up their permanent residence in Palestine.*

ART. 3.
The Mandatory shall, so far as circumstances permit, encourage local autonomy.

ART. 4.
An appropriate Jewish agency shall be recognised as a public body for the purpose of advising and co-operating with the Administration of Palestine in such economic,

social and other matters as may affect the establishment of the Jewish national home and the interests of the Jewish population in Palestine, and, subject always to the control of the Administration to assist and take part in the development of the country.

The Zionist organization, so long as its organization and constitution are in the opinion of the Mandatory appropriate, shall be recognised as such agency. It shall take steps in consultation with His Britannic Majesty's Government to secure the co-operation of all Jews who are willing to assist in the establishment of the Jewish national home.

ART. 5.
The Mandatory shall be responsible for seeing that no Palestine territory shall be ceded or leased to, or in any way placed under the control of the Government of any foreign Power.

ART. 6.
The Administration of Palestine, while ensuring that the rights and position of other sections of the population are not prejudiced, shall facilitate Jewish immigration under suitable conditions and shall encourage, in co-operation with the Jewish agency referred to in Article 4, close settlement by Jews on the land, including State lands and waste lands not required for public purposes.

ART. 7.
The Administration of Palestine shall be responsible for enacting a nationality law. There shall be included in this law provisions framed so as to facilitate the acquisition of Palestinian citizenship by Jews who take up their permanent residence in Palestine.

ART. 8.
The privileges and immunities of foreigners, including the benefits of consular jurisdiction and protection as formerly enjoyed by Capitulation or usage in the Ottoman Empire, shall not be applicable in Palestine.

Unless the Powers whose nationals enjoyed the afore-mentioned privileges and immunities on August 1st, 1914, shall have previously renounced the right to their re-establishment, or shall have agreed to their non-application for a specified period, these privileges and immunities shall, at the expiration of the mandate, be immediately reestablished in their entirety or with such modifications as may have been agreed upon between the Powers concerned.

ART. 9.
The Mandatory shall be responsible for seeing that the judicial system established in Palestine shall assure to foreigners, as well as to natives, a complete guarantee of their rights.

continues on page 64

continued from page 63

Respect for the personal status of the various peoples and communities and for their religious interests shall be fully guaranteed. In particular, the control and administration of Wakfs shall be exercised in accordance with religious law and the dispositions of the founders.

ART. 10.
Pending the making of special extradition agreements relating to Palestine, the extradition treaties in force between the Mandatory and other foreign Powers shall apply to Palestine.

ART. 11.
The Administration of Palestine shall take all necessary measures to safeguard the interests of the community in connection with the development of the country, and, subject to any international obligations accepted by the Mandatory, shall have full power to provide for public ownership or control of any of the natural resources of the country or of the public works, services and utilities established or to be established therein. It shall introduce a land system appropriate to the needs of the country, having regard, among other things, to the desirability of promoting the close settlement and intensive cultivation of the land.

The Administration may arrange with the Jewish agency mentioned in Article 4 to construct or operate, upon fair and equitable terms, any public works, services and utilities, and to develop any of the natural resources of the country, in so far as these matters are not directly undertaken by the Administration. Any such arrangements shall provide that no profits distributed by such agency, directly or indirectly, shall exceed a reasonable rate of interest on the capital, and any further profits shall be utilised by it for the benefit of the country in a manner approved by the Administration.

ART. 12.
The Mandatory shall be entrusted with the control of the foreign relations of Palestine and the right to issue exequaturs to consuls appointed by foreign Powers. He shall also be entitled to afford diplomatic and consular protection to citizens of Palestine when outside its territorial limits.

ART. 13.
All responsibility in connection with the Holy Places and religious buildings or sites in Palestine, including that of preserving existing rights and of securing free access to the Holy Places, religious buildings and sites and the free exercise of worship, while ensuring the requirements of public order and decorum, is assumed by the Mandatory, who shall be responsible solely to the League of Nations in all matters connected herewith, provided that nothing in this article shall prevent the

Mandatory from entering into such arrangements as he may deem reasonable with the Administration for the purpose of carrying the provisions of this article into effect; and provided also that nothing in this mandate shall be construed as conferring upon the Mandatory authority to interfere with the fabric or the management of purely Moslem sacred shrines, the immunities of which are guaranteed.

ART. 14.
A special commission shall be appointed by the Mandatory to study, define and determine the rights and claims in connection with the Holy Places and the rights and claims relating to the different religious communities in Palestine. The method of nomination, the composition and the functions of this Commission shall be submitted to the Council of the League for its approval, and the Commission shall not be appointed or enter upon its functions without the approval of the Council.

ART. 15.
The Mandatory shall see that complete freedom of conscience and the free exercise of all forms of worship, subject only to the maintenance of public order and morals, are ensured to all. No discrimination of any kind shall be made between the inhabitants of Palestine on the ground of race, religion or language. No person shall be excluded from Palestine on the sole ground of his religious belief.

The right of each community to maintain its own schools for the education of its own members in its own language, while conforming to such educational requirements of a general nature as the Administration may impose, shall not be denied or impaired.

ART. 16.
The Mandatory shall be responsible for exercising such supervision over religious or eleemosynary bodies of all faiths in Palestine as may be required for the maintenance of public order and good government. Subject to such supervision, no measures shall be taken in Palestine to obstruct or interfere with the enterprise of such bodies or to discriminate against any representative or member of them on the ground of his religion or nationality.

ART. 17.
The Administration of Palestine may organist on a voluntary basis the forces necessary for the preservation of peace and order, and also for the defence of the country, subject, however, to the supervision of the Mandatory, but shall not use them for purposes other than those above specified save with the consent of the Mandatory. Except for such purposes, no military, naval or air forces shall be raised or maintained by the Administration of Palestine.

continues on page 66

continued from page 65

Nothing in this article shall preclude the Administration of Palestine from contributing to the cost of the maintenance of the forces of the Mandatory in Palestine.

The Mandatory shall be entitled at all times to use the roads, railways and ports of Palestine for the movement of armed forces and the carriage of fuel and supplies.

ART. 18.
The Mandatory shall see that there is no discrimination in Palestine against the nationals of any State Member of the League of Nations (including companies incorporated under its laws) as compared with those of the Mandatory or of any foreign State in matters concerning taxation, commerce or navigation, the exercise of industries or professions, or in the treatment of merchant vessels or civil aircraft. Similarly, there shall be no discrimination in Palestine against goods originating in or destined for any of the said States, and there shall be freedom of transit under equitable conditions across the mandated area.

Subject as aforesaid and to the other provisions of this mandate, the Administration of Palestine may, on the advice of the Mandatory, impose such taxes and customs duties as it may consider necessary, and take such steps as it may think best to promote the development of the natural resources of the country and to safeguard the interests of the population. It may also, on the advice of the Mandatory, conclude a special customs agreement with any State the territory of which in 1914 was wholly included in Asiatic Turkey or Arabia.

ART. 19.
The Mandatory shall adhere on behalf of the Administration of Palestine to any general international conventions already existing, or which may be concluded hereafter with the approval of the League of Nations, respecting the slave traffic, the traffic in arms and ammunition, or the traffic in drugs, or relating to commercial equality, freedom of transit and navigation, aerial navigation and postal, telegraphic and wireless communication or literary, artistic or industrial property.

ART. 20.
The Mandatory shall co-operate on behalf of the Administration of Palestine, so far as religious, social and other conditions may permit, in the execution of any common policy adopted by the League of Nations for preventing and combating disease, including diseases of plants and animals.

ART. 21.
The Mandatory shall secure the enactment within twelve months from this date, and shall ensure the execution of a Law of Antiquities based on the following rules. This law shall ensure equality of treatment in the matter of excavations and archaeological research to the nationals of all States Members of the League of Nations.

(1) "Antiquity" means any construction or any product of human activity earlier than the year 1700 A. D.

(2) The law for the protection of antiquities shall proceed by encouragement rather than by threat.

   Any person who, having discovered an antiquity without being furnished with the authorization referred to in paragraph 5, reports the same to an official of the competent Department, shall be rewarded according to the value of the discovery.

(3) No antiquity may be disposed of except to the competent Department, unless this Department renounces the acquisition of any such antiquity.

   No antiquity may leave the country without an export licence from the said Department.

(4) Any person who maliciously or negligently destroys or damages an antiquity shall be liable to a penalty to be fixed.

(5) No clearing of ground or digging with the object of finding antiquities shall be permitted, under penalty of fine, except to persons authorised by the competent Department.

(6) Equitable terms shall be fixed for expropriation, temporary or permanent, of lands which might be of historical or archaeological interest.

(7) Authorization to excavate shall only be granted to persons who show sufficient guarantees of archaeological experience. The Administration of Palestine shall not, in granting these authorizations, act in such a way as to exclude scholars of any nation without good grounds.

(8) The proceeds of excavations may be divided between the excavator and the competent Department in a proportion fixed by that Department. If division seems impossible for scientific reasons, the excavator shall receive a fair indemnity in lieu of a part of the find.

ART. 22.
English, Arabic and Hebrew shall be the official languages of Palestine. Any statement or inscription in Arabic on stamps or money in Palestine shall be repeated in Hebrew and any statement or inscription in Hebrew shall be repeated in Arabic.

continues on page 68

continued from page 67

ART. 23.
The Administration of Palestine shall recognise the holy days of the respective communities in Palestine as legal days of rest for the members of such communities.

ART. 24.
The Mandatory shall make to the Council of the League of Nations an annual report to the satisfaction of the Council as to the measures taken during the year to carry out the provisions of the mandate. Copies of all laws and regulations promulgated or issued during the year shall be communicated with the report.

ART. 25.
In the territories lying between the Jordan and the eastern boundary of Palestine as ultimately determined, the Mandatory shall be entitled, with the consent of the Council of the League of Nations, to postpone or withhold application of such provisions of this mandate as he may consider inapplicable to the existing local conditions, and to make such provision for the administration of the territories as he may consider suitable to those conditions, provided that no action shall be taken which is inconsistent with the provisions of Articles 15, 16 and 18.

ART. 26.
The Mandatory agrees that, if any dispute whatever should arise between the Mandatory and another member of the League of Nations relating to the interpretation or the application of the provisions of the mandate, such dispute, if it cannot be settled by negotiation, shall be submitted to the Permanent Court of International Justice provided for by Article 14 of the Covenant of the League of Nations.

ART. 27.
The consent of the Council of the League of Nations is required for any modification of the terms of this mandate.

ART. 28.
In the event of the termination of the mandate hereby conferred upon the Mandatory, the Council of the League of Nations shall make such arrangements as may be deemed necessary for safeguarding in perpetuity, under guarantee of the League, the rights secured by Articles 13 and 14, and shall use its influence for securing, under the guarantee of the League, that the Government of Palestine will fully honour the financial obligations legitimately incurred by the Administration of Palestine during the period of the mandate, including the rights of public servants to pensions or gratuities.

> The present instrument shall be deposited in original in the archives of the League of Nations and certified copies shall be forwarded by the Secretary-General of the League of Nations to all members of the League.
>
> Done at London the twenty-fourth day of July, one thousand nine hundred and twenty-two.

Document Analysis

The Palestine Mandate begins with a specific affirmation of the principles outlined in the Balfour Declaration, the "establishment in Palestine of a national home for the Jewish people" based on their historical tie to Palestine. The British government has agreed to accept the mandate and administer it on behalf of the League of Nations. The specific terms of the mandate follow, giving the British "full powers of legislation and of administration" and requiring them to set up systems conducive to the establishment of a self-governing Jewish state. They are also required to "safeguard the civil and religious rights" of all people living in Palestine, of all religions. The Zionist organization will serve with the British administration, representing the "interests of the Jewish population," but ultimately under the control of the administration. The administration will work to "facilitate Jewish immigration under suitable conditions," and will settle them on land that is available. The rights of non-Jewish Palestinians are to be protected, though how this stipulation relates specifically to property rights is unclear.

Jewish immigrants to Palestine will be made citizens quickly, but foreigners will also have access to a judiciary that equally protects their rights. The administration is given the right to enact public ownership of "the natural resources of the country or of the public works," as well as to develop a system of efficient land use that encourages "close settlement and intensive cultivation." Public utilities can be constructed and operated by the Jewish agency assisting the administration.

Given the delicate nature of relations between people of different faiths in Palestine, each with their own claims to religious traditions and sites, it is perhaps not surprising that the mandate contains extensive provisions for allowing religious worship while "ensuring the requirements of public order and decorum" are maintained. The exception to this is "purely Moslem" sites, which are outside the mandate's area of responsibility. The mandate is given the responsibility of setting up a commission to study competing or overlapping claims to religious sites, and is also responsible for ensuring that religious freedom is maintained and that discrimination based on religion is not allowed. Still, the mandate has sweeping authority to supervise "religious or eleemosynary bodies of all faiths" to ensure public order, but should not obstruct them unreasonably.

The remainder of the mandate deals with trade issues, allows for a peacekeeping military force to be assembled, outlines the treatment of and authority over antiquities, and establishes the protection of the religious sites in Palestine as a League of Nations priority, even if the mandate is withdrawn or changed.

Essential Themes

On September 16, 1922, the Council of the League of Nations approved the additional memorandum concerning the ban on the application of the terms in the region known as Transjordan, establishing full support of the British Palestine Mandate and subsequently international support for the Balfour Declaration, its acceptance of a historical Jewish connection with Palestine, and its plan for a Jewish homeland there. Transjordan was not included in the plans for a Jewish homeland, though it made up a substantial percentage of the British Palestine mandate. On September 29, 1923, the mandate officially came into force, and with it an uncertain future for Palestine. The mandate was open-ended, and was seen by all as a temporary measure that would terminate when the League of Nations felt there was a viable self-determined government ready to take the reins. The Jewish people were eager to take advantage of the opportunity they had to establish themselves in Palestine before the mandate ended, and they began immigrating and acquiring land as quickly as possible. The Arab (and Christian, in far smaller numbers) people already living in Palestine were not eager to be displaced from their land by new settlers, and resented foreign interference. Tens of thousands of European Jews settled in Palestine in the decade following the end of the war, despite Great Britain's attempts to allow only as many settlers as could be placed on available land, and tensions between Palestinian Arabs and Jews increased dramatically.

Provisions for non-Jewish rights in the mandate were ambiguous. They were assured of religious liberty and access to their religious sites, and assured that discrimination would not be allowed based on their religion, but territorial rights and political rights were not included in these protections. Many Arabs in Palestine had viewed the Balfour Declaration, upon which the mandate was based, as a betrayal of promises made to them in exchange for their assistance in the defeat of the Ottoman Empire; they saw Great Britain's support of a Jewish homeland and their subsequent administration of Palestine as a profound betrayal of their nationalist ambitions and the promise of self-government. Instability in Palestine kept the area in limbo, with the British mandate continuing until 1948, when the state of Israel was established following World War II.

—*Bethany Groff Dorau*

Bibliography and Additional Reading

Barr, James. *A Line in the Sand: The Anglo-French Struggle for the Middle East, 1914–1948.* New York: Norton, 2012. Print.

Fromkin, David. *A Peace to End All Peace: The Fall of the Ottoman Empire and the Creation of the Modern Middle East.* New York: Holt, 2001. Print.

Pappé, Ilan. *A History of Modern Palestine: One Land, Two Peoples.* New York: Cambridge UP, 2004. Print.

Rogan, Eugene. *The Fall of the Ottomans: The Great War in the Middle East.* New York: Basic, 2015. Print.

White Paper of 1939

Date: May 23, 1939
Author: Malcolm MacDonald
Geographic region: Middle East, Palestine
Genre: Treaty; memorandum; proclamation

Summary Overview

The significance of the document examined here is not so much who authored it but which government produced it and when and why. On the eve of World War II, the 1939 White Paper was issued. It was not accepted—and then World War II broke out.

To understand the historical context, one needs to go back to the end of World War I, when Great Britain was given (and desired) a role in the Middle East. Britain was given control over Iraq and what was then Palestine. Palestine was made up of the current state of Israel and the land governed by the current Palestinian authority. Britain, in requesting the mandate (i.e., controlling authority), wanted to maintain its own power in the world, limit the influence of France, and preserve its pipeline to India. However, the British, particularly in Palestine, had their hands full. Jewish forces believed that they had been promised a Jewish homeland in the area under the Balfour Declaration of 1917, and Arab forces believed that they had been promised control under the exchange of letters known as the Hussein-McMahon correspondence. Jewish forces decided to migrate to the area and take control, and the British between 1919 and 1939 tried to limit that process while also balancing domestic political concerns. By 1939, the British were desperate for an answer, and this White Paper was their attempt at it.

Defining Moment

The drafting of the White Paper represents a defining moment in Middle Eastern history as far as the British are concerned because they needed to establish a policy regarding Palestine that work for all parties. They had largely created the problem themselves by announcing, in the 1917 Balfour Declaration, the intent to establish a Jewish homeland; and by agreeing, through the Hussein McMahon correspondence, to allow Arab control over Palestine. Between 1919 and 1939, Jews immigrated to the area and started buying land in order to assume control. In the 1920s, their goal was to buy enough land to control it. However, by the 1930s immigration was low yet problems mounted in Europe, as the threat of a major new war loomed. Soon, Jews sought to migrate anywhere outside of Europe, and Palestine was desirable because it overlapped with the ancient Jewish homeland. Arabs in the area, however, did not want more Jewish settlers, even though they were hardly consulted on the matter.

By 1939, the situation had become critical, as there were enough Jewish settlers in Palestine to be represent a sizable bloc of residents, but Britain was not yet prepared to commit to a two-state solution—one Arab/Palestinian and one Jewish. The British called a conference to try to negotiate a solution; but when the conference led to no significant change in Palestinian opinion (the Palestinians were not willing to accept the British ideas), the British simply announced their own intention to move ahead as they saw fit. The Palestinians did not accept the solution and so the situation remained at a standstill when World War II broke out. Complicating the issue was the fact that many European Jews had hoped to reach Palestine both before and during the outbreak of hostilities. Most nations would not accept Jewish migrants, and the British limited immigration in Palestine in order not to anger the Palestinians further. The Jews pointed out that they faced a grave danger in Europe, while the Palestinians pointed out that no one had asked them about giving up their land to help solve a problem they had not created.

Author Biography

The author of the White Paper of 1939 was Malcolm MacDonald, the British Colonial Secretary at the time. MacDonald was 37 years old then, fairly young for a high position. He was originally in the Labour Party, but joined the national government in the mid-1930s and was expelled. He became Colonial Secretary and oversaw an agreement with the Irish Free State, settling affairs there. He then oversaw the attempt to settle the issue of Palestine. In 1940, MacDonald left the office of Colonial Secretary, serving as Minister of Health for a while under Winston Churchill. In 1941 he served as High Commissioner to Canada. After 1946, he continued his career in colonial affairs, serving until the late 1960s in various roles.

The British government was led by Neville Chamberlain at the time. Chamberlain had become prime minister in 1937, when Stanley Baldwin, who had won election as Prime Minister in 1935, resigned. (This was after George VI became king when Edward VII abdicated to marry Wallis Simpson.) Chamberlain had a number of crises to deal with, including the Munich Crisis, in which Hitler demanded the Sudetenland and Chamberlain bowed to Hitler's wishes. Chamberlain worked hard to avoid war, but after France fell in 1940, he abdicated and Winston Churchill came to power.

HISTORICAL DOCUMENT: *White Paper of 1939*

In the statement on Palestine, issued on 9 November, 1938, His Majesty's Government announced their intention to invite representatives of the Arabs of Palestine, of certain neighboring countries and of the Jewish Agency to confer with them in London regarding future policy. It was their sincere hope that, as a result of full, free and frank discussions, some understanding might be reached. Conferences recently took place with Arab and Jewish delegations, lasting for a period of several weeks, and served the purpose of a complete exchange of views between British Ministers and the Arab and Jewish representatives. In the light of the discussions as well as of the situation in Palestine and of the Reports of the Royal Commission and the Partition Commission, certain proposals were formulated by His Majesty's Government and were laid before the Arab and Jewish Delegations as the basis of an agreed settlement. Neither the Arab nor the Jewish delegation felt able to accept these proposals, and the conferences therefore did not result in an agreement. Accordingly His Majesty's Government are free to formulate their own policy, and after careful consideration they have decided to adhere generally to the proposals which were finally submitted to and discussed with the Arab and Jewish delegations.

The Mandate for Palestine, the terms of which were confirmed by the Council of the League of Nations in 1922, has governed the policy of successive British Governments for nearly 20 years. It embodies the Balfour Declaration and imposes on the Mandatory four main obligations. These obligations are set out in Article 2, 6 and 13 of the Mandate. There is no dispute regarding the interpretation of one of these obligations, that touching the protection of and access to the Holy Places and religious building or sites. The other three main obligations are generally as follows:

> To place the country under such political, administrative and economic conditions as will secure the establishment in Palestine of a national home for the Jewish People. To facilitate Jewish immigration under suitable conditions, and to encourage, in cooperation with the Jewish Agency, close settlement by Jews on the Land.
>
> To safeguard the civil and religious rights of all inhabitants of Palestine irrespective of race and religion, and, whilst facilitating Jewish immigration and settlement, to ensure that the rights and position of other sections of the population are not prejudiced.
>
> To place the country under such political, administrative and economic conditions as will secure the development of self governing institutions.

The Royal Commission and previous commissions of Enquiry have drawn attention to the ambiguity of certain expressions in the Mandate, such as the expression 'a national home for the Jewish people', and they have found in this ambiguity and the resulting uncertainty as to the objectives of policy a fundamental cause of unrest and hostility between Arabs and Jews. His Majesty's Government are convinced that in the interests of the peace and well being of the whole people of Palestine a clear definition of policy and objectives is essential. The proposal of partition recommended by the Royal Commission would have afforded such clarity, but the establishment of self supporting independent Arab and Jewish States within Palestine has been found to be impracticable. It has therefore been necessary for His Majesty's Government to devise an alternative policy which will, consistent with their obligations to Arabs and Jews, meet the needs of the situation in Palestine. Their views and proposals are set forth below under three heads, Section I, "The Constitution", Section II. Immigration and Section III. Land.

Section I. "The Constitution"

It has been urged that the expression "a national home for the Jewish people" offered a prospect that Palestine might in due course become a Jewish State or

continues on page 74

continued from page 73

Commonwealth. His Majesty's Government do not wish to contest the view, which was expressed by the Royal Commission, that the Zionist leaders at the time of the issue of the Balfour Declaration recognized that an ultimate Jewish State was not precluded by the terms of the Declaration. But, with the Royal Commission, His Majesty's Government believe that the framers of the Mandate in which the Balfour Declaration was embodied could not have intended that Palestine should be converted into a Jewish State against the will of the Arab population of the country. That Palestine was not to be converted into a Jewish State might be held to be implied in the passage from the Command Paper of 1922 which reads as follows

> "Unauthorized statements have been made to the effect that the purpose in view is to create a wholly Jewish Palestine. Phrases have been used such as that 'Palestine is to become as Jewish as England is English.' His Majesty's Government regard any such expectation as impracticable and have no such aim in view. Nor have they at any time contemplated . . . the disappearance or the subordination of the Arabic population, language or culture in Palestine. They would draw attention to the fact that the terms of the (Balfour) Declaration referred to do not contemplate that Palestine as a whole should be converted into a Jewish National Home, but that such a Home should be founded IN PALESTINE."

But this statement has not removed doubts, and His Majesty's Government therefore now declare unequivocally that it is not part of their policy that Palestine should become a Jewish State. They would indeed regard it as contrary to their obligations to the Arabs under the Mandate, as well as to the assurances which have been given to the Arab people in the past, that the Arab population of Palestine should be made the subjects of a Jewish State against their will.

The nature of the Jewish National Home in Palestine was further described in the Command Paper of 1922 as follows:

> "During the last two or three generations the Jews have recreated in Palestine a community now numbering 80,000, of whom about one fourth are farmers or workers upon the land. This community has its own political organs; an elected assembly for the direction of its domestic concerns; elected councils in the towns; and an organization for the control of its schools. It has its elected Chief Rabbinate and Rabbinical Council for the direction of its religious affairs. Its business is conducted in Hebrew as a vernacular language, and a Hebrew press serves its needs. It has its distinctive intellectual life and displays considerable economic activity. This community, then, with its town and country population, its political, religious and social organizations, its own language, its own customs, its own life, has in fact 'national' characteristics.

When it is asked what is meant by the development of the Jewish National Home in Palestine, it may be answered that it is not the imposition of a Jewish nationality upon the inhabitants of Palestine as a whole, but the further development of the existing Jewish community, with the assistance of Jews in other parts of the world, in order that it may become a center in which the Jewish people as a whole may take, on grounds of religion and race, an interest and pride. But in order that this community should have the best prospect of free development and provide a full opportunity for the Jewish people to display its capacities, it is essential that it should know that it is in Palestine as of right and not on sufferance. That is the reason why it is necessary that the existence of a Jewish National Home in Palestine should be internationally guaranteed, and that it should be formally recognized to rest upon ancient historic connection."

His Majesty's Government adhere to this interpretation of the (Balfour) Declaration of 1917 and regard it as an authoritative and comprehensive description of the character of the Jewish National Home in Palestine. It envisaged the further development of the existing Jewish community with the assistance of Jews in other parts of the world. Evidence that His Majesty's Government have been carrying out their obligation in this respect is to be found in the facts that, since the statement of 1922 was published, more than 300,000 Jews have immigrated to Palestine, and that the population of the National Home has risen to some 450,000, or approaching a third of the entire population of the country. Nor has the Jewish community failed to take full advantage of the opportunities given to it. The growth of the Jewish National Home and its achievements in many fields are a remarkable constructive effort which must command the admiration of the world and must be, in particular, a source of pride to the Jewish people.

In the recent discussions the Arab delegations have repeated the contention that Palestine was included within the area in which Sir Henry McMahon, on behalf of the British Government, in October, 1915, undertook to recognize and support Arab independence. The validity of this claim, based on the terms of the correspondence which passed between Sir Henry McMahon and the Sharif of Mecca, was thoroughly and carefully investigated by the British and Arab representatives during the recent conferences in London. Their report, which has been published, states that both the Arab and the British representatives endeavored to understand the point of view of the other party but that they were unable to reach agreement upon an interpretation of the correspondence. There is no need to summarize here the arguments presented by each side. His Majesty's Government regret the misunderstandings which have arisen as regards some of the phrases used. For their part they can only adhere, for the reasons given by their representatives in the Report, to the view

continues on page 76

continued from page 75

that the whole of Palestine west of Jordan was excluded from Sir Henry McMahon's pledge, and they therefore cannot agree that the McMahon correspondence forms a just basis for the claim that Palestine should be converted into an Arab State.

His Majesty's Government are charged as the Mandatory authority "to secure the development of self governing institutions" in Palestine. Apart from this specific obligation, they would regard it as contrary to the whole spirit of the Mandate system that the population of Palestine should remain forever under Mandatory tutelage. It is proper that the people of the country should as early as possible enjoy the rights of self-government which are exercised by the people of neighbouring countries. His Majesty's Government are unable at present to foresee the exact constitutional forms which government in Palestine will eventually take, but their objective is self government, and they desire to see established ultimately an independent Palestine State. It should be a State in which the two peoples in Palestine, Arabs and Jews, share authority in government in such a way that the essential interests of each are shared.

The establishment of an independent State and the complete relinquishment of Mandatory control in Palestine would require such relations between the Arabs and the Jews as would make good government possible. Moreover, the growth of self governing institutions in Palestine, as in other countries, must be an evolutionary process. A transitional period will be required before independence is achieved, throughout which ultimate responsibility for the Government of the country will be retained by His Majesty's Government as the Mandatory authority, while the people of the country are taking an increasing share in the Government, and understanding and cooperation amongst them are growing. It will be the constant endeavor of His Majesty's Government to promote good relations between the Arabs and the Jews.

In the light of these considerations His Majesty's Government make the following declaration of their intentions regarding the future government of Palestine:

The objective of His Majesty's Government is the establishment within 10 years of an independent Palestine State in such treaty relations with the United Kingdom as will provide satisfactorily for the commercial and strategic requirements of both countries in the future. The proposal for the establishment of the independent State would involve consultation with the Council of the League of Nations with a view to the termination of the Mandate.

The independent State should be one in which Arabs and Jews share government in such a way as to ensure that the essential interests of each community are safeguarded.

The establishment of the independent State will be preceded by a transitional period throughout which His Majesty's Government will retain responsibility for the country. During the transitional period the people of Palestine will be given an increasing part in the government of their country. Both sections of the population will have an opportunity to participate in the machinery of government, and the process will be carried on whether or not they both avail themselves of it.

As soon as peace and order have been sufficiently restored in Palestine steps will be taken to carry out this policy of giving the people of Palestine an increasing part in the government of their country, the objective being to place Palestinians in charge of all the Departments of Government, with the assistance of British advisers and subject to the control of the High Commissioner. Arab and Jewish representatives will be invited to serve as heads of Departments approximately in proportion to their respective populations. The number of Palestinians in charge of Departments will be increased as circumstances permit until all heads of Departments are Palestinians, exercising the administrative and advisory functions which are presently performed by British officials. When that stage is reached consideration will be given to the question of converting the Executive Council into a Council of Ministers with a consequential change in the status and functions of the Palestinian heads of Departments.

> *The establishment of an independent State and the complete relinquishment of Mandatory control in Palestine would require such relations between the Arabs and the Jews as would make good government possible.*

His Majesty's Government make no proposals at this stage regarding the establishment of an elective legislature. Nevertheless they would regard this as an appropriate constitutional development, and, should public opinion in Palestine hereafter show itself in favour of such a development, they will be prepared, provided that local conditions permit, to establish the necessary machinery.

At the end of five years from the restoration of peace and order, an appropriate body representative of the people of Palestine and of His Majesty's Government will be set up to review the working of the constitutional arrangements during the transitional period and to consider and make recommendations regarding the constitution of the independent Palestine State.

His Majesty's Government will require to be satisfied that in the treaty contemplated by sub-paragraph (6) adequate provision has been made for:

> The security of, and freedom of access to the Holy Places, and protection of the interests and property of the various religious bodies.
>
> The protection of the different communities in Palestine in accordance with the obligations of His Majesty's Government to both Arabs and Jews and for the special position in Palestine of the Jewish National Home.

continues on page 78

continued from page 77

> Such requirements to meet the strategic situation as may be regarded as necessary by His Majesty's Government in the light of the circumstances then existing. His Majesty's Government will also require to be satisfied that the interests of certain foreign countries in Palestine, for the preservation of which they are at present responsible, are adequately safeguarded.
>
> His Majesty's Government will do everything in their power to create conditions which will enable the independent Palestine State to come into being within 10 years. If, at the end of 10 years, it appears to His Majesty's Government that, contrary to their hope, circumstances require the postponement of the establishment of the independent State, they will consult with representatives of the people of Palestine, the Council of the League of Nations and the neighboring Arab States before deciding on such a postponement. If His Majesty's Government come to the conclusion that postponement is unavoidable, they will invite the co-operation of these parties in framing plans for the future with a view to achieving the desired objective at the earliest possible date.
> During the transitional period steps will be taken to increase the powers and responsibilities of municipal corporations and local councils.
>
> Section II. Immigration
>
> Under Article 6 of the Mandate, the Administration of Palestine, "while ensuring that the rights and position of other sections of the population are not prejudiced," is required to "facilitate Jewish immigration under suitable conditions." Beyond this, the extent to which Jewish immigration into Palestine is to be permitted is nowhere defined in the Mandate. But in the Command Paper of 1922 it was laid down that for the fulfilment of the policy of establishing a Jewish National Home:
>
>> "It is necessary that the Jewish community in Palestine should be able to increase its numbers by immigration. This immigration cannot be so great in volume as to exceed whatever may be the economic capacity of the country at the time to absorb new arrivals. It is essential to ensure that the immigrants should not be a burden upon the people of Palestine as a whole, and that they should not deprive any section of the present population of their employment."
>
> In practice, from that date onwards until recent times, the economic absorptive capacity of the country has been treated as the sole limiting factor, and in the letter which Mr. Ramsay MacDonald, as Prime Minister, sent to Dr. Weizmann in February 1931 it was laid down as a matter of policy that economic absorptive

capacity was the sole criterion. This interpretation has been supported by resolutions of the Permanent Mandates Commissioner. But His Majesty's Government do not read either the Statement of Policy of 1922 or the letter of 1931 as implying that the Mandate requires them, for all time and in all circumstances, to facilitate the immigration of Jews into Palestine subject only to consideration of the country's economic absorptive capacity. Nor do they find anything in the Mandate or in subsequent Statements of Policy to support the view that the establishment of a Jewish National Home in Palestine cannot be effected unless immigration is allowed to continue indefinitely. If immigration has an adverse effect on the economic position in the country, it should clearly be restricted; and equally, if it has a seriously damaging effect on the political position in the country, that is a factor that should not be ignored. Although it is not difficult to contend that the large number of Jewish immigrants who have been admitted so far have been absorbed economically, the fear of the Arabs that this influx will continue indefinitely until the Jewish population is in a position to dominate them has produced consequences which are extremely grave for Jews and Arabs alike and for the peace and prosperity of Palestine. The lamentable disturbances of the past three years are only the latest and most sustained manifestation of this intense Arab apprehension. The methods employed by Arab terrorists against fellow Arabs and Jews alike must receive unqualified condemnation. But it cannot be denied that fear of indefinite Jewish immigration is widespread amongst the Arab population and that this fear has made possible disturbances which have given a serious setback to economic progress, depleted the Palestine exchequer, rendered life and property insecure, and produced a bitterness between the Arab and Jewish populations which is deplorable between citizens of the same country. If in these circumstances immigration is continued up to the economic absorptive capacity of the country, regardless of all other considerations, a fatal enmity between the two peoples will be perpetuated, and the situation in Palestine may become a permanent source of friction amongst all peoples in the Near and Middle East. His Majesty's Government cannot take the view that either their obligations under the Mandate, or considerations of common sense and justice, require that they should ignore these circumstances in framing immigration policy.

In the view of the Royal Commission the association of the policy of the Balfour Declaration with the Mandate system implied the belief that Arab hostility to the former would sooner or later be overcome. It has been the hope of British Governments ever since the Balfour Declaration was issued that in time the Arab population, recognizing the advantages to be derived from Jewish settlement and development in Palestine, would become reconciled to the further growth of the Jewish National Home. This hope has not been fulfilled. The alternatives before His Majesty's Government are either (i) to seek to expand the Jewish National Home indefinitely

continues on page 80

continued from page 79

by immigration, against the strongly expressed will of the Arab people of the country; or (ii) to permit further expansion of the Jewish National Home by immigration only if the Arabs are prepared to acquiesce in it. The former policy means rule by force. Apart from other considerations, such a policy seems to His Majesty's Government to be contrary to the whole spirit of Article 22 of the Covenant of the League of Nations, as well as to their specific obligations to the Arabs in the Palestine Mandate. Moreover, the relations between the Arabs and the Jews in Palestine must be based sooner or later on mutual tolerance and goodwill; the peace, security and progress of the Jewish National Home itself requires this. Therefore His Majesty's Government, after earnest consideration, and taking into account the extent to which the growth of the Jewish National Home has been facilitated over the last twenty years, have decided that the time has come to adopt in principle the second of the alternatives referred to above.

It has been urged that all further Jewish immigration into Palestine should be stopped forthwith. His Majesty's Government cannot accept such a proposal. It would damage the whole of the financial and economic system of Palestine and thus effect adversely the interests of Arabs and Jews alike. Moreover, in the view of His Majesty's Government, abruptly to stop further immigration would be unjust to the Jewish National Home. But, above all, His Majesty's Government are conscious of the present unhappy plight of large numbers of Jews who seek refuge from certain European countries, and they believe that Palestine can and should make a further contribution to the solution of this pressing world problem. In all these circumstances, they believe that they will be acting consistently with their Mandatory obligations to both Arabs and Jews, and in the manner best calculated to serve the interests of the whole people of Palestine, by adopting the following proposals regarding immigration:

Jewish immigration during the next five years will be at a rate which, if economic absorptive capacity permits, will bring the Jewish population up to approximately one third of the total population of the country. Taking into account the expected natural increase of the Arab and Jewish populations, and the number of illegal Jewish immigrants now in the country, this would allow of the admission, as from the beginning of April this year, of some 75,000 immigrants over the next five years. These immigrants would, subject to the criterion of economic absorptive capacity, be admitted as follows:

For each of the next five years a quota of 10,000 Jewish immigrants will be allowed on the understanding that a shortage one year may be added to the quotas for subsequent years, within the five year period, if economic absorptive capacity permits.

In addition, as a contribution towards the solution of the Jewish refugee problem, 25,000 refugees will be admitted as soon as the High Commissioner is satisfied that adequate provision for their maintenance is ensured, special consideration being given to refugee children and dependents.

The existing machinery for ascertaining economic absorptive capacity will be retained, and the High Commissioner will have the ultimate responsibility for deciding the limits of economic capacity. Before each periodic decision is taken, Jewish and Arab representatives will be consulted.

After the period of five years, no further Jewish immigration will be permitted unless the Arabs of Palestine are prepared to acquiesce in it.

His Majesty's Government are determined to check illegal immigration, and further preventive measures are being adopted. The numbers of any Jewish illegal immigrants who, despite these measures, may succeed in coming into the country and cannot be deported will be deducted from the yearly quotas.

His Majesty's Government are satisfied that, when the immigration over five years which is now contemplated has taken place, they will not be justified in facilitating, nor will they be under any obligation to facilitate, the further development of the Jewish National Home by immigration regardless of the wishes of the Arab population.

Section III. Land

The Administration of Palestine is required, under Article 6 of the Mandate, "while ensuring that the rights and position of other sections of the population are not prejudiced," to encourage "close settlement by Jews on the land," and no restriction has been imposed hitherto on the transfer of land from Arabs to Jews. The Reports of several expert Commissions have indicated that, owing to the natural growth of the Arab population and the steady sale in recent years of Arab land to Jews, there is now in certain areas no room for further transfers of Arab land, whilst in some other areas such transfers of land must be restricted if Arab cultivators are to maintain their existing standard of life and a considerable landless Arab population is not soon to be created. In these circumstances, the High Commissioner will be given general powers to prohibit and regulate transfers of land. These powers will date from the publication of this statement of policy and the High Commissioner will retain them throughout the transitional period.

The policy of the Government will be directed towards the development of the land and the improvement, where possible, of methods of cultivation. In the light of such development it will be open to the High Commissioner, should he be satisfied that the "rights and position" of the Arab population will be duly preserved, to review and modify any orders passed relating to the prohibition or restriction of the transfer of land.

continues on page 82

continued from page 81

> In framing these proposals His Majesty's Government have sincerely endeavored to act in strict accordance with their obligations under the Mandate to both the Arabs and the Jews. The vagueness of the phrases employed in some instances to describe these obligations has led to controversy and has made the task of interpretation difficult. His Majesty's Government cannot hope to satisfy the partisans of one party or the other in such controversy as the Mandate has aroused. Their purpose is to be just as between the two people in Palestine whose destinies in that country have been affected by the great events of recent years, and who, since they live side by side, must learn to practice mutual tolerance, goodwill and co operation. In looking to the future, His Majesty's Government are not blind to the fact that some events of the past make the task of creating these relations difficult; but they are encouraged by the knowledge that as many times and in many places in Palestine during recent years the Arab and Jewish inhabitants have lived in friendship together. Each community has much to contribute to the welfare of their common land, and each must earnestly desire peace in which to assist in increasing the well being of the whole people of the country. The responsibility which falls on them, no less than upon His Majesty's Government, to co operate together to ensure peace is all the more solemn because their country is revered by many millions of Moslems, Jews and Christians throughout the world who pray for peace in Palestine and for the happiness of her people.

GLOSSARY

Holy Places: the sacred areas of Jerusalem that were important to the three major faiths (Judaism, Christianity, and Islam) in the region

Jewish Agency: an organization representing the Jews of the world and seeking to help those wanting to relocate to Palestine

Jewish State: a state in Palestine run by Jews and promoting Jewish culture

Mandate: a grant of power under the League of Nations; an area so controlled or administered

National Home: in this context, a Jewish homeland in Palestine, but one that is not necessarily a sovereign state

Jewish demonstration against White Paper in Jerusalem, 1939.

Document Analysis

The document first notes why it was created. It lays out the conference and how it failed. To put a positive spin on it, the document argues that the failure of that meeting leaves the British government free to announce policy. The White Paper then looks at the history of the mandate and the original goals. It also honestly notes the difficulties with the mandate (these difficulties might have also been noted in order to give the British an out for not being any more successful there). The paper comments that the term "a national home for the Jewish people" was unclear and that a two-state solution was not possible. To justify this, in the first part of the paper, the author goes back to previous documents and argues that neither the Arabs, under the Hussein-McMahon correspondence, nor the Jews, under the Balfour Declaration, should get the entire area. The paper also argues that in line with the original League of Nations mandate, the whole area remains together. It states that only such a solution will allow the British the way out of the mandate, which, by this point, they were coming to desire.

After this, the White Paper moves into its goals, noting that the British wish to establish an independent state with both Arabs and Jews in it. This would be a government with "shared governance" involving both groups. The white paper notes the plan for creating such a government after a transitional period. The British would first lead and would then hand off the

Land classification and boundaries of land transfer regions as prescribed in 1940.

departments to the Palestinians, which here means both Arabs and Jews of the area. Unlike the executive, no plan is presented for a legislature, but the paper does indicate that the latter might be a good idea. A five-year transition period is proposed and the paper notes that Britain would need to be satisfied with the plans for protections of religious minorities and the holy sites of various religions before power was finally transferred. That period could take as long as ten years, it is noted.

On the subject of immigration, the White Paper notes that a continuation of the overall level of immigration is not desirable. After discussing why the Arabs are unhappy with the immigration currently, and noting the negative effects of the current level, the paper outlines three options. The first is to continue to allow immigration, which is not ideal given the wishes of the populace and also is contrary to the League of Nations. The second is to ban all immigration of Jews, which the paper denounces as contrary to the economic health of the region. Therefore, the paper proposes allowing 75,000 migrants in, with 10,000 per year and 25,000 refugees (at least under the first five years of the proposed transfer of power).

As for the land, the paper proposes that there should be no more transfers of land from the Arabs to the Jews. The two sides, in fact, are to be responsible for settling the issue of land rather than the British. The British basically have decided to end transfers and let the two sides sort out the past, as they will have to live together in the future. This is in accordance with the growing British interest in figuring a way out of the mandate, rather than continuing to be responsible for fixing all the problems regarding it.

Essential Themes

This document shows what the British might have done (or might have attempted to do) had World War II not broken out. Recall that there were various efforts afoot to prevent or limit a second world war from unfolding. Thus, the writers of this document were announcing what they wanted to do. It should be noted though that the British were trying to do this on their own, and their chances of success might have been limited because of it. After all, the reason why the British had to issue their own White Paper, rather than working with the local population, was that the Arabs had refused the agreement that the British suggested at the time. Thus, what the British were announcing had already been refuted.

There is also the matter of World War II, the threat of which was then looming over Europe. That threat shifted the focus of the British and most of the rest of the world. On the other hand, it caused the Jewish people in Europe to want to migrate more than ever. Although they were barred from entering a number of other countries, Jews did begin pouring into Palestine. This only increased the difficulty of the situation, and reduced the chance for finding an easy solution.

It is clear from the White Paper that the British wanted out of the area and also thought that there should be a Jewish homeland that could be governed jointly by Arabs and Jews. While that solution may have been unworkable, it was never really tried because of the British desire to be done with the matter and the onset of world war.

The paper, in fact, was written with an eye toward maintaining British influence in the region. That included relationships with Egypt, Iraq, and Saudi Arabia—even if these were not independent states at the time. If they had broken away, it could create an Axis powerhouse in the area given increased incursions from Germany and Italy. Moreover, much of the oil that the British planned to use in war came out of this area.

For the Arabs and the Jews, the White Paper did not serve their long-term interests. The Arabs were not ready to accept a Jewish homeland in the area, especially one thrust upon them; and the Jews considered that the homeland concept was not enough, that a state was what they needed. This conundrum would persist through the founding of Israel in 1948 and beyond.

—*Scott A. Merriman*

Bibliography and Additional Reading

Cohen, Michael Joseph. *Britain's Moment in Palestine: Retrospect and Perspectives, 1917–48*. London: Routledge/Taylor & Francis Group, 2014.

Matthews, Weldon C. *Confronting an Empire, Constructing a Nation: Arab Nationalists and Popular Politics in Mandate Palestine*. London: I.B. Tauris, 2006.

Neill, Lochery. "Review Article: Lion in the Sand: British Policy in the Middle East, 1945–67." *Middle Eastern Studies*, no. 5, 2008, p. 807.

Segev, Tom. *One Palestine, Complete: Jews and Arabs under the Mandate*. New York: Metropolitan Books, 2000.

Zweig, R. W. "British Policy to Palestine, May 1939 to 1943: The Fate of the White Paper." 1978. PhD Dissertation

Truman Statement on Immigration into Palestine

Date: October 4, 1946
Author: Harry S. Truman
Geographic region: Palestine
Genre: Government document

Summary Overview

In 1946, as the debate over whether Jews should be allowed to establish a homeland in Palestine raged, President Harry S. Truman advocated strongly in favor of the Jews' position. However, when a London conference on the issue abruptly ended without a clear series of recommendations for resolution, Truman issued a statement on the eve of Yom Kippur (the Day of Atonement in Judaism) expressing his disappointment about that conference's outcome. Truman reiterated his position that 100,000 displaced Jews should be allowed to immigrate to Palestine. He urged world leaders to endorse a peaceable solution to the Palestine issue and to create liberal immigration policies that would welcome Jews and other displaced groups to take up residence in their respective nations.

Defining Moment

When Adolf Hitler published his book *Mein Kampf* (1925, 1927), he outlined a personal philosophy that the Jews and other racial minorities were to be eradicated. Upon assuming power as chancellor (or Fuhrer) of Germany in 1933, Hitler quickly moved to make this idea a reality. By 1945, about six million of Europe's nine-and-a-half million Jews (a 1933 estimate) had died as a result of the Holocaust, with hundreds of thousands more displaced before and during World War II. Most of the survivors moved to the Western Hemisphere, but a sizable population still sought refuge in Europe.

One option for them had been under consideration for decades. In 1917, Russian-born Zionist Chaim Weizmann convinced the British government to honor the Jews, who had supported Britain against the Turks during World War I, by calling for a Jewish state in Palestine. However, by the 1930s, Jews escaping Hitler's genocide began entering Palestine, inciting a political backlash from the Arabs living there. Because Arabs already enjoyed a strong relationship with Britain (which, after World War I, controlled the region), Great Britain withdrew its support of the Jewish state. Zionist coalitions, feeling betrayed by the British change of course, turned to the United States for support.

President Franklin D. Roosevelt was supportive of the idea, particularly as the Holocaust showed the world the horrors to which the Jews were subjected. Near the end of World War II, Roosevelt's successor, Harry Truman, also showed great sympathy for the Zionist cause. He was, however, cognizant of the political risks of dividing Palestine into two distinct, autonomous states. In 1946, Truman worked with the Anglo-American Committee of Inquiry to address the issue in two areas: first, the Palestine issue, and second, the travel arrangements for 100,000 Jews who would be taken there.

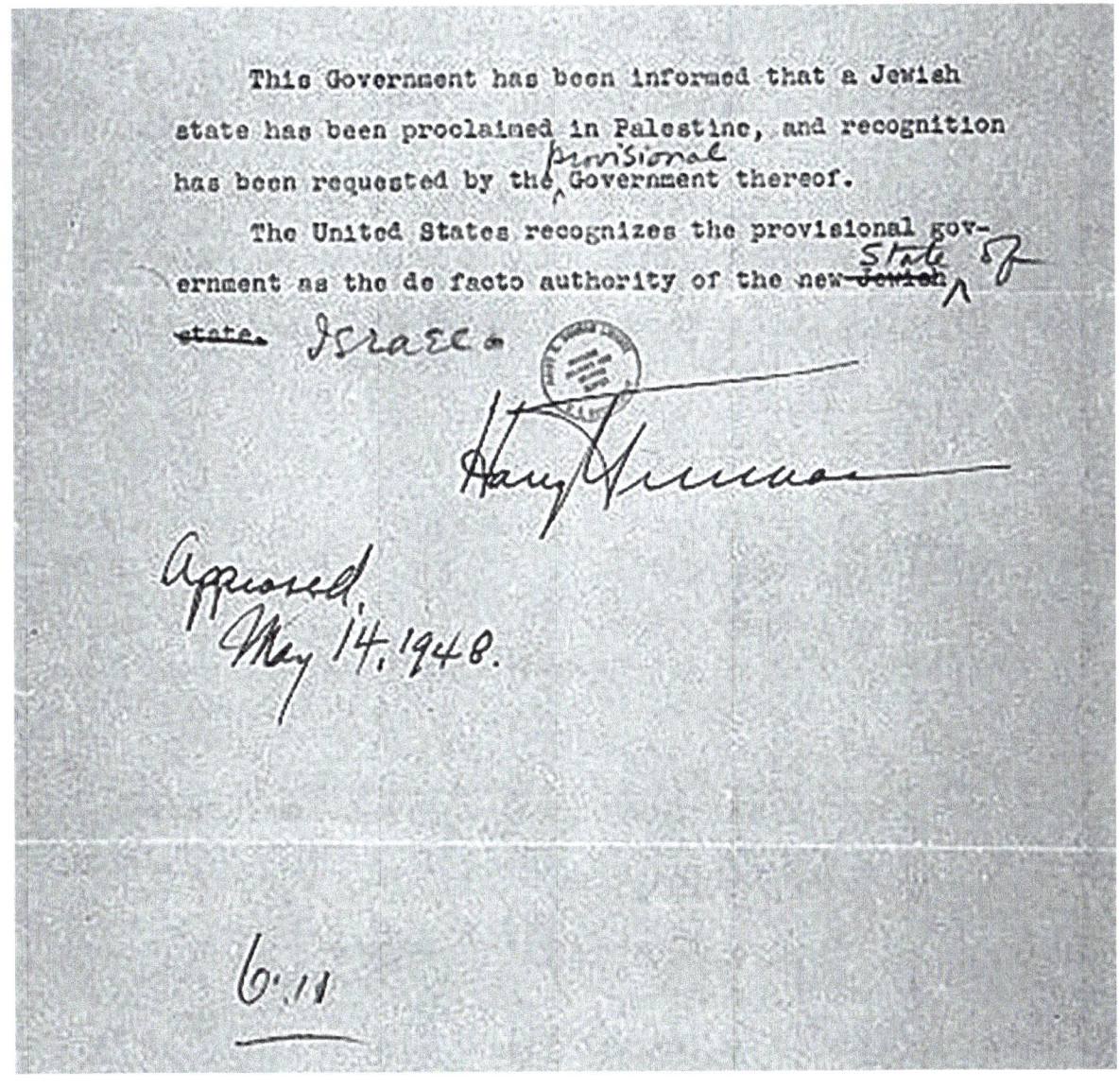

> This Government has been informed that a Jewish state has been proclaimed in Palestine, and recognition has been requested by the provisional Government thereof.
>
> The United States recognizes the provisional government as the de facto authority of the new State of ~~Jewish state.~~ ISRAEL.
>
> *Harry Truman*
>
> Approved
> May 14, 1948.
>
> 6:11

State Department Telegram to Diplomats and Consulates Record Group 59: Records of the Department of State National Archives and Records Administration.

In the United States, Congress was increasingly in favor of the idea of a Jewish state in Palestine. However, the manner by which the state would be established—whether a singular, all-inclusive state or a divided nation (one for Jews, the other for Arabs)—could not be settled. Truman, himself an advocate of a single state, believed that the partitioned model invited conflict and war. In an election year, Truman made the difficult decision of turning down the partition plan in Congress. Nevertheless, he continued to call for a Jewish state, which would be essential to harboring the 100,000 Jewish refugees whose fate had yet to be decided. In September 1946, a conference was held in London to bring a resolution to the

Palestinian issue. However, the conference only lasted three weeks, as a large number of its participants looked to attend the meeting of the United Nations General Assembly on October 23. The conference was adjourned abruptly, with its organizers planning to reconvene after the middle of December, though they did not ultimately meet again until February. Truman, in response, issued a statement in which he presented his thoughts on the adjournment and the issue as a whole.

Author Biography

Harry S. Truman was born on May 8, 1884, in Lamar, Missouri. He spent most of his childhood living in Independence, Missouri, outside of Kansas City. He enlisted in the National Guard and served from 1905 to 1911, rising to the rank of captain by World War I. In 1922, he won election as judge in Jackson County, Missouri. In 1934, Truman was elected to the US Senate and won reelection in 1940. In 1944, he was nominated Franklin D. Roosevelt's running mate in the presidential election. In 1945, after Roosevelt's sudden death, Truman assumed the role of president, overseeing the end of World War II and introducing the Fair Deal domestic economic reform package. He won reelection in 1948, faced with the Cold War, and during this term helped form the North Atlantic Treaty Organization (NATO). After his second term, Truman retired to Independence. He died on December 26, 1972.

HISTORICAL DOCUMENT: *Truman Statement on Immigration into Palestine*

I have learned with deep regret that the meetings of the Palestine Conference in London have been adjourned and are not to be resumed until December 16, 1946. In the light of this situation it is appropriate to examine the record of the administration's efforts in this field, efforts which have been supported in and not of Congress by members of both political parties, and to state my views on the situation as it now exists.

It will be recalled that, when Mr. Earl Harrison reported on September 29, 1945, concerning the condition of displaced persons in Europe, I immediately urged that steps be taken to relieve the situation of these persons to the extent at least of admitting 100,000 Jews into Palestine. In response to this suggestion the British Government invited the Government of the United States to cooperate in setting up a joint Anglo-American Committee of Inquiry, an invitation which this Government was happy to accept in the hope that its participation would help to alleviate the situation of the displaced Jews in Europe and would assist in finding a solution for the difficult and complex problem of Palestine itself. The urgency with which this Government regarded the matter is reflected in the fact that a 120-day limit was set for the completion of the Committee's task.

The unanimous report of the Anglo-American Committee of Inquiry was made on April 20, 1946, and I was gratified to note that among the recommendations contained in the Report was an endorsement of my previous suggestion that 100,000 Jews be admitted into Palestine. The administration immediately concerned itself with devising ways and means for transporting the 100,000 and caring for them upon their arrival. With this in mind, experts were sent to London in June 1946 to work out provisionally the actual travel arrangements. The British Government cooperated with this group but made it clear that in its view the Report must be considered as a whole and that the issue of the 100,000 could not be considered separately.

On June 11, I announced the establishment of a Cabinet Committee on Palestine and Related Problems, composed of the Secretaries of State, War, and Treasury, to assist me in considering the recommendations of the Anglo-American Committee of Inquiry. The alternates of this Cabinet Committee, headed by Ambassador Henry F. Grady, departed for London on July 10, 1946, to discuss with British Government representatives how the Report might best be implemented. The alternates submitted on July 24, 1946 a report, commonly referred to as the "Morrison plan," advocating a scheme of provincial autonomy which might lead ultimately to a bi-national state or to partition. However, opposition to this plan developed among members of the major political parties in the United States—both in the Congress and throughout the country. In accordance with the principle which I have consistently tried to follow, of having a maximum degree of unity within the country and between the parties on major elements of American foreign policy, I could not give my support to this plan.

> *In the light of the terrible ordeal which the Jewish people of Europe endured during the recent war and the crisis now existing, I cannot believe that a program of immediate action along the lines suggested above could not be worked out with the cooperation of all people concerned.*

I have, nevertheless, maintained my deep interest in the matter and have repeatedly made known and have urged that steps be taken at the earliest possible moment to admit 100,000 Jewish refugees to Palestine.

In the meantime, this Government was informed of the efforts of the British Government to bring to London representatives of the Arabs and Jews, with a view to finding a solution to this distressing problem. I expressed the hope that as a result of these conversations a fair solution of the Palestine problem could be found. While all the parties invited had not found themselves able to attend, I had hoped that there was still a possibility that representatives of the Jewish Agency might take part. If so, the prospect for an agreed and constructive settlement would have been enhanced.

continues on page 90

continued from page 89

The British Government presented to the Conference the so-called "Morrison plan" for provincial autonomy and stated that the Conference was open to other proposals. Meanwhile, the Jewish Agency proposed a solution of the Palestine problem by means of the creation of a viable Jewish state in control of its own immigration and economic policies in an adequate area of Palestine instead of in the whole of Palestine. It proposed furthermore the immediate issuance of certificates for 100,000 Jewish immigrants. This proposal received wide-spread attention in the United States, both in the press and in public forums. From the discussion which has ensued it is my belief that a solution along these lines would command the support of public opinion in the United States. I cannot believe that the gap between the proposals which have been put forward is too great to be bridged by men of reason and good-will. To such a solution our Government could give its support.

In the light of the situation which has now developed I wish to state my views as succinctly as possible:

1. In view of the fact that winter will come on before the Conference can be resumed I believe and urge that substantial immigration into Palestine cannot await a solution to the Palestine problem and that it should begin at once. Preparations for this movement have already been made by this Government and it is ready to lend its immediate assistance.

2. I state again, as I have on previous occasions, that the immigration laws of other countries, including the United States, should be liberalized with a view to the admission of displaced persons. I am prepared to make such a recommendation to the Congress and to continue as energetically as possible collaboration with other countries on the whole problem of displaced persons.

3. Furthermore, should a workable solution for Palestine be devised, I would be willing to recommend to the Congress a plan for economic assistance for the development of that country.

In the light of the terrible ordeal which the Jewish people of Europe endured during the recent war and the crisis now existing, I cannot believe that a program of immediate action along the lines suggested above could not be worked out with the cooperation of all people concerned. The administration will continue to do everything it can to this end.

Document Analysis

Even prior to his first term as president, Harry Truman had a reputation as a Zionist advocate. Truman and the rest of the international community had an opportunity to reach this goal at the end of World War II, as millions of refugees (a large number of whom were Jewish) sought safe havens after years of Nazi persecution. However, Truman was surprised and disappointed to learn that the international community could not come to an agreement on whether to allow 100,000 Jewish refugees to immigrate to Palestine. On the eve of Yom Kippur, Truman issued this statement, underscoring his commitment to peaceably enabling Jewish refugees to settle in the predominantly Arab region.

Truman begins his statement by expressing regret that the September Palestine Conference in London adjourned with no resolution and would not reconvene until the winter. Truman suggests that such an impasse undid the groundwork that he and other leaders laid over the course of decades. The preceding year, he says, Earl Harrison (the US representative of the Intergovernmental Committee on Refugees and dean of the University Pennsylvania Law School) issued a moving report depicting the plight of the Jews immediately after the Holocaust. Given the treatment the Jews had received by the Nazis and their continuing misery, Truman and the British government looked to relieve at least some of this suffering by giving 100,000 Jews entry into Palestine. As part of a bilateral commission, the US and British governments worked to generate attention about the Jews; Truman says that that commission's report suggested that these 100,000 refugees and their potential entry into Palestine could not be made a separate issue from the larger issue of postwar refugees.

Truman acknowledges, however, that the notion of moving a large number of Jews into the predominantly Arab area of Palestine was politically charged. The initial plan, dubbed the Morrison plan, entailed the division of Palestine into either two federated parts or two autonomous states. Truman says that, although he supports the Morrison plan in theory, neither the Republican nor the Democratic Party in Congress would agree to such a plan. He, therefore, begrudgingly abstains from supporting it. Nevertheless, he says, he will continue to advocate for the Palestine option. Other versions of the Morrison plan still existed, each of which calling for a Jewish state in Palestine and for the immigration of Jewish refugees to that state. Such proposals received a great deal of attention from the media and political leaders, he adds, ensuring that the issue itself remained highly relevant.

He argues that the US and other governments should liberalize their immigration policies to give safe haven to Jews and other wartime refugees. Second, according to him, the Palestine proposal should be immediately revisited and settled. Given the experiences of the Jews before and during the war, Truman says, it was only right that they be given prompt attention.

Essential Themes

President Harry Truman's statement served as a reiteration of his position on the plight of Europe's Jews. Truman expressed disappointment that the London conference adjourned without resolution. Keenly aware of the reports that came out of German-occupied territories before and during the war, Truman reiterated his call for to allow 100,000 Jewish refugees to enter and live in Palestine as well as the liberalization of international immigration policy to address the broader refugee crisis.

Truman used the opportunity to summarize the work that he, the US government, and their counterparts in Great Britain had performed to date in order to resolve this issue. He stated that there appeared to be forward momentum on the matter, particularly as the world was becoming increasingly aware of and sympathetic toward the plight of the Jews. However, he acknowledged, there were political forces at work that impeded the process. At home, during an election year, there was congressional partisanship with which to contend; Truman knew that were his effort to succeed, he needed not only congressional support, but the support of the voters as well. Internationally, the landscape was also challenging: the Arabs had successfully lobbied against the effort before, and the pressure was on the president to encourage a peaceful, diplomatic solution that would ensure that both Arabs and the increasing Jewish population would live in peace. Regardless how the Palestine concept would take shape—whether as a single state or as a bi-national state—it was imperative to address the refugees' welfare promptly.

The decisions made at that time continue to have resonance in the twenty-first century. The Palestinians were ultimately promised a state of their own, alongside that established for the Jewish people, Israel. However, wars soon ensued between the Palestinians and the Israelis, and the contentious debate over the "one-state solution" and the "two-state solution" remains.

—Michael P. Auerbach

Bibliography and Additional Reading

Benson, Michael T. *Harry S. Truman and the Founding of Israel*. Westport: Greenwood, 1997. Print.

"Jewish Population of Europe in 1945." *Holocaust Encyclopedia*. United States Holocaust Memorial Museum, 20 Jun. 2014. Web. 2 Jan. 2015.

Judis, John B. "Seeds of Doubt: Harry Truman's Concerns about Israel and Palestine Were Prescient—and Forgotten." *New Republic*. The New Republic, 15 Jan. 2014. Web. 2 Jan. 2015.

"London Conference on Palestine Suddenly Adjourns until after U.N. General Assembly." *JTA*. Jewish Telegraphic Agency, 2015. Web. 2 Jan. 2015.

McCullough, David. *Truman*. New York: Simon, 2003. Print.

"The Recognition of the State of Israel." *Harry S. Truman Library and Museum*. Harry S. Truman Library and Museum, 2014. Web. 2 Jan. 2015.

■ Declaration of the Establishment of the State of Israel

Date: May 14, 1948
Authors: David Ben-Gurion, Zvi Berenson, Yehuda Leib Maimon, Pinchas Rosen, Moshe Sharett, Aharon Zisling
Geographic region: Israel
Genre: Speech; declaration

Summary Overview

The declaration that the Jewish community living in the British protectorate of Palestine was forming an independent nation transformed international politics, not only in the Middle East, but across the world. Although it would take a few months to formally adopt a constitution, and even longer to gain control of its territories, the modern state of Israel began its existence on Mary 14, 1948, the last day the British ruled the area under a mandate given after World War I. During the seven decades since the declaration by the Jewish People's Council, the state of Israel has undergone major changes in its population, territory, and economy. Beginning with a war to secure the independence that had been declared, Israel's military has almost always been involved in ongoing operations, including four major wars against neighboring Arab states. The creation of the state of Israel, without the Palestinian Arabs taking the opportunity to create their own state in 1948, created uncertainty and an imbalance of power that has contributed to the ongoing hostility between Israel and its neighbors.

Defining Moment

With the Allied victory in World War II, the time came for the United Kingdom and France to make good on promises given to people in the Middle East during that war and during World War I. The British had governed the protectorate of Palestine since the end of World War I, directly, west of the Jordan River, and through a compliant monarchy east of the Jordan. In 1946, the territory east of the Jordan River became fully independent as the state of Jordan. West of the river, two groups had competing claims on the land and for statehood. Although Jewish groups and individuals had migrated throughout the world since antiquity, in the second century C.E., most Jews remaining in the Romans province of Palestine were expelled by the authorities. Since that time, the Jewish population in the region had been relatively small. However, the Zionist movement (which began in the late nineteenth century) had encouraged Jews to return to the area in which the Biblical states of Israel and Judea had been located, with the goal of creating a Jewish state. This goal had been reinforced by the Balfour Declaration (1917) in which the British government had endorsed the creation of a "national home for the Jewish people."

In 1946, a joint British-American commission recommended the creation of two states, one Jewish and one Arab, within the territory west of the Jordan River. However, President Truman made a statement supporting Jewish interests and ignoring the Arabs. The British stated that they would no longer administer the Palestinian Mandate, effective by August, 1948. In 1947, the

United Nations passed Resolution 181 which suggested the creation of two states in Palestine. The Arab states were opposed to this resolution and to later attempts to establish a Palestinian Arab state at the same time as the new Jewish state, because the proposed divisions seemed to favor the Jewish population. With civil unrest increasing, and a U.N. proposal in place, the United Kingdom announced that it was ending its protectorate at the end of the day on May 14, 1948. Thus, the Jewish leadership arranged for this declaration to be made that day, creating a temporary government for the territory identified as the new Jewish state of Israel in the United Nations' plan for partition. No comparable Arab government was in place, as the Palestinian Arabs and neighboring Arab states believed that the entire territory should be one state, which would have an Arab majority. (In 1945, the population was approximately 60 percent Muslim and 31 percent Jewish.) With the declaration that the state of Israel was established, conflict between Israel and its neighbors began with more than 13,000 Arab troops moving into Palestine to stop the creation of Israel as a viable state. When an armistice was finally negotiated, in 1949, between Israel and its four neighbors, Israel had increased in size by one third with the remainder of what had been proposed to be the Palestinian state then under the control of Jordan (West Bank) and Egypt (Gaza).

Author Biographies

David Ben-Gurion (1886–1973) was born (as David Gruen) in the Russian Empire/Poland. Raised in a Zionist family, by age 18 he was teaching a socialist form of Zionism in Warsaw. In 1906, he moved to Palestine and continued his activism. Exiled by the Ottoman Empire, he returned to Palestine after World War I. By 1935, he was the chairman of the principle Zionist organization in Palestine. After World War II, Ben-Gurion strengthened his work to create a Jewish state. He became Israel's first prime minister and defense minister. He served as prime minister from May 1948 to January 1954, and November 1955 to June 1963.

Zvi Berenson (1901–2001) was born in Palestine/Israel. A lawyer by training, he was an advisor to the General Labor Federation in Palestine, under the British. He wrote the first draft of the Declaration of the Establishment of the State of Israel. He served as Minister of Labor and later as a Supreme Court justice from 1954–1977.

Yehuda Leib Maimon (1875–1962) was born in the Russian Empire. A rabbi, he became a leader within the religious Zionist movement. He moved to Palestine in 1913, and was expelled by the Ottoman Empire, returning after World War I. He participated in every Zionist Congress from 1909 to 1948. After Israel was formed, he became the first Minister of Religions, serving until 1951.

Pinchas Rosen (1887–1978) was born in Germany and was a lawyer. Prior to World War I, he helped found a Zionist organization in Germany, and after the war became chairman of the Zionist Federation in Germany. Moving to Palestine, he was active in politics under the British, creating the New Aliyah Party. Upon independence, he became the first Minister of Justice, serving from 1948–51, 1952–56, and 1956–61.

Moshe Sharett (1894–1965) was born in the Russian Empire/Ukraine. He moved to Palestine in 1906 and later studied law in Constantinople. He worked in the Zionist movement, becoming a leader in 1933. Upon the creation of Israel, he was the first Foreign Minister and the second Prime Minister when Ben-Gurion retired.

Aharon Zisling (1901–64) was born in the Russian Empire/Belarus. He moved to Palestine, in 1904, becoming a leader in the Haganah, the Zionist para-military organization, which was the foundation for the Israel Defense Force. He initially served as Agricultural Minister, but broke with Ben-Gurion because of Ben-Gurion's treatment of Arab civilians in the 1948 Arab-Israeli War.

HISTORICAL DOCUMENT: *Declaration of the Establishment of the State of Israel*

ERETZ-ISRAEL (Hebrew—the Land of Israel, Palestine) was the birthplace of the Jewish people. Here their spiritual, religious and political identity was shaped. Here they first attained to statehood, created cultural values of national and universal significance and gave to the world the eternal Book of Books.

After being forcibly exiled from their land, the people kept faith with it throughout their Dispersion and never ceased to pray and hope for their return to it and for the restoration in it of their political freedom.

Impelled by this historic and traditional attachment, Jews strove in every successive generation to re-establish themselves in their ancient homeland. In recent decades they returned in their masses. Pioneers, ma'pilim (Hebrew—immigrants coming to Eretz-Israel in defiance of restrictive legislation0 and defenders, they made deserts bloom, revived the Hebrew language, built villages and towns, and created a thriving community controlling its own economy and culture, loving peace but knowing how to defend itself, bringing the blessings of progress to all the country's inhabitants, and aspiring towards independent nationhood.

In the year 5657 (1897), at the summons of the spiritual father of the Jewish State, Theodore Herzl, the First Zionist Congress convened and proclaimed the right of the Jewish people to national rebirth in its own country.

This right was recognized in the Balfour Declaration of the 2nd November, 1917, and re-affirmed in the Mandate of the League of Nations which, in particular, gave international sanction to the historic connection between the Jewish people and Eretz-Israel and to the right of the Jewish people to rebuild its National Home.

The catastrophe which recently befell the Jewish people—the massacre of millions of Jews in Europe—was another clear demonstration of the urgency of solving the problem of its homelessness by re-establishing in Eretz-Israel the Jewish State, which would open the gates of the homeland wide to every Jew and confer upon the Jewish people the status of a fully privileged member of the comity of nations.

Survivors of the Nazi holocaust in Europe, as well as Jews from other parts of the world, continued to migrate to Eretz-Israel, undaunted by difficulties, restrictions and dangers, and never ceased to assert their right to a life of dignity, freedom and honest toil in their national homeland.

In the Second World War, the Jewish community of this country contributed its full share to the struggle of the freedom and peace loving nations against the forces of Nazi wickedness and, by the blood of its soldiers and its war effort, gained the right to be reckoned among the peoples who founded the United Nations.

On the 29th November, 1947, the United Nations General Assembly passed a resolution calling for the establishment of a Jewish State in Eretz-Israel; the General Assembly required the inhabitants of Eretz-Israel to take such steps as were

continued from page 95

necessary on their part for the implementation of that resolution. This recognition by the United Nations of the right of the Jewish people to establish their State is irrevocable.

This right is the natural right of the Jewish people to be masters of their own fate, like all other nations, in their own sovereign State.

Accordingly we, members of the People's Council, representatives of the Jewish community of Eretz Israel and of the Zionist Movement, are here assembled on the day of the termination of the British Mandate over Eretz Israel and, by virtue of our natural and historic right and on the strength of the resolution of the United Nations General Assembly, hereby declare the establishment of a Jewish state in Eretz Israel, to be known as the State of Israel.

We declare that, with effect from the moment of the termination of the Mandate being tonight, the eve of Sabbath, the 6th Iyar, 5708 (15th May, 1948), until the establishment of the elected, regular authorities of the State in accordance with the Constitution which shall be adopted by the Elected Constituent Assembly not later than the 1st October 1948, the People's Council shall act as a Provisional Council of State, and its executive organ, the People's Administration, shall be the Provisional Government of the Jewish State, to be called "Israel".

> *This right is the natural right of the Jewish people to be masters of their own fate, like all other nations, in their own sovereign State.*

The State of Israel will be open for Jewish immigration and for the Ingathering of the Exiles; it will foster the development of the country for the benefit of all its inhabitants; it will be based on freedom, justice and peace as envisaged by the prophets of Israel; it will ensure complete equality of social and political rights to all its inhabitants irrespective of religion, race or sex; it will guarantee freedom of religion, conscience, language, education and culture; it will safeguard the Holy Places of all religions; and it will be faithful to the principles of the Charter of the United Nations.

The State of Israel is prepared to cooperate with the agencies and representatives of the United Nations in implementing the resolution of the General Assembly of the 29th November, 1947, and will take steps to bring about the economic union of the whole of Eretz-Israel.

We appeal to the United Nations to assist the Jewish people in the building-up of its State and to receive the State of Israel into the comity of nations.

We appeal—in the very midst of the onslaught launched against us now for months—to the Arab inhabitants of the State of Israel to preserve peace and participate in the upbuilding of the State on the basis of full and equal citizenship and due representation in all its provisional and permanent institutions.

We extend our hand to all neighbouring states and their peoples in an offer of peace and good neighbourliness, and appeal to them to establish bonds of cooperation and mutual help with the sovereign Jewish people settled in its own land. The State of Israel is prepared to do its share in a common effort for the advancement of the entire Middle East.

We appeal to the Jewish people throughout the Diaspora to rally round the Jews of Eretz-Israel in the tasks of immigration and upbuilding and to stand by them in the great struggle for the realization of the age-old dream—the redemption of Israel.

Placing our trust in the Almighty, we affix our signatures to this proclamation at this session of the provisional Council of State, on the soil of the Homeland, in the city of Tel-Aviv, on this Sabbath eve, the 5th day of Iyar, 5708 (14th May, 1948).

GLOSSARY

Herzl, Theodor: Austrian Jew who rejected assimilation and advocated for the creation of a Jewish state; he is considered the father of the modern Jewish state, although he died in 1904

Iyar, 5708: eighth month of the Jewish calendar from Rosh Hashanah, second counting from Nissan (month in which Passover falls), with the year based on ancient calculations of either creation or the expulsion of Adam from the Garden of Eden

Zionist: a supporter of the late nineteenth- and early twentieth-century political movement advocating the creation of a Jewish state; the term is derived from a Biblical name for the hill on which the Jewish temple was located

Document Analysis

This declaration was made to formally announce the creation of the state of Israel as well as to give justification for its creation. The authors sought to outline the long history of the Jewish people, as well as the origins of the Jewish state. Moving to more recent events, they gave their understanding of why a Jewish state was needed and why it should be located in what had been the British protectorate of Palestine. The Zionist forces within Judaism had been growing stronger each decade since the modern movement was established. Finally, they outlined what would be the transitional government, as well as giving assurances to all people that Israel would be a modern democracy, with rights extended to all its citizens, regardless of "religion, race or sex."

The declaration began with a statement of what had occurred in the ancient past, recounting Biblical stories of the development of the Jewish people, religion, and state. The fact that most of these things had occurred in this location (British Protectorate of Palestine) gave them, in their minds, a strong foundation for establishing the modern state of Israel in Palestine. In their declaration, the authors made indirect reference to parts of the Jewish liturgy in which those praying sought to celebrate holy days in Jerusalem, when they stated that Jews "in every successive generation" hoped to return to their homeland. In 1917, when the British Foreign Secretary, Arthur Balfour, communicated his government's support for the eventual establishment of a "national home for the Jewish people" in Palestine, it was an affirmation of these Jewish hopes. Thus, the committee established, to their satisfaction, that the protectorate of Palestine was the proper location of the new state.

The need for such a state was seen from two directions. For some, the temptation to assimilate into mainstream Western society was the primary reason a Jewish state was needed. The revival of the Hebrew language was but one illustration of the transformation that could happen in a Jewish state. However, for the majority, it was the Holocaust perpetuated by Nazis in World War II that illustrated the need for a Jewish state. While Jews had been somewhat assimilated in Western Europe, this had never been the case in Eastern Europe, nor did it seem, in Germany. Because there was no safe haven for Jews, many who hoped to flee persecution could not. By creating a state in which all Jews would automatically be eligible for citizenship, it was hoped that a repeat of the horrors of the concentration and extermination camps could be avoided.

The time for its creation was now, in 1948, in the eyes of the declaration's authors. World War II had ended and there was great support for the Jews who had suffered so much at the instigation of the Nazi leaders. It had been thirty years since the British had taken control of Palestine, and they were tiring of the financial and military costs of ruling the protectorate. The United Kingdom's announcement that it would no longer govern this portion of the Middle East had precipitated a crisis for many, due to the uncertainty that lay ahead. Negotiations at the newly formed United Nations resulted in Resolution 181, which called for a Jewish and an Arab (Muslim) state to be established in the territory that had been ruled by Britain. (The authors of the declaration conveniently forgot to mention the latter part of the United Nations' resolution.) While a resolution did not force the creation of these states, it did give a sense of what the world community thought would be best, even if the world community was only fifty-seven nations at that time. (The vote was thirty-three in favor, thirteen opposed—including all five Arab states; ten abstained, and one was not present.) Even though the British did not have a plan for the future of their protectorate of Palestine, once they left, they were among those voting against the resolution. Without any real alternative put forward by the British, or the United Nations, the Jewish leaders' decision to move forward in May 1948, seemed to them to be the best move.

With the creation of Israel, the authors of the declaration understood that there were certain responsibilities that would be placed upon the new government. As such, they pledged the new state to the ideals of the United Nations and the recommendations contained in Resolution 181. The committee pledged that the new state would act in the mold of modern liberal democracies, by respecting religious freedom and granting all equality before the law. Although they were consciously creating a Jewish state, and spent much time debating exactly how this should be reflected in the declaration and the government of the new state, the authors understood what it meant to be persecuted for one's religion. Thus, they pledged "freedom of religion, conscience, language, education, and culture." Even while ignoring the sections of Resolution 181 which recommended the creation of an Arab state, they did pledge that they would uphold the economic recommendations of Resolution 181, which had suggested that the two new states be unified in their economic development, creating an "economic union" such as was just starting in Western Europe. The committee offered "peace and good neighbourliness" to the surrounding Arab states, even though a low scale conflict had been simmering ever since the British had announced their departure from Palestine. (Within hours of the announcement of this declaration, this turned into a much larger military conflict.) With the public proclamation of this declaration creating the state of Israel, it was up to the Jewish people whether or not the state had a future.

Essential Themes

Having gathered in the Tel Aviv Museum of Art to announce this declaration to the world (this meeting was kept secret until almost the last minute due to security concerns), the Jewish People's Committee, which became the Provisional State Council, officially created the modern state of Israel. Gaining official recognition from the United States the day it was created, and the Union of Soviet Socialist Republics shortly thereafter, the leaders hoped that the future would be bright and that the conflict with the Arab states might be short-lived. However, as the decades have passed, it became clear that this was not the case. The fact that this was designated as a Jewish state has been one of the core issues of this conflict, just as it was one of the central points of the declaration. The suffering of the Jews down through the centuries was seen by Zionists as partially the result of not having a state to which they could immigrate, if needed. Reflecting Biblical history, as well as twentieth-century statements and events, the declaration sought to create Israel as a Jewish state, even while granting religious freedom to all people.

Although the United Nations was an untested organization, the Jewish leaders were hopeful that Resolution 181 would provide the foundation for international support for the state of Israel. By additionally pledging that all people would have basic human rights, the council hoped that this would increase support for the new state, as well as change the minds of some Arab leaders. The pledge of economic cooperation was another step in this direction. Although they recognized that the impending conflict was most probably going to occur, the council projected an optimistic vision for the future, even as they saw the "onslaught launched against us." However, for these individuals, their hope for the "redemption of Israel" was worth any struggle that might lie ahead.

—*Donald A Watt*

Bibliography and Additional Reading

Ben-Arieh, Alex. "Independence Day 1948" *Historama*. Tel Aviv: Historama, 2018. Web. 27 February 2018.

Morris, Benny. *1948: A History of the First Arab-Israeli War*. New Haven: Yale University Press, 2008. Print.

Office of the Historian. "The Arab-Israeli War of 1948" *Milestones in US Foreign Relations*. Washington: Department of State, 2018. Web. 27 February 2018.

SchlichimMetrowest. "Declaration of Independence of the State of Israel (English subtitles)" *YouTube*. San Bruno CA: YouTube, 2010. Web. 27 February 2018.

Shapira, Anita. (Anthony Berris, trans.) *Ben-Gurion: Father of Modern Israel*. (Jewish Lives) New Haven: Yale University Press, 2014. Print.

Shinder, Colin. *A History of Modern Israel*. 2nd ed. Cambridge: Cambridge University Press, 2013. Print.

CIA Summary of the Overthrow of Premier Mossadeq of Iran

Date: March 1954
Author: Donald N. Wilber
Genre: Government document

Summary Overview

In the late summer of 1953, British and American intelligence services worked together to orchestrate a coup to overthrow the democratically elected prime minister of Iran, Mohammad Mossadeq (also spelled Mosaddegh or Mosaddiq). The British relied heavily on Iranian oil, which they had controlled since 1909, and Mossadeq led a popular movement to nationalize the oil fields. The British responded to nationalization with a boycott, removing trained personnel from Iranian refineries and refusing to purchase or transport Iranian oil. This led to an economic crisis, and fears in the West that the Soviet Union would exploit this instability to gain influence in Iran through the Tudeh Party, Iran's Communist party. The shah, or monarch, of Iran was reluctant to support the coup plot, which hinged on a royal decree that would remove Mossadeq and install a pro-Western prime minister, Fazlollah Zahedi. After significant pressure from the CIA, the shah agreed to support the coup, which replaced Mossadeq with Zahedi and reopened Iranian oil to Western investment. The following year, one of the main CIA organizers of the coup, Donald N. Wilber, wrote a classified history of the event that was not made public until the year 2000.

Defining Moment

Great Britain's interest in Iranian oil began in earnest on May 28, 1901, when the shah granted the petroleum rights over vast areas of territory to a British citizen, William Knox D'Arcy. When oil was not immediately discovered, D'Arcy was forced to accept other investors. Significant quantities of oil were discovered in 1908, and in 1909, the Anglo-Persian Oil Company (APOC) which would later become British Petroleum, was formed. By 1913, a massive refinery in Abadan was pumping oil destined for the British Empire. Under the agreement with D'Arcy, the Iranian government's share of the oil profits was just 16 percent, and the company declined to open its books for inspection.

Just before World War I, the British navy upgraded their ships from coal to oil, and the British government gained a controlling interest in the APOC. The British economy and military were dependent on a steady flow of inexpensive Iranian oil. During the war, the British stationed troops in Iran to protect their pipelines and proposed in 1919 that Iran become a British protectorate. Though this was not accepted by Iran, the British continued to control the vast majority of Iranian territory, but not without opposition. In the 1920s and 1930s, the Iranian government fought to renegotiate the D'Arcy agreement and regain greater control of the nation's resources. In 1933, a new sixty-year agreement was reached, which increased payments to the Iranian

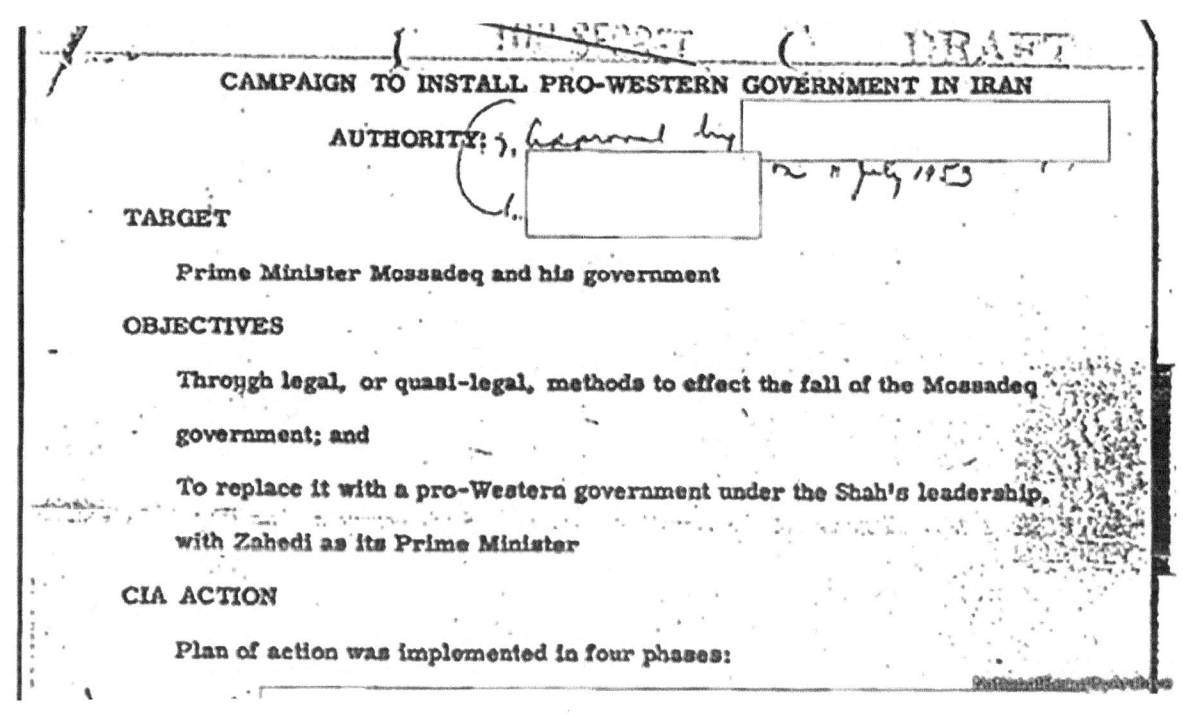

Confirmation for execution of Operation Ajax.

government and reduced the amount of land under direct APOC control.

Britain's relationship with Iran became even more complicated during World War II. The Soviet Union was a key British ally and was holding the Axis armies at bay on the Eastern Front, and this two-front war was key to Britain's survival. The Soviet Union depended on Iranian oil to resupply its army, and though Iran was neutral, the shah was suspected of Nazi sympathies. British and Soviet forces therefore invaded Iran in 1941. The ruler, Reza Shah, was deposed and replaced by his son, Mohammad Reza Pahlavi, who remained in power until 1979.

After the war, the Iranian parliament wanted greater control over the country's oil reserves. Mossadeq was the leader of the nationalization movement and was elected prime minister of Iran in 1951. On May 2, Mossadeq declared the oil fields to be the property of Iran alone. The response from Britain was to remove all trained personnel from the refineries and organize and international boycott of Iranian oil. Production and sales dropped precipitously, leading to an economic crisis and internal unrest. By 1952, British and American intelligence officers had begun to develop a plan to oust Mossadeq. Dwight D. Eisenhower, the newly elected president of the United States, was afraid that the Soviet Union would be able to take advantage of the instability in Iran and decided to support the coup.

Author Biography

Donald Newton Wilber was born in Wisconsin on November 14, 1907. He attended New Trier High School and then went to Princeton University, where he graduated with a BA in 1929, as well as an MFA and PhD in architecture in 1949. Wilber's area of scholarly expertise was the Middle East, and he traveled and wrote extensively in Iran, Afghanistan, and Sri Lanka. Wilber's book *Iran, Past and Present* was published in 1948, establishing him as an expert on Iranian history. These scholarly endeavors gave Wilbur cover for his activities with the CIA, which he joined in 1948. He was a primary planner of the overthrow of Mossadeq in favor of a government friendlier to Western interests. Wilber served in the CIA until 1970, while working with various prestigious universities. He died on February 2, 1997, in Princeton, New Jersey, survived by his wife and two daughters.

> ### HISTORICAL DOCUMENT: *CIA Summary of the Overthrow of Premier Mossadeq of Iran*
>
> SECRET
> Summary
>
> By the end of 1952, it had become clear that the Mossadeq government in Iran was incapable of reaching an oil settlement with interested Western countries; was reaching a dangerous and advanced stage of illegal, deficit financing; was disregarding the Iranian constitution in prolonging Premier Mohammed Mossadeq's tenure of office; was motivated mainly by Mossadeq's desire for personal power; was governed by irresponsible policies based on emotion; had weakened the Shah and the Iranian Army to a dangerous degree; and had cooperated closely with the Tudeh (Communist) Party of Iran. In view of these factors, it was estimated that Iran was in real danger of falling behind the Iron Curtain; if that happened it would mean a victory for the Soviets in the Cold War and a major setback for the West in the Middle East. No remedial action other than the covert action plan set forth below could be found to improve the existing state of affairs.
>
> It was the aim of the TPAJAX project to cause the fall of the Mossadeq government; to reestablish the prestige and power of the Shah; and to replace the Mossadeq government with one which would govern Iran according to constructive policies. Specifically, the aim was to bring power to a government which would reach equitable oil settlement, enabling Iran to become economically sound and financially solvent, and which would vigorously prosecute the dangerously strong Communist Party.
>
> Once it had been determined definitely that it was not in American interests for the Mossadeq government to remain in power and CIA had been so informed by the Secretary of State in March 1953, CIA began drafting a plan whereby the aims state above could be realized through covert action. An estimate entitled "Factors Involved in the Overthrow of Mossadeq" was completed on 16 April 1953. It was here determined that an overthrow of Mossadeq was possible through covert operations. In April it was determined that CIA should conduct the envisioned operation jointly with the British Secret Intelligence Service (SIS). By the end of April, it was

decided that CIA and SIS officers would draw up a plan on Cyprus which would be submitted to CIA and SIS Headquarters, and to the Department of State and the Foreign Office for final approval. On 3 June 1953, US ambassador Loy Wesley Henderson arrived in the United States where he was fully consulted with regard to the objective and aims, as stated above, as well as CIA's intentions to design covert means of achieving the objective and aims.

The plan was completed by 10 June 1953 at which time Mr. Kermit Roosevelt, Chief of the Near East and Africa Division, CIA (who carried with him the views of the Department of State, CIA, and Ambassador Henderson); Mr. Roger Goiran, CIA Chief of Station, Iran; and two CIA planning officers met in Beirut to consider the plan. With minor changes the operational proposal was submitted to the SIS in London on 14 June 1953.

On 19 June 1953, the final operational plan, agreed upon by Mr. Roosevelt for the CIA and by British Intelligence in London, was submitted in Washington to the Department of State; to Mr. Allen W. Dulles, Director of CIA; and to Ambassador Henderson for approval. Simultaneously, it was submitted to the British Foreign Office by SIS for approval. The Department of State wanted to be assured of two things before it would grant approval of the plan:

In view of these factors, it was estimated that Iran was in real danger of falling behind the Iron Curtain; if that happened it would mean a victory for the Soviets in the Cold War and a major setback for the West in the Middle East.

1. That the United States Government could provide adequate grant aid to a successor Iranian Government so that such a government could be sustained until an oil settlement was reached.
2. That the British Government would signify in writing, to the satisfaction of the Department of State, its intentions to reach an early oil settlement with a successor Iranian Government in a spirit of good will and equity. The Department of State satisfied itself on both of these scores.

In mid-July 1953, the Department of State and the British Foreign Office granted authorization for the implementation of the TPAJAX project, and the Director of CIA obtained the approval of the President of the United States. The SIS, with the concurrence of the CIA Director and Ambassador Henderson, proposed that

continues on page 104

continued from page 103

Mr. Roosevelt assume field command in Tehran of the final phases of the operation. It was determined by the Department of State that it would be advisable for Ambassador Henderson to postpone his return to Iran, from Washington consultation, until the operation had been concluded. Arrangements were made jointly with SIS whereby operational liaison would be conducted on Cyprus where a CIA officer would be temporarily stationed, and support liaison would be conducted in Washington. Rapid three-way communications were arranged through CIA facilities between Tehran, Cyprus, and Washington. The time set for the operation was mid-August.

In Iran, CIA and SIS propaganda assets were to conduct an increasingly intensified propaganda effort through the press, handbills, and the Tehran clergy in a campaign designed to weaken the Mossadeq government in any way possible. In the United States, highranking US officials were to make official statements which would shatter any hopes held by Premier Mossadeq that American economic aid would be forthcoming, and disabuse the Iranian public of the Mossadeq myth that the United States supported his regime.

General Fazlollah Zahedi, a former member of Mossadeq's cabinet, was chosen as the most suitable successor to the Premier since he stood out as the only person of stature who had consistently been openly in opposition to Mossadeq and who claimed any significant following. Zahedi was to be approached by CIA and be told of our operation and its aim of installing him as the new prime minister. He was to name a military secretariat with which CIA would conclude a detailed staff plan of action.

From the outset, the cooperation of the Shah was considered to be an essential part of the plan. His cooperation was necessary to assure the action required of the Tehran militart garrisons, and to legalize the succession of a new prime minister. Since the Shah had shown himself to be a man of indecision, it was determined that pressure on him to cooperate would take the following forms:

1. The Shah's dynamic and forceful twin sister, Princess Ashraf Pahlavi, was to come from Europe to urge the Shah to dismiss Mossadeq. She would say she had been in contact with US and UK officials who had requested her to do so.
2. Arrangements were made for a visit to Iran by General H. Norman Schwarzkopf, former head of the US Gendarme Mission, who the Shah liked and respected. Schwarzkopf was to explain the proposed project and get from the Shah signed firmans (royal decrees) dismissing Mossadeq, appointing Zahedi, and calling on the Army to remain loyal to the crown.

3. The principal indigenous British agent, who bona fides had been established with the Shah, was to reinforce the Shah that this was a joint US-UK action.
4. Failing results from the above, Mr. Roosevelt, representing the President of the United States, would urge the Shah to sign the above-mentioned firmans. When received, the firmans would be released by CIA to Zahedi on the day called for in the plan. On D-Day, the Shah was to be at some location outside of Tehran so that Zahedi, armed with the royal firmans and with military support, could take over the government without danger of the Sha's reversing his stand, and to avoid any attempt on the Shah's life.

Through agents in the Tehran military, CIA was to ensure, to the degree possible, Tehran Army cooperation in support of the Shah-appointed new prime minister.

The following public statements made in the United States had tremendous impact on Iran and Mossadeq, and contributed greatly to Mossadeq's downfall:

1. The publication, on 9 June 1953, of President Eisenhower's 29 June 1953 letter to Premier Mossadeq made it clear that increased aid would not be forthcoming to Iran.
2. The Secretary of State's press conferences of 28 July 1953 stated that ". ... The growing activities of the illegal Communist Party in Iran and the toleration fo them by the Iranian Government has caused our government concern. These developments make it more difficult to grant aid to Iran."
3. The President's Seattle speech at the Governors' convention, in which he stated that the United States would not sit by and see Asian countries fall behind the Iron Curtain, had definite effect.

In cooperation with the Department of State, CIA had several articles planted in major American newspapers and magazines which, when reproduced in Iran, had the desired psychological effect in Iran and contributed to the war of nerves against Mossadeq.

After considerable pressure from Princess Ashraf and General Schwarzkopf, and after several meetings with Mr. Roosevelt, the Shah finally signed the required firmans on 15 August 1953. Action was set for 16 August. However, owing to a security leak in the Iranian military, the chief of the Shah's bodyguard, assigned to seize Mossadeq qith the help of two truckloads of pro-Shah soldiers, was overwhelmed by superior armed forces still loyal to Mossadeq. The balance of the military plan was thus frustrated for that day. Upon hearing that the plan has misfired, the Shah flew to Baghdad. This was an act of prudence and had been at least partially foreseen in the plan. Zahedi remained in hiding in CIA custody. With his key officers, he eluded Mossadeq's security forces which were seeking to apprehend the major opposition elements.

continues on page 106

continued from page 105

> Early in the afternoon of 17 August 1953 Ambassador Henderson returned to Tehran. General Zahedi, through a CIA-arranged secret press conferences and through CIA covert printing facilities, announced to Iran that he was legally prime minister and that Mossadeq had staged an illegal coup against him. CIA agents disseminated a large quantity of photographs of the firmans, appointing Zahedi prime minister and dismissing Mosssadeq. This had tremendous impact on the people of Tehran who had already been shocked and angered when they realized that the Shah had been forced to leave Iran because of Mossadeq's actions. US Ambassador Burton Y. Berry, in Baghdad, contacted the Shah and stated that he had confidence that the Shah would return soon to Iran despite the apparent adverse situation at the time. Contact was also established with the Shah in Rome after he had flown there from Baghdad. Mr. Roosevelt and the station consistently reported that Mossadeq's apparent victory was misleading; that there were very concrete signs that the Army was still loyal to the Shah; and that a favorable reversal of the situation was possible. The station further urged both the British Foreign Office and the Department of State to make a maximum effort to persuade the Shah to make public statements encouraging the Army and populace to reject Mossadeq and to accept Zahedi as prime minister.
> On 19 August 1953, a pro-Shah demonstration, originating in the bazaar area, took on overwhelming proportions. The demonstration appeared to start partially spontaneously, revealing the fundamental prestige of the Shah and the public alarm at the undisguised republican move being started by the Communists as well as by certain National Frontists. Station political action assets also contributed to the beginnings of the Pro-Shah demonstrations. The Army very soon joined the pro-Shah movement and by noon of that day it was clear that Tehran, as well as certain provincial areas, were controlled by pro-Shah street groups and Army units. The situation was such that the above-mentioned military plan could then be implemented. At the station's signal, Zahedi came out of hiding to lead the movement. He first broadcast over Radio Tehran and announced that the government was his. The General Staff offices were then seized, Mossadeq's home was gutted, and pro-Mossadeq politicians and officers arrested. By the end of 19 August, the country was in the hands of the new Premier, Zahedi, and members of the Mossadeq government were either in hiding or were incarcerated.
> The Shah returned shortly to Iran where he was given a rousing popular reception. The Shah was deeply moved by the fact that his people and Army had revolted in the face of adversity against a vindictive Mossadeq and a Communist Party riding the crest of a temporary victory and clearly planning to declare Iran a republic. The Shah felt for the first time that he had the mandate of his people, and he returned determined to regain firm control of the Army.

In order to give Zahedi badly needed immediate financial assistance so that the month-end payrolls could be met before the United States could provide large scale grant aid, CIA covertly made available $5,000,000 within two days of Zahedi's assumption of power.

[The C.I.A.'s secret history of the 1953 coup in Iran was a nearly 200-page document, comprising the author's own account of the operation and a set of planning documents he attached. *The New York Times* on the Web is publishing the introduction and many of the planning documents. But the Times decided not to publish the main body of text after consulting prominent historians who believed there might be serious risk that some of those named as foreign agents would face retribution in Iran.

Because the introductory summary and the main body of the document are inconsistent on a few dates and facts, readers may note discrepancies between accounts. In its reporting, the *Times* has relied upon details in the C.I.A. document not published here. In addition, certain names and identifying descriptions have been removed from the documents available on the Web.]

Document Themes and Analysis

This selection is the introduction and summary of Wilber's CIA history of the coup. It begins with a brief recap of the reasons that the CIA and British intelligence had decided to remove Mossadeq from power. The first sentence outlines perhaps the principal British concern: "By the end of 1952, it had become clear that the Mossadeq government in Iran was incapable of reaching an oil settlement with interested Western countries." They believed furthermore that Mossadeq was acting recklessly, contrary to the constitution of Iran, and was in danger of leading the nation "behind the Iron Curtain," or into Soviet-style Communism—perhaps the principal American concern. If Iran turned to Communism, it would advance Soviet interests in the Middle East at the expense of the West, and so the decision was made to replace the Mossadeq government with one that would "govern Iran according to constructive policies."

By April 1953, a coup was agreed upon as the best course of action, and plans were drawn up for a joint operation between the CIA and British Secret Intelligence Services. By mid-July 1953, the plan was approved by both governments; in the United States, the operation was named TPAJAX, or Operation Ajax.

The lead-up to the coup involved a propaganda war, with US officials making clear in public statements that economic aid would not be offered to Mossadeq's Iran. At the same time, opposition to Mossadeq was fomented inside the country, particularly through the media. A top army general, Fazlollah Zahedi, was picked to replace Mossadeq as prime minister. However, the plot also hinged on the cooperation of the shah, Mohammad Reza Pahlavi, who was extremely reluctant to involve himself in a plot by foreign powers and is described by Wilber as "a man of indecision." The report lays out the ways that pressure was brought to bear on the shah, from bringing his sister and US

Army general H. Norman Schwarzkopf Sr. to negotiate with him, to readying the orders for him to sign and promising to spirit him away while the coup was taking place. On August 15, under considerable pressure, the shah signed the decrees needed to oust Mossadeq.

The plot seemed doomed from the beginning. A security leak meant that the element of surprise was lost, and Mossadeq initially escaped capture. The shah fled to Iraq, and the CIA worked to gather support for the newly appointed Zahedi by disseminating copies of the decrees replacing Mossadeq. On August 19, with the help of some CIA agents, a pro-shah demonstration in the streets of Tehran gathered momentum. By the end of the day, the capital was in the hands of supporters of Zahedi and the shah, and Mossadeq and his supporters were arrested.

The report ends by noting that the CIA secretly transferred five million dollars to Zahedi's government within two days in order to keep the government running until promised US grant aid was forthcoming.

The Iranian coup of 1953 was the first of several CIA operations that sought to encourage rivals of obstreperous or Communist-leaning leaders during the Cold War; for example, the following year, in 1954, the CIA engineered a coup in Guatemala to overthrow the democratically elected government of Jacobo Arbenz, and in 1961, the CIA backed the ill-fated Bay of Pigs Invasion intended to oust Fidel Castro, the Communist leader of Cuba. When the extent of US intervention in these countries was suspected, or confirmed, it led to long-term resentment and distrust of US policy in these regions. The overthrow of Mossadeq was no exception.

The shah continued to rule until 1979 in close association with the United States and Britain. When he was overthrown by militants led by Ayatollah Khomeini in 1979, the depth of animosity toward the United States in Iran was made clear. The American Embassy was attacked and the staff taken hostage, accused of spying and manipulating the Iranian people. Tensions with Iran remain high in part because of the historical distrust sewn during the 1953 coup.

—*Bethany Groff Dorau*

Bibliography and Additional Reading

Abrahamian, Ervand. *The Coup: 1953, the CIA, and the Roots of Modern US-Iranian Relations.* New York: New, 2013. Print.

Bowie, Robert R. & Richard H. Immerman. *Waging Peace: How Eisenhower Shaped an Enduring Cold War Strategy.* New York: Oxford UP, 1998. Print.

Gasiorowski, Mark J. *Mohammad Mosaddeq and the 1953 Coup in Iran.* Syracuse, NY: Syracuse UP, 2004. Print.

Baghdad Pact

Date: February 25, 1955
Authors: Various
Geographic region: Kingdom of Iraq; Republic of Turkey; United Kingdom; Dominion of Pakistan; Kingdom of Iran
Genre: Treaty

Summary Overview

In the 1950s, United States foreign policy was concerned primarily with halting the spread of Communism throughout the world. Asia, Europe, and the Middle East all bordered the Soviet Union, and had great strategic importance for the United States, Great Britain, and their allies. The Middle East, in particular, with its vast oil reserves and its proximity to the Soviet Union, seemed ripe for a Communist incursion, and the maintenance of pro-Western governments was of great concern to the United States and Great Britain.

In 1953, US secretary of state John Foster Dulles traveled to several Middle Eastern capitals, gathering support for a pro-Western defense alliance similar to the North Atlantic Treaty Organization (NATO). This ultimately led to the formation of the Baghdad Pact, or Middle East Treaty Organization (METO), between Turkey, Pakistan, Iraq, Iran, and the United Kingdom. The United States did not ultimately sign the treaty, as it was reluctant to antagonize Egypt and wary of being perceived as anti-Israel, but remained involved in the organization. Though it was a milestone in the containment policies of the United States, the agreement proved to be short-lived and generally unsuccessful. After Iraq withdrew from the pact in 1959, the alliance changed its name to the Central Treaty Organization (CENTO), but when Iran withdrew in 1979 it dissolved completely.

Defining Moment

The United States and the Soviet Union had clashed over control of the oil-rich land of the Middle East since the end of World War II. Initially allies, Russian, British, and American forces occupied Iran to keep its resources out of German hands. After the war, however, relations between the Soviet Union and its former allies were in precipitous decline, and the Soviet Union refused to withdraw its troops from the region. Under increasing international pressure, they withdrew in March 1946, but their interest in the Middle East was clear. Later that month, Turkey and Iraq signed a Treaty of Friendship and Good Neighbourhood, the first in a sequence of separate mutual assistance treaties signed over the following decade between Turkey, Pakistan, Iraq, Iran, the United Kingdom, and the United States.

The United States eventually signed separate agreements with all of the nations who would join the Baghdad Pact. In 1954 Pakistan and Turkey signed a security agreement, followed by Iraq and Turkey in February 1955. Yet both the United States and the United Kingdom wanted a broader regional mutual defense pact, along the lines of NATO or the Southeast Asia Treaty Organization (SEATO). Such alliances were vital to the Western powers' strategy of containment of Communism, which relied on pro-Western governments in nations surrounding the Soviet Union in order to block the spread of Soviet influence. Containment was the main policy of the United States during the Cold War, and would significantly shape international relations. The United States and Great Britain were hopeful that Jordan and Syria would also join a potential agreement, which would complete the regional barrier to Communist expansion in what became known as the Northern Tier area of the Middle East.

Direct negotiation with Middle Eastern nations was tricky for the United States, however, as it enjoyed a special relationship with Israel, which was suspicious of Western treaties with nations antagonistic toward it. In addition, the pact faced strong opposition from Arabs in the anti-colonialist movement, especially Egyptian president Gamal Abdel Nasser and his followers. Nasser saw the Baghdad Pact as a threat to his leadership in the Middle East and resented Western influence in the region. He denounced it in the press. Jordan and Syria, facing significant public pressure, did not join. The United Kingdom joined Iraq and Turkey's earlier alliance in February 1955 along with Pakistan and Iran, forming the official Baghdad Pact, but the United States did not sign the agreement.

Although not formally a member, the United States was intimately involved in the creation of the Baghdad Pact. It achieved a major strategic goal for the United States policy of containment, linking Turkey, the southernmost member of NATO, with the westernmost member of SEATO, Pakistan, to form a bloc along the southwestern border of the Soviet Union.

Document Information

The Baghdad Pact, as a multinational treaty, had no single author, but was crafted through the work of the governments involved. It began in February 1955 as a cooperation agreement between Turkey and Iraq, designed to provide a framework for mutually opposing any aggression from foreign powers. The two allies then invited other nations to join; the United Kingdom did so in April 1955, followed by Pakistan in September and Iran in October. The place of signing—Iraq's capital, Baghdad—lent the pact its name.

Although the United States did not sign the Baghdad Pact, it was instrumental in forming the alliance. Most notably, US secretary of state John Foster Dulles, appointed by President Dwight D. Eisenhower in 1953, played a key role in shaping the agreement in accord with US goals in the region. British foreign secretary Anthony Eden was another important figure representing the Western powers in the development of the Baghdad Pact.

HISTORICAL DOCUMENT: *Baghdad Pact*

Whereas the friendly and brotherly relations existing between Iraq and Turkey are in constant progress, and in order to complement the contents of the Treaty of Friendship and Good Neighbourhood concluded between His Majesty the King of Iraq and his Excellency the President of the Turkish Republic signed in Ankara on March 29, 1946, which recognised the fact that peace and security between the two countries is an integral part of the peace and security of all the nations of the world and in particular the nations of the Middle East, and that it is the basis for their foreign policies;

Whereas article 11 of the Treaty of Joint Defence and Economic Co-operation between the Arab League States provides that no provision of that treaty shall in any way affect, or is designed to affect, any of the rights and obligations accruing to the Contracting Parties from the United Nations Charter;

And having realised the great responsibilities borne by them in their capacity as members of the United Nations concerned with the maintenance of peace and security in the Middle East region which necessitate taking the required measures in accordance with article 51 of the United Nations Charter;

They have been fully convinced of the necessity of concluding a pact fulfilling these aims, and for that purpose have appointed as their plenipotentiaries . . . who having communicated their full powers, found to be in good and due form, have agreed as follows:-

> *Consistent with article 51 of the United Nations Charter the High Contracting Parties will co-operate for their security and defence. Such measures as they agree to take to give effect to this co-operation may form the subject of special agreements with each other.*

ARTICLE 1

Consistent with article 51 of the United Nations Charter the High Contracting Parties will co-operate for their security and defence. Such measures as they agree to take to give effect to this co-operation may form the subject of special agreements with each other.

ARTICLE 2

In order to ensure the realization and effect application of the co-operation provided for in article 1 above, the competent authorities of the High Contracting Parties will determine the measures to be taken as soon as the present pact enters into force. These measures will become operative as soon as they have been approved by the Governments of the High Contracting Parties.

ARTICLE 3

The High Contracting Parties undertake to refrain from any interference whatsoever in each other's internal affairs. They will settle any dispute between themselves in a peaceful way in accordance with the United Nations Charter.

ARTICLE 4

The High Contracting Parties declare that the dispositions of the present pact are not in contradiction with any of the international obligations contracted by either of

continues on page 112

continued from page 111

them with any third State or States. They do not derogate from and cannot be interpreted as derogating from, the said international obligations. The High Contracting Parties undertake not to enter into any international obligation incompatible with the present pact.

ARTICLE 5

This pact shall be open for accession to any member of the Arab League or any other State actively concerned with the security and peace in this region and which is fully recognized by both of the High Contracting Parties. Accession shall come into force from the date of which the instrument of accession of the State concerned is deposited with the Ministry for Foreign Affairs of Iraq.

Any acceding State party to the present pact may conclude special agreements, in accordance with article 1, with one or more States parties to the present pact. The competent authority of any acceding State may determine measures in accordance with article 2. These measures will become operative as soon as they have been approved by the Governments of the parties concerned.

ARTICLE 6

A Permanent Council at ministerial level will be set up to function within the framework of the purposes of this pact when at least four Powers become parties to the pact.

The Council will draw up its own rules of procedure.

ARTICLE 7

This pact remains in force for a period of five years renewable for other five-year periods. Any Contracting Party may withdraw from the pact by notifying the other parties in writing of its desire to do so six months before the expiration of any of the above-mentioned periods, in which case the pact remains valid for the other parties.

ARTICLE 8

This pact shall be ratified by the contracting parties and ratifications shall be exchanged at Ankara as soon as possible. Thereafter it shall come into force from the date of the exchange of ratifications.

In witness whereof, the said plenipotentiaries have signed the present pact in Arabic, Turkish and English, all three texts being equally authentic except in the case of doubt when the English text shall prevail.

Done in duplicate at Bagdad this second day of Rajab 1374 Hijri corresponding to the twenty-fourth day of February 1955.

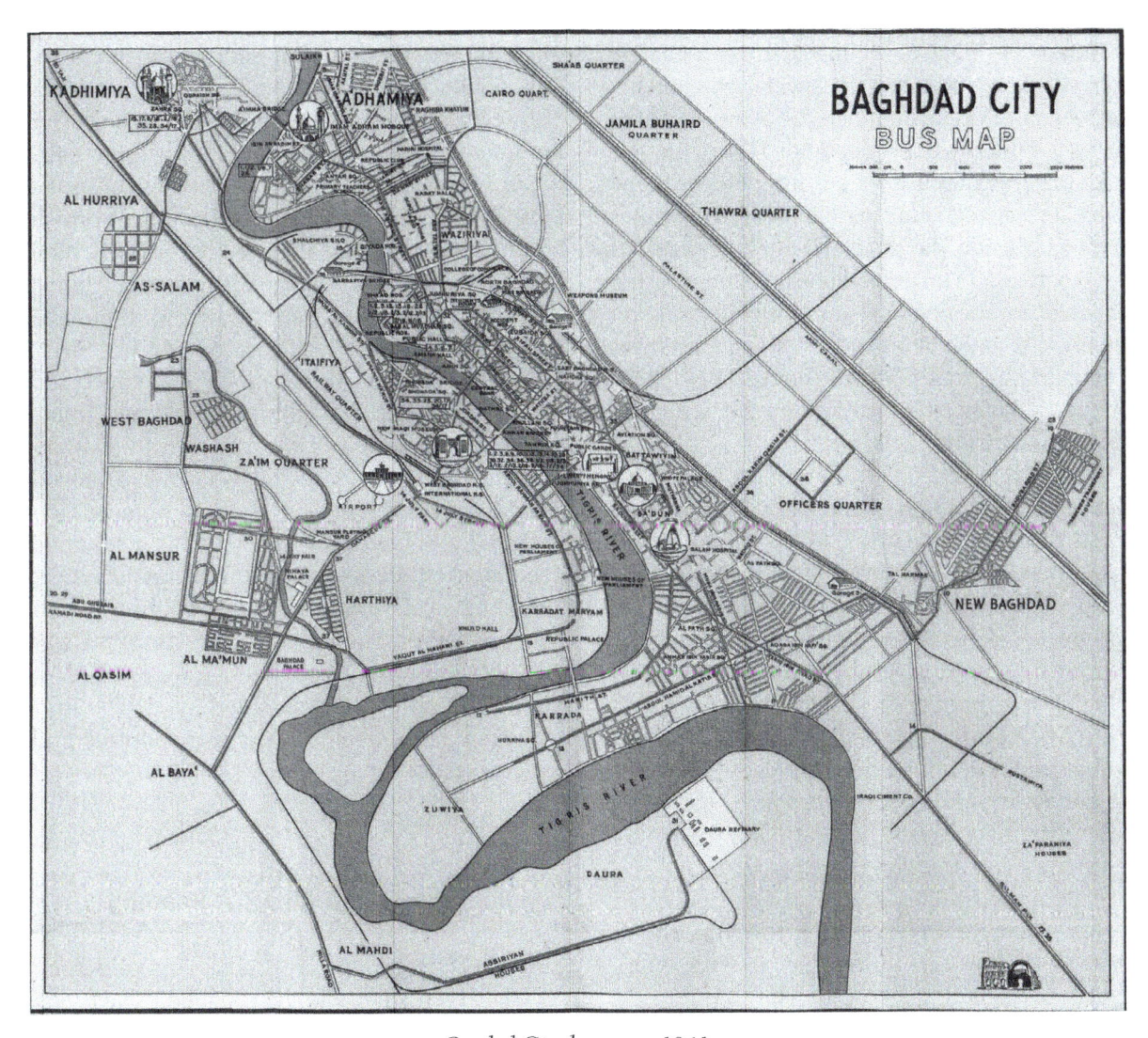

Bagdad City bus map, 1961.

Document Analysis

The Baghdad Pact begins by referencing the Treaty of Friendship and Good Neighbourhood signed by Iraq and Turkey in 1946. It recognizes that the earlier treaty acknowledged that world peace was not possible without peace in the Middle East, and that "the friendly and brotherly relations existing between Iraq and Turkey are in constant progress." It also mentions the signing nations' submission to the authority of both the Arab League and the United Nations, and their adherence to international law, reinforcing the Baghdad Pact as one of many interrelated treaties and alliances created after World War II.

Critically, the pact references the primary goal of "the maintenance of peace and security in the Middle East region." The pact's eight articles outline the ways in which this goal is intended to be achieved. Signers will "cooperate for their security and defense," and "refrain from any interference whatsoever in each other's internal affairs." It states that special agreements between individual members are allowed as long as they work toward cooperation. Likewise, the pact ensures that it does not interfere with any member's agreements or alliances with other nations outside the pact. The governments of each participant are left responsible for enacting the treaty at the practical level—significantly, no mention is made of an overarching hierarchy of command or shared armed forces. This meant the pact did not provide an outright structure for mutual defense.

The pact is left open to anyone who has an active interest in the security of the Middle East, particularly members of the Arab League. It further states that once four nations have ratified the pact, a permanent council will be set up to administer its application, though it leaves the procedure of the council open. For a long-term structure, the pact states that it can be renewed every five years after it comes into force. It also confirms the right of any member to withdraw, and that it will remain valid even after a member leaves the treaty. The treaty was ratified by all parties by October 1955.

The United States was pursuing a policy of containment in 1955, encouraging the formation of alliances to thwart the Soviet Union's ability to expand and spread. The Middle East seemed particularly vulnerable, but was also a sensitive area for US foreign policy. The Baghdad Pact was designed, encouraged, and promoted by the United States, working closely with Great Britain, but in the end the United States was not a signatory. This absence points to the complex political climate in the region, with Arab nationalism, pro-Western dictatorships, Israeli territorial instability, and encroaching Communism all in the mix.

After the pact went into effect, the United States continued to support the alliance, even joining as an associate member and serving on its military committee in an attempt to bolster its influence. However, the Baghdad Pact never proved effective in containing Communism or promoting peace in the Middle East. The seizure of the Suez Canal in 1956 by Egyptian forces under Nasser led to the decline of British influence in the region, and the Soviet Union successfully aligned itself with several Middle Eastern countries. Iraq withdrew from the pact in 1959 after its government was overthrown, and the other nations abandoned the Baghdad Pact title in favor of the Central Treaty Organization, or CENTO.

The headquarters of CENTO were moved to Ankara, Turkey, and the organization generally served as a vehicle for economic cooperation rather than a military alliance. Although Pakistan attempted to gain the support of other members during its 1965 war with India, no mutual defense was provided. CENTO officially disbanded in 1979 after the Iran withdrew following its revolution and Pakistan also left.

—*Bethany Groff Dorau*

Bibliography and Additional Reading

Ashton, Nigel John. "The Hijacking of a Pact: The Formation of the Baghdad Pact and Anglo American Tensions in the Middle East, 1955–1958." *Review of International Studies* 19.2 (1993): 123–37. Print.

Lansford, Tom. *The Lords of Foggy Bottom: American Secretaries of State and the World They Shaped.* Baldwin Place: Encyclopedia Soc., 2001. Print.

Sanjian, Ara. "The Formulation of the Baghdad Pact." *Middle Eastern Studies* 33.2 (1997): 226–66. Print.

Yeşilbursa, B. Kemal. *The Baghdad Pact: Anglo-American Defence Policies in the Middle East, 1950–1959.* New York: Cass, 2005. Print.

The Nationalization of the Suez Canal

Date: July 26, 1956
Author: Gamal Abdel Nasser
Geographic region: Egypt
Genre: Speech

Summary Overview

From its opening in 1869, the Suez Canal was a vital link for European trade with Asia and many parts of the Middle East. Anything that might upset the flow of ships, and the goods they transported, would precipitate a major crisis. Thus, when Nasser created great uncertainty by announcing the nationalization of the Suez Canal Company, many members of the global community reacted strongly. While the speech Nasser gave on July 26, 1956, dealt with the economic matter of the purchase of all shares of the Universal Company of the Suez Maritime Canal by the government of Egypt, and the continuation of operations, it also represented a political slap in the face to the British and French, who had been running the canal. The turmoil that developed among members of the international community resulted in the political and military conflict known as the Suez Crisis. Within months, British, French, and Israeli forces invaded Egypt to try to force Egypt to relinquish control of the canal to its previous owners (mainly British and French), and hopefully to overthrow Nasser. By obtaining the backing of the United States and the Soviet Union, Egypt not only successfully weathered these events, kept control of the canal, and strengthened its position in the Middle East, but also pushed the country into a leadership role within the non-aligned movement.

Defining Moment

The Suez Canal Company was originally developed in 1858 as a joint venture between French entrepreneurs and the Ottoman Empire's regional governor in Egypt. However, under political pressure, the Ottoman Empire gave Egypt partial independence in 1867, and then financial problems forced the Egyptian viceroy (khedive) to sell Egypt's 44 percent of the company's stock to the British government in 1875. From that point forward the British, which controlled trade going around the horn of Africa, sought to control trade going through the canal as well. Invited in to help the Egyptian government put down a revolt, British troops took control not only of that situation but of the canal as well. Thus, from 1882 the Suez Canal was both owned by European interests and managed on a day-to-day basis by them. Several times in the decades prior to 1956 the British had been asked to leave, and Egyptian leaders had sought a larger role in canal operations. The British had been slowly removing their troops and had agreed to the transfer of leadership in canal operations in the future. The final withdrawal of British troops (negotiated with Nasser in 1954) occurred on July 18, 1956.

Nasser had come into power after a 1952 coup against King Farouk, who had lost popular support owing to his lavish lifestyle. Nasser sought to develop Egypt economically, through the construction of a dam on the Nile River at Aswan. As a former military leader, he also wanted to strengthen the military for possible use against Israel. Trying to be neutral in the Cold War, Nasser traded with, and accepted assistance from, both Western and Communist nations. While the United States and the United Kingdom had initially pledged funds to build the dam, when Nasser bought weapons from a Communist source, both nations pulled out of the project. Nasser had previously pressed for greater Egyptian control of the Suez Canal, and the end of US support for the dam gave him one excuse to take over the operations of the canal. The money earned from its operations would, according to Nasser's plan, be used to build the Aswan Dam. With the last foreign troops (British) having been withdrawn from Egypt eight days prior to this speech, Nasser felt secure in making the move. His dramatic step not only resulted in Egypt gaining control of canal operations (technically, it had always owned the land on which the canal was built) but helped Egypt and Nasser become leaders within the Arab and non-aligned communities.

Author Biography

Gamal Abdel Nasser (January 15, 1918—September 28, 1970) was born into what might be considered a middle-class family, with his father working as a postal supervisor in a variety of offices. While in school, Nasser became active in anti-British, anti-colonial demonstrations that ended up with him being wounded and acquiring a criminal record. Although he remained a strong nationalist, when demonstrations died out after a new British-Egyptian treaty was signed, Nasser completed school and began to study law. Dropping out, he sought entrance into the military but was denied owing to his criminal record. Gaining support from a high government official, he was admitted to the military college and was commissioned in 1938. At his first posting (Mankabad) he met other young officers with a similar nationalist orientation and they began discussing how to rid the nation of the British and to advance a modern political/economic agenda. During the 1948 Arab-Israeli War, Nasser became a national hero as commander of a small Egyptian force surrounded by Israeli troops, which held its position until negotiations for that territory were concluded between the leaders of the respective governments. Later, He was among those sent to negotiate the final agreement ending hostilities.

After the war, Nasser expanded the group that had formed in Mankabad, with it becoming the Association of Free Officers. Slowly developing his network of allies, Colonel Nasser finally led a coup in 1952, although politically he remained in the background and pushed General Naguib to be the head of the government. Nasser was more radical in the economic reforms he desired, and by 1954 he had pushed Naguib out of power, although he did not himself become president until June 1956. The nationalization of the canal made Nasser very popular among Egyptians. During his reign he pushed through many economic changes and major construction projects. He was a leader in the Arab world and a major player on the world stage. However, his strong leadership also meant that many human right violations occurred during his rule. He ruled until his death in 1970.

HISTORICAL DOCUMENT: *The Nationalization of the Suez Canal*

In the Name of the Nation

The President of the Republic, Considering the two firmans issued on November 30, 1854 and January 5, 1856 (respectively) concerning the preferential rights relating to the administration of the Suez Canal Transit Service and the establishment of an Egyptian joint-stock company to operate it; and Law No. 129 of 1947 concerning public utility concessions; and Law No. 317 of 1952 concerning individual labor contracts; and Law No. 26 of 1954 concerning joint-stock companies, limited partnerships by shares and limited liability companies; with the advice of the State Council; has issued the following law:

Article I

The Universal Company of the Suez Maritime Canal (Egyptian joint-stock company) is hereby nationalized. All its assets, rights and obligations are transferred to the Nation and all the organizations and committees that now operate its management are hereby dissolved.

Stockholders and holders of founders' shares shall be compensated for the ordinary or founders shares they own in accordance with the value of the shares shown in the closing quotations of the Paris Stock Exchange on the day preceding the effective date of the present law.

The payment of said indemnity shall be effected after the Nation has taken delivery of all the assets and properties of the nationalized company.

Article II

An independent organization endowed with juristic personality and annexed to the Ministry of Commerce, shall take over the management of the Suez Canal Transit Service. The composition of the organization and the remuneration of its members shall be fixed in an order of the President of the Republic. In so far as managing the Transit Service is concerned the organization shall have all the necessary powers required for the purpose without being restricted by Government regulations and procedures.

Without prejudice to the auditing of its final accounts by the State Audit Department, the organization shall have an independent budget prepared in accordance with the rules in force for commercial concerns. Its financial year shall begin on July 1 and end on June 30 each year. The budget and final accounts shall be approved by an order of the President of the Republic. The first financial year shall begin on the effective date of the present law and end with June 30, 1957.

The organization may delegate one or several of its members to implement its decisions or to discharge any duty assigned to these members.

It may also set up from among its own members or from among other people, a technical committee to assist it in its own research work and studies.

> *The Universal Company of the Suez Maritime Canal (Egyptian joint-stock company) is hereby nationalized. All its assets, rights and obligations are transferred to the Nation and all the organizations and committees that now operate its management are hereby dissolved.*

continues on page 118

continued from page 117

The chairman of the organization shall represent it before the courts, government agencies, and other places, and in its dealings with third parties.

Article III
The assets and rights of the nationalized company in the Republic of Egypt and abroad are hereby frozen. Without specific permission obtained in advance from the organization provided for in Article II above, banks, organizations and private persons are hereby prohibited from disposing of those assets or making any payment requested them or due by them.

Article IV
The organization shall retain all the present officials, employees and laborers of the nationalized company at their posts; they shall have to continue with the discharge of their duties; no one will be allowed to leave his work or vacate his post in any manner and for any reason whatsoever except with the permission of the organization provided for in Article II above.

Article V
All violations of the provisions of Article III above shall be punished by imprisonment and a fine equal to three times the value of the amount involved in the offense. All violations of the provisions of Article IV shall be punished by imprisonment in addition to the forfeiture by the offender of all rights to compensation, pension or indemnity.

Article VI
The present order shall be published in the Official Gazette and shall have the force of law. It shall come into force on the date of its publication. The Minister of Commerce shall issue the necessary administrative orders for its implementation.
It shall bear the Seal of the State and be implemented as one of the State laws.

Given this 18th day of Zull Heggah, 1375 A.H. [July 26, 1956]
Gamal Abdel Nasser

GLOSSARY

firman: a ruler's administrative order or edict; the term originated during the Ottoman Empire

juristic personality: a legal entity capable of making all forms of legal agreements and undertaking corporate operations

Egyptian forces crossing the Suez Canal on October 7, 1973.

Document Themes and Analysis

On July 26 Nasser spoke to a large crowd for more than two and a half hours, with the central point of his speech being the nationalization of the Suez Canal. Nasser had been studying politics, especially the politics of revolution, for more than twenty years when he made the decision to take control of canal operations. He understood the repercussions of taking control from the Europeans, and sought to mitigate these by paying the previous owners a fair price for their asset. In addition, he made it clear that the canal would continue to function and that Egypt was totally committed to this move. Contemporaneous records indicated that Nasser only fully developed this plan a few days prior to its announcement; he was seeking to give his action a basic legal foundation and a means to domestically enforce the decision.

Egyptian leaders since the time of the pharaohs had desired, and some attempted, to build

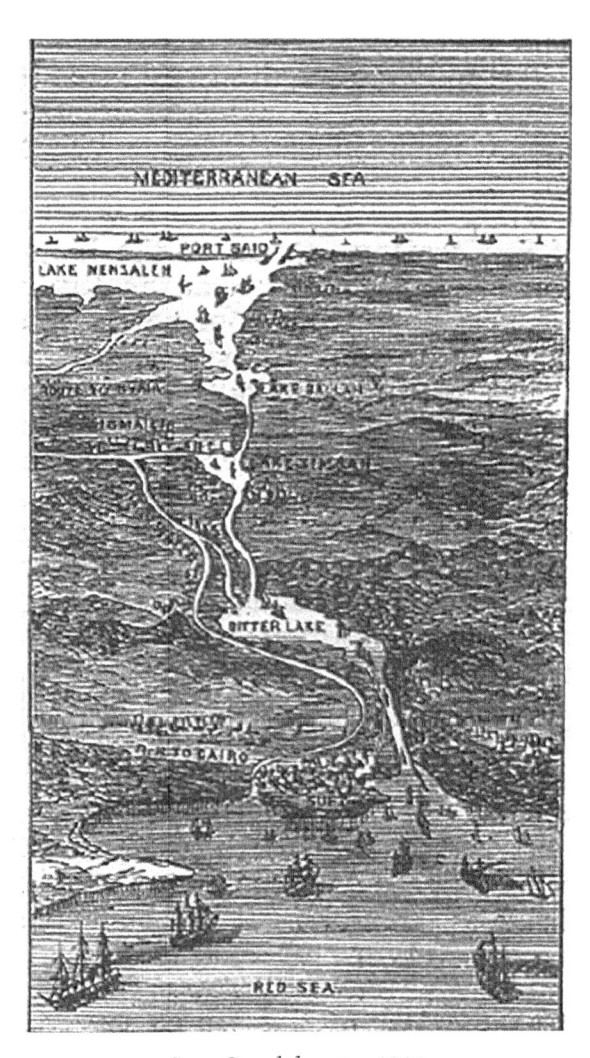

Suez Canal drawing 1881.

a canal connecting the Red Sea and the Nile River or Mediterranean Sea. A few attempts had been successful in temporarily connecting the Nile and the Red Sea, but none were lasting. Thus, when Europeans entrepreneurs proposed the creation of a canal in the 1850s, they were following in the footsteps of previous generations. As part of his speech, Nasser pointed out that most of the canal had been dug by Egyptians, and used this as part of the underlying reason why Egypt should have control of the canal operations. (He conveniently ignored the fact that Egypt had originally owned

Israeli soldiers in the Sinai wave at a passing French plane.

part of the company operating the canal.) In the introduction to this official document, Nasser outlined the executive orders that had created the "joint-stock company" operating the canal. Thus, he made certain there could be no legal action based on a lack of clarity as to what was being nationalized.

Articles I and III stated that all assets of the operating company were being nationalized, not just those within Egypt. Nasser understood that it would be harder to nationalize things outside of Egypt, but their clear inclusion in Article III gave a legal foundation for any legal actions necessary in other countries. In Article I, the Universal Company of the Suez Maritime Canal was told that what might be termed a hostile takeover had occurred, with the assets of this company being merged into Egypt's Ministry of Commerce. As in normal mergers/takeovers, the stockholders of the company would be paid for their stock, based on the last price of the previous day's trading on, in this case, the Paris Stock Exchange. Nasser was trying to smooth the takeover of the canal, by doing away with what would have been a major obstacle, if no payment had been made. Nasser anticipated that some shareholders, and European politicians, would object to his action. He believed that this compensation would weaken these objections substantially. Paying for the stock was a key step—the carrot—in the eventual acceptance of his action by the global community. Conversely, the stick that he wielded was contained in Article V, which allowed for "imprisonment and a fine" for those who failed to follow the orders dictated by Article III.

Articles II, IV, and V outlined how the continuing operation of the canal would be implemented. The second article specified the relationship between the new "Suez Canal Transit Service" and the government of Egypt. It also made provision for replacing the private corporation's board of directors with "an independent organization endowed with juristic personality" that would oversee the operations of the canal. The fourth and fifth articles insured that those handling the day to day operations of the canal would remain in their positions, until the new management decided to replace them. Article IV mandated that these individuals remain in place, while Article V outlined the types of punishments that could be imposed upon individuals who failed to follow the regulations outlined in Article IV. The scope of possible punishment ranged from "forfeiture" of monetary items to actual incarceration. While virtually all Egyptians working for the canal would have no reason to quit their jobs because of the nationalization, Nasser hoped that this would keep the foreign workers in place until an orderly transition could be established to replace those who might desire to leave.

The last article, Article VI, was included to follow a common legal formulation in which a new law, or executive order, had to be announced publically through an established process. While Nasser's speech in Alexandria told people what was happening, and it did happen on the day of the speech, the written publication of the edict "in the Official Gazette" made it clearly a law under the established procedures of the Egyptian government. Nasser wanted to ensure that this dramatic act, which would transform the international shipping industry and global commerce, was not thwarted by a legal technicality. (By following the technicalities in the process for the implementation of a new law, Nasser hoped it would quiet some international and domestic objections.) Whether or not under Egyptian law Nasser had the power to nationalize the canal operations and abrogate an international agreement, he did have the backing of the military and Egyptian people when he nationalized the canal. Domestically, this was all that was needed for the nationalization to be successful.

When Nasser stepped forward in Alexandria to speak to the audience gathered to hear him, his primary message was simple: the operation of the Suez Canal was being taken over by the Egyptian government. However, he added two auxiliary messages that he hoped would insure a tranquil transition, in canal operations and in Egypt's relationships with other nations. Nasser's statement that the company running canal operations "is hereby nationalized" gave the essential point of this speech. Even though the agreement that had established the company running the canal had another twelve years on its lease, and the owners of the company had expected another twelve years of income from this concession, Nasser put an end to this arrangement. While he went on to clarify how the canal company was being brought into the government (via the Ministry of Commerce), this was secondary to the fact that canal operations were being nationalized.

Nasser understood that there would be resistance to this dramatic action. In order to try to keep friendly relations with the United Kingdom and France and various influential individuals, Nasser clearly stated that the current owners of company stock would be paid for their shares, based on the value from the preceding day's transactions. By making this secondary point a part of the speech, he hoped to undercut any negative reaction from stock owners or the European governments. Obviously, the invasion by British and French forces three months later showed that this was a false hope in terms of the governments. However, for the individuals who owned the stock, his decision to pay market value for their shares reduced many complications that might have arisen had he seized the assets of the company without payment.

The other secondary message was that canal operations would continue without interruption, by his proclamation that anyone working for the canal had to remain working for the canal administration, unless the Egyptian government gave permission for a worker to leave. This was a multi-purpose point, assuring workers that they still had jobs, assuring the shipping industry that competent individuals would still be running the canal, and ensuring that the operations could not be sabotaged by certain key individuals leaving their posts. Although foreign workers had less to fear, by holding their pensions hostage Nasser made sure that they would remain during the transition.

As Nasser announced this bold step, undertaken to make Egypt more self-sufficient, he was establishing himself, and his nation, as a role model for others seeking to move from colonial status to true independence. Although the move did not go as smoothly as he had hoped—for example, the Sinai was temporarily lost to invading forces—Nasser was ultimately successful in nationalizing the canal's operations and, except in times of warfare, it has operated efficiently under Egyptian control. While there were at first some serious obstacles to overcome, in the long run the nationalization of the canal has worked out well for Egypt.

—Donald A Watt

Bibliography and Additional Reading

Aburish, Said K. *Nasser: The Last Arab.* New York: Thomas Dunne Books, 2004. Print.

Adel, Ezzat. "The Day Nasser Nationalised the Canal." *BBC News.* London: The British Broadcasting Corporation, 2006. Web. 2 March 2018.

Doran, Michael. *Ike's Gamble: American's Rise to Dominance in the Middle East.* New York: Free Press, 2016. Print.

Kyle, Keith. *Suez.* New York: St. Martin's Press, 1991. Print.

Milner, Laurie. "History: The Suez Crisis." *BBC.* London: The British Broadcasting Corporation, 2014. Web. 28 February 2018.

Slany, William Z. "Foreign Relations of the United States, 1955–1957, Suez Crisis, July 26-December 31, 1956, Volume XVI." *Office of the Historian: Department of State.* Washington: United States Department of State, 2018. Web. 2 March 2018.

The Eisenhower Doctrine

Date: January 5, 1957
Author: Dwight D. Eisenhower
Geographic region: Middle East
Genre: Speech

Summary Overview

President Eisenhower announced what would become known as the Eisenhower Doctrine in January 1957 in a speech to a joint session of Congress. He called for a new relationship with nations in the increasingly unstable Middle East, in order to protect them from the threat of Communist incursion. Eisenhower made funds and military support available to any nation that felt that its independence was threatened, and he singled out the Soviet Union as being particularly eager for control of the area. Congress approved the spending and the authority necessary to carry this out in March 1957. The Eisenhower Doctrine placed the Middle East squarely in the middle of the Cold War conflict between the United States and the Soviet Union. Where the French and English had previously been the controlling Western powers in the Middle East, the United States was now pledged to defend the volatile region from Soviet incursion.

Defining Moment

The Middle East was increasingly unstable in the months leading up to Eisenhower's speech. In particular, Egyptian leader Gamal Abdel Nasser had sparked an anti-Western, anti-Israeli, pan-Arab movement that threatened to undermine US and European interests in the area; his provocations came to an explosive head in the Suez Canal Crisis of October 1956.

The crisis began on July 19, 1956, when the United States announced that it would not offer Egypt financial aid in the construction of the Aswan Dam over the Nile River. Nearly seventy million dollars had been pledged by the United States and Great Britain in December 1955 to Nasser's government, but the offer was revoked because of both Nasser's increasing ties to the Soviet Union and vitriolic anti-Western agenda. It was hoped that financial aid would temper Nasser's nationalist goals and weaken his ties to the Soviets, but Nasser continued to purchase Soviet weapons through Czechoslovakia, and his attacks on Western colonialism and imperialism continued unabated. Nasser was enraged by the withdrawal of support, and the Soviet Union quickly offered aid of its own. The British were also taken by surprise at the US announcement and saw it as a dangerous maneuver, destined to strengthen Nasser and further damage British relations with the Egypt.

Nasser responded to the withdrawal of US support for the Aswan Dam by announcing, on July 26, 1956, that the Suez Canal Company, the operators of a vital trade route for Middle Eastern petroleum that was managed by the French and British governments and was held by the British, would be nationalized—that is, declared the property of the Egyptian government. All the company's assets were seized, and

Egypt closed the canal to all Israeli shipping. The British and French were outraged, and the United States, hoping to avoid an armed conflict that could ignite hostilities with the Soviet Union and perhaps even lead to a nuclear war, attempted to broker a compromise deal that would divide ownership equally between Egypt, France, and Britain, along with other interested nations. None of the parties involved were interested in this compromise, and Britain, France, and Israel began secretly planning an invasion of Egypt to retake the Suez Canal.

On October 29, 1956, Israel attacked Egypt across the Sinai Peninsula and advanced rapidly toward the Suez Canal. Two days later, British and French forces joined the Israeli army. The United States was in the difficult position of condemning recent Soviet intervention in Hungary, which was also in turmoil, but not wishing to condemn its allies in Egypt or support an escalation that would lead to increased Soviet involvement in the conflict. The Eisenhower administration urged the belligerents to accept United Nations intervention, with a ceasefire on November 6, and even voted for a measure in the U.N. condemning the invasion. The Americans urged the Soviet Union not to involve itself in the conflict and pressured US allies to withdraw from Egypt. The British and French left in December. The Israeli army remained in Egypt until March 1957, after the declaration of the Eisenhower Doctrine. Relations between the United States and its allies Britain and France were cooled by this episode, with both sides feeling that they had been deceived by the other. The Eisenhower Doctrine was articulated just two months after the end of hostilities as a US effort to fill the power vacuum left by receding British and French influence in the region.

Author Biography

Dwight David Eisenhower was born in Denison, Texas, on October 14, 1890. He was the third of seven sons, and when he was two years old, his parents moved to Abilene, Kansas. Eisenhower graduated from Abilene High School in 1909 and was accepted to West Point in 1911. He was an officer in the US Army during World War I but was not sent overseas. He continued his military career after the war and became a brigadier general on October 3, 1941. Eisenhower went on to command the Allied landing in North Africa in November 1942. In 1943, President Franklin D. Roosevelt made Eisenhower supreme Allied commander in Europe, and he was in charge of the Allied forces that invaded occupied France on June 6, 1944, D-Day. After a postwar position as the military commander of occupied Germany, Eisenhower was named chief of staff of the Army, until becoming president of Columbia University in 1948. He was named supreme commander of the North Atlantic Treaty Organization (NATO) in 1950, but he retained the presidency of Columbia until 1953, when he became president of the United States. After serving a second term as president, Eisenhower retired to Pennsylvania, where his German American family originated. He died of congestive heart failure on March 28, 1969, and is buried on the grounds of the Eisenhower Presidential Library in Abilene, Kansas.

HISTORICAL DOCUMENT: *The Eisenhower Doctrine*

First may I express to you my deep appreciation of your courtesy in giving me, at some inconvenience to yourselves, this early opportunity of addressing you on a matter I deem to be of grave importance to our country.

In my forthcoming State of the Union Message, I shall review the international situation generally. There are worldwide hopes which we can reasonably entertain, and there are worldwide responsibilities which we must carry to make certain that freedom—including our own—may be secure.

There is, however, a special situation in the Middle East which I feel I should, even now, lay before you.

Before doing so it is well to remind ourselves that our basic national objective in international affairs remains peace—a world peace based on justice. Such a peace must include all areas, all peoples of the world if it is to be enduring. There is no nation, great or small, with which we would refuse to negotiate, in mutual good faith, with patience and in the determination to secure a better understanding between us. Out of such understandings must, and eventually will, grow confidence and trust, indispensable ingredients to a program of peace and to plans for lifting from us all the burdens of expensive armaments. To promote these objectives, our government works tirelessly, day by day, month by month, year by year. But until a degree of success crowns our efforts that will assure to all nations peaceful existence, we must, in the interests of peace itself, remain vigilant, alert and strong.

I.

The Middle East has abruptly reached a new and critical stage in its long and important history. In past decades many of the countries in that area were not fully self-governing. Other nations exercised considerable authority in the area and the security of the region was largely built around their power. But since the First World War there has been a steady evolution toward self-government and independence. This development the United States has welcomed and has encouraged. Our country supports without reservation the full sovereignty and independence of each and every nation of the Middle East.

The evolution to independence has in the main been a peaceful process. But the area has been often troubled. Persistent crosscurrents of distrust and fear with raids back and forth across national boundaries have brought about a high degree of instability in much of the Mid East. Just recently there have been hostilities involving Western European nations that once exercised much influence in the area. Also the relatively large attack by Israel in October has intensified the basic differences between that nation and its Arab neighbors. All this instability has been heightened and, at times, manipulated by International Communism.

continued from page 125

II.

Russia's rulers have long sought to dominate the Middle East. That was true of the Czars and it is true of the Bolsheviks. The reasons are not hard to find. They do not affect Russia's security, for no one plans to use the Middle East as a base for aggression against Russia. Never for a moment has the United States entertained such a thought.

The Soviet Union has nothing whatsoever to fear from the United States in the Middle East, or anywhere else in the world, so long as its rulers do not themselves first resort to aggression.

That statement I make solemnly and emphatically.

Neither does Russia's desire to dominate the Middle East spring from its own economic interest in the area. Russia does not appreciably use or depend upon the Suez Canal. In 1955 Soviet traffic through the Canal represented only about three fourths of 1% of the total. The Soviets have no need for, and could provide no market for, the petroleum resources which constitute the principal natural wealth of the area. Indeed, the Soviet Union is a substantial exporter of petroleum products.

The reason for Russia's interest in the Middle East is solely that of power politics. Considering her announced purpose of Communizing the world, it is easy to understand her hope of dominating the Middle East.

This region has always been the crossroads of the continents of the Eastern Hemisphere. The Suez Canal enables the nations of Asia and Europe to carry on the commerce that is essential if these countries are to maintain well-rounded and prosperous economies. The Middle East provides a gateway between Eurasia and Africa.

It contains about two thirds of the presently known oil deposits of the world and it normally supplies the petroleum needs of many nations of Europe, Asia and Africa. The nations of Europe are peculiarly dependent upon this supply, and this dependency relates to transportation as well as to production! This has been vividly demonstrated since the closing of the Suez Canal and some of the pipelines. Alternate ways of transportation and, indeed, alternate sources of power can, if necessary, be developed. But these cannot be considered as early prospects.

These things stress the immense importance of the Middle East. If the nations of that area should lose their independence, if they were dominated by alien forces hostile to freedom, that would be both a tragedy for the area and for many other free nations whose economic life would be subject to near strangulation. Western Europe would be endangered just as though there had been no Marshall Plan, no North Atlantic Treaty Organization. The free nations of Asia and Africa, too, would be placed in serious jeopardy. And the countries of the Middle East would lose the markets upon which their economies depend. All this would have the most adverse, if not disastrous, effect upon our own nation's economic life and political prospects.

Then there are other factors which transcend the material. The Middle East is the birthplace of three great religions-Moslem, Christian and Hebrew. Mecca and Jerusalem are more than places on the map. They symbolize religions which teach that the spirit has supremacy over matter and that the individual has a dignity and rights of which no despotic government can rightfully deprive him. It would be intolerable if the holy places of the Middle East should be subjected to a rule that glorifies atheistic materialism.

International Communism, of course, seeks to mask its purposes of domination by expressions of good will and by superficially attractive offers of political, economic and military aid. But any free nation, which is the subject of Soviet enticement, ought, in elementary wisdom, to look behind the mask.

Remember Estonia, Latvia and Lithuania! In 1939 the Soviet Union entered into mutual assistance pacts with these then dependent countries; and the Soviet Foreign Minister, addressing the Extraordinary Fifth Session of the Supreme Soviet in October 1939, solemnly and publicly declared that "we stand for the scrupulous and punctilious observance of the pacts on the basis of complete reciprocity, and we declare that all the nonsensical talk about the Sovietization of the Baltic countries is only to the interest of our common enemies and of all anti-Soviet provocateurs." Yet in 1940, Estonia, Latvia and Lithuania were forcibly incorporated into the Soviet Union.

Soviet control of the satellite nations of Eastern Europe has been forcibly maintained in spite of solemn promises of a contrary intent, made during World War II.

Stalin's death brought hope that this pattern would change. And we read the pledge of the Warsaw Treaty of 1955 that the Soviet Union would follow in satellite countries "the principles of mutual respect for their independence and sovereignty and noninterference in domestic affairs." But we have just seen the subjugation of Hungary by naked armed force. In the aftermath of this Hungarian tragedy, world respect for and belief in Soviet promises have sunk to a new low. International Communism needs and seeks a recognizable success.

Thus, we have these simple and indisputable facts:

> *There is no nation, great or small, with which we would refuse to negotiate, in mutual good faith, with patience and in the determination to secure a better understanding between us.*

continues on page 128

continued from page 127

1. The Middle East, which has always been coveted by Russia, would today be prized more than ever by International Communism.
2. The Soviet rulers continue to show that they do not scruple to use any means to gain their ends.
3. The free nations of the Mid East need, and for the most part want, added strength to assure their continued independence.

III.

Our thoughts naturally turn to the United Nations as a protector of small nations. Its charter gives it primary responsibility for the maintenance of international peace and security. Our country has given the United Nations its full support in relation to the hostilities in Hungary and in Egypt. The United Nations was able to bring about a cease-fire and withdrawal of hostile forces from Egypt because it was dealing with governments and peoples who had a decent respect for the opinions of mankind as reflected in the United Nations General Assembly. But in the case of Hungary, the situation was different. The Soviet Union vetoed action by the Security Council to require the withdrawal of Soviet armed forces from Hungary. And it has shown callous indifference to the recommendations, even the censure, of the General Assembly. The United Nations can always be helpful, but it cannot be a wholly dependable protector of freedom when the ambitions of the Soviet Union are involved.

IV.

Under all the circumstances I have laid before you, a greater responsibility now devolves upon the United States. We have shown, so that none can doubt, our dedication to the principle that force shall not be used internationally for any aggressive purpose and that the integrity and independence of the nations of the Middle East should be inviolate. Seldom in history has a nation's dedication to principle been tested as severely as ours during recent weeks.

There is general recognition in the Middle East, as elsewhere, that the United States does not seek either political or economic domination over any other people. Our desire is a world environment of freedom, not servitude. On the other hand many, if not all, of the nations of the Middle East are aware of the danger that stems from International Communism and welcome closer cooperation with the United States to realize for themselves the United Nations goals of independence, economic well-being and spiritual growth.

If the Middle East is to continue its geographic role of uniting rather than separating East and West; if its vast economic resources are to serve the well-being of the peoples there, as well as that of others; and if its cultures and religions and their shrines are to be preserved for the uplifting of the spirits of the peoples, then the United States must make more evident its willingness to support the independence of the freedom-loving nations of the area.

V.

Under these circumstances I deem it necessary to seek the cooperation of the Congress. Only with that cooperation can we give the reassurance needed to deter aggression, to give courage and confidence to those who are dedicated to freedom and thus prevent a chain of events which would gravely endanger all of the free world.

There have been several Executive declarations made by the United States in relation to the Middle East. There is the Tripartite Declaration of May 25, 1950, followed by the Presidential assurance of October 31, 1950, to the King of Saudi Arabia. There is the Presidential declaration of April 9, 1956, that the United States will within constitutional means oppose any aggression in the area. There is our Declaration of November 29, 1956, that a threat to the territorial integrity or political independence of Iran, Iraq, Pakistan, or Turkey would be viewed by the United States with the utmost gravity.

Nevertheless, weaknesses in the present situation and the increased danger from International Communism, convince me that basic United States policy should now find expression in joint action by the Congress and the Executive. Furthermore, our joint resolve should be so couched as to make it apparent that if need be our words will be backed by action.

VI.

It is nothing new for the President and the Congress to join to recognize that the national integrity of other free nations is directly related to our own security.

We have joined to create and support the security system of the United Nations. We have reinforced the collective security system of the United Nations by a series of collective defense arrangements. Today we have security treaties with 42 other nations which recognize that our peace and security are intertwined. We have joined to take decisive action in relation to Greece and Turkey and in relation to Taiwan.

Thus, the United States through the joint action of the President and the Congress, or, in the case of treaties, the Senate, has manifested in many endangered areas its purpose to support free and independent governments—and peace—against external menace, notably the menace of International Communism. Thereby we have helped to maintain peace and security during a period of great danger. It is now essential that the United States should manifest through joint action of the President and the Congress our determination to assist those nations of the Mid East area, which desire that assistance.

continues on page 130

continued from page 129

The action which I propose would have the following features.

It would, first of all, authorize the United States to cooperate with and assist any nation or group of nations in the general area of the Middle East in the development of economic strength dedicated to the maintenance of national independence.

It would, in the second place, authorize the Executive to undertake in the same region programs of military assistance and cooperation with any nation or group of nations which desires such aid.

It would, in the third place, authorize such assistance and cooperation to include the employment of the armed forces of the United States to secure and protect the territorial integrity and political independence of such nations, requesting such aid, against overt armed aggression from any nation controlled by International Communism.

These measures would have to be consonant with the treaty obligations of the United States, including the Charter of the United Nations and with any action or recommendations of the United Nations. They would also, if armed attack occurs, be subject to the overriding authority of the United Nations Security Council in accordance with the Charter.

The present proposal would, in the fourth place, authorize the President to employ, for economic and defensive military purposes, sums available under the Mutual Security Act of 1954, as amended, without regard to existing limitations.

The legislation now requested should not include the authorization or appropriation of funds because I believe that, under the conditions I suggest, presently appropriated funds will be adequate for the balance of the present fiscal year ending June 30. I shall, however, seek in subsequent legislation the authorization of $200,000,000 to be available during each of the fiscal years 1958 and 1959 for discretionary use in the area, in addition to the other mutual security programs for the area hereafter provided for by the Congress.

VII.

This program will not solve all the problems of the Middle East. Neither does it represent the totality of our policies for the area. There are the problems of Palestine and relations between Israel and the Arab States, and the future of the Arab refugees. There is the problem of the future status of the Suez Canal. These difficulties are aggravated by International Communism, but they would exist quite apart from that threat. It is not the purpose of the legislation I propose to deal directly with these problems. The United Nations is actively concerning itself with all these matters, and we are supporting the United Nations. The United States has made clear, notably by Secretary Dulles' address of August 26, 1955, that we are willing to do much to assist the United Nations in solving the basic problems of Palestine.

The proposed legislation is primarily designed to deal with the possibility of Communist aggression, direct and indirect. There is imperative need that any lack of power in the area should be made good, not by external or alien force, but by the increased vigor and security of the independent nations of the area.

Experience shows that indirect aggression rarely if ever succeeds where there is reasonable security against direct aggression; where the government disposes of loyal security forces, and where economic conditions are such as not to make Communism seem an attractive alternative. The program I suggest deals with all three aspects of this matter and thus with the problem of indirect aggression.

It is my hope and belief that if our purpose be proclaimed, as proposed by the requested legislation, that very fact will serve to halt any contemplated aggression. We shall have heartened the patriots who are dedicated to the independence of their nations. They will not feel that they stand alone, under the menace of great power. And I should add that patriotism is, throughout this area, a powerful sentiment. It is true that fear sometimes perverts true patriotism into fanaticism and to the acceptance of dangerous enticements from without. But if that fear can be allayed, then the climate will be more favorable to the attainment of worthy national ambitions.

And as I have indicated, it will also be necessary for us to contribute economically to strengthen those countries, or groups of countries, which have governments manifestly dedicated to the preservation of independence and resistance to subversion. Such measures will provide the greatest insurance against Communist inroads. Words alone are not enough.

VII.

Let me refer again to the requested authority to employ the armed forces of the United States to assist to defend the territorial integrity and the political independence of any nation in the area against Communist armed aggression. Such authority would not be exercised except at the desire of the nation attacked. Beyond this it is my profound hope that this authority would never have to be exercised at all.

Nothing is more necessary to assure this than that our policy with respect to the defense of the area be promptly and clearly determined and declared. Thus the United Nations and all friendly governments, and indeed governments which are not friendly, will know where we stand.

If, contrary to my hope and expectation, a situation arose which called for the military application of the policy which I ask the Congress to join me in proclaiming, I would of course maintain hour-by-hour contact with the Congress if it were in session. And if the Congress were not in session, and if the situation had grave implications, I would, of course, at once call the Congress into special session.

continues on page 132

continued from page 131

> In the situation now existing, the greatest risk, as is often the case, is that ambitious despots may miscalculate. If power-hungry Communists should either falsely or correctly estimate that the Middle East is inadequately defended, they might be tempted to use open measures of armed attack. If so, that would start a chain of circumstances which would almost surely involve the United States in military action. I am convinced that the best insurance against this dangerous contingency is to make clear now our readiness to cooperate fully and freely with our friends of the Middle East in ways consonant with the purposes and principles of the United Nations. I intend promptly to send a special mission to the Middle East to explain the cooperation we are prepared to give.
>
> ### IX.
>
> The policy which I outline involves certain burdens and indeed risks for the United States. Those who covet the area will not like what is proposed. Already, they are grossly distorting our purpose. However, before this Americans have seen our nation's vital interests and human freedom in jeopardy, and their fortitude and resolution have been equal to the crisis, regardless of hostile distortion of our words, motives and actions.
>
> Indeed, the sacrifices of the American people in the cause of freedom have, even since the close-of World War II, been measured in many billions of dollars and in thousands of the precious lives of our youth. These sacrifices, by which great areas of the world have been preserved to freedom, must not be thrown away.
>
> In those momentous periods of the past, the President and the Congress have united, without partisanship, to serve the vital interests of the United States and of the free world.
>
> The occasion has come for us to manifest again our national unity in support of freedom and to show our deep respect for the rights and independence of every nation—however great, however small. We seek not violence, but peace. To this purpose we must now devote our energies, our determination, ourselves.

Document Themes and Analysis

Eisenhower's speech to the joint session of Congress begins with a promise to review the most pressing international concern of the hour, the "special situation" in the Middle East. Eisenhower reiterates that the fundamental objective in all international relations is the pursuit of peace. He argues that the Middle East is at a particularly vulnerable stage in its development. It is emerging from centuries of colonial rule, which he downplays as "other nations exercis[ing] considerable authority in the area." While colonial powers had once been responsible for the defense and security of their Middle Eastern territory, the move toward independence and self-determination in these

U.S. Marine sits in a foxhole and points a machine gun towards Beirut, Lebanon, in the distance.

countries meant increasing conflict and border disputes. The Suez Canal Crisis, which he refers to as "hostilities involving Western European nations" has exacerbated these tensions, particularly with Israel. The Soviet Union, at the head of "international Communism," had also exploited these tensions and therefore has responsibility for some of the outbreak of violence.

The bulk of this speech addresses the Soviet Union's reasons for wanting to control the Middle East and the reasons it must be prevented from doing so. Eisenhower notes that unlike Western Europe, which depends heavily on Middle Eastern petroleum, Russia has its own oil reserves. Thus, they do not need to use the trade route that the Suez Canal provides. Their desire to control the Middle East is ideological and not born of economic necessity. He says the Soviet Union is motivated by its "announced purpose of Communizing the world." Eisenhower warns the nations of the Middle East not to fall for Soviet promises of aid with no strings attached. Independent nations had been absorbed by the Soviet Union by force after such promises had been made. He gives examples of the Baltic States during World War II and the Eastern European nations after the war, most notably Hungary, where the Soviet Union had intervened militarily to prop up the Communist puppet government there. The United Nations was unable to intervene, since the Soviet Union was able to use its veto on the U.N. Security Council. In addition, Eisenhower reminds Congress that the officially atheist Soviet Union does not respect religious freedom. He asks: How would it treat the holy sites of Christianity, Islam, and Judaism if it controlled the region?

It is no secret that the "national integrity of other free nations is directly related to our own security," and therefore, Eisenhower proposes a plan that would work with the United Nations to build economic support for the Middle East and to provide it with "programs of military assistance." Eisenhower indicates that he will ask for two hundred million dollars for aid to the Middle East in the upcoming years, a commitment that he felt would encourage nations in the region to resist Soviet overtures or aggression.

The Eisenhower Doctrine firmly established the United States' interest in the Middle East, supplanting the influence of former colonial powers in the region, most notably France and Great Britain. The ongoing conflict between the United States and the Soviet Union would increasingly be played out in the Middle East (among other parts of the developing world), and the area remained unstable and volatile.

The military intervention promised in the Eisenhower Doctrine was requested once, by Lebanon, in July 1958. Lebanese president Camille Chamoun aroused the ire of Nasser and anti-Western pan-Arabs by refusing to cut diplomatic ties with Western nations during the Suez Crisis. Fearing a revolution with outside (Soviet) support, Chamoun went to the U.N. Security Council for help, and when that body failed to provide support, he called on the United States for help. The United States sent ships and troops to protect transportation and trade centers in Beirut, notably the seaport and airport. The troops were withdrawn in October 1958.

—*Bethany Groff Dorau*

Bibliography and Additional Reading

Ambrose, Stephen E. *Eisenhower, Vol. II: The President*. New York: Simon, 1984. Print.

Thomas, Evans. *Ike's Bluff: President Eisenhower's Secret Battle to Save the World*. New York: Little, Brown, 2012. Print.

Walker, Martin. *The Cold War: A History*. New York: Holt, 1993. Print.

Arab Voices in Opposition

Skepticism toward the West had long existed in the Muslim world, but by the middle of the twentieth century anti-Western attitudes were beginning to gain a broader hearing. Egypt's Muslim Brotherhood, an Islamic organization, initially supported the presidency of Gamal Abdul Nasser but soon learned that the feeling was not mutual. The group's chief ideologue, Sayyid Qutb, who had spent two years in the United States, deplored Nasser's secular approach to government and denounced the West in militant terms. In numerous critical publications, Qutb popularized the concept of *jihad,* or uncompromising struggle against unjust rulers for the purpose of implementing "true" Islamic rule. Nasser's regime arrested and imprisoned Qutb, released him after ten years (in 1964), and finally put him on trial and hanged him (1966) for conspiring against the state. Qutb's brother, Muhammad, nevertheless spread his message from a secret haven for Muslim Brothers in Saudi Arabia. Among those who would be influenced by that message were Ayman al-Zawahiri and Osama bin Laden, eventual leaders of the al-Qaeda terrorist network and organizers of the 9/11 attacks against the United States.

This, of course, represents just one strand of Arab opposition to western capitalism in general and the United States in particular; but it is one of the most momentous strands from the perspective of the United States.

Charter of the Arab League

Date: March 22, 1945
Author: Mustafa al-Nahhas Pasha
Geographic region: Syria, Transjordan, Iraq, Saudi Arabia, Lebanon, Egypt, and Yemen
Genre: Charter

Summary Overview

The Charter of the Arab League lists the founding principles for a pan-Arab organization stretching across North Africa and the Middle East. The original members of the league gathered in response to the dissolution of the Ottoman Empire and concerns about divisions of territory after World War II, in particular regarding the creation of a Jewish state in Palestine. The purpose of the league has been to strengthen ties between countries within the region and to coordinate among members on matters of common interest. This charter provides for members to cooperate on shared economic, political, and social issues; it also endows the League with the ability to mediate military conflicts between or with member states. However, the charter's emphasis on recognizing national sovereignty above all else has drawn criticism since it limits the ability of the member states to act collectively. Since the original countries ratified the pact in 1945, the League has grown to twenty-two members and has attempted to reorganize into a more potent international organization after a wave of popular uprisings across the Arab world in 2011.

Defining Moment

The origins of the Arab League can be traced at least to the end of World War I and the "balkanization," i.e. division into smaller parts, of the Ottoman Empire. The Treaty of Lausanne, which was signed in 1923, defined the borders of the modern Turkish state and ceded many former territories in the Levant and North Africa into the control of the Allies as zones of influence. Arab leaders were immediately dissatisfied since the dissolution of Ottoman power resulted not in Arab independence, but an exchange of colonial control. Additionally, the Sykes-Picot Agreement of 1916, in which the United Kingdom, France, and Russia determined which Middle Eastern regions would fall under their spheres of influence, appeared to be a motivating force in how the European leaders divided the former Ottoman Empire among themselves with little attention to regional differences. The Balfour Declaration, in which Britain expressed support for the creation of a new Jewish state in 1917, would also have huge ramifications for nascent Arab nationalism.

Several Arab leaders had been considering the merits of a pan-Arab state, or at very least promulgated the ideology of pan-Arab unity. Major proponents of pan-Arabism included Zaki al-Arsuzi and Michel Aflaq, two Syrians thinkers who helped establish the Ba'ath Party, as well as Abdullah I of Jordan, a ruler with expansionist hopes who was first Emir under a British Mandate and later king of the independent nation. Surprisingly, Britain became a supporter of a pan-Arab organization to foment unity at the start of World War II. The Allies needed to secure support against the Axis drive into North Africa, and they could not combat both anti-British sentiment in the Middle Eastern territories or risk losing local support to the Axis powers. The League of Nations, although it had failed in its mission to prevent another world war, provided a paradigm for a consortium of governments that could gather to work on shared issues. In 1941 British Foreign Minister Anthony Eden announced his country's support for recognizing the independence of the Lebanese and Syrians, and he expressed hope that these new Arab countries would build economic and political ties with each other.

It was only during the spring of 1943 that an Arab leader, Nuri al-Said of Iraq, came forward with a plan for Arab unity. Al-Said proposed that Iraq and Syria initially form an "Arab League" that would be open to other Arab states to join; he also suggested that this "Arab League" would have a permanent council that could pass decisions on many issues, including currency control, foreign affairs, education, and protection of minority rights. The leaders of Egypt and Transjordan had different ideas about what Arab unity would look like, and serious questions about the form of this new organization stymied progress. Nahhas Pasha, the premier of Egypt, decided that his government ought to mediate the question of regional Arab cooperation; he announced a joint conference that would be held in Alexandria on September 25, 1944. The Alexandria Protocol resulted from this conference, and became the prototype of the later Charter of the League of Arab States. In this earlier protocol, five nations (Egypt, Iraq, Syria, Jordan, and Lebanon) set the groundwork for strengthening relations between themselves. However, this protocol also stressed protection for independent sovereignty, a right that had been relatively recently acquired for all participating member states. This concern would become one of the fundamental organizing guidelines for the later Charter and one of the greatest obstacles in encouraging political unity and more concerted action between member states.

Author Biography

Seven countries signed the initial charter to form the League of Arab States, but the composition of the pact was due in large part to the work of Nahhas Pasha, Egyptian premier at the time. Mustafa al-Nahhas Pasha (1879–1965) began his career first as a lawyer and then as a judge until he was dismissed and exiled in 1919 for joining the Wafd, an Egyptian nationalist party. He rejoined Egyptian government in 1923, and climbed the ranks of government quickly; he first served as prime minister for a short tenure in 1928. Nahhas Pasha frequently clashed with both the Egyptian king and the British over his nationalist sympathies and desire to curtail the sovereign's power. When he was appointed prime minister for a third time in 1936, Nahhas Pasha helped negotiate the Anglo-Egyptian Treaty in London, which ended British occupation of Egypt and established an alliance. He would not hold onto his third premiership for long, since the new king Farouk I disagreed with his domestic and foreign policies. The outbreak of World War II and British pressure compelled the king to appoint the controversial Nahhas Pasha again to be prime minister in 1942. During this premiership, he instituted important social policies on labor and played a central role in gathering Arab leaders to the conference that resulted in the Alexandria Protocol in 1944. He studied the activities of other nascent pan-regional conferences, such as the Organization of American Republics, in order to help draft the document that would serve as the blueprint for the later Charter of the Arab League. However, two days after the Alexandria Protocol was signed in order to guide a new pan-Arab association, the Egyptian king removed Nahhas Pasha from his position; the Syrian and the Jordanian prime ministers who had joined the conference were also dismissed from their posts in their respective countries. Nahhas Pasha served one last term as prime minister in 1950, during which time he abrogated the Anglo-Egyptian Treaty in favor of the Egyptian king, but growing dissatisfaction with the Wafd Party led to his final dismissal in 1952. Nahhas Pasha and his wife were arrested and charged with corruption and imprisoned for a year, after which he lived out the rest of his life as a private citizen.

HISTORICAL DOCUMENT: *Charter of the Arab League*

His Excellency the President of the Syrian Republic,
His Royal Highness the Emir of Transjordan,
His Majesty the King of Iraq,
His Majesty the King of Saudi-Arabia,
His Excellency the President of the Lebanese Republic,
His Majesty the King of Egypt;
His Majesty the King of Yemen,

With a view to strengthen[ing] the close relations and numerous ties which bind the Arab States,

And out of concern for the cementing and reinforcing of these bonds on the basis of respect for the independence and sovereignty of theme Stated,

And in order to direct their efforts toward[s] the goal of the welfare of all the Arab States, their common weal, the guarantee of their future and the realization of their aspirations

And in response to Arab public opinion in all the Arab countries,

Have agreed to conclude a pact to this effect and have delegated as their plenipotentiaries those whose names are given below:

Who, after the exchange of the credentials granting them full authority, which were found valid and in proper form, have agreed upon the following:

Article 1.

The League of Arab States shall be composed of the: independent Arab States that have signed this Pact.

Every independent Arab State shall have the right to adhere to the League. Should it desire to adhere, it shall present an application to this effect which shall be filed with the permanent General Secretariat and submitted to the Council at its first meeting following the presentation of the application.

Article 2.

The purpose of the League is to draw closer the relations between member States and co-ordinate their political activities with the aim of realizing a close collaboration between them, to safeguard their independence and sovereignty, and to consider in a general way the affairs and interests of the Arab countries.

It also has among its purposes a close co-operation of the member States with due regard to the structure of each of these States and the conditions prevailing therein, in the following matters:

(a) Economic and financial matters, including trade, customs, currency, agriculture and industry;
(b) (communications, including railways, roads, aviation, navigation, and posts and telegraphs;
(c) Cultural matters;
(d) Matters connected with nationality, passports, visas, execution of judgments and extradition;
(e) Social welfare matters;
(f) Health matters.

Article 3.

The League shall have a Council composed of the representatives of the member States. Each State shall have one vote, regardless of the number of its representatives.

The Council shall be entrusted with the function of realizing the purpose of the League and of supervising the execution of the agreements concluded between the member States on matters referred to in the preceding article or on other matters.

It shall also have the function of determining the means whereby the League will collaborate with the international organizations which may be created in the future to guarantee peace and security and organize economic and social relations.

> *The purpose of the League is to draw closer the relations between member States and co-ordinate their political activities with the aim of realizing a close collaboration between them, to safeguard their independence and sovereignty, and to consider in a general way the affairs and interests of the Arab countries.*

continues on page 140

continued from page 139

Article 4.

A special Committee shall be formed for each of the categories enumerated in article 2, on which the member States shall be represented. These Committees shall be entrusted with establishing the basis and scope of co-operation in the form of draft agreements which shall be submitted to the Council for its consideration preparatory to their being submitted to the States referred to.

Delegates representing the other Arab countries may participate in these Committees as members. The Council shall determine the circumstances in which the participation of these representatives shall be allowed as well as the basis of the representation.

Article 5.

The recourse to force for the settlement of disputes between two or more member States shall not be allowed. Should there arise among them a dispute that does not involve the independence of a State, its sovereignty or its territorial integrity, and should the two contending parties apply to the Council for the settlement of this dispute, the decision of the Council shall then be effective and obligatory.

In this case, the States among whom the dispute has arisen shall not participate in the deliberations and decisions of the Council.

The Council shall mediate in a dispute which may lead to war between two member States or between a member State and another State in order to conciliate them

The decisions relating to arbitration and mediation shall be taken by a majority vote.

Article 6.

In case of aggression or threat of aggression by a State against a member State, the State attacked or threatened with attack may request an immediate meeting of the Council.

The Council shall determine the necessary measures to repel this aggression. Its decision shall be taken unanimously. If the aggression is committed by a member State the vote of that State will not be counted in determining unanimity.

If the aggression is committed in such a way as to render the Government of the State attacked unable to communicate with the Council, the representative of that State in the Council may request the Council to convene for the purpose set forth in the preceding paragraph. If the representative is unable to communicate with the Council, it shall be the right of any member State to request a meeting of the Council.

Article 7.

The decisions of the Council taken by a unanimous vote shall be binding on all the member States of the League; those that are reached by a majority vote shall bind only those that accept them.

In both cases the decisions of the Council shall be executed in each State in accordance with the fundamental structure of that State.

Article 8.

Every Member State of the League shall respect the form of government obtaining in the other States of the League, and shall recognize the form of government obtaining as one of the rights of those States, and shall pledge itself not to take any action tending to change that form.

Article 9.

The States of the Arab League that are desirous of establishing among themselves closer collaboration and stronger bonds than those provided for in the present Pact, may conclude among themselves whatever agreements they wish for this purpose.

The treaties and agreements already concluded or that may be concluded in the future between a member State and any other State shall not be binding on the other members.

Article 10.

The permanent seat of the League of Arab States shall be Cairo. The Council of the League may meet at any other place it designates.

Article 11.

The Council of the League shall meet in ordinary session twice a year, during the months of March and October. It shall meet in extraordinary session at the request of two member States whenever the need arises.

Article 12.

The League shall have a permanent General Secretariat, composed of a Secretary-General, Assistant Secretaries and an adequate number of officials.

The Secretary-General shall be appointed by the Council upon the vote of two-thirds of the States of the League. The Assistant Secretaries and the principal officials shall be appointed by the Secretary-General with the approval of the Council.

The Council shall establish an internal organization for the General Secretariat as well as the conditions of service of the officials.

The Secretary-General shall have the rank of Ambassador; and the Assistant Secretaries the rank of Ministers Plenipotentiary.

continues on page 142

continued from page 141

The first Secretary-General of the League is designated in an annex to the present Pact.

Article 13.

The Secretary-General shall prepare the draft of the budget of the League and submit it for approval to the Council before the beginning of each fiscal year.

The Council shall determine the share of each of the States of the League in the expenses. It shall be allowed to revise the share if necessary.

Article 14.

The members of the Council of the League, the members of its Committees and such of its officials as shall be designated in the internal organization, shall enjoy, in the exercise of their duties, diplomatic privileges and immunities.

The premises occupied by the institutions of the League shall be inviolable.

Article 15.

The council shall meet the first time at the invitation of the Head of the Egyptian Government. Later meetings shall be convoked by the Secretary-General.

In each ordinary session the representatives of the States of the League shall assume the chairmanship of the Council in rotation.

Article 16.

Except for the cases provided for in the present Pact, a majority shall suffice for decisions by the Council effective in the following matters:

(a) Matters concerning the officials.
(b) The approval of the budget of the League.
(c) The internal organization of the Council, the Committees and the General Secretariat.
(d) The termination of the sessions.

Article 17.

The member States of the League shall file with the General Secretariat copies of all treaties and agreements which they have concluded or will conclude with any other State, whether a member of the League or otherwise.

Article 18.

If one of the member States intends to withdraw from the League, the Council shall be informed of its intention one year before the withdrawal takes effect

The Council of the League may consider any State that is not fulfilling the obligations resulting from this Pact as excluded from the League, by a decision taken by a unanimous vote of all the States except the State referred to.

Article 19.

The present Pact may be amended with the approval of two-thirds of the members of the League in particular for the purpose of strengthening the ties between them, of creating an Arab Court of Justice, and of regulating the relations of the League with the international organizations that may be created in the future to guarantee security and peace

No decision shall be taken as regards an amendment except in the session following that in which it is proposed.

Any State that does not approve an amendment may withdraw from the League when the amendment becomes effective, without being bound by the provisions of the preceding article.

Article 20.

The present Pact and its annexes shall be ratified in accordance with the fundamental form of government in each of the contracting States.

The instruments of ratification shall be filed with the General Secretariat and the present Pact shall become binding on the States that ratify in fifteen days after the Secretary-General receives instruments of ratification from four States.

The present Pact has been drawn up in the Arabic language in Cairo and dated 8 Rabi al Thani 1364 (March 22, 1945), in a single text which shall be deposited with the General Secretariat.

A certified copy shall be sent to each of the States of the League.

ANNEX ON PALESTINE

At the end of the last Great War, Palestine, together with the other Arab States, was separated from the Ottoman Empire. She became independent, not belonging to any other State.

The Treaty of Lausanne proclaimed that her fate should be decided by the parties concerned in Palestine.

Even though Palestine was not able to control her own destiny, it was on the basis of the recognition of her independence that the Covenant of the League of Nations determined a system of government for her.

Her existence and her independence among the nations can, therefore, no more be questioned de jure than the independence of any of the other Arab States.

continues on page 144

continued from page 143

Even though the outward signs of this independence have remained veiled as a result of force majeure, it is not fitting that this should be an obstacle to the participation of Palestine in the work of the League.

Therefore, the States signatory to the Pact of the Arab League consider that in view of Palestine's special circumstances, the Council of the League should designate an Arab delegate from Palestine to participate in its work until this country enjoys actual independence.

ANNEX ON CO-OPERATION WITH ARAB COUNTRIES NOT MEMBERS OF THE COUNCIL OF THE LEAGUE

Whereas the member States of the League will have to deal either in the Council or in the Committees with questions affecting the interests of the entire Arab world

And whereas the Council cannot fail to take into account the aspirations of the Arab countries not members of the Council and to work toward their realization, the States signatory to the Pact of the Arab League strongly urge that the Council of the League should cooperate with them as far as possible in having them participate in the Committees referred to in the Pact, and in other matters should not spare any effort to learn their needs and understand their aspirations and should moreover work for their common weal and the guarantee of their future by whatever political means available.

ANNEX ON THE APPOINTMENT OF SECRETARY-GENERAL OF THE LEAGUE

The States signatory to the present Pact have agreed to appoint Abd Al Rahman Azzam Bey Secretary General of the League of Arab States.

His appointment shall be for a term of two years. The Council of the League shall later determine the future organization of the General Secretariat.

Document Themes and Analysis

Many of the critiques of the Arab League focus on its inability to foment positive unity and change among the relations of its member states. However, the wording of the Charter itself clarifies that the League was never meant to have its own supranational ideology: the terms characterize the League as a reactive device for solving disputes rather than a proactive entity in international affairs.

Even in the preamble of the charter, it is clear that there is no overarching political ideology guiding the organization. The first two lines of the preamble show how the pact intends to create a device for improving regional relations. The

Arab League of states establishment memorial stamp. Showing flags of the 8 establishing countries: Kingdom of Egypt, Kingdom of Saudi Arabia, Mutwakilite Kingdom of Yemen, Hashimite Kingdom of Syria, Hashimite Kingdom of Iraq, Hashimite Kingdom of Jordan, Republic of Lebanon and Palestine.

signatory countries have agreed upon the following articles "With a view to strengthen[ing] the close relations and numerous ties which bind the Arab States," which reveals that the charter intends to confirm the existing relationships, rather than create new ties that may transcend existing connections or divisions. The next line of the preamble is even clearer regarding this purpose. "And out of concern for the cementing and reinforcing of these bonds on the basis of respect for the independence and sovereignty of theme Stated": the Charter does not restrict which types of sovereignty the League respects, but leaves the language general. This permitted the League to include authoritarian regimes among its members for many years. Article 8 reinforces that the League will not attempt to change the form of a member state's government, and yet does not consider the ramifications should a member state's government be repressive. Furthermore, Article 7 undermines the ability of the League to take any proactive stance, since it stipulates that decisions of the Council will only apply to the members who vote on a decision. Article 9 similarly negates any possibility for the League to have a proactive function, since this article stipulates that member states "may conclude among themselves whatever agreements they wish" for the purposes of collaboration. Again, this does not guard against potentially unjust alliances, and has permitted factionalism within the League to stymie its efforts to proactively resolve military confrontations.

The Charter comes closest to stipulating a guiding ideology for the Arab League in its Annex on Palestine. By agreeing to this addendum, members of the Arab League profess to the right of sovereign self-determination in the face of unjust occupation. However, the previous articles of the Charter do not bind the Arab states to cooperate on this principle. Thus, Egypt was free to make independent peace agreements with Israel, and the League had difficulty in forcefully responding to Iraq's invasion of Kuwait. In this way, the Arab League has reflected its most immediate predecessor, the League of Nations, in its ability to respond to difficult political and military matters; in smaller economic and social matters, the Charter has reflected its close contemporary, the United Nations, in creating substantive change.

The Charter's emphasis on recognizing the sovereignty of its member states above all has

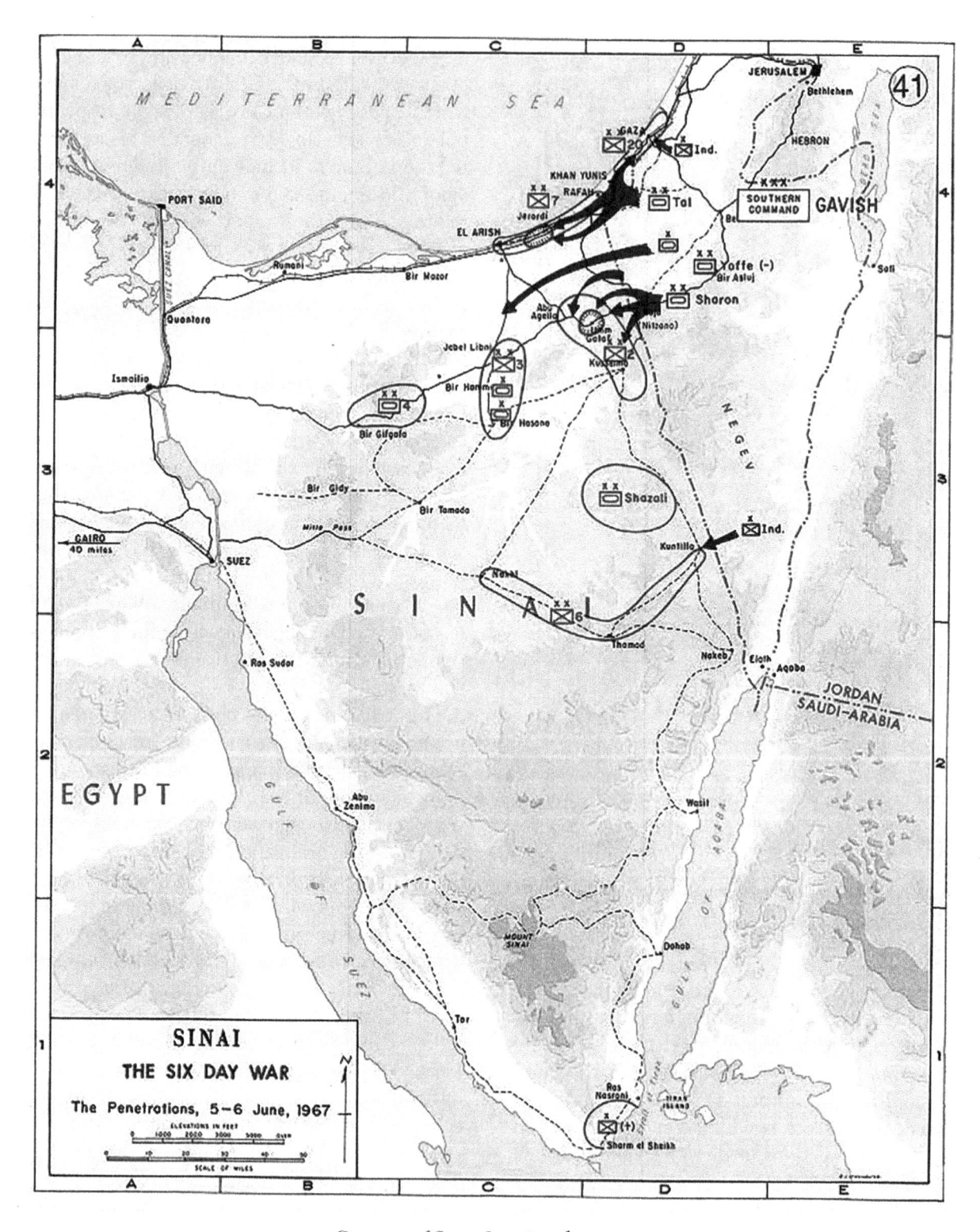

Conquest of Sinai, June 5 and 6, 1967

contributed to charges of disunity, disorganization, and ineffectiveness against the League. The decline of British and French spheres of influence, the rise of the strategic importance of oil reserves, and Cold War rivalries undermined the message of Arab unity. The issue of Palestine has remained one of the few ideologically unifying components of the Charter's principles. After the Six-Day War with Israel in 1967, the Arab League passed the Khartoum Resolution: this stipulated that the League would have no peace with Israel, would not recognize Israel, and would not negotiate with it; the League has also maintained an official boycott of Israeli goods since 1948, although recent enforcement has not been as strict. Egypt's leadership in the League in particular has been tested by the nation's evolving relationship with Israel. In 1977 Egyptian President Anwar Sadat opened up unilateral peace negotiations with Israel; in turn, the League voted to suspend Egypt's membership and moved its headquarters from Cairo to Tunis. Egypt was only readmitted into the League in 1989 and the headquarters moved back to Cairo in 1990. Internal divisions similarly beset the Arab League during Iraq's invasion of Kuwait in 1990, the United States' involvement during the first Gulf War (1990–91), and the American invasion of Iraq in 2003. Some members approved of Western involvement, including powerful members like Egypt, Saudi Arabia, and Syria; others opposed foreign encroachment, and some members took neither side.

The failure of the Arab League to coordinate on military issues rendered important bodies like the Joint Defense Council effectively purposeless. However, popular uprisings across the Arab world in 2011 gave the League an opportunity to reform its policies; the appointment of Egyptian Nabil al-Araby as secretary-general in the same year was also seen as a turning point in the organization. Not only did the League support U.N. action against Muammar Gaddafi, the former authoritarian leader of Libya, but the League also supported a no-fly zone over Libya that helped in Gaddafi's overthrow. After Gaddafi's end, the League approached the deteriorating civil war in Syria. After Bashar al-Assad, President of Syria, continued to oppress peaceful protesters of his regime and violated the Arab League's peace agreement, the League stripped Syria of its membership. Still, the old divisions remain: allies of Assad have blocked the Syrian opposition government from fully participating in the organization, and others have looked askance at the League's willingness to work with the United Nations as "internationalizing" a regional problem. Although the original principles of the League's charter were in response to a time when spheres of influence and external aggression were serious threats to the independence of the new Arab states, the stress on independent sovereignty continues to hamper the ability of the member states to rise above their regional differences and act together as a supranational entity.

—Ashleigh Fata

Bibliography and Additional Reading

Addi, Lahouari. *Radical Arab Nationalism and Political Islam*. Translated by Anthony Roberts, Washington, DC: Georgetown University Press, 2017.

Doran, Michael. *Pan-Arabism Before Nasser: Egyptian Power Politics and the Palestinian Question*. New York: Oxford University Press, 1999.

MacDonald, Robert W. *The League of Arab States: A Study in Dynamics of Regional Organization*. Princeton: Princeton University Press, 1965.

Wien, Peter. *Arab Nationalism: The Politics of History and Culture in the Modern Middle East*. New York: Routledge, 2017.

■ Palestinian National Charter

Date: July 1968
Author: Ahmed Shukeiri
Geographic region: Palestine
Genre: Charter

Summary Overview

Because Arab leaders refused to create a government in 1947–48, when the state and government of Israel were created, the Arab Palestinian people were left without a state and without established leaders. In 1964, with Egypt and Jordan ruling most of what had been the proposed Palestinian state, the Arab League held a meeting that recommended a Palestinian organization be established. It was to eventually create a Palestinian state, and in the interim to assist the Palestinian people in their conflict with Israel. The Palestinian National Council was thus created, which adopted the first version of the Palestinian National Charter. In 1968, after a decisive Arab military defeat by Israeli forces, this charter was expanded, generally with stronger statements against the existence of Israel.

The Palestinian National Charter was the first concrete step that Arab leaders had taken toward the creation of an Arab state in what had been the British protectorate west of the Jordan River. Prior to the charter's being written and adopted, Arab and Palestinian leaders had made statements about how an Arab majority state should exist in the region, yet no official group had come together to explicitly organize for that eventuality. While the charter was not a constitution, in terms of outlining the specifics of a system of government, it did recognize the Palestine Liberation Organization (PLO) as the official representative for all Palestinians. For the first time, there was an organization charged with the responsibilities of leadership of the Palestinians and with creating a situation in which a viable Palestinian state could come into existence.

Defining Moment

Under the League of Nations, the United Kingdom was given mandates to rule various areas in the Middle East, with the goal of helping them to prepare for independence. Civil unrest in the British protectorate of Palestine made the British eager to withdraw from that area after the end of World War II. The territory east of the Jordan River gained independence in 1946, with strong divisions west of the river inhibiting the creation of a state in that region. The United Kingdom announced that it was withdrawing from that region by the middle of 1948, turning the situation over to the United Nations. In November 1947, the United Nations passed a resolution recommending the division of the area west of the Jordan River into two states, one Jewish and one Arab (Muslim). On the day the British withdrew their last troops from the protectorate of Palestine, Jewish leaders announced the creation of the state of Israel, with its borders to be those recommended by the United Nations. The Arab leaders rejected the division and refused to create a government for the area which was to become the Arab state of Palestine. Neighboring nations attacked Israel, which successfully responded, repelling the invading armies and expanding the territory of Israel by about a third. The other areas that were to have been part of the Palestinian state were taken by Egypt and Jordan. This war created the first wave of Palestinian refugees.

Twenty years after the creation of Israel, there was still no Palestinian state. The Six Day War, in 1967, gave Israel control of the entire area that had been proposed as a Palestinian state, as well as parts of Egypt, Jordan, and Syria. This also created a second wave of Palestinian refugees. Without any Arab government in control of what had been considered Palestinian territory, many believed that a radical step was needed to confront Israel. The 1968 Palestinian National Charter included revisions that gave justification for military operations against any Israeli unit or locale, as well as abandoning the 1947 proposal for a two-state solution. The PLO intensified its efforts to wear down the Israeli government by a constant series of small attacks or conflicts, including targeting civilians. The Palestinian National Charter not only gave the PLO formal status, at least vis-à-vis Arab states and their allies, but the ability to fight or use peaceful means to reach the goal of defeating Israel.

However, as stated in the charter, military actions were seen by the Palestinian leaders to be the only way in which Israel could be forced out of Palestine, and out of existence.

Author Biography

Ahmed Shukeiri (1908—1980) was born in the Ottoman Empire, where his father, an Ottoman legislator, represented part of what became the Palestine protectorate. Ahmed was well educated and went on to graduate from law school in Britain. As a respected lawyer, he advocated for independence, during the British rule. After World War II, he worked in various Arab causes, including as a delegate to the United Nations for Syria. As assistant Secretary General of the Arab League, in 1964, he was given the responsibility for organizing the Palestinians into a more united body. He convened the meeting which adopted the 1964 Charter, having written most of it himself. He was elected the Chairman of the PLO, and served until December 1967. Although he was not personally responsible for Israel's dramatic victory in the Six Day War, many Palestinian leaders blamed him for the loss. After his resignation he continued to support Palestinian and Arab causes, working as an author until his death.

HISTORICAL DOCUMENT: *Palestinian National Charter*

Article 1. Palestine is the homeland of the Arab Palestinian people; it is an indivisible part of the greater Arab homeland, and the Palestinian people are an integral part of the Arab nation.

Article 2: Palestine, with the boundaries it had during the British Mandate, is an indivisible territorial unit.

Article 3: The Palestinian Arab people possess the legal right to their homeland and to self-determination after the completion of the liberation of their country in accordance with their wishes and entirely of their own accord and will.

continued from page 149

Article 4: The Palestinian identity is a genuine, essential, and inherent characteristic; it is transmitted from fathers to children. The Zionist occupation and the dispersal of the Palestinian Arab people, through the disasters which befell them, do not make them lose their Palestinian identity and their membership in the Palestinian community, nor do they negate them.

Article 5: The Palestinians are those Arab nationals who, until 1947, normally resided in Palestine regardless of whether they were evicted from it or stayed there. Anyone born, after that date, of a Palestinian father—whether in Palestine or outside it—is also a Palestinian.

Article 6: The Jews who had normally resided in Palestine until the beginning of the Zionist invasion are considered Palestinians.

Article 7: There is a Palestinian community and that it has material, spiritual, and historical connection with Palestine are indisputable facts. It is a national duty to bring up individual Palestinians in an Arab revolutionary manner. All means of information and education must be adopted in order to acquaint the Palestinian with his country in the most profound manner, both spiritual and material, that is possible. He must be prepared for the armed struggle and ready to sacrifice his wealth and his life in order to win back his homeland and bring about its liberation.

Article 8: The phase in their history, through which the Palestinian people are now living, is that of national (watani) struggle for the liberation of Palestine. Thus the conflicts among the Palestinian national forces are secondary, and should be ended for the sake of the basic conflict that exists between the forces of Zionism and of colonialism on the one hand, and the Palestinian Arab people on the other. On this basis the Palestinian masses, regardless of whether they are residing in the national homeland or in Diaspora (mahajir) constitute—both their organizations and the individuals—one national front working for the retrieval of Palestine and its liberation through armed struggle.

Article 9: Armed struggle is the only way to liberate Palestine. This is the overall strategy, not merely a tactical phase. The Palestinian Arab people assert their absolute determination and firm resolution to continue their armed struggle and to work for an armed popular revolution for the liberation of their country and their return to it. They also assert their right to normal life in Palestine and to exercise their right to self-determination and sovereignty over it.

> *The Palestinian Arab people possess the legal right to their homeland and to self-determination after the completion of the liberation of their country in accordance with their wishes and entirely of their own accord and will.*

Article 10: Commando (Feday'ee) action constitutes the nucleus of the Palestinian popular liberation war. This requires its escalation, comprehensiveness, and the mobilization of all the Palestinian popular and educational efforts and their organization and involvement in the armed Palestinian revolution. It also requires the achieving of unity for the national (watani) struggle among the different groupings of the Palestinian people, and between the Palestinian people and the Arab masses, so as to secure the continuation of the revolution, its escalation, and victory.

Article 11: Palestinians have three mottoes: national unity, national (al-qawmiyya) mobilization, and liberation.

Article 12: The Palestinian Arab people believe in Arab unity. In order to contribute their share toward the attainment of that objective, however, they must, at the present stage of their struggle, safeguard their Palestinian identity and develop their consciousness of that identity, oppose any plan that may dissolve or impair it.

Article 13: Arab unity and the liberation of Palestine are two complementary goals, the attainment of either of which facilitates the attainment of the other. Thus, Arab unity leads to the liberation of Palestine, the liberation of Palestine leads to Arab unity; and the work toward the realization of one objective proceeds side by side with work toward the realization of the other.

Article 14: The destiny of the Arab Nation, and indeed Arab existence itself, depend upon the destiny of the Palestinian cause. From this interdependence springs the Arab nation's pursuit of, and striving for, the liberation of Palestine. The people of Palestine play the role of the vanguard in the realization of this sacred (qawmi) goal.

Article 15: The liberation of Palestine, from an Arab viewpoint, is a national (qawmi) duty and it attempts to repel the Zionist and imperialist aggression against the Arab homeland, and aims at the elimination of Zionism in Palestine. Absolute responsibility for this falls upon the Arab nation—peoples and governments-with the Arab people of Palestine in the vanguard. Accordingly, the Arab nation must mobilize all its military, human, moral, and spiritual capabilities to participate actively with the Palestinian people in the liberation of Palestine. It must, particularly, in the phase of the armed Palestinian revolution, offer and furnish the Palestinian people with all possible help, and material and human support, and make available to them the means and opportunities that will enable them to continue to carry out their leading role in the armed revolution, until they liberate their homeland.

Article 16: The liberation of Palestine, from a spiritual viewpoint, will provide the Holy Land with an atmosphere of safety and tranquillity, which in turn will safeguard the country's religious sanctuaries and guarantee freedom of worship and of visit to all, without discrimination of race, color, language, or religion. Accordingly, the Palestinian people look to all spiritual forces in the world for support.

continues on page 152

continued from page 151

Article 17: The liberation of Palestine, from a human point of view, will restore to the Palestinian individual his dignity, pride, and freedom. Accordingly, the Palestinian Arab people look forward to the support of all those who believe in the dignity of man and his freedom in the world.

Article 18: The liberation of Palestine, from an international point of view, is a defensive action necessitated by the demands of self-defense. Accordingly, the Palestinian people, desirous as they are of the friendship of all people, look to freedom-loving and peace-loving states for support in order to restore their legitimate rights in Palestine, to re-establish peace and security in the country, and to enable its people to exercise national sovereignty and freedom.

Article 19: The partition of Palestine in 1947, and the establishment of the state of Israel are entirely illegal, regardless of the passage of time, because they were contrary to the will of the Palestinian people and its natural right in their homeland, and were inconsistent with the principles embodied in the Charter of the United Nations, particularly the right to self-determination.

Article 20: The Balfour Declaration, the Palestine Mandate, and everything that has been based on them, are deemed null and void. Claims of historical or religious ties of Jews with Palestine are incompatible with the facts of history and the conception of what constitutes statehood. Judaism, being a religion, is not an independent nationality. Nor do Jews constitute a single nation with an identity of their own; they are citizens of the states to which they belong.

Article 21: The Arab Palestinian people, expressing themselves by armed Palestinian revolution, reject all solutions which are substitutes for the total liberation of Palestine and reject all proposals aimed at the liquidation of the Palestinian cause, or at its internationalization.

Article 22: Zionism is a political movement organically associated with international imperialism and antagonistic to all action for liberation and to progressive movements in the world. It is racist and fanatic in its nature, aggressive, expansionist and colonial in its aims, and fascist in its methods. Israel is the instrument of the Zionist movement, and the geographical base for world imperialism placed strategically in the midst of the Arab homeland to combat the hopes of the Arab nation for liberation, unity, and progress. Israel is a constant source of threat vis-à-vis peace in the Middle East and the whole world. Since liberation of Palestine will destroy the Zionist and imperialist presence and will contribute to the establishment of peace in the Middle East. That is why the Palestinian people look to the progressive and peaceful forces and urge them all, irrespective of their affiliations and beliefs, to offer the Palestinian people all aid and support in their just struggle for the liberation of their homeland.

Article 23: The demand of security and peace, as well as the demand of right and justice, require all states to consider Zionism an illegitimate movement, to outlaw its existence, and to ban its operations, in order that friendly relations among peoples may be preserved, and the loyalty of citizens to their respective homelands safeguarded.

Article 24: The Palestinian people believe in the principles of justice, freedom, sovereignty, self-determination, human dignity, and the right of peoples to exercise them.

Article 25: For the realization of the goals of this Charter and its principles, the Palestine Liberation Organization will perform its role in the liberation of Palestine.

Article 26: The Palestine Liberation Organization, the representative of the Palestinian revolutionary forces, is responsible for the Palestinian Arab peoples movement in its struggle—to retrieve its homeland, liberate and return to it and exercise the right to self-determination in it—in all military, political, and financial fields and also for whatever may be required by the Palestinian cause on the inter-Arab and international levels.

Article 27: The Palestine Liberation Organization shall cooperate with all Arab states, each according to its potentialities; and will adopt a neutral policy among them in light of the requirements of the battle of liberation; and on this basis does not interfere in the internal affairs of any Arab state.

Article 28: The Palestinian Arab people assert the genuineness and independence of their national revolution and reject all forms of intervention, trusteeship, and subordination.

Article 29: The Palestinian people possess the fundamental and genuine legal right to liberate and retrieve their homeland. The Palestinian people determine their attitude toward all states and forces on the basis of the stands they adopt vis-à-vis the Palestinian revolution to fulfill the aims of the Palestinian people.

Article 30: Fighters and carriers of arms in the war of liberation are the nucleus of the popular army which will be the protective force for the gains of the Palestinian Arab people.

Article 31: This Organization shall have a flag, an oath of allegiance, and an anthem. All this shall be decided upon in accordance with a special law.

Article 32: A law, known as the Basic Statute of the Palestine Liberation Organization, shall be annexed to this Covenant. It will lay down the manner in which the Organization, and its organs and institutions, shall be constituted, the respective competence of each; and the requirements of its obligation under the Charter.

Article 33: This Charter shall not be amended save by [vote of] a majority of two-thirds of the total membership of the National Council of the Palestine Liberation Organization [taken] at a special session convened for that purpose.

> **GLOSSARY**
>
> **commando action:** small-scale raids, some of which might be called terrorist acts, intended to cause harm to Israelis or Israeli targets, without seeking to retain control of the area attacked
>
> **Zionism:** the political movement during the late nineteenth and early twentieth centuries that advocated for the creation of a Jewish homeland in Palestine; once Israel was created, it was seen as the push for its full development

Document Analysis

The Arab League called together nearly four hundred representatives of the Palestinian people, in 1964, to begin the process of developing a Palestinian state. Knowing that this was a process, they included in their charter the provision that it could be amended. In 1968, the National Council of the PLO amended the original charter, adopting several more aggressive provisions in the struggle against Israel. The focus of this charter was the assertion that Israel had no right to exist, since all the territory west of the Jordan River was part of the yet to be formed Palestinian state. Israel was "illegal," from the Palestinian point of view. As such, "armed struggle" was the manner by which Palestine could be freed, since it was clear Israel was not going to voluntarily disband. All Arabs should be unified, according to the charter, especially in support of the Palestinian cause. Once Palestine was liberated, then Palestinians would work with other Arabs in creating a more unified Middle East. However, until that time the PLO would focus on opposing all who supported Israel and work toward gaining justice and freedom for the Palestinian people through any means which might lead to the collapse of Israel.

The Palestinian National Charter defined a Palestinian quite broadly, as any Arab who "normally" lived in Palestine, or was descended from a person who had lived in the territory as of 1947. (Jews who lived in Palestine prior to the beginnings of the Zionist movement, in the 1890s, were also defined as Palestinians.) These were the individuals to whom the land belonged, and who should be allowed to create a state that included all the territory of the British mandate west of the Jordan River. The gathering that adopted this document believed that these people had a "material, spiritual, and historical connection" with the land, and each with one another. Thus, the Diaspora created by the imposition of the state of Israel upon this territory, according to the Palestinian National Council, needed to be tempered by educating the children as Palestinians not as citizens of wherever the family resided.

The charter was divided in terms of the view of the Palestinian leadership that it presented to the world. The main perception which was projected was one regarding the strong support which it gave to using violence to obtain the goal of a Palestinian state. This was clearly stated in Articles 7, 9, 10, 15, 21, 26, 29, and 30. The "revolutionary force," or the PLO's operational wing, was to bring a "war of liberation" to Israel. Stating that "commando action constitutes the nucleus of the Palestinian popular liberation war," the charter authorized virtually any type of armed action against Israel and its supporters. As noted, some of these articles were added in the 1968 version and others were strengthened. Through this process, the final vision became

The founder of the PLO, Ahmad Shukeiri.

that of an all-or-nothing struggle. Either Israel was destroyed, or the Palestinian cause would fail.

At the same time that the charter supports strong military actions, it also tries to communicate the idea that the values of the Western democratic tradition are a part of the Palestinian worldview. Thus, the charter contains assurances that Palestinians believe in "justice, freedom, sovereignty, human dignity, and the right of peoples to exercise them." Variations of this statement were included in several articles of the charter. To many who read the charter, these ideals can seem overshadowed by the advocacy of violent action against Israel. The articles reflecting a firm resolve for the use of violent methods to achieve the goal of a Palestinian state tend to outweigh the promised "tranquility" that a Palestinian state would be expected bring.

Many articles (i.e. 3, 4, 8, 15, 19, 20, 22, and 23) illustrate a worldview holding that none of the arguments supporting the existence of Israel, or even Israel itself, are valid. Not just Palestinians, but the entire global community should understand, according to the charter, that Zionism is "an illegitimate movement." The division of the territory into two states, whether as the result of United Nations' actions, or by any other means, is deemed unacceptable, or illegal, according to the charter. All of this reflects the goal of the destruction of Israel and the institution of the state of Palestine in all the territory that the United Kingdom had given to the United Nations in 1948, when the state of Israel had been declared to exist. According to the charter, there is no room in the Middle East for the state of Israel.

In line with the thought of the 1960s, Arab unity plays a strong role within the charter. It serves a dual purpose. First, it is one justification for broader Arab support of the Palestinian cause and movement. If the broader Arab community accepts the assertion that "Arab existence itself" is possible only if Israel is destroyed and the new Arab state of Palestine replaces it, then a strong argument is created for all Arab states to contribute to the Palestinian cause. The Palestinians as the vanguard in the struggle against hostile forces are depicted as the first wave in the reunification of all Arabs, as well. Even though the military forces of the major Arab nations had recently been embarrassed in a war with Israel, the Palestinian charter advocates for putting the combined military and economic forces of the Arab community at the disposal of the leaders and allies of the Palestinian cause. The long-term pledge by the Palestinian leadership is that they will support a future pan-Arab order.

As might be expected in a charter of this kind, the focus of the Palestinian National Charter was the creation of a Palestinian state. However, in this case the Palestinians believed that the only way the state of Palestine could be created would be if Israel was totally destroyed. The "national struggle" outlined in this charter does not allow for a compromise on this score. Violent revolution was the path, the only path, to liberation, according to the Palestine National Council and its charter.

Essential Themes

When the Palestinian leaders watched all the territory they claimed come under Israeli control, they responded with a strong statement of opposition. They outlined who, in their eyes, had a legitimate claim to the territory that had been the "British Mandate," and then proclaimed not only the right for the Palestinian people to use force against Israel, but indicated that it was their duty. "Armed struggle" would allow Palestine to come to life, or at least the Palestinian leaders hoped this would be the case. There was a strong global condemnation of the emphasis upon violence, as most nations had hoped that a negotiated settlement might have been possible. However, in the 1960s this was not considered by the Palestinians. With the statement that Israel was an illegal entity, Israeli leaders were not ready for negotiations either. Since reasonable people understood that Israel was not going to disappear, the Palestinian stance was not viable in the long-term.

When secret negotiations between the PLO and Israel became public negotiations in the early 1990s, the PLO had to renounce some or all of several articles in this charter. While PLO leaders have given written statements assuring this to be the case, it was unclear to some if the official text of the charter was ever changed according to the rule outlined in Article 33. However, the 1994 agreement between the PLO and Israel, leading to the creation of the Palestinian National Authority, was based in part upon the PLO renouncing the most militant articles of the charter. Although the Oslo Accords, as the 1994 agreement is known, have allowed Israel and the Palestinian Authority to cooperate, the issues of the borders outlined in the charter are far from resolved. There are also groups, such as Hamas, which have maintained a more militant stance, and have continued violent acts toward Israel. However, the PLO, in creating the Palestinian Authority and allowing it to cooperate with Israel, has moved the Palestinian cause forward by gaining control of some of the territory promised in the 1947 United Nations' resolution. Although the 1994 agreement proved that significant progress toward coexistence could be made, events since then have demonstrated that there is still a long way to go before any lasting solution is reached.

—Donald A Watt

Bibliography and Additional Reading

Baracskay, Daniel. *The Palestine Liberation Organization: Terrorism and Prospects for Peace in the Holy Land.* (Praeger Security International) Santa Barbara CA: Praeger, 2011. Print.

Jamal, Amal. *The Palestinian National Movement.* Bloomington IN: Indiana University Press, 2005. Print.

Palestine Ministry of Information. "The Palestinian Charter." *Palestine Affairs Council.* Houston: Palestine American Council, 2018. Web. 7 March 2018.

Shukeiry, Ahmed. "Palestine Liberation Organization: The Original Palestine National Charter (1964)." Jewish Virtual Library. Washington: American-Israeli Cooperative Enterprise, 2018. Web. 7 March 2018.

UCC Palestine Solidarity Campaign. "Ahmad Shukairi." *Palestine: Information with Provenance (PIWP database).* Cork IE: UCC Palestine Solidarity Campaign, 2018. Web. 7 March 2018.

Islam and Universal Peace

Date: 1977
Author: Sayyid Qutb
Genre: Book; religious tract

Summary Overview

In the document examined here, the influential Egyptian author and activist Sayyid Qutb develops his thoughts on jihad, or struggle in defense of Islam. After spending some time in the United States and Europe, Sayyid Qutb returned to his home nation of Egypt. He eventually joined the Muslim Brotherhood, which took an oppositional approach to the Egyptian governments before and after the 1952 Egyptian Revolution. He was jailed multiple times for his activism and executed in 1966. An avid writer, much of his work was edited and published posthumously by his brother Muhammad Qutb. Included within these posthumous works is the book *Islam and Universal Peace*, from which this excerpt is taken. In this document, which has been translated from the original Arabic, Qutb details his understanding of jihad. Qutb's conceptualization of jihad here and elsewhere influenced many jihadis, including those who led the attacks on September 11, 2001, Ayman al-Zawahiri and Osama bin Laden.

Defining Moment

Sayyid Qutb and his writing have played an influential role in the history of the Muslim Brotherhood and in the strain of Islamic thought that derives its name from his, Qutbism.

The Society of the Muslim Brotherhood was founded by Hassan al-Banna in Egypt in the year 1928. The Brotherhood did—and still does—promulgate Islam through grassroot politics and charity work. It spread from Egypt across the Sunni world and influenced other groups such as Hamas. Today the Brotherhood officially advertises itself as peaceful and denounces violence, but members throughout its history have employed violence to further the group's agenda. It was officially banned in Egypt in the 1930s after railing against British imperial rule. It continued to thrive, however, in opposition to Egypt's Muhammad Ali Dynasty, which had become a puppet regime for Great Britain before and after the Second World War. The Brotherhood initially supported the 1952 Egyptian Revolution. Sayyid Qutb, the author of this document and a major player in the Brotherhood, carried on a close relationship with Gamal Abdel Nasser, Egypt's reformist president. Upon realizing the extent to which Nasser was secularizing Egypt, the Brotherhood dropped its support and took up an oppositional role. Qutb spent the majority of his final decade jailed before his execution in 1966. However, his writing survived him and formed the foundations for Qutbism.

Following Sayyid's execution, his younger brother Muhammad Qutb moved from Egypt to Saudi Arabia where he helped spread Sayyid's writing and thinking. Ayman al-Zawahiri was Muhammad Qutb's student, and through Muhammad Qutb, al-Zawahiri became well acquainted with Sayyid Qutb's writing. Al-Zawahiri, in turn, mentored Osama bin Laden, and since bin Laden's death, he has led

Sayyid Qutb.

[Source: Sayyid Qutb, *Islam and Universal Peace*. Oak Brook, IL: American Trust Publishing, 1977; p. 72.]

al-Qaeda. Both al-Zawahiri and bin Laden have explicitly expressed their adherence to Qutbism. Among Qutbism's main tenets is the belief that the world is divided between those pursuing Islam and those that have sunken into Jahiliyya, or godlessness/ignorance. The attraction of Jahiliyya, according to Qutbism, is strong, and Muslims must, therefore, take an aggressive approach in eliminating it, hence jihad, or holy war. On September 11, 2001, Osama bin Laden coordinated the attacks against the twin towers and the pentagon, vaulting these men and their beliefs into the American consciousness. After almost two decades of war since, al-Qaeda and Qutbism live on.

Author Biography

Sayyid Qutb became an influential political and religious thinker and major player in Egypt's Muslim Brotherhood. Born in Musha, a village in Upper Egypt, on October 9, 1906, Qutb moved to Cairo in his twenties to study literature. After the Second World War, he spent two years in the United States and some time traveling around Europe. Upon his return, he railed against the Western culture he witnessed firsthand. He joined the Muslim Brotherhood and rose to the top echelons of the organization. He utilized his education and background in literature to edit the group's weekly publication *Al-Ikhwan al-Muslimin* and take charge of the group's marketing and propaganda efforts. He wrote profusely. When Gamal Abdel Nasser and his allies overthrew Egypt's government in 1952, the Brotherhood initially supported their efforts. The Brotherhood viewed Egypt's former government as too influenced by Western power, and Qutb and Nasser enjoyed a close, personal relationship. The relationship soon soured, however, as the Brotherhood realized Nasser's incipient government was shaping up to be far more secular than they had expected. In 1954, Qutb and other members were jailed for plotting Nasser's assassination. He continued to write from jail and was released in 1964. His most influential works are *Milestones* and his thirty-volume commentary on the Quran, *In the Shade of the Quran*. Less than a year after his release, he was arrested again. On August 26, 1966, he was hanged by Nasser's government.

HISTORICAL DOCUMENT: From *Islam and Universal Peace*

Muslims are first commanded to defend their brothers against deception and materialism. Second, they are ordered to defend the liberty of thought and to invite others to their belief. To this end they are commanded to eliminate any oppressive force that would suppress the propagation of Islam. Third, they are to establish the sovereignty of God on earth and to repel any aggression against it. Those who claim the right to legislate for people and exclude God's legislation are aggressors and are liable to divine punishment. Fourth, Muslims are required to establish justice in the world and to allow all peoples to enjoy this justice as individuals, as members of a society, as citizens of a nation and as members of the international community. Thus, Muslims are commanded to fight against injustice wherever it may be; whether it be individual, social, national or international.

The struggle to establish the sovereignty of God on earth is called jihad. Jihad is achieved by giving men the chance to emancipate themselves from their oppressors and to restore their human rights granted by God to all mankind.

"Those who believe fight in the Cause of God, and those who reject faith fight in the cause of Evil..." (Q[uran] IV 76)

The fundamental Islamic principles are revolutionary. It was a revolution against the deification of men, against injustice, and against political, economic, racial, and religious prejudice.

Naturally, the Islamic revolution met with individual, class, and state resistance. But the Islamic revolution overcame all opposition. It was inevitable that Muslims would declare jihad. They had to save humanity—individuals and societies—from prevailing injustices. They had to fight in order to establish peace, not only among states, but within these states as well. Islamic philosophy aims at dignifying man. Slavery under any guise, therefore, is unacceptable and people living under governments which deprive them of their human rights are entitled to Muslims' help to attain justice and check oppression.

Jihad, then is a means to achieve a universal change by establishing peace of conscience, domestic peace, national peace and international peace. This universal peace cannot endure unless it is founded on universal justice.

Jihad, then is a means to achieve a universal change by establishing peace of conscience, domestic peace, national peace and international peace. This universal peace cannot endure unless it is founded on universal justice.

Document Themes and Analysis

This document is an excerpt from *Islam and Universal Peace*, a book by Sayyid Qutb published posthumously by his brother Muhammad Qutb. In it, Sayyid Qutb develops his thinking on jihad, or holy war. Qutb's understanding of Islam, known later as Qutbism, influenced jihadis such as Ayman Al-Zawahiri and Osama bin Laden. This excerpt utilizes the themes of revolution and justice to construct its conceptualization of jihad.

Before even mentioning the word revolution or its cognates, Qutb assumes a revolutionary outlook. The excerpt begins by enumerating what Muslims must do to save humanity and establish world peace. Third on the list is: "[Muslims] are to establish the sovereignty of God on earth and to repel any aggression against it." Such a step would constitute a vast reworking of the globe, of which Qutb himself is well aware. He later discusses revolution more directly: "The fundamental Islamic principles are revolutionary. It was a revolution against the deification of men, against injustice, and against political, economic, racial, and religious prejudice." Qutb connects his agenda with Islam's origins. The religion which Muhammad brought to life in the seventh century initiated a revolution, one that spread rapidly from Mecca across the Middle East and beyond. Qutb is hoping to reignite the revolution thirteen centuries later. He describes jihad in a particularly revolutionary way: "Jihad, then is a means to achieve a universal change by establishing peace of conscience, domestic peace, national peace and international peace." To Qutb, jihad is not an end unto itself but a means of achieving stable peace.

Qutb understands jihad to operate upon a foundation of justice. He evokes justice throughout the excerpt. In the first paragraph, he ordains that "Muslims are required to establish justice in the world and to allow all peoples to enjoy this justice as individuals, as members of a society, as citizens of a nation and as members of the international community." He continues, outlining the inverse: "Thus, Muslims are commanded to fight against injustice wherever it may be; whether it be individual, social, national or international." In this way, jihad is glossed as necessary and just. Later he contrasts justice with slavery and oppression: "Slavery under any guise, therefore, is unacceptable and people living under governments which deprive them of their human rights are entitled to Muslims' help to attain justice and check oppression." Finally, the universal peace which jihad intends to set up requires justice: "This universal peace cannot endure unless it is founded on universal justice." To outsiders and critics, jihad seems inherently cruel and unjust, but to Qutb and his adherents, jihad requires justice, and justice requires jihad.

—Anthony Vivian

Bibliography and Additional Reading

Bergensen, Albert J., ed. *The Sayyid Qutb Reader: Selected Writings on Politics, Religion, and Society*. London: Routledge, 2008. Print.

Qutb, Muhammad. *Islam: The Misunderstood Religion*. Riyadh, Saudi Arabia: International Islamic Publishing House, 1991. Print.

Qutb, Sayyid. *Milestones*. New York: Islamic Book Service, 2006. Print.

Qutb, Sayyid. *Islam and Universal Peace*. Oak Brook, IL: American Trust Publishing, 1977. Print.

Yusuf, Badmas 'Lanre. *Sayyid Qutb: A Study of his Tafsir*. Selangor, Malaysia: Islamic Book Trust, 2009. Print.

■ *Islam: The Misunderstood Religion*

Date: 1991
Author: Muhammad Qutb
Genre: Book; religious tract

Summary Overview

Sayyid and Muhammad Qutb are the founders of the conceptualization of Islam that now bears their name, Qutbism. Among other tenets, Qutbism advocates for members to actively spread Islam. Their calls for jihad, or holy war, have inspired some of the world's most famous jihadis, including Ayman al-Zawahiri and Osama bin Laden. Sayyid Qutb, Muhammad's older brother, was an active member of the Muslim Brotherhood in Egypt. He initiated the movement with his profuse writing and was executed by the Egyptian government in 1966. Muhammad carried on his brother's legacy, publishing much of his unpublished works posthumously and penning works of his own. This document is an excerpt from Muhammad Qutb's 1991 book *Islam: The Misunderstood Religion*. In this excerpt, Qutb connects his contemporary world with the one on the eve of Islam's birth in the seventh century. This allows him to construct his own revolutionary agenda in the tradition of Islam's origins.

Defining Moment

The story of Qutbism begins with the Qutb brothers, Sayyid and Muhammad. Born in Egypt, they became active members of the Muslim Brotherhood. Through his writing, Sayyid Qutb developed the doctrine that became known as Qutbism. This thread of Islam posits that the world is split between Islam and Jahiliyya, which translates to "godlessness" or "ignorance." Qutbism calls upon Muslims to take an active role in defeating Jahiliyya and spreading Islam. It is only then, the doctrine holds, that world peace can be obtained. However, the means to this peace was jihad, or holy war. Although the Muslim Brotherhood, the Qutb brothers included, initially welcomed the 1952 Egyptian Revolution, they soon returned to their antagonistic role when the new government became more secular than the Brotherhood had hoped. Sayyid and Muhammad Qutb were arrested along with other members of the Muslim Brotherhood. Muhammad and others escaped, but Sayyid Qutb was executed in 1966.

Qutbism, still in its infancy, travelled from Egypt to Saudi Arabia with Muhammad Qutb. He edited and published much of his late brother's unreleased writings. He delineated the contours of his brother's thinking, publishing books of his own and working as a university professor. He served as the bridge between his brother's thinking and the most prominent adherents of Qutbism, Ayman al-Zawahiri and Osama bin Laden. Qutbism should be distinguished from Wahhabism, another conservative thread of Sunni Islam proliferating particularly in Saudi Arabia. The attacks on September 11, 2001 marked a major victory in the eyes of bin Laden and al-Zawahiri. The United States government's 9/11 commission cited Qutbism as foundational to the thinking of the attackers.

Author Biography

Muhammad Qutb was born in 1919 in the Egyptian village of Musha. He lived in Egypt for his first four-plus decades, where he became affiliated with the Muslim Brotherhood. He, his older brother Sayyid, and other members of the Brotherhood were arrested in 1965 by the Egyptian government. His brother, a prominent Islamic writer, was hanged on August 29, 1966. Muhammad Qutb and other members of the Brotherhood escaped the same fate and emigrated to Saudi Arabia. There, Qutb published many of his brother's works and otherwise spread his brother's thinking. He worked as a university professor and wrote books of his own. Among his more influential works is *Islam: The Misunderstood Religion*, from which this document is excerpted. Several of his students went on to become high profile terrorists, including Ayman al-Zawahiri, the current leader of al-Qaeda and mentor of Osama bin Laden. Qutb died in Mecca on April 4, 2014.

HISTORICAL DOCUMENT: From *Islam: The Misunderstood Religion*

Let none dare say that the revival of Islam is an impossible and hopeless undertaking, as the human race has in the past proved beyond any doubt that it is quite capable of rising above a purely animal level. And surely what once was possible in the past must still be possible in the present, for mankind has temperamentally not undergone any change ever since. The world of humanity had sunk then, as now, to quite as low level and was as much taken up with sensual pleasure as it at present seems to be. There is no difference between its present and past save the outwardly visible forms of voluptuousness or the names of the luxuries indulged in. Ancient Rome was no less rotten morally than its modern counterparts—Paris, London, and the cities of America. Similarly, in ancient Persia sexual anarchy was as rank as is at present associated with the communist countries. It was in this historical perspective that Islam was revealed to the world. It brought about a complete change, lifted mankind from the abyss of moral degradation, gave human life a lofty purpose, dynamism, movement, and infused into it a spirit to strive hard in the way of truth and goodness. Humanity under Islam flourished, prospered and there was set afoot a dynamic intellectual and spiritual movement that encompassed the East as well as the West. No forces of evil and mischief dared check the onward march of Islam with the result that the whole outside look of human life was radically transformed. Thus the world of Islam became the headspring of light, excellence and progress in the world for a long time to come. During this long period of its dominance never did the Islamic world find itself lagging behind materially, intellectually or spiritually for the simple reason that it did not encourage moral corruption, sexual anarchy or Godlessness. Its followers were looked upon as symbols of goodness and excellence in all sphere of human activity till they ceased to reflect in their lives the noble and exalted ideal of Islam and became mere slaves to their whims and animal desires.

It was then that all their glory and power came to an end in accordance with the immutable law of God.

The modern Islamic movement that is still gathering force derives its strength from the past and makes use of all the modern available resources with its gaze fixed on the future. It has great potentialities and as such has a bright future ahead, for it is fully capable of performing that great miracle which has once been already effected by Islam making man look higher and beyond animal pleasures with his feet planted firmly on the earth and with his gaze fixed beyond the heavens.

> *Thus the world of Islam became the headspring of light, excellence and progress in the world for a long time to come.*

[Source: Muhammad Qutb, *Islam: The Misunderstood Religion*. Riyadh, Saudi Arabia: International Islamic Publishing House, 1991; pp. 18–19.]

Document Themes and Analysis

Muhammad Qutb refined and spread his brother Sayyid Qutb's understanding of Islam. The resultant doctrine, Qutbism, has had and continues to have a strong influence. In this excerpt from Muhammad Qutb's *Islam: The Misunderstood Religion*, which has been translated from the original Arabic, Qutb displays his conceptualization of Islam. To do so, he develops the themes of continuity with the past and the exceptionalism of Islam.

In this book as well as in other writings, Muhammad Qutb calls for a global revolution in the name of Islam. He understands the daunting nature of this agenda but advocates for its feasibility by comparing it to Islam's original, rapid spread: "And surely what once was possible in the past must still be possible in the present, for mankind has temperamentally not undergone any change ever since." Part of this connection rests upon Qutb's understanding of the relationship between the world pre-Islam and his contemporary world: "The world of humanity had sunk then, as now, to quite as low level and was as much taken up with sensual pleasure as it at present seems to be." Qutb sees a vacuum that called for Islam's initial inception, and he understands the times in which he lives to exhibit a similar vacuum. Not only is the circumstance the same to Qutb, but he also sees Islam's origin story as powering the revolution he seeks. "The modern Islamic movement that is still gathering force derives its strength from the past and makes use of all the modern available resources with its gaze fixed on the future." Islam's founding, therefore, stands as a positive example of what is possible and directly fuels his agenda.

Since Qutb draws such a close connection between the initial rise of Islam and the revolution for which he calls, we can look to his description of the early days of Islam to understand what he wants and expects from an Islamic revival. Of Islam's origins he says: "It brought about a complete change, lifted mankind from the abyss of moral degradation, gave human life a lofty purpose, dynamism, movement, and infused into it a spirit to strive hard in the way of truth and goodness. Humanity under Islam flourished, prospered and there was set afoot a dynamic intellectual and spiritual movement that encompassed the East as well as the West." In opposition to some the caricatures of Islamic society, Qutb describes it as a society thriving on intellectuality and morality. He continues, "Thus the world of Islam became the headspring of light, excellence and progress in the world for a long time to come. During this long period of its dominance never did the Islamic world find itself lagging behind materially, intellectually or spiritually for the simple reason that it did not encourage moral corruption, sexual anarchy or Godlessness." The society that he describes is one which his critics and opponents might be surprised by how much it coincides with their understanding of a favorable society.

It is more the means that Muhammad Qutb and his brother advocate for realizing this ideal society than the description of the society itself that gives Qutbism's critics pause.

—Anthony Vivian

Bibliography and Additional Reading

Bergensen, Albert J., ed. *The Sayyid Qutb Reader: Selected Writings on Politics, Religion, and Society*. London: Routledge, 2008. Print.

Qutb, Muhammad. *Islam: The Misunderstood Religion*. Riyadh, Saudi Arabia: International Islamic Publishing House, 1991. Print.

Qutb, Sayyid. *Milestones*. New York: Islamic Book Service, 2006. Print.

Qutb, Sayyid. *Islam and Universal Peace*. Oak Brook, IL: American Trust Publishing, 1977. Print.

Yusuf, Badmas 'Lanre. *Sayyid Qutb: A Study of his Tafsir*. Selangor, Malaysia: Islamic Book Trust, 2009. Print.

Saudi Arabia: A Country Study

Date: December 1, 1993
Author: Helen Chapin Metz
Genre: Book

Summary Overview

This excerpt from a 1990s study of Saudi Arabia offers an American perspective on the alliance between the House of Saud and Wahhabism. In 1744, the Saud Family, also known as the House of Saud, made an alliance with the religious leader Muhammad ibn Abd al-Wahhab. The latter had constructed a very strict interpretation of Islam. Central to this interpretation was the elimination of false idolatry, which ibn Abd al-Wahhab saw as rampant among Muslims. Wahhabis, also known as Muwahhids (which translates to "unitarians"), often take an offensive approach to spreading their strict interpretation of Islam. In fact, shortly after the alliance of 1744, the newly formed First Saudi State began expanding across the Arabian Peninsula. This expansion came with violence and destruction, as the Saudis were keen to destroy sacred shrines and items that they interpreted as false idols in accordance with ibn Abd al-Wahhab's teachings. The political-religious alliance between the House of Saud and ibn Abd al-Wahhab's interpretation of Islam survived the religious leader's life. Much of the Arabian Peninsula has been under Saudi rule off and on since 1744. The strict doctrine of Wahhabism still influences the Kingdom of Saudi Arabia's society and culture today.

Defining Moment

The Arabian Peninsula is the birthplace of not only Islam but also Wahhabism and the House of Saud. A 1744 treaty forged an alliance between Wahhabism and the House of Saud that has proved influential to this day on the Peninsula and beyond.

Muhammad's journey in 622 to Medina constitutes the first event of the Islamic calendar. In the decades that followed the new religion over the Arabian Peninsula and across large swath of Asia, Africa, and Europe. Shortly after Muhammad's death, a conflict over succession led to the Shia-Sunni split, which still divides Muslims today. Cycles of living side by side peacefully and intermittent violent conflicts have defined the two groups' long coexistence.

In the eighteenth century, Muhammad ibn Abd al-Wahhab ended a period of peace between the groups living on the Arabian Peninsula.

Ibn Abd al-Wahhab was an Islamic scholar who developed a unitarian message. He advocated an orthodox "pure" Sunni Islam, with strict adherence to Sharia Law. Various Shia and Sunni Muslims had incorporated the reverence of shrines and/or holy objects into their religious practices. Ibn Abd al-Wahhab considered this to be false idolatry and railed vehemently against it. He encouraged his followers to take an aggressive approach in stamping out this practice, with Shia Muslims becoming a common target. His understanding of Islam came to be called Wahhabism and his followers Wahhabis, although many of them prefer the label Muwahhid, or unitarian.

The Saud family traces its lineage back to figures in the fifteenth century; however, their political relevance rose prominently in the eighteenth century from their alliance with ibn Abd al-Wahhab. In 1744, Muhammad ibn Saud, the leader of the Saud family at the time, struck an alliance with ibn Abd al-Wahhab. The former gave the latter a political platform from which to spread his belief-system, and the latter gave the former and his family a distinct, and ultimately influential, religious message. The alliance marked the beginning of the First Saudi State, or Emirate of Diriyah, which immediately began to expand across the Arabian Peninsula. The First Saudi State fell to the Ottomans in 1818. A Second Saudi State, also known as Emirate of Najd, rose up in its wake but fell, in turn, in 1891.

The Third Saudi State, or Kingdom of Saudi Arabia, formed in the early twentieth century. Abdulaziz Ibn Saud unified much of the Arabian Peninsula under his leadership, and the Kingdom of Saudi Arabia officially came into being in 1932.

This document was composed in the 1990s as an official *Country Study Handbook* for the Library of Congress. It looks at the alliance of ibn Abd al-Wahhab and the House of Saud from an American perspective.

Author Biography

Helen Chapin Metz was born on April 13, 1928. Graduating from Vassar College and the American University of Beirut, Metz went on to a successful career at the Library of Congress' Federal Research Division. She edited fifteen different Country Study Handbooks, including one for Saudi Arabia, from which this document is excerpted. She passed away on May 13, 2011.

HISTORICAL DOCUMENT: From *Saudi Arabia: A Country Study*

The Saud Family and Wahhabi Islam, 1500–1818

The Al Saud originated in Ad Diriyah, in the center of Najd, close to the modern capital of Riyadh. Around 1500 ancestors of Saud ibn Muhammad took over some date groves, one of the few forms of agriculture the region could support, and settled there. Over time the area developed into a small town, and the clan that would become the Al Saud came to be recognized as its leaders.

The rise of Al Saud is closely linked with Muhammad ibn Abd al Wahhab (died 1792), a Muslim scholar whose ideas form the basis of the Wahhabi movement. He grew up in Uyaynah, an oasis in southern Najd, where he studied with his grandfather Hanbali Islamic law, one of the strictest Muslim legal schools. While still a young man, he left Uyaynah to study with other teachers, the usual way to pursue higher education in the Islamic world. He studied in Medina and then went to Iraq and to Iran.

To understand the significance of Muhammad ibn Abd al Wahhab's ideas, they must be considered in the context of Islamic practice. There was a difference between the established rituals clearly defined in religious texts that all Muslims perform and popular Islam. The latter refers to local practice that is not universal.

The Shia practice of visiting shrines is an example of a popular practice. The Shia continued to revere the Imams even after their death and so visited their graves to ask favors of the Imams buried there. Over time, Shia scholars rationalized the practice and it became established.

Some of the Arabian tribes came to attribute the same sort of power that the Shia recognized in the tomb of an Imam to natural objects such as trees and rocks. Such beliefs were particularly disturbing to Muhammad ibn Abd al Wahhab. In the late 1730s he returned to the Najdi town of Huraymila and began to write and preach against both Shia and local popular practices. He focused on the Muslim principle that there is only one God, and that God does not share his power with anyone—not Imams, and certainly not trees or rocks. From this unitarian principle, his students began to refer to themselves as muwahhidun (unitarians). Their detractors referred to them as "Wahhabis"—or "followers of Muhammad ibn Abd al Wahhab," which had a pejorative connotation.

The idea of a unitary god was not new. Muhammad ibn Abd al Wahhab, however, attached political importance to it. He directed his attack against the Shia. He also sought out local leaders, trying to convince them that this was an Islamic issue. He expanded his message to include strict adherence to the principles of Islamic law. He referred to himself as a "reformer" and looked for a political figure who might give his ideas a wider audience.

> *If the Al Saud had remained in Najd, the world would have paid them scant attention. But capturing the Hijaz brought the Al Saud empire into conflict with the rest of the Islamic world.*

Lacking political support in Huraymila, Muhammad ibn Abd al Wahhab returned to Uyaynah where he won over some local leaders. Uyaynah, however, was close to Al Hufuf, one of the Twelve Shia centers in eastern Arabia, and its leaders were understandably alarmed at the anti-Shia tone of the Wahhabi message. Partly as a result of their influence, Muhammad ibn Abd al Wahhab was obliged to leave Uyaynah, and headed for Ad Diriyah. He had earlier made contact with Muhammad ibn Saud, the leader in Ad Diriyah at the time, and two of Muhammad's brothers had accompanied him when he destroyed tomb shrines around Uyaynah.

Accordingly, when Muhammad ibn Abd al Wahhab arrived in Ad Diriyah, the Al Saud was ready to support him. In 1744 Muhammad ibn Saud and Muhammad ibn Abd al Wahhab swore a traditional Muslim oath in which they promised to work together to establish a state run according to Islamic principles. Until that time the Al Saud had been accepted as conventional tribal leaders whose rule was based on longstanding but vaguely defined authority.

continues on page 168

continued from page 167

Muhammad ibn Abd al Wahhab offered the Al Saud a clearly defined religious mission to which to contribute their leadership and upon which they might base their political authority. This sense of religious purpose remained evident in the political ideology of Saudi Arabia in the 1990s.

Muhammad ibn Saud began by leading armies into Najdi towns and villages to eradicate various popular and Shia practices. The movement helped to rally the towns and tribes of Najd to the Al Saud-Wahhabi standard. By 1765 Muhammad ibn Saud's forces had established Wahhabism—and with it the Al Saud political authority—over most of Najd.

After Muhammad ibn Saud died in 1765, his son, Abd al Aziz, continued the Wahhabi advance. In 1801 the Al Saud-Wahhabi armies attacked and sacked Karbala, the Shia shrine in eastern Iraq that commemorates the death of Husayn. In 1803 they moved to take control of Sunni towns in the Hijaz. Although the Wahhabis spared Mecca and Medina the destruction they visited upon Karbala, they destroyed monuments and grave markers that were being used for prayer to Muslim saints and for votive rituals, which the Wahhabis consider acts of polytheism. In destroying the objects that were the focus of these rituals, the Wahhabis sought to imitate Muhammad's destruction of pagan idols when he reentered Mecca in 628.

If the Al Saud had remained in Najd, the world would have paid them scant attention. But capturing the Hijaz brought the Al Saud empire into conflict with the rest of the Islamic world. The popular and Shia practices to which the Wahhabis objected were important to other Muslims, the majority of whom were alarmed that shrines were destroyed and access to the holy cities restricted.

Moreover, rule over the Hijaz was an important symbol. The Ottoman Turks, the most important political force in the Islamic world at the time, refused to concede rule over the Hijaz to local leaders. At the beginning of the nineteenth century, the Ottomans were not in a position to recover the Hijaz, because the empire had been in decline for more than two centuries, and its forces were weak and overextended. Accordingly, the Ottomans delegated the recapture of the Hijaz to their most ambitious client, Muhammad Ali, the semi-independent commander of their garrison in Egypt. Muhammad Ali, in turn, handed the job to his son Tursun, who led a force to the Hijaz in 1816; Muhammad Ali later joined his son to command the force in person.

Meanwhile, Muhammad ibn Abd al Wahhab had died in 1792, and Abd al Aziz died shortly before the capture of Mecca. The movement had continued, however, to recognize the leadership of the Al Saud and so followed Abd al Aziz's son, Saud, until 1814; after Saud died in 1814, his son, Abd Allah, ruled. Accordingly, it was Abd Allah ibn Saud ibn Abd al Aziz who faced the invading Egyptian army.

Tursun's forces took Mecca and Medina almost immediately. Abd Allah chose this time to retreat to the family's strongholds in Najd. Muhammad Ali decided to pursue him there, sending out another army under the command of his other son, Ibrahim. The Wahhabis made their stand at the traditional Al Saud capital of Ad Diriyah, where they managed to hold out for two years against superior Egyptian forces and weaponry. In the end, however, the Wahhabis proved no match for a modern army, and Ad Diriyah—and Abd Allah with it—fell in 1818.

[Source: US Library of Congress, *Saudi Arabia: A Country Study*, ed. Helen Chapin Metz, 1992.]

GLOSSARY

Hijaz, the: also Hejaz, a region in what is today western Saudi Arabia, containing the important Islamic holy sites of Mecca and Medina

Najd: a region in what is today central Saudi Arabia

Document Themes and Analysis

This document, an excerpt from a Country Study Handbook on Saudi Arabia, shows the Wahhabite foundation of Saudi Arabia from an American perspective. The author tells this history with the themes of alliance and destruction.

The major date in this document is 1744. Before that date, Muhammad ibn Abd al Wahhab had a reputation but not a secure home, the House of Saud, meanwhile, had limited authority and no religious doctrine. That changed with their alliance: "In 1744 Muhammad ibn Saud and Muhammad ibn Abd al Wahhab swore a traditional Muslim oath in which they promised to work together to establish a state run according to Islamic principles." This alliance fundamentally altered the nature of Saudi rule: "Until that time the Al Saud had been accepted as conventional tribal leaders whose rule was based on longstanding but vaguely defined authority." The First Saudi State marks this date as its beginning. The alliance influences Saudi policy to this day.

Ibn Abd al Wahhab conceptualized a strict, conservative interpretation of Islam. As the document details, he viewed the reverence of shrines and objects as false idolatry. His zeal helped fuel the First Saudi State's expansion, which in turn led to much destruction: "Although the Wahhabis spared Mecca and Medina the destruction they visited upon Karbala, they destroyed monuments and grave markers that were being used for prayer to Muslim saints and for votive rituals, which the Wahhabis consider acts of polytheism." The conquerors rooted their violence in the past: "In destroying the objects that were the focus of these rituals, the Wahhabis sought to imitate Muhammad's destruction of pagan idols when he reentered Mecca in 628." The document showcases how Wahhabi's strict interpretation of Islam and desire to spread this doctrine can lead to destruction.

The strict strain of Wahhabi Islam that first became associated with the House of Saud in 1744 still undergirds Saudi Arabia's conservative society and culture today. This conservatism has led to what outsiders consider human rights violations in areas such as women's and LGBTQ rights. However, Saudi Arabia's vast supply of oil and geo-political influence in the region has curbed western nations from trying to discourage such violations.

Saudi Arabia's Wahhabism has also brought it in close contact with terrorist groups such as al Qaeda and the Islamic State of Iraq and Syria, also known as ISIS. Fifteen of the nineteen September 11th hijackers were from Saudi Arabia. The government of Saudi Arabia's alleged role in the attack has not been officially confirmed. However, in 2016 Congress passed the Justice Against Sponsors of Terrorism Act which allows families of that day's victims to carry out a lawsuit against the nation Saudi Arabia alleging its involvement in the attack.

—Anthony Vivian

Bibliography and Additional Reading

Ayoob, Mohammed & Hasan Kosebalaban, eds. *Religion and Politics in Saudi Arabia: Wahhabism and the State*. Boulder, CO: Lynne Rienner Publishers, 2008. Print.

Firro, Tarik. *Wahhabism and the Rise of the House of Saud*. Sussex: Sussex Academic Press, 2018. Print.

Metz, Helen Chapin, ed. *Saudi Arabia: A Country Study*. Ann Arbor, MI: University of Michigan Library, 1993. Print.

Valentine, Simon Ross. *Force and Fanaticism: Wahhabism in Saudi Arabia and Beyond*. London: Hurst, 2015. Print.

LATE TWENTIETH-CENTURY WARS AND PEACE ACCORDS

By the mid-1960s, the United States had not yet formed close relationships with Arab nations beyond Saudi Arabia. The Six-Day War (1967) between Israel and several Arab states only toughened Washington's position. The war left Israel in control of Jerusalem, the West Bank (adjacent to Jerusalem), and other Palestinian territories, most of which Israel still claims today. Jewish-Arab relations have remained tense, spawning another war over the status of the Palestinians in 1973. Peace accords were signed between Egypt and Israel in 1979, and between Jordan and Israel in 1994. The Oslo Accords (1993 and 1995) sought peace between the Israelis and the Palestinians, presenting a two-state solution. Despite their promise, however, the accords ultimately proved to be unworkable in the context of ongoing hostilities between the two parties and events occurring in the surrounding region.

In 1970, the Palestine Liberation Organization (PLO) moved its headquarters to Lebanon and began military raids into northern Israel. The Christian-dominated Lebanese government attempted to stop them, and in response the PLO sided with Lebanon's Muslims in their conflict with Christians. A vicious civil war ensued, pitting numerous political and religious factions against each other. Syrian and U.N. troops worked to maintain a cease-fire from 1976 to 1982, but in 1982 Israeli forces invaded the country in an effort to drive out Palestinian forces. After 1985 the Israeli's maintained a buffer zone inside Lebanon, but guerrillas from the Lebanese Shia militia Hezbollah clashed regularly with Israeli troops. The Israelis withdrew from Lebanon in 2000, but tensions remained high—and government in Lebanon has remained fragile.

In Iran, in 1978, a revolution unfolded in which the shah—a friend of the United States, albeit a highly controversial one—was toppled and an Islamic Republic was declared under the leadership of the ultra-conservative Shiite cleric Ayatollah Khomeini. Iran and the United States have been on hostile footing toward each other for most of the intervening 40 years. For its part, the Iranian government has continued to fund a range of militant Islamic groups, such as Hezbollah in Lebanon and Shiite oppositional forces in Iraq.

Barely a year after the Iranian Revolution, the Soviet Union invaded Afghanistan—seeking a puppet state in the region. Afghan oppositional forces, known as mujahedeen, soon began receiving political support and weapons—notably, hand-held rocket launchers—from the Reagan administration in the United States as a bulwark against communist encroachment. When, after nearly ten years, the Soviets finally pulled out (1989), beaten by bands of guerrilla fighters, the US armaments remained in the country, and Afghanistan spiraled into chaos, with tribal warlords fighting against one another to establish local territorial control. This is the context in which the Taliban—a violent Islamist political movement—along with Osama bin-Laden and his al-Qaeda terrorist network, would emerge in the 1990s.

Throughout most of the 1980s, Iran and Iraq fought a bitter, costly war over territory and influence. Although Iraq was headed by a brutal dictator, Saddam Hussein, the United States supported him and his regime as the lesser of two evils. However, even as members of the Reagan administration indicated to Saddam that they would seek to curtail the flow of weapons into Iran from international sources, the same administration was busy supplying weapons, illegally, to Iran through back channels and using the profits from those sales to fund, illegally, rightist forces in faraway Nicaragua as part of a civil war there. This was the so-called Iran-Contra affair (1985–87), an American political scandal of major proportions and one that served to further complicate the picture regarding US–Middle East relations. The United States seemed to be playing it both ways, even as it stood up publicly for truth, democracy, and efforts toward peace.

Through it all, the US backing of Saddam Hussein gave the despot cause to think it safe for him to operate as before. In 1990, therefore, he launched a military invasion of Kuwait in a territorial grab. After doing so, to his surprise the then US president George H.W. Bush pledged, "this will not stand" and embarked on a war—the Gulf War—to eject Iraqi forces from the small but oil-rich country to Iraq's south. A coalition of Arab countries (and others) also fought in support of the US effort, and managed to prevent Israel from participating and to argue for the retention of Saddam in power after the war. Saddam's forces were easily defeated. In the post–Gulf War period Iraq was required to submit to United Nations monitoring of its weapons and military capabilities to insure against a replay of the Kuwait episode, or worse.

U.N. Security Council Resolution 242 on the Arab-Israeli Conflict

Date: November 22, 1967
Authors: Hugh M. Foot; Arthur Goldberg; Eugene Rostow
Geographic region: Middle East; Egypt; Jordan; Syria
Genre: Legislation; report

Summary Overview

In June, 1967, with tension rising in the Middle East, and Egyptian, Jordanian, and Syrian military forces being mobilized and stationed along their borders with Israel, Israel mobilized its forces and attacked these three nations, winning a decisive military victory in six days. Israel occupied territory belonging to these three nations when a cease-fire was signed. A solution was needed to ease, or perhaps end, the tensions between the Arabs and the Israelis. The U.N. resolution reprinted here was designed to address that situation.

Resolution 242 addressed both a basic problem from before the war (the existence of Israel) and a major problem as a result of the war (Israel occupying non-Israeli territory). The compromise offered through this resolution was that Israel would return the lands it had conquered in exchange for the Arab states recognizing Israel and its right to exist. Although this compromise would not have solved all the tensions that had arisen in the region since World War II, the full implementation of the resolution would have peacefully resolved major disputes that these nations were facing.

Defining Moment

One reason the United Nations was founded, as stated in its charter, was to settle "international disputes by peaceful means." Resolution 242 was one attempt to implement this aspect of the charter; in this instance by settling the dispute between Israel and its neighbors, Egypt, Jordan, and Syria. When the British had announced that they were giving up their protectorate of Palestine during 1948, the existing Arab countries in that region had desired the creation of one new state in that area, Palestine. If this had been done it would have been a majority Arab/Muslim state, with a significant Jewish minority. However, Jewish settlers in that area, and Jews around the world, advocated for the creation of a Jewish state in those sections of the protectorate in which Jews were the majority. A two-state division of the area was recommended by the United Nations, and Jewish leaders declared the creation of Israel in 1948. After repelling Arab troops, Israel was established with most of the area that was to have been a Palestinian state incorporated into Egypt and Jordan.

During the spring of 1967, increased violence was directed toward Israel, in the form of both guerilla raids by Palestinians and larger efforts such as Syria's artillery bombardment of northern Israel. Egypt closed Israel's access to the Red Sea. By early June, when the Israeli leadership believed (as did most other global leaders) that the Arab states were about to attack Israel (reinforcements were on the way to Jordan from Iraq), Israel made a pre-emptive attack against them destroying their air forces and many of their tanks and other mechanized forces. Once the Israelis had advanced far enough to secure defensible physical borders, they accepted a cease-fire, ending the fighting but not ending the hostility between the two sides. As the organization that had brokered the cease-fire on June 11, the United Nations, and its leaders sought to find a way to create a more stable situation for Israel and its neighbors. After five months of discussion, debate, and negotiations, the fifteen members of the Security Council unanimously adopted Resolution 242 at the 1382nd meeting of the Security Council.

The resolution was directed toward the nations of the Middle East, where it received a cool reception. Although it contained points that each side could accept, those that were acceptable to the Israelis seemed to be unacceptable to the Arabs, and vice versa. As such, although it did contain a potential path toward long-term peace and stability, the resolution produced no great progress. However, the basic premise of the resolution, land for peace, was the foundation for later agreements that Israel made with individual Arab states. As such, it was a seed that eventually did bear fruit, even if not in the form that had been articulated by the Security Council.

Author Biographies

Hugh M. Foot (1907–90) was a British diplomat who grew up in a liberal, politically active family. (His father and three brothers were all, at various times, members of Parliament.) He was an administrator in British Palestine and during World War II served as a military administrator in the Mediterranean. Except for a short time when he resigned over the British policy in Rhodesia, he served as a representative for the United Kingdom from 1961 to 1970. In 1964, he was made a life peer.

Arthur Goldberg (1908–90) was the American ambassador to the United Nations. He grew up in a family of modest means but eventually earned a law degree. Prior to his work at the U.N., he had been a labor lawyer and Secretary of Labor, and had served as an Associate Justice of the Supreme Court. After his time at the U.N., Goldberg tried, and failed, to win elective office, subsequently returning to private practice.

Eugene Rostow (1913–2002) was from a socialist family but became a conservative Democrat and supported a number of unpopular causes. He became a law professor at Yale, and in 1945, as an advisor to the State Department, published an article against Japanese-American internment. He eventually became Dean of the Yale Law School, serving there until 1965. During the Johnson administration he was an under-secretary of state and a strong defender of US actions in the Vietnam War. It was in this capacity, as under-secretary, that he became involved in the U.N. action regarding the Six Day War in the Middle East. Rostow later led the US Arms Control and Disarmament Agency.

HISTORICAL DOCUMENT: *U.N. Security Council Resolution 242 on the Arab-Israeli Conflict*

The Security Council,

Expressing its continuing concern with the grave situation in the Middle East,

Emphasizing the inadmissibility of the acquisition of territory by war and the need to work for a just and lasting peace in which every State in the area can live in security,

Emphasizing further that all Member States in their acceptance of the Charter of the United Nations have undertaken a commitment to act in accordance with Article 2 of the Charter,

1. Affirms that the fulfillment of Charter principles requires the establishment of a just and lasting peace in the Middle East which should include the application of both the following principles:

   (i) Withdrawal of Israeli armed forces from territories occupied in the recent conflict;

   (ii) Termination of all claims or states of belligerency and respect for and acknowledgement of the sovereignty, territorial integrity and political independence of every State in the area and their right to live in peace within secure and recognized boundaries free from threats or acts of force;

2. Affirms further the necessity

   (a) For guaranteeing freedom of navigation through international waterways in the area;

   (b) For achieving a just settlement of the refugee problem;

   (c) For guaranteeing the territorial inviolability and political independence of every State in the area, through measures including the establishment of demilitarized zones;

3. Requests the Secretary General to designate a Special Representative to proceed to the Middle East to establish and maintain contacts with the States concerned in order to promote agreement and assist efforts to achieve a peaceful and accepted settlement in accordance with the provisions and principles in this resolution;

4. Requests the Secretary-General to report to the Security Council on the progress of the efforts of the Special Representative as soon as possible.

> *Emphasizing the inadmissibility of the acquisition of territory by war and the need to work for a just and lasting peace in which every State in the area can live in security.*

Document Analysis

The Security Council of the United Nations sought to end the tension in the Middle East caused by the withdrawal of the British from Palestine without the status of the territory, and borders of any new states, having been agreed to by all interested parties. In 1948, when the Jewish leaders announced the creation of the state of Israel within borders recommended by a 1947 U.N. resolution, there was not a comparable Arab/Palestinian organization ready to establish a government within the remaining territory, nor were the Arab Palestinians ready to accept the proposed arrangement. The resulting turmoil and new borders led to twenty years of ongoing tension between Israel and its neighbors. The members of the Security Council rightly understood that unless this underlying tension was resolved, the pressures that had brought about the Six Day War would result in future wars. Thus, the Council not only called for a "just and lasting peace in which every State in the area can live in security," but tried to provide a foundation on which this might occur. Without mandating a timeline or other specifics, the resolution proposed that a long-term peace would be attained through the resolution of basic four issues. These would be the withdrawal from occupied territory (Israel), mutual recognition of states and previous boundaries (all participants, but especially the Arab states), following agreements regarding international waterways (Egypt), and a solution to the refugee crisis resulting from the displacement of many Palestinians (mainly Jordan and Israel). While no specific temporal order was assigned to resolving these issues, it was understood that these were not totally independent concerns and certain solutions might have to be implemented simultaneously.

The creators of this resolution understood that the goal of peace was not simple, or it would have already been accomplished. However, with the Six Day War ceasefire a new opportunity presented itself. Both sides in the conflict had something the other wanted. The Arab states wanted their lands back, or at least for Israel not to have it, while Israel wanted diplomatic recognition and the ability to undertake normal economic endeavors. Those opposing Israel looked at the first major point in the introduction and the first clause, which stated that Israel should withdraw from "territories occupied in the recent conflict." The initial thought was that this was a first step, to be followed by other actions. These leaders demanded that Israel take the first step. Israel's response was to point to the next clause, which mandated that everyone in the Middle East should make an "acknowledgement of the sovereignty, territorial integrity and political independence of every State" within the region. Israel countered, then, that the first step should be the implementation of the second clause declaring that secure national borders must be established along with the acceptance of Israel's right to exist. Israel's position was that the Arab states' rejection of Israel had been the source of tension prior to the war. The Security Council, however, believed that with each side having something to trade, Israel should be able to obtain diplomatic recognition in exchange for giving up the occupied territory.

It was assumed that if the border issue were resolved, then opening the Straits of Tiran (connecting the Gulf of Aqaba and the Red Sea) would be assured, as was the case when Egypt and Israel signed a peace treaty in 1978. (Since Israel held the Sinai Peninsula after the Six Day War, this was temporarily not an issue.) The first three clauses laying out issues to be settled were all important to Israel—and to at least one of the Arab states. However, the fourth issue, "the refugee problem," was not a top concern for any national leader at the time. Israel seemed to think that the refugees could transform into residents in whatever nation they found themselves. The Arab nations believed that, while some refugees might meld into their populations, most would return to Palestine (the Gaza Strip or the West Bank) and become part of the new Palestinian state, whenever that was created. Thus, all of the leaders considered the refugees as someone else's problem, and therefore they took few steps to try to solve this issue.

Although a Special Representative was to be appointed to assist with any negotiations, and a report submitted to the Security Council, those measures were not expected to resolve any serious issues not otherwise addressed. Officials were sent and offers to mediate were made, but none of these efforts were eagerly received by the nations in the conflict. In addition, the exact meaning of this fairly simple resolution was debated. For example, a dispute over the exact meaning of the clause instructing Israel to withdraw seems to have been present from the start. Israel and Arthur Goldberg, one of the authors, interpreted this statement as meaning that Israel should withdraw from some of, but not necessarily all, the territory. On the other side, the Arab nations and Eugene Rostow, another author, believed that to fulfill the resolution Israel had to withdraw from all territory acquired during the 1967 war. While there are no modifiers on the term "withdrawal" in the resolution, those supporting a partial withdrawal pointed to the fact that the Security Council had voted against a Soviet Union proposal that had included the word "total" as a modifier to "withdrawal," instead adopting the British proposal without that modifier. The resolution was not complex, and clearly related to Article 2 Clause 3 of the U.N. Charter, which affirmed that settlement of disputes should be "by peaceful means," and Clause 4's affirmation of "territorial integrity." Nevertheless, exactly how the resolution was to be implemented to achieve this goal was not a matter of settled opinion.

Essential Themes

At the heart of Resolution 242 was the proposal to end the conflict by means of what has been called a "land for peace" deal. Israel held territory that had been part of, or was claimed by, the three major belligerents on the Arab side. Although none of the four active participants in the war responded to the resolution by giving it a wholehearted endorsement, Israel, Egypt, and Jordan were inclined to see it as a positive proposal and something that might work. Syria was adamant that it would not consider discussing other issues while Israel held Syrian territory. Although Resolution 242 initially received a tepid reception, it did play an important role in future talks and treaties.

The 1979 peace treaty signed by Egyptian and Israeli leaders reflected the core of Resolution 242. While additional issues and safeguards were included in the later agreement, Israel returned the Sinai Peninsula to Egypt and Egypt recognized Israel and its right to exist. The Gaza Strip, which had been governed by Egypt from 1948 to 1967, was left in Israel's control, to become a future Palestinian state. Although Jordan had annexed the West Bank after the 1948 Arab-Israeli conflict, in 1988 it officially renounced this annexation, turning over the territory to the Palestinian people, even though at that time it was under Israel's control. Thus, the Jordanian-Israeli treaty, signed in 1994, returned only a small amount of territory to Jordan in exchange for its recognition of Israel and normalization of economic and political relations between the two states. Syria and Israel have never signed a peace treaty, although they did have an agreement leading to military "disengagement" along their border. The Syrian leadership has always demanded that Israel withdraw from all occupied territory before they would consider further discussions regarding a peace treaty. Still, even aspects of the "disengagement" plan echoed Resolution 242, in that

Israel partially withdrew in return for a small move toward more peaceful relations between the two nations.

The final issue that Resolution 242 sought to advance was the "refugee problem." While Jordan had the largest group of displaced Palestinians within its borders, once Israel had taken control of the Gaza Strip and the West Bank it acquired not only this territory and the original inhabitants, but thousands of refugees as well. As illustrated by the situation more than fifty years later, the refugee issue was not then at the forefront of matters requiring a quick solution. Yet, on this issue, and on the related issue of a Palestinian state, Resolution 242 established the pattern for what was to be accomplished. The Palestinian slogan of the "right to return" was not in the resolution, nor was any specific reference to Palestinians. But under the 1993 Oslo Accords, Israel gave the Palestinian National Authority control over much of the occupied territory, and in exchange the PLO and the Palestinian National Authority recognized the right of Israel to exist. Thus, although no nation that participated in the Six Day War received Resolution 242 with enthusiasm, it has ended up playing a role in a variety of later events and agreements.

—Donald A Watt

Bibliography and Additional Reading

Black, Eric. "Resolution 242 and the Aftermath of 1967." *Frontline*. Boston: WGBH Educational Foundation, 1995. Web. 6 March 2018.

Gilbert, Martin. *Israel: A History.* New York: Harper Perennial, 1998 and 2008. Print.

Jewish Virtual Library. "U.N. Security Council: The Meaning of Resolution 242." *Jewish Virtual Library.* Chevy Chase MD: American-Israeli Cooperative Enterprise, 2018. Web. 7 March 2018.

Odeh, Adnan Abu (ed.) *U.N. Security Council Resolution 242: The Building Block of Peacemaking: A Washington Institute Monograph.* Washington: Washington Institute for Near East Policy. 1993. Print.

Robins, Philip. *A History of Jordan.* Cambridge: Cambridge University Press, 2004. Print.

Robenne, Meir. "Understanding U.N. Security Council Resolution 242." *Jerusalem Center for Public Affairs: Israeli Security, Regional Diplomacy, and International Law.* Jerusalem: Jerusalem Center for Public Affairs, 2018. Web. 7 March 2018.

Rostow, Eugene V. "The Drafting of Security Council Resolution 242: The Role of Non-Regional Actors." *Yale Law School Legal Scholarship Repository: Faculty Scholarship Series.* New Haven: Yale Law School, 1993. Web. 6 March 2018.

Camp David Accords

Date: September 17, 1978
Authors: Anwar al-Sadat and Menachem Begin (signatories)
Geographic Region: Middle East
Genre: Treaty

Summary Overview

In the fall of 1978, Egyptian president Anwar al-Sadat and Israeli prime minister Menachem Begin, with US president Jimmy Carter acting as facilitator, signed a landmark peace accord that helped establish peace between Egypt and Israel. The Egypt-Israel peace framework formed one part of the agreement and was by far the most successful; the other part was a framework for resolution of the wider Arab-Israeli conflict, mainly the political and territorial issues between Israel and the Palestinian Arabs. This part of the agreement was far less successful, as it was rejected by the Palestinians, who were given no part in the negotiations, and by the United Nations, which objected to it on several grounds.

Defining Moment

When the United Nations voted in 1947 to partition Palestine into Jewish and Arab territories, the action helped foster decades of distrust, political instability, violence, and war. Shortly after Israel's declaration of independence in 1948, forces from multiple neighboring states (Egypt, Syria, Iraq, Lebanon, Saudi Arabia, and Jordan) invaded the new nation. Israel was able to repel the Arab attackers before a series of localized armistices temporarily halted the violence. Egypt retained control over the Gaza Strip, a piece of land along the southern coast of Israel, and Jordan held the West Bank along Israel's eastern border with that nation. This uneasy peace held until 1967.

In 1967, tensions rose again when Egypt moved troops into the Sinai Peninsula, which borders Israel, and compelled U.N. peacekeepers to leave. Israel responded by launching a pre-emptive strike against Egypt in June. Jordan, Syria, and Iraq then attacked Israel, and over the course of six days Israeli forces decisively defeated these powers, capturing the Gaza Strip and Sinai Peninsula from Egypt, the West Bank from Jordan, and the Golan Heights from Syria. In the wake of the Six-Day War, as it became known, the U.N. Security Council adopted Resolution 242, calling for Israel to return the territories it had occupied in exchange for the Arab nations' recognition of Israel's territorial integrity and political independence. This resolution became the foundation of future diplomatic efforts to resolve the Arab-Israeli conflict.

Those efforts were again interrupted by war, however, when Egypt and Syria again attacked Israel and were again repelled in the 1973 Yom Kippur War. Although defeated, Egyptian and Syrian forces performed better than expected in the conflict. Egyptian president Sadat opted to use his increased prestige following the conflict to try to move toward peace with Israel. Meanwhile, in 1977, Israel elected a new prime minister, Menachem Begin, who was also interested in a peace initiative. In November of 1977,

Sadat became the first Arab leader to visit Israel. In the summer of 1978, Begin returned the gesture, visiting Cairo. In September of 1978, US president Jimmy Carter, recognizing the opportunity that these gestures created, invited Begin and Sadat to Camp David, a presidential retreat in Maryland. Located a safe distance from the lights and publicity of Washington, DC, Camp David would provide the three leaders with the seclusion needed for the frank exchange of ideas necessary to broker peace.

Author Biographies

Muhammad Anwar al-Sadat was born in Mit Abu al-Kawm, Egypt, on December 25, 1918. He played an active role in the fight against British dominance in Egypt, helping to depose the pro-British King Farouk in 1952. He became President Gamal Abdel Nasser's vice president in 1969, and when Nasser died the following year, Sadat became president. During his tenure, he loosened Egypt's ties to the Soviet Union and drew it closer to the United States. A strong proponent of the Middle East peace process, Sadat was assassinated in 1981 by Egyptian extremists who were opposed to his peace initiatives.

Menachem Wolfovitch Begin was born on August 16, 1913, in Brest-Litovsk in the Russian Empire (now in Belarus). Begin was a major figure in the Betar Zionist youth movement before World War II. During the war, he joined a Soviet-backed Polish army unit that was sent to Palestine, where he was released from service and joined the fight for an independent Israel. After independence, he rose in Israeli politics, becoming chairman of the conservative Likud party in 1973. In 1977, he became prime minister, a post he held until 1983. He died on March 9, 1992.

HISTORICAL DOCUMENT: Camp David Accords

The Framework for Peace in the Middle East

Muhammad Anwar al-Sadat, President of the Arab Republic of Egypt, and Menachem Begin, Prime Minister of Israel, met with Jimmy Carter, President of the United States of America, at Camp David from September 5 to September 17, 1978, and have agreed on the following framework for peace in the Middle East. They invite other parties to the Arab-Israel conflict to adhere to it.

Preamble

The search for peace in the Middle East must be guided by the following:
  The agreed basis for a peaceful settlement of the conflict between Israel and its neighbors is United Nations Security Council Resolution 242, in all its parts.
  After four wars during 30 years, despite intensive human efforts, the Middle East, which is the cradle of civilization and the birthplace of three great religions, does not enjoy the blessings of peace. The people of the Middle East yearn for peace so that the vast human and natural resources of the region can be turned to the pursuits of peace and so that this area can become a model for coexistence and cooperation among nations.

The historic initiative of President Sadat in visiting Jerusalem and the reception accorded to him by the parliament, government and people of Israel, and the reciprocal visit of Prime Minister Begin to Ismailia, the peace proposals made by both leaders, as well as the warm reception of these missions by the peoples of both countries, have created an unprecedented opportunity for peace which must not be lost if this generation and future generations are to be spared the tragedies of war.

The provisions of the Charter of the United Nations and the other accepted norms of international law and legitimacy now provide accepted standards for the conduct of relations among all states. To achieve a relationship of peace, in the spirit of Article 2 of the United Nations Charter, future negotiations between Israel and any neighbor prepared to negotiate peace and security with it are necessary for the purpose of carrying out all the provisions and principles of Resolutions 242 and 338.

Peace requires respect for the sovereignty, territorial integrity and political independence of every state in the area and their right to live in peace within secure and recognized boundaries free from threats or acts of force. Progress toward that goal can accelerate movement toward a new era of reconciliation in the Middle East marked by cooperation in promoting economic development, in maintaining stability and in assuring security.

> **P**eace requires respect for the sovereignty, territorial integrity and political independence of every state in the area and their right to live in peace within secure and recognized boundaries free from threats or acts of force.

Security is enhanced by a relationship of peace and by cooperation between nations which enjoy normal relations. In addition, under the terms of peace treaties, the parties can, on the basis of reciprocity, agree to special security arrangements such as demilitarized zones, limited armaments areas, early warning stations, the presence of international forces, liaison, agreed measures for monitoring and other arrangements that they agree are useful.

Framework

Taking these factors into account, the parties are determined to reach a just, comprehensive, and durable settlement of the Middle East conflict through the conclusion of peace treaties based on Security Council resolutions 242 and 338 in all their parts. Their purpose is to achieve peace and good neighborly relations. They recognize that for peace to endure, it must involve all those who have been most deeply affected by the conflict. They therefore agree that this framework, as appropriate, is

continues on page 182

continued from page 181

intended by them to constitute a basis for peace not only between Egypt and Israel, but also between Israel and each of its other neighbors which is prepared to negotiate peace with Israel on this basis. With that objective in mind, they have agreed to proceed as follows:

West Bank and Gaza

Egypt, Israel, Jordan and the representatives of the Palestinian people should participate in negotiations on the resolution of the Palestinian problem in all its aspects. To achieve that objective, negotiations relating to the West Bank and Gaza should proceed in three stages:

Egypt and Israel agree that, in order to ensure a peaceful and orderly transfer of authority, and taking into account the security concerns of all the parties, there should be transitional arrangements for the West Bank and Gaza for a period not exceeding five years. In order to provide full autonomy to the inhabitants, under these arrangements the Israeli military government and its civilian administration will be withdrawn as soon as a self-governing authority has been freely elected by the inhabitants of these areas to replace the existing military government. To negotiate the details of a transitional arrangement, Jordan will be invited to join the negotiations on the basis of this framework. These new arrangements should give due consideration both to the principle of self-government by the inhabitants of these territories and to the legitimate security concerns of the parties involved. Egypt, Israel, and Jordan will agree on the modalities for establishing elected self-governing authority in the West Bank and Gaza. The delegations of Egypt and Jordan may include Palestinians from the West Bank and Gaza or other Palestinians as mutually agreed. The parties will negotiate an agreement which will define the powers and responsibilities of the self-governing authority to be exercised in the West Bank and Gaza. A withdrawal of Israeli armed forces will take place and there will be a redeployment of the remaining Israeli forces into specified security locations. The agreement will also include arrangements for assuring internal and external security and public order. A strong local police force will be established, which may include Jordanian citizens. In addition, Israeli and Jordanian forces will participate in joint patrols and in the manning of control posts to assure the security of the borders.

When the self-governing authority (administrative council) in the West Bank and Gaza is established and inaugurated, the transitional period of five years will begin. As soon as possible, but not later than the third year after the beginning of the transitional period, negotiations will take place to determine the final status of the West Bank and Gaza and its relationship with its neighbors and to conclude a peace treaty between Israel and Jordan by the end of the transitional period. These negotiations will be conducted among Egypt, Israel, Jordan and the elected representatives of the inhabitants of the West Bank and Gaza. Two separate but related committees will be convened, one committee, consisting of representatives of the four parties which will negotiate and agree on the final status of the West Bank and Gaza, and its relationship with its neighbors, and the second committee, consisting of representatives of Israel and representatives of Jordan to be joined by the elected representatives of the inhabitants of the West Bank and Gaza, to negotiate the peace treaty between Israel and Jordan, taking into account the agreement reached in the final status of the West Bank and Gaza. The negotiations shall be based on all the provisions and principles of U.N. Security Council Resolution 242. The negotiations will resolve, among other matters, the location of the boundaries and the nature of the security arrangements. The solution from the negotiations must also recognize the legitimate right of the Palestinian peoples and their just requirements. In this way, the Palestinians will participate in the determination of their own future through:

The negotiations among Egypt, Israel, Jordan and the representatives of the inhabitants of the West Bank and Gaza to agree on the final status of the West Bank and Gaza and other outstanding issues by the end of the transitional period.

Submitting their agreements to a vote by the elected representatives of the inhabitants of the West Bank and Gaza.

Providing for the elected representatives of the inhabitants of the West Bank and Gaza to decide how they shall govern themselves consistent with the provisions of their agreement.

Participating as stated above in the work of the committee negotiating the peace treaty between Israel and Jordan.

All necessary measures will be taken and provisions made to assure the security of Israel and its neighbors during the transitional period and beyond. To assist in providing such security, a strong local police force will be constituted by the self-governing authority. It will be composed of inhabitants of the West Bank and Gaza. The police will maintain liaison on internal security matters with the designated Israeli, Jordanian, and Egyptian officers.

During the transitional period, representatives of Egypt, Israel, Jordan, and the self-governing authority will constitute a continuing committee to decide by agreement on the modalities of admission of persons displaced from the West Bank and Gaza in 1967, together with necessary measures to prevent disruption and disorder. Other matters of common concern may also be dealt with by this committee. Egypt and Israel will work with each other and with other interested parties to establish agreed procedures for a prompt, just and permanent implementation of the resolution of the refugee problem.

continues on page 184

continued from page 183

Egypt-Israel

Egypt-Israel undertake not to resort to the threat or the use of force to settle disputes. Any disputes shall be settled by peaceful means in accordance with the provisions of Article 33 of the U.N. Charter.

In order to achieve peace between them, the parties agree to negotiate in good faith with a goal of concluding within three months from the signing of the Framework a peace treaty between them while inviting the other parties to the conflict to proceed simultaneously to negotiate and conclude similar peace treaties with a view the achieving a comprehensive peace in the area. The Framework for the Conclusion of a Peace Treaty between Egypt and Israel will govern the peace negotiations between them. The parties will agree on the modalities and the timetable for the implementation of their obligations under the treaty.

Associated Principles

Egypt and Israel state that the principles and provisions described below should apply to peace treaties between Israel and each of its neighbors—Egypt, Jordan, Syria and Lebanon. Signatories shall establish among themselves relationships normal to states at peace with one another. To this end, they should undertake to abide by all the provisions of the U.N. Charter. Steps to be taken in this respect include:

full recognition;

abolishing economic boycotts;

guaranteeing that under their jurisdiction the citizens of the other parties shall enjoy the protection of the due process of law.

Signatories should explore possibilities for economic development in the context of final peace treaties, with the objective of contributing to the atmosphere of peace, cooperation and friendship which is their common goal.

Claims commissions may be established for the mutual settlement of all financial claims. The United States shall be invited to participate in the talks on matters related to the modalities of the implementation of the agreements and working out the timetable for the carrying out of the obligations of the parties.

The United Nations Security Council shall be requested to endorse the peace treaties and ensure that their provisions shall not be violated. The permanent members of the Security Council shall be requested to underwrite the peace treaties and ensure respect or the provisions. They shall be requested to conform their policies and actions with the undertaking contained in this Framework.

For the Government of Israel: Menachem Begin
For the Government of the Arab Republic of Egypt: Muhammed Anwar al-Sadat
Witnessed by: Jimmy Carter, President of the United States of America

Framework for the Conclusion of a Peace Treaty between Egypt and Israel

In order to achieve peace between them, Israel and Egypt agree to negotiate in good faith with a goal of concluding within three months of the signing of this framework a peace treaty between them: It is agreed that:

> The site of the negotiations will be under a United Nations flag at a location or locations to be mutually agreed.
> All of the principles of U.N. Resolution 242 will apply in this resolution of the dispute between Israel and Egypt.
> Unless otherwise mutually agreed, terms of the peace treaty will be implemented between two and three years after the peace treaty is signed.

The following matters are agreed between the parties:

> the full exercise of Egyptian sovereignty up to the internationally recognized border between Egypt and mandated Palestine;
> the withdrawal of Israeli armed forces from the Sinai;
> the use of airfields left by the Israelis near al-Arish, Rafah, Ras en-Naqb, and Sharm el-Sheikh for civilian purposes only, including possible commercial use only by all nations;
> the right of free passage by ships of Israel through the Gulf of Suez and the Suez Canal on the basis of the Constantinople Convention of 1888 applying to all nations; the Strait of Tiran and Gulf of Aqaba are international waterways to be open to all nations for unimpeded and nonsuspendable freedom of navigation and overflight;
> the construction of a highway between the Sinai and Jordan near Eilat with guaranteed free and peaceful passage by Egypt and Jordan; and the stationing of military forces listed below.

Stationing of Forces

No more than one division (mechanized or infantry) of Egyptian armed forces will be stationed within an area lying approximately 50 km. (30 miles) east of the Gulf of Suez and the Suez Canal. Only United Nations forces and civil police equipped with light weapons to perform normal police functions will be stationed within an

continues on page 186

continued from page 185

area lying west of the international border and the Gulf of Aqaba, varying in width from 20 km. (12 miles) to 40 km. (24 miles).

In the area within 3 km. (1.8 miles) east of the international border there will be Israeli limited military forces not to exceed four infantry battalions and United Nations observers.

Border patrol units not to exceed three battalions will supplement the civil police in maintaining order in the area not included above.

The exact demarcation of the above areas will be as decided during the peace negotiations. Early warning stations may exist to insure compliance with the terms of the agreement.

United Nations forces will be stationed:
in part of the area in the Sinai lying within about 20 km. of the Mediterranean Sea and adjacent to the international border, and in the Sharm el-Sheikh area to insure freedom of passage through the Strait of Tiran; and these forces will not be removed unless such removal is approved by the Security Council of the United Nations with a unanimous vote of the five permanent members.

After a peace treaty is signed, and after the interim withdrawal is complete, normal relations will be established between Egypt and Israel, including full recognition, including diplomatic, economic and cultural relations; termination of economic boycotts and barriers to the free movement of goods and people; and mutual protection of citizens by the due process of law.

Interim Withdrawal

Between three months and nine months after the signing of the peace treaty, all Israeli forces will withdraw east of a line extending from a point east of El-Arish to Ras Muhammad, the exact location of this line to be determined by mutual agreement.

For the Government of the Arab Republic of Egypt: Muhammed Anwar al-Sadat
For the Government of Israel: Menachem Begin
Witnessed by: Jimmy Carter, President of the United States of America

Document Analysis

The first part of the Camp David Accords is an ambitious "Framework for Peace in the Middle East." It begins by recognizing U.N. Security Council Resolutions 242 as the basis for peace negotiations, and by further acknowledging that "peace requires respect for the sovereignty,

From left to right: Menachem Begin, Jimmy Carter and Anwar Sadat, in Camp David.

territorial integrity and political independence of every state in the area." This framework, it is hoped, will not just lead to peace between the signatories, Israel and Egypt, but "between Israel and each of its other neighbors which is prepared to negotiate peace with Israel on this basis."

Following this preamble, the document attempts to address the heart of the Arab-Israeli conflict: the fate of the Palestinian territories of the West Bank and Gaza Strip, whose Arab inhabitants had essentially been stateless refugees ever since the establishment of Israel in 1948, and who had been living under Israeli occupation since 1967. Therefore, it is proposed that Egypt and Israel (as well as Jordan and representatives of the Palestinians themselves, although neither is a party to this agreement) work together to facilitate the granting of political autonomy to Gaza and the West Bank, over a transitional period of five years. As an independent Palestinian government is negotiated and elected, the Israeli occupation is to end, with Israeli forces withdrawn and mutual security arrangements put in place.

The second part of the agreement is a "Framework for the Conclusion of a Peace Treaty between Egypt and Israel." This treaty, with an ambitious timeline for conclusion of three months following the signing of this document, is to involve the full withdrawal of Israeli forces from the Sinai and the peninsula's return to Egyptian sovereignty. Israeli military airfields established in the Sinai are to be repurposed for civilian use, and the Suez Canal and other waterways around the Sinai are to be open to international travel. Detailed provisions are also laid out for the stationing of military forces a safe distance from sensitive borders. The United Nations is to maintain a peacekeeping presence near some key waterways to ensure they remain open. Once all of these provisions

Egyptian President Anwar Sadat and Israeli Prime Minister Menachem Begin acknowledge applause during a joint session of Congress in Washington, D.C., during which President Jimmy Carter announced the results of the Camp David Accords, September 18, 1978.

are implemented, Egypt and Israel are to establish normal diplomatic relations, "including full recognition, including diplomatic, economic and cultural relations; termination of economic boycotts and barriers to the free movement of goods and people; and mutual protection of citizens by the due process of law."

Essential Themes

The second part of the Camp David Accords—the part that applied exclusively to the two signatories—was carried out in full: the Egypt-Israel Peace Treaty was signed the following year, 1979, again by Sadat and Begin in the presence of Carter, in Washington, DC. Egypt was the first Arab state to conclude a peace agreement with Israel, and the treaty remains in force. In recognition of this accomplishment, Begin and Sadat were jointly awarded the 1978 Nobel Peace Prize. Carter received the Nobel Peace Prize in 2002, and the Camp David Accords were listed among his accomplishments.

However, the first part of the agreement, aimed at resolving the status of the Palestinian Arabs, was roundly rejected by all the parties not present, including the Palestinians themselves and all the other Arab states. In fact, the United Nations itself rejected this portion of the agreement, as it was concluded without consulting the people it most directly affected, the Palestinians, thus violating the principle of self-determination, as well as a number of U.N. resolutions regarding the Palestinian issue. The other Arab states were outraged that Egypt had broken the united Arab front against Israel, and in 1979 Egypt's membership in the Arab League was suspended (it was readmitted in 1989). Sadat himself paid the ultimate price at the hands of Arab extremists when he was shot to death during a military parade in 1981 by members of his own presidential guard. However, Sadat also showed that peace with Israel was possible, and despite Jordan's umbrage at being named in the Camp David Accords, that country became the second Arab state to conclude peace with Israel, in 1994. The issue of Palestinian statehood, however, remains as unresolved and fraught with violence in the twenty-first century as it was in the twentieth.

—Michael P. Auerbach

Bibliography and Additional Reading

Feron, James. "Menachem Begin, Guerilla Leader Who Became Peacemaker." *New York Times*. New York Times, 10 Mar. 1992. Web. 30 Mar. 2016.

Friedman, Uri. "The 'Peace Process': A Short History." *Foreign Policy*. Foreign Policy, 27 Feb. 2012. Web. 30 Mar. 2016.

Pace, Eric. "Anwar el-Sadat, the Daring Arab Pioneer of Peace with Israel." *New York Times*. New York Times, 7 Oct. 1981. Web. 30 Mar. 2016.

"Peace Talks at Camp David, September 1978." *PBS*. WGBH, n.d. Web. 30 Mar. 2016.

Pressman, Jeremy. "Explaining the Carter Administration's Israeli-Palestinian Solution." *Diplomatic History* 37.5 (2013): 1117–47. Print.

Egypt-Israel Peace Treaty

Date: March 26, 1979
Authors: Anwar al-Sadat and Menachem Begin (signatories)
Geographic Region: Middle East
Genre: Treaty

Summary Overview

On March 26, 1979, after three decades of declared war between their two nations, Egyptian president Anwar al-Sadat and Israeli prime minister Menachem Begin signed the Egypt-Israel Peace Treaty. The treaty was signed at the White House and was overseen by US president Jimmy Carter, who had arranged for the meeting that led to the treaty and played a crucial role in negotiations. The framework for peace that led to the treaty, called the Camp David Accords, was a result of over a year of high-level diplomatic negotiations, culminating in a two-week summit at Camp David, in rural Maryland, beginning on September 5, 1978. Egypt and other Arab nations had been at war with Israel since the latter had declared its independence in 1948. After the Six-Day War of 1967, Israel occupied the Egyptian-controlled Gaza Strip and the Sinai Peninsula. The United Nations issued Resolution 242, which called for Israel's withdrawal from these and other occupied areas in exchange for peace with its Arab neighbors and an equitable settlement for displaced Palestinians. For a decade, no agreement was reached, and unrest in the Middle East continued. Sadat and Begin were awarded the 1978 Nobel Peace Prize for their work on the Camp David Accords and the treaty that followed.

Defining Moment

Conflict between Egypt and what became Israel can be traced back to the end of World War I. When the Ottoman Empire collapsed at the end of the war, Palestine, which it had controlled for four centuries, was placed under British control, and planning for a Jewish homeland in the region began. After World War II, the United Nations adopted a plan to partition the region into three separate areas, which was accepted by the Jewish community but not the Arab world. There would be an independent Israel, an independent Palestine, and the contested cities of Jerusalem and Bethlehem would be internationally administered by the United Nations. The region disintegrated into civil war after Israel declared its independence on May 14, 1948. The fighting continued for ten months, and Israel was left in control of a larger area than had initially been included in the United Nations partition plan. There was no independent Palestinian state, and the remainder of the territory was divided up between Israel's neighbors. Hundreds of thousands of Palestinian Arabs left their lands in the newly created Israeli state and fled to neighboring countries, while hundreds of thousands of Jewish people from across the world settled in Israel. This massive demographic upheaval exacerbated long-standing resentment between Israel and its neighbors, and sporadic violence flared up in the decades that followed.

Arab resistance to Israel was led by Egyptian president Gamal Abdel Nasser until his death in 1970. During his tenure, Egypt lost the Sinai Peninsula and the Gaza Strip to Israel during the 1967 Six-Day War; Syria lost the Golan Heights and Jordan lost the West Bank. When hostilities ended on June 11, 1967, the Egyptian air force was destroyed, and Israel occupied more than three times as much territory as it had held before the war. The United Nations passed Security Council Resolution 242 in November, calling for Israel to leave occupied areas and settle the refugee crisis, and for Israel's neighbors to seek peace and recognize Israel's right to exist.

A stalemate quickly developed as Israel waited to withdraw its troops until it had received official recognition from its Arab neighbors, which was not forthcoming. When Sadat became president of Egypt after Nasser's death, he was eager to regain the territory lost in the Six-Day War, and also believed that even if unsuccessful, an attack could put him in a more favorable position to set terms of peace. On October 6, 1973, the Yom Kippur War began, as Egypt and Syria attacked Israel with support from Jordan and Iraq. Israel quickly mobilized and pushed back the allies, and on October 25, 1973, a ceasefire was declared. After the war, Sadat, who had been heavily supported by the Soviet Union, moved away from Soviet influence and made overtures toward Israel and the West. In 1974, a portion of the Sinai Peninsula was returned to Egypt, and in 1977, Sadat traveled to Jerusalem. He was the first Arab leader to ever visit Israel, and his visit outraged many hard-line pan-Arabists. After it seemed that peace talks were faltering, Carter, the president of the United States in 1977, invited Sadat and Begin to meet at Camp David, the presidential retreat in rural Maryland. There, they hashed out a road map that would lead to peace between the two nations, and both signed the Egypt-Israel Peace Treaty on March 26, 1979.

Author Biographies

The Egypt-Israel Peace Treaty was signed on March 26, 1979, in Washington, DC. The treaty was witnessed by Jimmy Carter, president of the United States since 1977, and was signed by Egyptian president Anwar al-Sadat and Israeli prime minister Menachem Begin.

Sadat had played a major role in the fight against British rule in Egypt in the 1940s and 1950s, in some cases facing imprisonment. After aiding in Gamal Abdel Nasser's coup that overthrew the British in 1952, he succeeded in being named to the vice presidency under Nasser in 1964 and again in 1969. Upon Nasser's death, he was elected president in 1970 and quickly began making serious efforts to establish peace between Egypt and Israel. However, facing increased domestic disapproval following the treaty signed in 1979, he was assassinated in 1981.

Begin had been head of the Betar, a Revisionist-Zionist youth movement, and fought with an underground militant group to attain an independent Israeli state. In 1977, when his Likud party won a majority in the Knesset (the Israeli parliament), he was elected prime minister. He resigned from his post in 1983 and died in 1992.

HISTORICAL DOCUMENT: *Egypt-Israel Peace Treaty*

The Government of the Arab Republic of Egypt and the Government of the State of Israel;

PREAMBLE

Convinced of the urgent necessity of the establishment of a just, comprehensive and lasting peace in the Middle East in accordance with Security Council Resolutions 242 and 338;

Reaffirming their adherence to the "Framework for Peace in the Middle East Agreed at Camp David," dated September 17, 1978;

Noting that the aforementioned Framework as appropriate is intended to constitute a basis for peace not only between Egypt and Israel but also between Israel and each of its other Arab neighbors which is prepared to negotiate peace with it on this basis;

Desiring to bring to an end the state of war between them and to establish a peace in which every state in the area can live in security;

Convinced that the conclusion of a Treaty of Peace between Egypt and Israel is an important step in the search for comprehensive peace in the area and for the attainment of settlement of the Arab- Israeli conflict in all its aspects;

Inviting the other Arab parties to this dispute to join the peace process with Israel guided by and based on the principles of the aforementioned Framework;

Desiring as well to develop friendly relations and cooperation between themselves in accordance with the United Nations Charter and the principles of international law governing international relations in times of peace;

Agree to the following provisions in the free exercise of their sovereignty, in order to implement the "Framework for the Conclusion of a Peace Treaty Between Egypt and Israel";

ARTICLE I The state of war between the Parties will be terminated and peace will be established between them upon the exchange of instruments of ratification of this Treaty. Israel will withdraw all its armed forces and civilians from the Sinai behind the international boundary between Egypt and mandated Palestine, as provided in the annexed protocol (Annex I), and Egypt will resume the exercise of its full sovereignty over the Sinai. Upon completion of the interim withdrawal provided for in Annex I, the parties will establish normal and friendly relations, in accordance with Article III (3).

ARTICLE II The permanent boundary between Egypt and Israel in the recognized international boundary between Egypt and the former mandated territory of Palestine, as shown on the map at Annex II, without prejudice to the issue of the status of the Gaza Strip. The Parties recognize this boundary as inviolable. Each will respect the territorial integrity of the other, including their territorial waters and airspace.

Article III The Parties will apply between them the provisions of the Charter of the United Nations and the principles of international law governing relations among states in times of peace. In particular: They recognize and will respect each other's sovereignty, territorial integrity and political independence; They recognize and will respect each other's right to live in peace within their secure and recognized boundaries; They will refrain from the threat or use of force, directly or indirectly, against each other and will settle all disputes between them by peaceful means. Each Party undertakes to ensure that acts or threats of belligerency, hostility, or violence do not originate from and are not committed from within its territory, or by any forces subject to its control or by any other forces stationed on its territory, against the population, citizens or property of the other Party. Each Party also undertakes to refrain from organizing, instigating, inciting, assisting or participating in acts or threats of belligerency, hostility, subversion or violence against the other Party, anywhere, and undertakes to ensure that perpetrators of such acts are brought to justice. The Parties agree that the normal relationship established between them will include full recognition, diplomatic, economic and cultural relations, termination of economic boycotts and discriminatory barriers to the free movement of people and goods, and will guarantee the mutual enjoyment by citizens of the due process of law. The process by which they undertake to achieve such a relationship parallel to the implementation of other provisions of this Treaty is set out in the annexed protocol (Annex III).

Article IV In order to provide maximum security for both Parties on the basis of reciprocity, agreed security arrangements will be established including limited force zones in Egyptian and Israeli territory, and United Nations forces and observers, described in detail as to nature and timing in Annex I, and other security arrangements the Parties may agree upon. The Parties agree to the stationing of United Nations personnel in areas described in Annex I. The Parties agree not to request withdrawal of the United Nations personnel and that these personnel will not be removed unless such removal is approved by the Security Council of the United Nations, with the affirmative vote of the five Permanent Members, unless the Parties otherwise agree. A Joint Commission will be established to facilitate the implementation of the Treaty, as provided for in Annex I. The security arrangements provided for in paragraphs 1 and 2 of this Article may at the request of either party be reviewed and amended by mutual agreement of the Parties.

Article V Ships of Israel, and cargoes destined for or coming from Israel, shall enjoy the right of free passage through the Suez Canal and its approaches through the Gulf of Suez and the Mediterranean Sea on the basis of the Constantinople Convention of 1888, applying to all nations, Israeli nationals, vessels and cargoes, as well as persons, vessels and cargoes destined for or coming from Israel, shall be accorded

continues on page 194

continued from page 193

non-discriminatory treatment in all matters connected with usage of the canal. The Parties consider the Strait of Tiran and the Gulf of Aqaba to be international waterways open to all nations for unimpeded and non-suspendable freedom of navigation and overflight. The parties will respect each other's right to navigation and overflight for access to either country through the Strait of Tiran and the Gulf of Aqaba.

ARTICLE VI This Treaty does not affect and shall not be interpreted as affecting in any way the rights and obligations of the Parties under the Charter of the United Nations. The Parties undertake to fulfill in good faith their obligations under this Treaty, without regard to action or inaction of any other party and independently of any instrument external to this Treaty. They further undertake to take all the necessary measures for the application in their relations of the provisions of the multilateral conventions to which they are parties, including the submission of appropriate notification to the Secretary General of the United Nations and other depositaries of such conventions. The Parties undertake not to enter into any obligation in conflict with this Treaty. Subject to Article 103 of the United Nations Charter in the event of a conflict between the obligation of the Parties under the present Treaty and any of their other obligations, the obligations under this Treaty will be binding and implemented.

ARTICLE VII Disputes arising out of the application or interpretation of this Treaty shall be resolved by negotiations. Any such disputes which cannot be settled by negotiations shall be resolved by conciliation or submitted to arbitration.

ARTICLE VIII The Parties agree to establish a claims commission for the mutual settlement of all financial claims.

ARTICLE IX This Treaty shall enter into force upon exchange of instruments of ratification. This Treaty supersedes the Agreement between Egypt and Israel of September, 1975. All protocols, annexes, and maps attached to this Treaty shall be regarded as an integral part hereof. The Treaty shall be communicated to the Secretary General of the United Nations for registration in accordance with the provisions of Article 102 of the Charter of the United Nations.

Annex I
Protocol Concerning Israeli Withdrawal and Security Agreements

ARTICLE I CONCEPT OF WITHDRAWAL Israel will complete withdrawal of all its armed forces and civilians from the Sinai not later than three years from the date of exchange of instruments of ratification of this Treaty. To ensure the mutual security of the Parties, the implementation of phased withdrawal will be accompanied by the military measures and establishment of zones set out in this Annex and in Map 1, hereinafter referred to as "the Zones." The withdrawal from the Sinai will be accomplished in two phases: The interim withdrawal behind the line from east of El-Arish to Ras Mohammed as delineated on Map 2 within nine months from the date of exchange of instruments of ratification of this Treaty. The final withdrawal from the Sinai behind the international boundary not later than three years from the date of exchange of instruments of ratification of this Treaty. A Joint Commission will be formed immediately after the exchange of instruments of ratification of this Treaty in order to supervise and coordinate movements and schedules during the withdrawal, and to adjust plans and timetables as necessary within the limits established by paragraph 3, above. Details relating to the Joint Commission are set out in Article IV of the attached Appendix. The Joint Commission will be dissolved upon completion of final Israeli withdrawal from the Sinai.

ARTICLE II DETERMINATION OF FINAL LINES AND ZONES In order to provide maximum security for both Parties after the final withdrawal, the lines and the Zones delineated on Map 1 are to be established and organized as follows:

Zone A is bounded on the east by line A (red line) and on the west by the Suez Canal and the east coast of the Gulf of Suez, as shown on Map 1. An Egyptian armed force of one mechanized infantry division and its military installations, and field fortifications, will be in this Zone. The main elements of that Division will consist of: Three mechanized infantry brigades. One armed brigade. Seven field artillery battalions including up to 126 artillery pieces. Seven anti-aircraft artillery battalions including individual surface-to-air missiles and up to 126 anti-aircraft guns of 37 mm and above. Up to 230 tanks. Up to 480 armored personnel vehicles of all types. Up to a total of twenty-two thousand personnel.

Zone B
  Zone B is bounded by line B (green line) on the east and by line A (red line) on the west, as shown on Map 1. Egyptian border units of four battalions equipped

Convinced that the conclusion of a Treaty of Peace between Egypt and Israel is an important step in the search for comprehensive peace in the area and for the attainment of settlement of the Arab-Israeli conflict in all its aspects;

continues on page 196

continued from page 195

with light weapons and wheeled vehicles will provide security and supplement the civil police in maintaining order in Zone B. The main elements in the four Border Battalions will consist of up to a total of four thousand personnel. Land based, short range, low power, coastal warning points of the border patrol units may be established on the coast of this Zone. There will be in Zone B field fortifications and military installations for the four border battalions.

Zone C

Zone C is bounded by line B (green line) on the west and the International Boundary and the Gulf of Aqaba on the east, as shown on Map 1. Only United Nations forces and Egyptian civil police will be stationed in Zone C. The Egyptian civil police armed with light weapons will perform normal police functions within this Zone. The United Nations Force will be deployed within Zone C and perform its functions as defined in Article VI of this annex. The United Nations Force will be stationed mainly in camps located within the following stationing areas shown on Map 1, and will establish its precise locations after consultations with Egypt: In that part of the area in the Sinai lying within about 20 Km. of the Mediterranean Sea and adjacent to the International Boundary. In the Sharm el Sheikh area.

Zone D

Zone D is bounded by line D (blue line) on the east and the international boundary on the west, as shown on Map 1. In this Zone there will be an Israeli limited force of four infantry battalions, their military installations, and field fortifications, and United Nations observers. The Israeli forces in Zone D will not include tanks, artillery and anti-aircraft missiles except individual surface-to-air missiles. The main elements of the four Israeli infantry battalions will consist of up to 180 armored personnel vehicles of all types and up to a total of four thousand personnel. Access across the international boundary shall only be permitted through entry check points designated by each Party and under its control. Such access shall be in accordance with laws and regulations of each country. Only those field fortifications, military installations, forces, and weapons specifically permitted by this Annex shall be in the Zones.

ARTICLE III AERIAL MILITARY REGIME Flights of combat aircraft and reconnaissance flights of Egypt and Israel shall take place only over Zones A and D, respectively. Only unarmed, non-combat aircraft of Egypt and Israel will be stationed in Zones A and D, respectively. Only Egyptian unarmed transport aircraft will take off and land in Zone B and up to eight such aircraft may be maintained in Zone B. The Egyptian border unit may be equipped with unarmed helicopters to perform their functions in Zone B. The Egyptian civil police may be equipped with unarmed police helicopters to perform normal police functions in Zone C. Only civilian airfields maybe built in the Zones. Without prejudice to the provisions of this Treaty, only those military aerial activities specifically permitted by this Annex shall be allowed in the Zones and the airspace above their territorial waters.

Article IV Naval Regime Egypt and Israel may base and operate naval vessels along the coasts of Zones A and D, respectively. Egyptian coast guard boats, lightly armed, may be stationed and operate in the territorial waters of Zone B to assist the border units in performing their functions in this Zone. Egyptian civil police equipped with light boats, lightly armed, shall perform normal police functions within the territorial waters of Zone C. Nothing in this Annex shall be considered as derogating from the right of innocent passage of the naval vessels of either party. Only civilian maritime ports and installations may be built in the Zones. Without prejudice to the provisions of this Treaty, only those naval activities specifically permitted by this Annex shall be allowed in the Zones and in their territorial waters.

Article V Early Warning Systems Egypt and Israel may establish and operate early warning systems only in Zones A and D respectively.

Article VI United Nations Operations The Parties will request the United Nations to provide forces and observers to supervise the implementation of this Annex and employ their best efforts to prevent any violation of its terms. With respect to these United Nations forces and observers, as appropriate, the Parties agree to request the following arrangements: Operation of check points, reconnaissance patrols, and observation posts along the international boundary and line B, and within Zone C. Periodic verification of the implementation of the provisions of this Annex will be carried out not less than twice a month unless otherwise agreed by the Parties. Additional verifications within 48 hours after the receipt of a request from either Party. Ensuring the freedom of navigation through the Strait of Tiran in accordance with Article V of the Treaty of Peace. The arrangements described in this article for each zone will be implemented in ones A, B, and C by the United Nations Force and in Zone D by the United Nations Observers. United Nations verification teams shall be accompanied by liaison officers of the respective Party. The United Nations Force and observers will report their findings to both Parties. The United Nations Force and Observers operating in the Zones will enjoy freedom of movement and other facilities necessary for the performance of their tasks. The United Nations Force and Observers are not empowered to authorize the crossing of the international boundary. The Parties shall agree on the nations from which

continues on page 198

continued from page 197

the United Nations Force and Observers will be drawn. They "will be drawn from nations other than those which are permanent members of the United Nations Security Council. The Parties agree that the United Nations should make those command arrangements that will best assure the effective implementation of its responsibilities.

ARTICLE VII LIAISON SYSTEM Upon dissolution of the Joint Commission, a liaison system between the Parties will be established. This liaison system is intended to provide an effective method to assess progress in the implementation of obligations under the present Annex and to resolve any problem that may arise in the course of implementation, and refer other unresolved matters to the higher military authorities of the two countries respectively for consideration. It is also intended to prevent situations resulting from errors or misinterpretation on the part of either Party. An Egyptian liaison office will be established in the city of El-Arish and an Israeli liaison office will be established in the city of Beer-Sheba. Each office will be headed by an officer of the respective country, and assisted by a number of officers. A direct telephone link between the two offices will be set up and also direct telephone lines with the United Nations command will be maintained by both offices.

ARTICLE VIII RESPECT FOR WAR MEMORIALS Each Party undertakes to preserve in good condition the War Memorials erected in the memory of soldiers of the other Party, namely, those erected by Egypt in Israel, and shall permit access to such monuments.

ARTICLE IX INTERIM ARRANGEMENTS The withdrawal of Israeli armed forces and civilians behind the interim withdrawal line, and the conduct of the forces of the Parties and the United Nations prior to the final withdrawal, will be governed by the attached Appendix and Map 2 . . .

ANNEX II *Map of Israel-Egypt International Boundary*
ANNEX III *Protocol Concerning Relations of the Parties*

ARTICLE 1 DIPLOMATIC AND CONSULAR RELATIONS The Parties agree to establish diplomatic and consular relations and to exchange ambassadors upon completion of the interim withdrawal.

ARTICLE 2 ECONOMIC AND TRADE RELATIONS The Parties agree to remove all discriminatory barriers to normal economic relations and to terminate economic boycotts of each other upon completion of the interim withdrawal. As soon as possible, and not later than six months after the completion of the interim withdrawal, the Parties will enter negotiations with a view to concluding an agreement on trade and commerce for the purpose of promoting beneficial economic relations.

ARTICLE 3 CULTURAL RELATIONS The Parties agree to establish normal cultural relations following completion of the interim withdrawal. They agree on the desirability of cultural exchanges in all fields, and shall, as soon as possible and not later than six months after completion of the interim withdrawal, enter into negotiations with a view to concluding a cultural agreement for this purpose.

ARTICLE 4 FREEDOM OF MOVEMENT Upon completion of the interim withdrawal, each Party will permit the free movement of the nationals and vehicles of the other into and within its territory according to the general rules applicable to nationals and vehicles of other states. Neither Party will impose discriminatory restrictions on the free movement of persons and vehicles from its territory to the territory of the other. Mutual unimpeded access to places of religious and historical significance will be provided on a non- discriminatory basis.

ARTICLE 5 COOPERATION FOR DEVELOPMENT AND GOOD NEIGHBORLY RELATIONS The Parties recognize a mutuality of interest in good neighbourly relations and agree to consider means to promote such relations. The Parties will cooperate in promoting peace, stability and development in their region. Each agrees to consider proposals the other may wish to make to this end. The Parties shall seek to foster mutual understanding and tolerance and will, accordingly, abstain from hostile propaganda against each other.

ARTICLE 6 TRANSPORTATION AND TELECOMMUNICATIONS The Parties recognize as applicable to each other the rights, privileges and obligations provided for by the aviation agreements to which they are both party, particularly by the Convention on International Civil Aviation, 1944 ("The Chicago Convention") and the International Air Services Transit Agreement, 1944. Upon completion of the interim withdrawal any declaration of national emergency by a party under Article 89 of the Chicago Convention will not be applied to the other party on a discriminatory basis. Egypt agrees that the use of airfields left by Israel near El-Arish, Rafah, Ras El-Nagb and Sharm El- Sheikh shall be for civilian purposes only, including possible commercial use by all nations. As soon as possible and not later than six months after the completion of the interim withdrawal, the Parties shall enter into negotiations for the purpose of concluding a civil aviation agreement. The Parties will reopen and maintain roads and railways between their countries and will consider further road

continues on page 200

continued from page 199

and rail links. The Parties further agree that a highway will be constructed and maintained between Egypt, Israel and Jordan near Eilat with guaranteed free and peaceful passage of persons, vehicles and goods between Egypt and Jordan, without prejudice to their sovereignty over that part of the highway which falls within their respective territory. Upon completion of the interim withdrawal, normal postal, telephone, telex, data facsimile, wireless and cable communications and television relay services by cable, radio and satellite shall be established between the two Parties in accordance with all relevant international conventions and regulations. Upon completion of the interim withdrawal, each Party shall grant normal access to its ports for vessels and cargoes of the other, as well as vessels and cargoes destined for or coming from the other. Such access will be granted on the same conditions generally applicable to vessels and cargoes of other nations. Article 5 of the Treaty of Peace will be implemented upon the exchange of instruments of ratification of the aforementioned treaty.

ARTICLE 7 ENJOYMENT OF HUMAN RIGHTS The Parties affirm their commitment to respect and observe human rights and fundamental freedoms for all, and they will promote these rights and freedoms in accordance with the United Nations Charter.

ARTICLE 8 TERRITORIAL SEAS Without prejudice to the provisions of Article 5 of the Treaty of Peace each Party recognizes the right of the vessels of the other Party to innocent passage through its territorial sea in accordance with the rules of international law . . .

For the Government of the Arab Republic of Egypt: Muhammed Anwar al-Sadat
For the Government of Israel: Menachem Begin
Witnessed by: Jimmy Carter, President of the United States of America

Document Analysis

The Egypt-Israel Peace Treaty begins with an affirmation of the need for peace between not only Israel and Egypt, but all of Israel's neighbors in the Middle Eastern region. The opening lines of the treaty also affirm the desire of both nations to come into compliance with U.N. Security Resolution 242, which called for the withdrawal of Israel from occupied lands and the recognition of Israel by Arab states. Egypt feels that it must lead other nations in this regard, as "a Treaty of Peace between Egypt and Israel is an important step in the search for comprehensive peace in the area and for the attainment of settlement of the Arab-Israeli conflict in all its aspects." Other Arab states are invited to join the peace process as outlined in the Camp David Accords, and both nations desire to comply with the U.N. Charter.

The two most contentious points in any conversation between Israel and its neighbors were always the return of occupied lands and the recognition of Israel's sovereignty. The body of the treaty deals primarily with the mechanics of the return of the Sinai Peninsula to Egypt and the simultaneous official recognition of the state of Israel. The withdrawal of Israeli troops and civilians is addressed in great detail, and the Egyptians agree to hold Sinai as a demilitarized area once they regain control of it. The treaty does not address the issue of the Palestinians, and leaves the issue of Gaza, the other occupied territory formerly under Egypt's control, to be revisited "without prejudice," exempting it from the required return of territory to Egypt. In fact, the Camp David Accords dealt with the transition of the West Bank and Gaza Strip to a self-governing Palestinian state, so there was no need to include such language in the treaty.

In addition to the agreement to withdraw from the Sinai Peninsula, with its very specific requirements for access and buffer zones on both sides, the treaty addresses two specific points crucial to a healthy trade relationship. Egypt agrees to free passage of Israeli vessels through the Suez Canal, the Strait of Tiran, and the Gulf of Aqaba. This access was crucial to the delivery of supplies, particularly oil, to Israel. In addition, Israel would now be allowed to purchase Egyptian oil on the open market, a trade relationship that was impossible during the declared war of the previous years. In further hope of preventing future conflicts related to such deep-seated issues, the treaty also specifies that any possible disputes over these stipulations should be handled through diplomacy rather than military action.

Essential Themes

Egypt was a very large and relatively developed and wealthy nation compared to some of its Arab neighbors, and the world had good reason to hope that the signing of the Egypt-Israeli Peace Treaty in 1979 would be the first step to a general thawing of tensions between Israel and its Middle Eastern neighbors. Egypt would be the only neighbor to recognize Israel for years, however. Sadat returned to find many of his former allies outraged at the treaty and refusing to accept the Camp David Accords and their peace process. In 1979, Egypt was suspended from membership in the Arab League, whose headquarters were moved to Tunisia, even as Sadat and Begin were jointly awarded the Nobel Peace Prize for their work on the Camp David Accords. Sadat was assassinated by members of the Egyptian Islamic Jihad on October 6, 1981, as he attended a parade commemorating Egypt's crossing of the Suez Canal during the Yom Kippur War of 1973. Relations between Egypt and Israel continued to evolve, however, and in 1982, full diplomatic relations were established between the two nations. Egypt was the only nation to recognize Israel until 1994, when Jordan signed a peace treaty with Israel.

—*Bethany Groff Dorau*

Bibliography and Additional Reading

Lesch, David W. *1979: The Year That Shaped the Modern Middle East*. Boulder: Westview, 2001. Print.

Meital, Yoram. *Peace in Tatters: Israel, Palestine, and the Middle East*. Boulder: Rienner, 2006. Print.

Wright, Lawrence. *Thirteen Days in September: Carter, Begin, and Sadat at Camp David*. New York: Knopf, 2014. Print.

■ "Crisis of Confidence"

Date: July 15, 1979
Author: Jimmy Carter
Genre: Speech

Summary Overview

Over the course of the 1970s, the United States faced a host of economic, political, and social problems that coalesced by the end of the decade into what President Jimmy Carter called a "crisis of confidence." Though the Carter presidency could easily be remembered for a number of foreign-policy achievements, some have characterized his administration in terms of two events: the taking of more than sixty Americans hostage inside the American embassy in Tehran, Iran, and the televised address that Carter made on July 15, 1979, which many have called his "malaise speech" (though he never used the term in the address). Though the majority of the speech was about Carter's plans to achieve greater energy independence, and he had hoped that the speech would rally the American people to meet the nation's challenges, the speech captured a particular negative mood in the United States in the late 1970s. This allowed conservatives to craft a contrasting message of hope as the presidential election the next year drew near.

Defining Moment

In the aftermath of America's withdrawal from the decade-long war in Vietnam, the nation was faced with a number of economic, political, and social crises. These crises, along with a general sense of discontent with the political status quo, which had brought Jimmy Carter to the presidency in 1976, persisted through his term in office. Although Carter had concentrated largely on foreign policy achievements, such as the Camp David Accords between Israel and Egypt and the signing of the SALT II arms control treaty with the Soviet Union, back at home many Americans had lost faith in the federal government, which they saw as bloated and corrupt. Additionally, the economic problems that had plagued the nation for much of the decade had persisted, with inflation easily outpacing the rise in income for most Americans.

Exacerbating the situation was yet another round of oil price hikes by the Organization of the Petroleum Exporting Countries (OPEC), largely made up of Middle Eastern nations. The "energy crisis" was nothing new, having been a topic on the national agenda for the better part of the decade. But the escalating price and shrinking supply of oil on the world market were combining to compound the problems facing the American economy. Americans were having to wait in long lines at gas stations to fill their tanks, and the prices had gone up sharply. In the Northeast, where many people heated their homes in the winter with heating oil, prices had also increased rapidly. Carter decided to address the nation on the topic of energy and the ideas he had to lead the nation to energy independence as quickly as possible.

Before making the speech, Carter followed the counsel of some of his closest advisers and went to Camp David for the weekend to listen to what a selected group of Americans from various walks of life had to say about the energy crisis and its effects on the economy. However, what Carter heard from those who spoke with him was much more. The cross section of people with whom he consulted—from the worlds of business, religion, labor, and education—spoke not just about energy and the economy, but about the general direction of the nation, the quality of his personal leadership as president, and, most troubling to Carter, a deep moral and spiritual crisis that seemed to threaten to change the fundamental character of what it meant to be an American. It became clear to Carter that these factors were having a disastrous impact on the spirit of the American people, which he addressed in this nationally televised speech on July 15, 1979.

Author Biography

When Jimmy Carter was elected president in 1976, he was expected to be different from the line of presidents that had preceded him. Unlike Gerald Ford, Richard M. Nixon, Lyndon B. Johnson, and John F. Kennedy, Carter was a complete outsider to the world of Washington, DC, politics. Carter had been a one-term governor of Georgia and a peanut farmer before that. If the American people were looking for someone to take the nation in a different direction, Carter seemed like a good choice. He was a man of principle, a southern governor who had taken the opportunity of his 1971 inaugural address to declare that the time for racial discrimination and segregation was over. On his way to his inauguration as president in 1977, Carter did not ride in the limousine; rather, he got out and walked. This plain style worked well with the public for a time, but it did nothing to solve the serious problems that the nation faced in the late 1970s.

HISTORICAL DOCUMENT: *"Crisis of Confidence"*

Good evening.

This is a special night for me. Exactly 3 years ago, on July 15, 1976, I accepted the nomination of my party to run for President of the United States. I promised you a President who is not isolated from the people, who feels your pain, and who shares your dreams and who draws his strength and his wisdom from you.

During the past 3 years I've spoken to you on many occasions about national concerns, the energy crisis, reorganizing the Government, our Nation's economy, and issues of war and especially peace. But over those years the subjects of the speeches, the talks, and the press conferences have become increasingly narrow, focused more and more on what the isolated world of Washington thinks is important. Gradually, you've heard more and more about what the Government thinks or what the Government should be doing and less and less about our Nation's hopes, our dreams, and our vision of the future.

continued from page 203

Ten days ago I had planned to speak to you again about a very important subject—energy. For the fifth time I would have described the urgency of the problem and laid out a series of legislative recommendations to the Congress. But as I was preparing to speak, I began to ask myself the same question that I now know has been troubling many of you. Why have we not been able to get together as a nation to resolve our serious energy problem?

It's clear that the true problems of our Nation are much deeper—deeper than gasoline lines or energy shortages, deeper even than inflation or recession. And I realize more than ever that as President I need your help. So, I decided to reach out and listen to the voices of America.

I invited to Camp David people from almost every segment of our society—business and labor, teachers and preachers, Governors, mayors, and private citizens. And then I left Camp David to listen to other Americans, men and women like you. It has been an extraordinary 10 days, and I want to share with you what I've heard.

First of all, I got a lot of personal advice. Let me quote a few of the typical comments that I wrote down.

This from a southern Governor: "Mr. President, you are not leading this Nation—you're just managing the Government."

"You don't see the people enough any more."

"Some of your Cabinet members don't seem loyal. There is not enough discipline among your disciples."

"Don't talk to us about politics or the mechanics of government, but about an understanding of our common good."

"Mr. President, we're in trouble. Talk to us about blood and sweat and tears."

"If you lead, Mr. President, we will follow."

Many people talked about themselves and about the condition of our Nation. This from a young woman in Pennsylvania: "I feel so far from government. I feel like ordinary people are excluded from political power."

And this from a young Chicano: "Some of us have suffered from recession all our lives."

"Some people have wasted energy, but others haven't had anything to waste."

And this from a religious leader: "No material shortage can touch the important things like God's love for us or our love for one another."

And I like this one particularly from a black woman who happens to be the mayor of a small Mississippi town: "The big-shots are not the only ones who are important. Remember, you can't sell anything on Wall Street unless someone digs it up somewhere else first."

This kind of summarized a lot of other statements: "Mr. President, we are confronted with a moral and a spiritual crisis."

Several of our discussions were on energy, and I have a notebook full of comments and advice. I'll read just a few.

"We can't go on consuming 40 percent more energy than we produce. When we import oil we are also importing inflation plus unemployment."

"We've got to use what we have. The Middle East has only 5 percent of the world's energy, but the United States has 24 percent."

And this is one of the most vivid statements: "Our neck is stretched over the fence and OPEC has a knife."

"There will be other cartels and other shortages. American wisdom and courage right now can set a path to follow in the future."

This was a good one: "Be bold, Mr. President. We may make mistakes, but we are ready to experiment."

And this one from a labor leader got to the heart of it: "The real issue is freedom. We must deal with the energy problem on a war footing."

And the last that I'll read: "When we enter the moral equivalent of war, Mr. President, don't issue us BB guns."

These 10 days confirmed my belief in the decency and the strength and the wisdom of the American people, but it also bore out some of my longstanding concerns about our Nation's underlying problems.

I know, of course, being President, that government actions and legislation can be very important. That's why I've worked hard to put my campaign promises into law—and I have to admit, with just mixed success. But after listening to the American people I have been reminded again that all the legislation in the world can't fix what's wrong with America. So, I want to speak to you first tonight about a subject even more serious than energy or inflation. I want to talk to you right now about a fundamental threat to American democracy.

I do not mean our political and civil liberties. They will endure. And I do not refer to the outward strength of America, a nation that is at peace tonight everywhere in the world, with unmatched economic power and military might.

The threat is nearly invisible in ordinary ways. It is a crisis of confidence. It is a crisis that strikes at the very heart and soul and spirit of our national will. We can see this crisis in the growing doubt about the meaning of our own lives and in the loss of a unity of purpose for our Nation.

> *So, I want to speak to you first tonight about a subject even more serious than energy or inflation. I want to talk to you right now about a fundamental threat to American democracy.*

continues on page 206

continued from page 205

The erosion of our confidence in the future is threatening to destroy the social and the political fabric of America.

The confidence that we have always had as a people is not simply some romantic dream or a proverb in a dusty book that we read just on the Fourth of July. It is the idea which founded our Nation and has guided our development as a people. Confidence in the future has supported everything else—public institutions and private enterprise, our own families, and the very Constitution of the United States. Confidence has defined our course and has served as a link between generations. We've always believed in something called progress. We've always had a faith that the days of our children would be better than our own.

Our people are losing that faith, not only in government itself but in the ability as citizens to serve as the ultimate rulers and shapers of our democracy. As a people we know our past and we are proud of it. Our progress has been part of the living history of America, even the world. We always believed that we were part of a great movement of humanity itself called democracy, involved in the search for freedom, and that belief has always strengthened us in our purpose. But just as we are losing our confidence in the future, we are also beginning to close the door on our past.

In a nation that was proud of hard work, strong families, close-knit communities, and our faith in God, too many of us now tend to worship self-indulgence and consumption. Human identity is no longer defined by what one does, but by what one owns. But we've discovered that owning things and consuming things does not satisfy our longing for meaning. We've learned that piling up material goods cannot fill the emptiness of lives which have no confidence or purpose.

The symptoms of this crisis of the American spirit are all around us. For the first time in the history of our country a majority of our people believe that the next 5 years will be worse than the past 5 years. Two-thirds of our people do not even vote. The productivity of American workers is actually dropping, and the willingness of Americans to save for the future has fallen below that of all other people in the Western world.

As you know, there is a growing disrespect for government and for churches and for schools, the news media, and other institutions. This is not a message of happiness or reassurance, but it is the truth and it is a warning.

These changes did not happen overnight. They've come upon us gradually over the last generation, years that were filled with shocks and tragedy.

We were sure that ours was a nation of the ballot, not the bullet, until the murders of John Kennedy and Robert Kennedy and Martin Luther King, Jr. We were taught that our armies were always invincible and our causes were always just, only to suffer the agony of Vietnam. We respected the Presidency as a place of honor until the shock of Watergate.

We remember when the phrase "sound as a dollar" was an expression of absolute dependability, until 10 years of inflation began to shrink our dollar and our savings. We believed that our Nation's resources were limitless until 1973, when we had to face a growing dependence on foreign oil.

These wounds are still very deep. They have never been healed.

Looking for a way out of this crisis, our people have turned to the Federal Government and found it isolated from the mainstream of our Nation's life. Washington, DC, has become an island. The gap between our citizens and our Government has never been so wide. The people are looking for honest answers, not easy answers; clear leadership, not false claims and evasiveness and politics as usual.

What you see too often in Washington and elsewhere around the country is a system of government that seems incapable of action. You see a Congress twisted and pulled in every direction by hundreds of well-financed and powerful special interests. You see every extreme position defended to the last vote, almost to the last breath by one unyielding group or another. You often see a balanced and a fair approach that demands sacrifice, a little sacrifice from everyone, abandoned like an orphan without support and without friends.

Often you see paralysis and stagnation and drift. You don't like it, and neither do I. What can we do?

First of all, we must face the truth, and then we can change our course. We simply must have faith in each other, faith in our ability to govern ourselves, and faith in the future of this Nation. Restoring that faith and that confidence to America is now the most important task we face. It is a true challenge of this generation of Americans.

One of the visitors to Camp David last week put it this way: "We've got to stop crying and start sweating, stop talking and start walking, stop cursing and start praying. The strength we need will not come from the White House, but from every house in America."

We know the strength of America. We are strong. We can regain our unity. We can regain our confidence. We are the heirs of generations who survived threats much more powerful and awesome than those that challenge us now. Our fathers and mothers were strong men and women who shaped a new society during the Great Depression, who fought world wars, and who carved out a new charter of peace for the world.

We ourselves are the same Americans who just 10 years ago put a man on the Moon. We are the generation that dedicated our society to the pursuit of human rights and equality. And we are the generation that will win the war on the energy problem and in that process rebuild the unity and confidence of America.

We are at a turning point in our history. There are two paths to choose. One is a path I've warned about tonight, the path that leads to fragmentation and self-interest.

continues on page 208

continued from page 207

Down that road lies a mistaken idea of freedom, the right to grasp for ourselves some advantage over others. That path would be one of constant conflict between narrow interests ending in chaos and immobility. It is a certain route to failure.

All the traditions of our past, all the lessons of our heritage, all the promises of our future point to another path, the path of common purpose and the restoration of American values. That path leads to true freedom for our Nation and ourselves. We can take the first steps down that path as we begin to solve our energy problem.

Energy will be the immediate test of our ability to unite this Nation, and it can also be the standard around which we rally. On the battlefield of energy we can win for our Nation a new confidence, and we can seize control again of our common destiny.

In little more than two decades we've gone from a position of energy independence to one in which almost half the oil we use comes from foreign countries, at prices that are going through the roof. Our excessive dependence on OPEC has already taken a tremendous toll on our economy and our people. This is the direct cause of the long lines which have made millions of you spend aggravating hours waiting for gasoline. It's a cause of the increased inflation and unemployment that we now face. This intolerable dependence on foreign oil threatens our economic independence and the very security of our Nation.

The energy crisis is real. It is worldwide. It is a clear and present danger to our Nation. These are facts and we simply must face them:

What I have to say to you now about energy is simple and vitally important.

Point one: I am tonight setting a clear goal for the energy policy of the United States. Beginning this moment, this Nation will never use more foreign oil than we did in 1977—never. From now on, every new addition to our demand for energy will be met from our own production and our own conservation. The generation-long growth in our dependence on foreign oil will be stopped dead in its tracks right now and then reversed as we move through the 1980s, for I am tonight setting the further goal of cutting our dependence on foreign oil by one-half by the end of the next decade—a saving of over 4 1/2 million barrels of imported oil per day.

Point two: To ensure that we meet these targets, I will use my Presidential authority to set import quotas. I'm announcing tonight that for 1979 and 1980, I will forbid the entry into this country of one drop of foreign oil more than these goals allow. These quotas will ensure a reduction in imports even below the ambitious levels we set at the recent Tokyo summit.

Point three: To give us energy security, I am asking for the most massive peacetime commitment of funds and resources in our Nation's history to develop America's own alternative sources of fuel—from coal, from oil shale, from plant products for gasohol, from unconventional gas, from the Sun.

I propose the creation of an energy security corporation to lead this effort to replace 2 1/2 million barrels of imported oil per day by 1990. The corporation will issue up to $5 billion in energy bonds, and I especially want them to be in small denominations so that average Americans can invest directly in America's energy security.

Just as a similar synthetic rubber corporation helped us win World War II, so will we mobilize American determination and ability to win the energy war. Moreover, I will soon submit legislation to Congress calling for the creation of this Nation's first solar bank, which will help us achieve the crucial goal of 20 percent of our energy coming from solar power by the year 2000.

These efforts will cost money, a lot of money, and that is why Congress must enact the windfall profits tax without delay. It will be money well spent. Unlike the billions of dollars that we ship to foreign countries to pay for foreign oil, these funds will be paid by Americans to Americans. These funds will go to fight, not to increase, inflation and unemployment.

Point four: I'm asking Congress to mandate, to require as a matter of law, that our Nation's utility companies cut their massive use of oil by 50 percent within the next decade and switch to other fuels, especially coal, our most abundant energy source.

Point five: To make absolutely certain that nothing stands in the way of achieving these goals, I will urge Congress to create an energy mobilization board which, like the War Production Board in World War II, will have the responsibility and authority to cut through the red tape, the delays, and the endless roadblocks to completing key energy projects.

We will protect our environment. But when this Nation critically needs a refinery or a pipeline, we will build it.

Point six: I'm proposing a bold conservation program to involve every State, county, and city and every average American in our energy battle. This effort will permit you to build conservation into your homes and your lives at a cost you can afford.

I ask Congress to give me authority for mandatory conservation and for standby gasoline rationing. To further conserve energy, I'm proposing tonight an extra $10 billion over the next decade to strengthen our public transportation systems. And I'm asking you for your good and for your Nation's security to take no unnecessary trips, to use carpools or public transportation whenever you can, to park your car one extra day per week, to obey the speed limit, and to set your thermostats to save fuel. Every act of energy conservation like this is more than just common sense—I tell you it is an act of patriotism.

Our Nation must be fair to the poorest among us, so we will increase aid to needy Americans to cope with rising energy prices. We often think of conservation only in terms of sacrifice. In fact, it is the most painless and immediate way of rebuilding our Nation's strength. Every gallon of oil each one of us saves is a new form of

continues on page 210

continued from page 209

production. It gives us more freedom, more confidence, that much more control over our own lives.

So, the solution of our energy crisis can also help us to conquer the crisis of the spirit in our country. It can rekindle our sense of unity, our confidence in the future, and give our Nation and all of us individually a new sense of purpose.

You know we can do it. We have the natural resources. We have more oil in our shale alone than several Saudi Arabias. We have more coal than any nation on Earth. We have the world's highest level of technology. We have the most skilled work force, with innovative genius, and I firmly believe that we have the national will to win this war.

I do not promise you that this struggle for freedom will be easy. I do not promise a quick way out of our Nation's problems, when the truth is that the only way out is an all-out effort. What I do promise you is that I will lead our fight, and I will enforce fairness in our struggle, and I will ensure honesty. And above all, I will act.

We can manage the short-term shortages more effectively and we will, but there are no short-term solutions to our long-range problems. There is simply no way to avoid sacrifice.

Twelve hours from now I will speak again in Kansas City, to expand and to explain further our energy program. Just as the search for solutions to our energy shortages has now led us to a new awareness of our Nation's deeper problems, so our willingness to work for those solutions in energy can strengthen us to attack those deeper problems.

I will continue to travel this country, to hear the people of America. You can help me to develop a national agenda for the 1980s. I will listen and I will act. We will act together. These were the promises I made 3 years ago, and I intend to keep them.

Little by little we can and we must rebuild our confidence. We can spend until we empty our treasuries, and we may summon all the wonders of science. But we can succeed only if we tap our greatest resources—America's people, America's values, and America's confidence.

I have seen the strength of America in the inexhaustible resources of our people. In the days to come, let us renew that strength in the struggle for an energy secure nation.

In closing, let me say this: I will do my best, but I will not do it alone. Let your voice be heard. Whenever you have a chance, say something good about our country. With God's help and for the sake of our Nation, it is time for us to join hands in America. Let us commit ourselves together to a rebirth of the American spirit. Working together with our common faith we cannot fail.

Thank you and good night.

Document Analysis

In this speech, President Jimmy Carter addresses the American people knowing full well what they are thinking about the energy crisis. Although the energy crisis is, indeed, the central topic of the speech, Carter has something much more personal to communicate. The problems the nation faces, he says, are much deeper than simply securing cheap, dependable domestic energy sources; they are more sociological in nature, as the American character seems to be under attack. He relates the energy crisis to a greater crisis by asking, "Why have we not been able to get together as a nation to solve our serious energy problem?"

Carter then describes his ten-day fact-finding mission with the American people, reading through a long list of grievances against both the government in general and himself personally, over his inability to inspire people, his inability to do more about the energy crisis, and what, to Carter, were even more serious problems: a diminished faith in the American government, a gulf that people felt existed between their needs and concerns and what Carter and others talked about in Washington. Agreeing with one of his interviewees, he concludes that the nation faces a "moral and spiritual crisis," or, a "crisis of confidence." Understanding this crisis is vitally important, says Carter, because it strikes "at the very heart and soul and spirit of our national will." It is so serious that it is causing Americans to question the nation's leadership role in the progress of humankind, and the idea that life for the next generation will be better than the one before. Carter then took on a scolding tone, stating that "too many of us now tend to worship self-indulgence and consumption."

This crisis of confidence is larger than the energy crisis, but Carter argues that the energy crisis will test the nation's ability to unite and solve a practical problem of importance to everyone. Carter's speech then becomes more conventional, outlining the need for increased coal and oil production, along with a call for conservation of energy resources and increased use of public transit. Energy conservation, the president argues, is a matter of patriotism, and the crisis could only be met by an attitude of wartime sacrifice. Carter concludes that he has no doubt in the outcome, however, because he has unwavering faith in "our greatest resources—America's people, America's values, and America's confidence."

Essential Themes

In the immediate aftermath of Carter's speech, polling showed a more than 10 percent increase in his job-approval rating. Calls poured in to the White House switchboard, supporting the president's identification of the crisis as a spiritual one. It seemed that Americans were ready for the message that the president wanted them to hear. However, shortly thereafter, Carter determined to reshape his cabinet, demanding the resignation of several key officials. This did away with any good will that the president had garnered as a result of his speech. The public perception was that the administration was rudderless and that Carter could not seem to figure out how to right the ship.

Within four months of this speech, the area that had been Carter's strongest, foreign policy, experienced a shock that did nothing to help the US domestic malaise. In November 1979, radical Islamic students in Iran took more than sixty Americans hostage in the American embassy in Tehran. Whereas Carter had seemed capable of fostering world peace despite his domestic challenges, now it seemed that the president had lost his grip on foreign as well as domestic policy. The Iranian hostage crisis would plague the rest of his presidency.

By the time the 1980 presidential campaign began, the prospect of a second term for

Carter was looking dim. He faced a strong primary challenge from within his own party from Senator Edward Kennedy. Barely managing to gain the Democratic nomination, Carter was then confronted by a revitalized conservative movement within the Republican Party, whose standard bearer was former California governor Ronald Reagan. Reagan, a former actor, seemed much more at home in front of the camera, and seemed to have a much more optimistic vision for the nation than Carter. The incumbent president won only six states and the District of Columbia in the Reagan landslide of 1980, ushering in twelve years of Republicans in the White House.

—Steven L. Danver

Bibliography and Additional Reading

Carter, Jimmy. *White House Diary*. New York: Farrar, 2010. Print.

Dumbrell, John. *The Carter Presidency: A Re-Evaluation*. 2nd ed. New York: Manchester UP, 1995. Print.

Hargrove, Erwin C. *Jimmy Carter as President: Leadership and the Politics of the Public Good*. Baton Rouge: Louisiana State UP, 1988. Print.

Horowitz, Daniel. *Jimmy Carter and the Energy Crisis of the 1970s: The "Crisis of Confidence" Speech of July 15, 1979*. Boston: Bedford, 2004. Print.

Mattson, Kevin. *"What the Heck Are You Up To, Mr. President?": Jimmy Carter, America's "Malaise," and the Speech That Should Have Changed the Country*. New York: Bloomsbury, 2010. Print.

■ "The Great Satan"

Date: November 5, 1979
Author: Ruhollah Khomeini
Geographic region: Iran
Genre: Speech

Summary Overview

On November 4, 1979, a mob of Iranian militants, many of them university students, seized the United States Embassy in Tehran, Iran, taking over sixty people hostage. The following day, Ayatollah Ruhollah Khomeini, a cleric and leader of the Iranian Revolution, gave a speech praising the actions of the revolutionaries and denouncing the United States and its influence in Iran. He famously called the United States the Great Satan for its alleged role in manipulating Iran, including supporting the unpopular, authoritarian shah (king). The shah had been ousted in January 1979 amid widespread rioting, and the ayatollah installed a regime governed by Islamic law in his place. The ayatollah's anti-Western speech would set the tone for Iran's relations with the United States for decades to come.

Defining Moment

American involvement in Iran can be traced to Iran's ties to Great Britain and the discovery of significant quantities of oil in Iran in the early 1900s. In 1909 the Anglo-Persian Oil Company (APOC), which would later become British Petroleum (BP), was formed. The British economy and military were dependant on a steady flow of inexpensive Iranian oil, and during World War I the British stationed troops in Iran to protect their pipelines. Though Iran was technically an independent nation, the British controlled large amounts of its territory.

The United States became involved in Iran as an ally of Great Britain during World War II. Though Iran was neutral, the shah was suspected of Nazi sympathies. Combined British and other Allied forces invaded Iran and the shah, Reza Shah Pahlavi, was deposed and replaced by his son, Mohammad Reza Shah Pahlavi.

In 1951 the popular nationalist Mohammad Mossadeq was elected prime minister of Iran and announced that he would nationalize the nation's oil production. Fearing the loss of these strategic oil reserves, British and US intelligence orchestrated a coup that replaced Mossadeq with a pro-Western leader and restored the power of the shah. The shah returned most of Iran's oil wealth to the United States and Britain and headed a secular government that attempted to modernize and westernize the nation. He received vast amounts of foreign aid in return for his loyalty, but was seen by many Iranians as a puppet of the United States who brutally suppressed his own people.

In 1963 the shah clashed with a group of conservative Islamic clerics led by Ayatollah Ruhollah Khomeini, who preached a return to a religious state that would throw off Western oppression. The uprising was suppressed, and Khomeini imprisoned and then exiled to Iraq, but discontent with the shah's autocratic regime continued to grow. Protests erupted throughout Iran during the 1970s, and government crackdowns could not prevent the growing instability. On January 6, 1979, the shah fled to Egypt, and on February 1, 1979, Khomeini returned to cheering crowds. Under his leadership an Islamic state was established, with the ayatollah declared its supreme leader for life. He reinstated Islamic law and purged the government and civil service of opposition to his new regime, killing thousands.

Anti-American fervor swept the country as Khomeini gave impassioned speeches about purging the nation of Western influence. On November 4, 1979, a group of militant protestors scaled the walls of the United States Embassy in Tehran and took more than sixty hostages, demanding the extradition of the shah, who was in the United States for cancer treatment. The next day Khomeini gave a memorable speech in support of their efforts against what he viewed as Iran's greatest enemy.

Author Biography

Ruhollah Khomeini was born on September 24, 1902 in Khomeyn, Iran. He was from a family of Shia Islamic mullahs and was educated in a series of Islamic schools. After World War I he studied at a seminary until he moved with his religious teacher to the city of Qom in 1922. He studied history, philosophy, and religion, and was a lecturer and noted scholar of Shia Islam in Qom. He wrote prodigiously on Islamic law and philosophy, and was an outspoken critic of the shah. He was made an ayatollah, or religious leader, in the 1950s, and a supreme religious leader or grand ayatollah, in 1963.

Khomeini was imprisoned for antigovernment protests in 1963 and then exiled, first to Iraq and then to France, where he continued to communicate with his followers in Iran and call for an Islamic republic. When the shah was overthrown in 1979, Khomeini returned to Iran as the leader of the revolution and installed a strict Islamic regime while suppressing opposition. He was the political and religious ruler of Iran until his death on June 3, 1989.

HISTORICAL DOCUMENT: *"The Great Satan"*

In the name of God, the merciful, the compassionate

[America, the Great Satan]
I have in mind a story in which on the day the Prophet attained prophethood, that Great Satan shouted and gathered all the devils around himself to say that we are facing some difficulties. In this revolution, the Great Satan, which is the United States, is gathering the devils around himself with a shout. And he has gathered both the baby devils who are in Iran, and the devils outside of Iran, and has started a ruckus.

You all know that during the reign of these two evil men [reference to the two Shahs of the Pahalavi dynasty]—whose reign was also against the law—Iran was at one period captive to Britain, and at another, to the United States. I mean, mostly, the US. The British brought Reza Khan and made him an officer over us, and

Mohammad Reza, when the Allied Forces came to Iran—as they said—it was best that Mohammad Reza remains. Of course, they did not see what is best for the nation; they meant what is best for themselves. During this time extensive problems affected our nation—whether women or men—you all know. Many of you don't remember much of it, which I do remember, that they, during the time of Reza Khan, in the name of unity in form, in the name of lifting the veil, the things they did, what calamities they bestowed on this country. What bullying, what children were aborted as a result of their attacks on women to pull off their veils. That period passed in bitterness, and those same Allied Forces that had brought him—meaning the British—those same people took him from here. And they announced it, too. On the Dehli Radio, which at that time was in their hands, they announced that we brought him and after he betrayed us, we took him. And later, he gathered up his jewelry and packed his bags and placed them in the ship to take with him, on the way—as told by one of his companions –they approached his ship with a special ship for carrying animals, and they took Reza Khan to that place where he belonged. And he said "the luggage?" and they said "they will come later." He was taken to that island and they took the luggage for themselves.

Then it was this second one's turn for plundering, which most of you remember. I mean, all of you remember the end. Also the beginning, many of you remember what they did, and what crimes they committed in this country, and with what deceptive names. Unfortunately, some people believed their extensive propaganda, and some who are partners in their crimes and are still active. These are those same devils who now, with the shouts of the US, have become active, who are busy with deviousness. And our nation must neutralize these conspiracies with vigilance and astuteness.

[Deception and gossip of the enemy]

It is important, these conspiracies . . . these deceptions, this gossip-mongering that is now common. Many rumors for weakening the spirits of the nation. Imagine several thieves kill some people in a place. Then we see that the news arrives that they've killed 100 people somewhere, they've beheaded 25 people. The second time, 400 people were killed, although none of this happened. They want to create rumors to weaken. "All the destroyed checkpoints, all that happened"; it's all to create some mischief and weaken your spirits, our spirits.

Including things that keep being said, and keep being promulgated from around that "a revolution has taken place, but nothing really happened, it's just a revolution and things went from a monarchy form to a mullah form. But nothing's changed." This is something that I also said yesterday. And again I submit to you: that what the nation wanted, all of that has taken place. What did the nation want? When the nation roared, what was it saying? Wasn't it saying "freedom and independence and Islamic

continues on page 216

continued from page 215

Republic"? Which one hasn't happened? Right now there is freedom, such that you and I can sit here and talk. Could we do this five years ago? Independence is there. Right now, this ruckus that the US has created and all this noise that this Great Satan screams and gathers the other devils around itself, this is because its hands have been tied. Its hands from taking our resources; they've been tied from its interest here. And it is afraid that its hands will be tied until the end; that's why it is conspiring.

[Occupying the American nest of spies (e.g. US embassy)]
And that center that our youngsters went and took over—as they informed us—was the center of spying and conspiracy. America expects that it can take the Shah over there, to be busy with conspiracies, and also create a base here for conspiracies, and that our youngsters [will] just sit and watch. Again the rotten roots became active to get us to intervene and tell the youth that "you should come out of the place" where they went. The youth did something because they saw, because they upset these youngsters. A Shah that plundered this country for fifty years and looted it and gave it away, given others to take, and taken himself, and more important than this, has killed so much, has killed civilians—the 15th of *Khordad*—the way it became infamous—fifteen thousand people were murdered. On the day of the 15th of *Khordad* and from that time until now, maybe we have had one hundred thousand dead and several hundred thousand wounded, who we are everyday faced with these injured ones. Just now they told me that there are some injured here who, on the day of the *aid-e Qadir*, the injured are one segment of them. Many of them are the same ones injured during the revolution, at their hands. They said that on the day of *aid-e Qadir*, "they're having a meeting, you should come, too. " Of course I will also go there. They expect that a person who, for fifty years, has done that to this nation, and now the US, with a silly excuse, has taken him and is safeguarding him, and has provided his comfort, and in the name of being sick, or in reality being sick—it makes no difference—has taken him over there and is keeping him, and our youth that protested there, they dispersed them or jailed them. In these two or three days that on that Statue of Liberty—which is a bald-faced lie in the US, "liberty"—our young people went there and chained themselves there and placed a banner there that you must return the Shah. The police went and dispersed them and apprehended several of them. They expect to take our first-rate criminal and keep him there and support him, and also create a center of conspiracy here, and create a center for distributing things that are conspiracy, I don't know, do all the things they want to do, and our nation, and our youth, and our young people from the university, and our devout young people sit and watch so that the blood of this one hundred thousand people, approximately—more or less—is wasted, in order to show respect for Mr. Carter and others like him. There must be no conspiracies. But of course if there were no

conspiracies, if these sabotages did not exist, if that corrupt act didn't exist, all the people are free to be present here. But when there is a conspiracy at play, when those kinds of corrupt acts take place, it upsets our youth. Young people expect that in this world where their country—for which they have made so much effort—is in their own hands. When they see a conspiracy where they want to return to the previous situation and again all their things are lost to the wind, they cannot sit still. There must not be an expectation that they sit still and watch. And they plundered, now carry out their conspiracies, and this conspiracy grows and whatnot. Our young people must destroy these conspiracies with all their focus and with strength.

[Underground and hidden conspiracies]

Today is not a day for us to sit and watch. Today, the situation is a little deeper, a little worse, than the time when Mohammad Reza was there. At that time, it was clear that this traitor was standing up against the nation. And the nation knew him and was standing up against him. Today, there are underground betrayals. Specifically, underground betrayals are being fomented in the very embassies that exist, the most important and the majority of which belong to the Great Satan, which is the US And you cannot sit still and they carry out their conspiracy. One day we realize that a country was destroyed, and with irrelevant talk like 'democracy' and the like, deceives us that the country is a democracy, and anybody has the right to stay here; has the right to foment a conspiracy. This irrelevant talk has to be set aside. And our nation, just as it has happened up to now, must continue the same way from now on and cut off the hands of these people. And if these people don't get it, and don't return the Shah who has taken our treasures and placed large sums in banks—that we may be aware of some of them—has placed them in banks, and it all belongs to the nation, unless they return him,

Right now, this ruckus that the US has created and all this noise that this Great Satan screams and gathers the other devils around itself, this is because its hands have been tied.

and if they don't return him, we will deal with them in a different way. We will deal with Britain in a different way, as well. They shouldn't imagine that we are just sitting still and listening and they can do whatever they damn please. No, it's not like this. The issue is, again, the revolution. A larger revolution than the first one will take place. They must sit in their place and return this traitor. And that other traitor; the traitor Bakhtiar, they must return him. Not that they take that traitor Bakhtiar there and he can sit down and foment a conspiracy and gather people around himself and—I

continues on page 218

continued from page 217

submit to you—write a newspaper and create information, and the British government to arrest and incarcerate our young people for protesting against the Shah or against Bakhtiar. If they don't let go of them and deliver these criminals, or at least expel them from their countries, we have another duty and will act on that duty.

[Not showing weakness in front of conspiracies]
We must go forward with power. If we show weakness, if they sense that we have become weak, if these diminutions that our unfair writers make of our nation, if they feel that these writings have affected us, if they feel this, they will be emboldened and will attack. They will do worse things. Don't feel weakness in yourselves. The more these writers write that "Nothing's happened and this country is in the same place as before", and, like it's written in a piece that I saw the day before yesterday, that "in the previous regime, political activists were jailed, were imprisoned, and now too political activists are imprisoned, this has not changed with them, in the previous regime, there was suffocation and the like, now is the same way". Well, this is to weaken our spirits. Now we will take this under consideration.

[The difference between prisoners during the monarchy and the Islamic Republic]
In the previous regime, some people were imprisoned. Some people were captive. Now, too, some people are imprisoned. No doubt. But who are they? In the previous regime, who was imprisoned, and in the current regime, who are imprisoned? Which groups were executed in the previous regime? Let's look at who was executed in the previous regime and who is executed in the current regime? They don't look at that. They just say all this and think that our youth will be tricked by these words. In the previous regime, the ones they killed, [were] the best of our young people, committed, religious, because they said don't violate, they said don't ruin our country. They were Islamic scholars. This Mr. Montazeri was in jail for ages. That late Mr. Taleghani was in jail, and many like them. The ones who were executed, who were they? The late Sa'eidi was executed, and people like him. These same clerics that they took from around these people and sometimes, they were in jail. This, Mr. Lahouti who is now in the *Sepah*, he was imprisoned for a long time. And what calamities has this man witnessed, and what insults he has endured. In exile, scholars from this *howzeh*, the learned men of this *howzeh*, the scientists of this *howzeh*, were in exile. Here, there, they took them and exiled them. Those who were jailed back then, were these kinds of people. And the ones who were executed were these kinds of people. And the ones exiled were these kinds of people. Now let's look at this side of the story, that there is no difference between now and then. Has been executed: Hoveyda, Nasiri. They are tearing their hearts out for him. These who are writing that there has been no change; these are the same people who in the US,

they speak of that why? Why? Why? And those unjust advocates of human rights are calling out, why is he executed? Those same people who when he is writing "why are there executions in Iran?" do not write about many places where there are genocides by this corrupt US, and they don't say a word about that. But here, that they executed Hovayda, or executed Nasiri, or these corrupt individuals, they are making a lot of noise. And the ones here who are of their kind, they write that there is no difference; now there are executions, back then there were executions, too. Who are the ones imprisoned? Who were they back then? Do you find one imprisoned individual today who is a decent person and is in prison? Do you find a person who is a religious person, a nationalistic person, a person? Back then when they were imprisoned, all the nationalists were imprisoned. And all, I submit to you, like that. And now, who is imprisoned? Those who have committed many crimes and all those crimes, these are in prison. Now see the situation of the imprisonment of these criminals, with the situation of presents back then with those criminals, with these devout people. The situation of then was such that you have to hear from the people who were in prison how things were. These things, as much as we have information, the most important of which is Tehran, the people who are there, and we have constantly instructed, will never abuse anyone. Prison terms are not the kinds that create dissatisfaction. It's prison, but these unfair [writers] write that the prisons are worse than that time, at that place, in those prisons. In one of those prisons, they sawed off the leg of one of our scholars—as has been said. Now these prisons are worse than those? These are all the same devils that Carter has gathered around himself by a great shout, because, in the same way that that Great Satan is scared of the Quran and Islam, now they, too, are afraid of this movement, which is an Islamic movement. And, following that Great Satan, are busy with treachery to weaken the spirit of our people. Our nation, our valorous youth, must go forward with complete strength and not fear these conspiracies. These are not humans that humans should be afraid of.

[Hands behind the veil in Kurdistan unrest]

And these disturbances that sometimes these same devils cause, and the followers of these depraved causes, resolving these, too, is not a problem. They imagine that the situation of Kurdistan is a situation that cannot be resolved. The situation in Kurdistan, if they were not mixed with the Kurdish people, and were not amongst the young and the women and children, we don't want even one innocent person to get killed, if they weren't there, then it would be nothing to mow them down and annihilate them. But unfortunately, it's like this, right now. You have heard, for sure, that these unfair [people] use women and children as shields, and by using them as shields, killed our young people. And those brave young men, so as not to kill the

continues on page 220

continued from page 219

innocent, did not resist. Well, if they were not mixed with them, it would be no effort to destroy them. They are not much of a force. They are a bunch of hoodlums. These hoodlums, we were faced with them in the past, too. These are a bunch of hooligans that are thieves. Sometimes they kidnap, or kill people, too. They are not a force now against the force of the government, or against the force of the nation. We, whenever we want, all the people may go up to Kurdistan and destroy them, but we want the situation to be fixed in peace. These unfair [people] won't let us. Now a group has gone to resolve the problem in peace, to see "what do you want?" The things that they want, we gave to them. Will give. But they want America. They, if you ask them directly, what they want in their hearts, the Democrat Party [*Hezb-e democrat*] will say that we "want the interests of the masses." Meaning, they express a tendency for the Left, but all of them are right-wing, the dishonest right.

Be strong brothers, sisters, be strong with strength. Islam is behind you. The elevated and sublime God is behind you. Go forth with power and strength and build this country yourselves. The country must be build by your hands. May God bless you all.

Imam Khomeini.

Document Themes and Analysis

Khomeini begins his speech with a traditional Islamic invocation, known as the Basmala, which calls on the name of God. He relates a story from the Qur'an about the Prophet Mohammed, who challenged evil so much that Satan summoned his demons for assistance. He draws a parallel to Iran's challenge to the United States: the Iranian revolution has caused the United States, which he directly calls "the Great Satan," to attempt to gather support among "devils" both inside and outside of Iran. In this way he immediately positions the United States and Iran as mortal enemies grounded in religious conflict.

Khomeini then gives a brief overview of the history of Western involvement in Iran. He describes the last two shahs as "evil men" and pawns of the United States and Britain, who have only their own interests at heart. He describes the "calamities bestowed on this country" by the pro-Western shahs, focusing on the literal and symbolic "lifting of the veil," or traditional Islamic dress for women, as the destruction of moral and cultural values. Khomeini notes that there were some Iranians who cooperated with the shahs and now sympathize with the United States. He claims that these forces are still at work, and they must be found and destroyed.

Khomeini warns his audience not to listen to rumors and Western propaganda, particularly suggestions that the ayatollah's supporters are committing crimes or that the revolution has simply replaced the monarchy with religious authority. These are only the murmurs of a desperate United States, he claims, and proof that the Great Satan is worried. He asserts that the fact that he is able to make this speech, which surely would not have been allowed by the shah, is evidence that the revolution is succeeding in throwing off Western control and providing freedom.

The ayatollah then addresses the seizure of the US Embassy—which he calls a "center of spying and conspiracy"—by revolutionaries as a noble act by young people who could not sit idly by and watch the shah escape punishment and continue to conspire with the United States against the Iranian people. Khomeini announces that he will not intervene to release the hostages or make the revolutionaries leave the embassy. The United States is defending a murderer, he argues, who for fifty years has executed his own countrymen. Western powers must return the shah and other figures from the pro-Western Iranian government for trial. Khomeini also warns that the enemies of the state are harder to identify but even more dangerous now that they are not in power and are trying to bring down the righteous government through spying and intrigue disseminated through embassies.

Khomeini also addresses the issue of the mass imprisonments and executions in Iran, drawing a distinction between those before and after the revolution. He argues that good people, especially religious leaders and scholars, were imprisoned and executed by the shah, but that the revolutionaries have only imprisoned and executed corrupt thieves and spies. He claims that Western onlookers and human rights activists criticizing his regime are hypocritical both for ignoring this difference and for failing to condemn atrocities committed by the United States.

He closes his speech with a description of the Kurdish rebellion, which he claims is incited by Western disruption. Khomeini says the rebellion is little threat and could be put down easily, except they use women and children as shields. The speech ends, as it began, with an Islamic invocation and the assurance that "Islam is behind you."

The Iran hostage crisis and Khomeini's hostile rhetoric led to great tension between Iran and the United States and consequences on both sides, including American economic sanctions against Iran and the failure of US President Jimmy Carter's re-election bid when he was unable to resolve the hostage situation. Of the sixty-six hostages taken, thirteen were quickly released and another was freed later. The remaining fifty-two hostages were held for 444 days and released soon after President Carter left office in 1981. Khomeini continued to lead an anti-Western theocracy and refer to the United States as Iran's greatest enemy, the Great Satan. He was also hostile to the world's other superpower, the Soviet Union, calling it the Lesser Satan, while Israel was termed the Little Satan. The ayatollah further encouraged militant Islamic revolution in neighboring countries, and Iran was at war with Iraq for eight years.

Khomeini dismantled many of the economic drivers that had supported Iran's prosperity under the shah. Trade with the West was virtually eliminated and oil production plummeted. During the war with Iraq, Khomeini liquidated much of the nation's gold reserves and inflation skyrocketed. Despite bread lines and war, Khomeini was the undisputed leader of Iran for the remainder of his life, and he embodied the principal of rule by those who carried out Islamic law. The term "Great Satan" would become a lasting symbol of Islamic resistance to Western power.

—*Bethany Groff Dorau*

Bibliography and Additional Reading

Axworthy, Michael. *Revolutionary Iran: A History of the Islamic Republic*. New York: Oxford UP, 2016. Print.

Kinzer, Stephen. *All the Shah's Men: An American Coup and the Roots of Middle East Terror*. Hoboken: Wiley, 2003. Print.

Lesch, David W. *1979: The Year That Shaped the Modern Middle East*. Boulder: Westview, 2001. Print.

Documents Relating to the Soviet Invasion of Afghanistan

Date(s): September 23, 1980; November 5, 1982; March 21, 1986
Authors: Central Intelligence Agency (CIA), Defense Intelligence Agency (DIA), President Ronald Reagan
Geographic region: Afghanistan
Genre: Report

Summary Overview

During the Cold War, two sizeable military conflicts each directly involved one of the two superpowers: Vietnam (the United States) and Afghanistan (the Soviet Union). Earlier in the 1970s, communism had expanded in Vietnam after the United States decided to withdraw its forces. In Afghanistan in the late 1970s, the government was transformed from a non-aligned one into a Communist-headed one, even while much of the rest of the country stood at odds with that result. Factional fighting and political assassinations ensued, and in December 1979 Soviet troops entered Afghanistan to install a Soviet-backed regime and extend its authority to the rest of the nation. Many Americans, both inside and outside the government, advocated not only a forceful diplomatic response but also military assistance to the Afghani *mujahedeen* fighters resisting the Soviet occupation. The CIA and Defense Intelligence Agency (DIA) sought to learn more about what was happening, and which Afghan groups' interests might align with those of the United States. Thus did the CIA/DIA produce reports such as the ones reprinted here, while also arranging the shipment of military supplies to anti-Soviet groups in Afghanistan. Meanwhile, President Reagan made public statements intended to keep pressure on the Soviets to withdraw their troops. If the Soviets prevailed, it was thought, it could give them a significant victory in the ongoing Cold War.

Defining Moment

Throughout the Cold War, both the United States and the Soviet Union tried to expand their spheres of influence and block each other's geopolitical maneuvers. Entering the 1970s, Afghanistan had been a non-aligned country and was relatively inactive on the international stage. This changed in 1973, however, when a coup overthrew the Afghan monarchy. King Mohammad Zahir Shah had recently appointed a prime minister who was anti-Communist and who advocated instituting some liberal Western ideas. Mohammad Daoud Khan, a former prime minister, led the 1973 coup and was more open to communist ideas. Strongly supported by the Soviet Union, Daoud Khan tried to balance Soviet interests against American desires. In 1978, the Soviets seemed to tire of dealing with him, resulting in a Communist takeover under Nur Mohammad Taraki. Taraki signed a treaty with the Soviet Union, which the Soviets used as justification for their invasion in December 1979. However, in September 1979, Taraki was overthrown and killed by Hafizullah Amin. On December 27th, Amin himself was overthrown by Soviet-backed forces and replaced by a strong friend of the Soviet Union, Babrak Karmal. The Afghan Communist Party now firmly controlled the government, and during the last week of 1979 about 40,000 Soviet troops entered Afghanistan to insure that Karmal stayed in power and carried out policies in line with Soviet desires.

Prior to 1978, the central government in Afghanistan had allowed tribal and regional leaders a substantial amount of freedom in the handling of local affairs. Karmal and his Soviet allies, on the other hand, wanted total control of the nation. Although not everyone in every region opposed that idea, there was widespread opposition to the attempt to radically strengthen the central government. The effort to enforce the central government's policy of total control placed a heavy burden on Soviet troops charged with enforcing the policy. In addition, Moscow's policy virtually insured that the United States would provide supplies and assistance to those opposing the Communists. The CIA coordinated most of the American assistance going to the anti-Soviet leaders. After Reagan was elected president, he supported many anti-Communist efforts, through both covert and overt means.

Author Biographies

The Central Intelligence Agency, a civilian agency, was created in 1948 to gather information on foreign governments and foreign operatives both openly and covertly. It grew out of the Office of Strategic Services, a World War II agency. The Directorate of Analysis was established in 1952 and reorganized in 1981, with several sub-offices including Political Analysis.

The Defense Intelligence Agency was established in the early 1961. It is a joint operation of all branches of the military. Its mission is to provide needed information for the Department of Defense and the armed forces, not the government as a whole.

Ronald Wilson Reagan (1911–2004) was born in Illinois, although most of his adult life was spent in California, where he served as governor (1966–73). He was president of the United States from 1981 to 1989, being noted for his political vision and conservative views.

HISTORICAL DOCUMENT: *Documents Relating to the Soviet Invasion of Afghanistan*

[Central Intelligence Agency, Directorate of Intelligence, Office of Political Analysis]

23 September 1980
MEMORANDUM
SUBJECT: The Soviets and the Tribes of Southwest Asia

SUMMARY

The Tribes

There are hundreds of tribes belonging to more than a dozen ethnic groups in Afghanistan and neighboring areas of Iran and Pakistan. Most are loosely organized with little or no central authority, but in some the power of the tribal chief is nearly absolute. Some have only a few thousand members; others, several hundred thousand. Some tribesmen are nomadic, most are settled farmers, and a few have abandoned the tribal way of life almost entirely.

These variations occur even with tribes. Pushtun [or Pashtun] Mohmands (living on both sides of the Pakistan-Afghan border near the Khyber Pass) include both nomads and farmer, and some members of the tribe have broken with traditional ways altogether to become urban laborers or even physicians or lawyers.

Tribes in Afghanistan

Tribal loyalties have more importance among the Pushtun of eastern and southern Afghanistan than among most of the other ethnic groups. Among the Uzbeks of northern Afghanistan, for example, tribal ties are weak, and they probably are not much stronger for many of the Turkmen of northwest Afghanistan. Even for the Pushtuns, tribal membership usually means little more than a feeling of identity with others in the tribe. Organized action by an entire tribe is rare. An attack on one part of a tribe may bring some response from other tribesmen not directly affected, but each extended family or village usually determines its own course without reference to the rest of the tribe or to the ostensible tribal leaders.

Those who cling most closely to the tradition tribal ways are the least likely to be influenced by Communism. To the extent that the tribesmen have an ideology it is a belief that a combination of Islam and even older tribal traditions is the proper guide for action. Among most tribes, the traditional views include such things as the obligation to seek revenge, masculine superiority, an emphasis on personal bravery and honor, and suspicion of outsiders. Tradition also tends to sanctify everything from rules governing property ownership to ways of treating illness. Any change in the traditional way of life is considered wrong, and modern ideas–whether Communist or Western–are seen as a threat.

The Afghan insurgency has been strongest among the most traditionally minded such as the Pushtuns of Paktia Province and the Nuristanis and Tajiks farther north along the Pakistani border. They resist the Afghan Marxists and the Soviets more to preserve their old ways than to fight Communism. Some of the reforms that have incensed the tribes–education of women, for example–are neither Communist nor anti-Islamic, but they conflict with the tribesman's perceptions of what is right. . . .

In the tribal villages, it is in the interests of the most influential men–local landowners, religious leaders, or both–to reject reforms, especially Communist ones, that threaten both their property and their political power. Nevertheless, Communist programs might have some appeal to the settled tribes. . . .

continues on page 226

continued from page 225

A major problem for the Soviets is to convince the tribes that it is to their advantage to support the government. The Soviets can bolster their arguments with offers of weapons and money. They can also threaten retaliation against tribesmen who will not cooperate, or threaten to support their traditional enemies. . . .

Even were the tribesmen motivated by more than an opportunity to steal, they would probably regard any arrangement with the Soviets as a temporary expedient and would turn against them as soon as it seemed advantageous to do so. . . In the past, tribesmen fighting for outsiders have changed alliance in response to offers of better pay, or even when they decided their pay [was] inadequate. A recent book review published in Tashkent made much of Britain's problems in the 19th century in trying to keep Afghan tribes loyal.

* * *

[Defense Intelligence Agency, Directorate for Research, 5 November 1982]

Assessment of Insurgent Equipment

All six major resistance groups appear to have adequate supplies of modern assault weapons and ammunition but still lack the heavier weaponry needed to turn the military situation in their favor. Smaller groups in isolated provinces, however, are still affected by shortages of small arms and ammunition.

While Soviets can and do temporarily disrupt the two-way flow of men and supplies through the major mountain passes, we do not believe the Soviets can permanently seal off Afghanistan from the rest of the world. The rugged terrain, limited manpower thus far available to Soviet/Afghan commanders, hostility of the local populace and the resourcefulness of the resistance argue against a successful effort to permanently close the passes.

Insurgent Equipment Deficiencies

Major military equipment deficiencies among resistance forces include more and better surface-to-air missiles and anti-aircraft guns, heavy machine guns, antitank missiles, antitank mines, man-pack mortars and tactical radio equipment. . . .

Resolve of the Resistance Forces

The resistance forces could continue the insurgency for the foreseeable future at its present level against current Soviet forces. We believe the Soviets would have to double their strength to break the current stalemate . . .

Proclamation 5450—Afghanistan Day, 1986
March 21, 1986

By the President of the United States of America

A Proclamation

The people of Afghanistan celebrate March 21 as the beginning of their new year. In ordinary times, it is an occasion of joy, renewal, and hope for a better future. March 21, 1986, however, does not mark the passage of an ordinary year, nor does it bring cause to celebrate. For the heroic Afghan people it marks the beginning of yet another year in their struggle for national liberation against the ruthless Soviet military force that seeks to conquer them.

Over six years ago, on December 27, 1979, the Soviet army invaded Afghanistan, a small, friendly, nonaligned, and deeply religious neighbor. For six long years, the Soviets have sought to obliterate Afghan culture and remold that ancient nation into a replica of their own system, causing millions of Afghan refugees to flee the country. To achieve their goals, the Soviets installed the quisling regime of Babrak Karmal, in which Soviet advisors now man the key positions. They have transported thousands of young Afghans to the Soviet Union for reeducation in summer camps, universities, and specialized institutions, and they have set up a secret police apparatus matched in brutality only by their own KGB.

These tactics hardly begin to describe the continuing horror of the Soviet attempt to subjugate Afghanistan, a violation of international law repeatedly condemned by the United Nations. Despite calculated destruction of crops, irrigation systems, and livestock, indiscriminate air and artillery bombardments of civilian areas, brutal reprisals against noncombatants, and other unspeakable atrocities, the Afghan people remain

> *Those who cling most closely to the tradition tribal ways are the least likely to be influenced by Communism. To the extent that the tribesmen have an ideology it is a belief that a combination of Islam and even older tribal traditions is the proper guide for action.*

continues on page 228

continued from page 227

determined to defend their liberty. The resistance has in fact become more effective than ever.

The Soviet failure to quell the Afghan people is not surprising. The Afghans have a long history of resisting invasion and of defending their homes, their faith, and their culture. Since December 1979, resistance fighters have acquitted themselves well in many engagements against larger and better armed Soviet forces. The Afghan freedom fighters have shown they can render all of their country unsafe for the invader. After six years of hard, bloody fighting, the Soviets are far from achieving their military goals.

Recently the Afghan resistance has taken major steps toward achieving unity and making its presence felt on the international scene, strengthening its ability to publicize the Afghan cause. We welcome these developments. With the support of the community of civilized nations, the Afghan resistance has also increased its efforts to aid civilians remaining inside Afghanistan. This will improve the Afghan people's ability to carry on the fight and counter the deliberate Soviet attempt to drive the civilian population away from resistance-controlled areas.

Throughout the period of their brutal occupation, the Soviets have tried—but failed—to divide the international supporters of the cause of Afghan freedom. They cannot be divided. The overwhelming votes in the United Nations General Assembly, year after year, are but one expression of the ongoing commitment of the world community to this cause. For our part we reaffirm our commitment to support this just struggle until the Soviets withdraw; until the people of Afghanistan regain their liberties, their independence, and the right to self-determination; and until the refugees can return in safety to their native land. Only such a settlement can command the support of the Afghan people; a settlement that does not command their support will not end this war.

Today, we pay tribute to the brave men, women, and children of Afghanistan and remind them that their sacrifice is not and will not be forgotten.

The Congress, by Senate Joint Resolution 272, has authorized and requested the President to issue a proclamation designating March 21, 1986, as "Afghanistan Day."

Now, Therefore, I, Ronald Reagan, President of the United States of America, do hereby proclaim March 21, 1986, as Afghanistan Day.

In Witness Whereof, I have hereunto set my hand this twenty-first day of March, in the year of our Lord nineteen hundred and eighty-six, and of the Independence of the United States of America the two hundred and tenth.

Ronald Reagan

Mujahideen in Kunar, Afghanistan.

Document Themes and Analysis

Although the United States was officially an outside observer, these documents demonstrate that the Americans were involved in the Afghan wars of the 1980s. The first two documents were for internal use by government agencies, while the proclamation by Reagan was for the general public. American intelligence agencies sought out weaknesses in the Soviet position and ways to help the resistance. The American president conducted a public relations campaign that likewise helped the resistance. Although few Americans paid much attention to Afghanistan prior to the Soviet invasion in 1979, throughout the 1980s events in and related to Afghanistan moved to the forefront of public awareness.

The CIA analysis of the socio-political situation in Afghanistan was necessary because, previously, the United States had had only moderate involvement with the country. Although formal diplomatic relations had been established in 1921, there was little interaction prior to the onset of the Cold War, and even then it was limited to a few economic projects. While some were intended to strengthen the central government, as can be seen from the CIA analysis, this had not happened in this case. Tribal loyalties took precedence over national ones, although even tribes were "loosely organized." The CIA accurately understood this to be a positive factor in resisting the Communist incursion, as most local tribal and religious leaders were ready to help the highest bidder, provided it did not interfere in local affairs. In 1980, then, this fit American needs perfectly.

The DIA report represents the more controversial aspect of American involvement in

Afghanistan: providing weapons to the resistance. The DIA's analysis of what weapons and weapon systems were available to the tribes fighting the Soviets, was at the heart of this matter. The 1982 list of resistance groups' "deficiencies" in military equipment was basically a requisition by the DIA for the weapons listed. The DIA accurately understood that local forces resisting the non-native troops could sustain a conflict at a much lower cost than could those from the outside. Thus, it was left to the Soviets as to how much of their resources they were willing to expend to obtain a military victory.

President Reagan campaigned on a strong anti-Communist platform. In Afghanistan, this included covert operations supporting the resistance. In addition, he also harshly criticized Communism in public forums. Thus the proclamation of Afghanistan Day in 1986 was not a simple statement applauding Afghan society. What he issued was a short history of the Soviet incursion into that country and the resulting war—at that time more than six years old. Reagan closed with the dramatic statement of tribute, "to the brave men, women, and children of Afghanistan and remind them that their sacrifice is not and will not be forgotten." The Afghan sacrifice as opposed to the brutality of the Soviets was the president's constant message. This message was designed to strengthen support for the Afghan resistance both within the United States and internationally. In the end, the Soviet Union did not want to increase its effort to the level reflected in the DIA report, and, facing strong international opposition, the Soviets withdrew from Afghanistan in 1989.

Examining the three documents, in the Historical Document section, it can be seen that each one has a central theme. The CIA report's theme is the tribal nature of the country, and the advantages that that gives to those resisting the central government. For the DIA, it is the types of heavy weapons needed to augment those already available in the nation (mostly side arms). Finally, for Reagan, it is the dichotomy between the heroic Afghan people and the invading forces of the Soviet Union, which three years earlier he had called the "Evil Empire." In spite of the fact that each document differs in its specifics, the group is united in so far as seeking ways to support the anti-Communist movement.

The fact that Afghanistan has never been a strongly unified nation is seen in these documents as key to being able to develop anti-Soviet forces. Tradition normally triumphs over change in Afghanistan, and the implication in the CIA document is that the US could assist this through giving the right type of support. The slightly later DIA document focuses on military items that might be supplied to the tribal divisions for them to prevail in the conflict. Sticking to military matters, the DIA's analysis projected a positive outcome for the resistance, unless the Soviets decide to greatly increase their support of the Afghan government.

President Reagan, in his proclamation, very definitely interprets the situation from an American, anti-Communist, point of view. (As is often the case, one person's "freedom fighter" is another person's "terrorist.") Ultimately, the hopeful optimism of the DIA report and Reagan's observations proved correct. The Soviets could not bear up under the long-term strain of a foreign war. However, when the United States became involved in Afghanistan as a result of the September 11 al-Qaida attacks on American targets, things in Afghanistan were both the same and yet different. One can recognize in the 1980 CIA analysis a picture of tribal and regional differences that still held true in 2001 (and after), the main difference being the growth of the Taliban and al-Qaida.

—*Donald A. Watt*

Bibliography and Additional Reading

Braithwaite, Rodric. *Afgantsy: The Russians in Afghanistan 1979–89*. Oxford: Oxford UP, 2011. Print.

Feifer, Gregory. *The Great Gamble: The Soviet War in Afghanistan*. New York: HarperCollins, 2009. Print.

Office of the Historian. "The Soviet Invasion of Afghanistan and the US Response, 1978–1980." *US Department of State: Bureau of Public Affairs*. Washington: US Department of State, 2016. Web.

Savranskaya, Svetlana. "The Soviet Experience in Afghanistan: Russian Documents and Memoirs." *The September 11th Sourcebooks: Volume II: Afghanistan: Lessons from the Last War*. Washington: The National Security Archive, 2016. Web.

Wilson Center. "Soviet Invasion of Afghanistan." *Wilson Center Digital Archive: International History Declassified*. Washington, DC: Woodrow Wilson International Center for Scholars, 2016. Web.

Remarks on the Attack in Beirut

Date: October 24, 1983
Author: Ronald Reagan
Genre: Speech; news conference

Summary Overview

Upon returning to the White House on the evening of Sunday, October 23, 1983, President Ronald Reagan made a short 204-word statement of sorrow and outrage in connection with the bombing of the US Marine barracks in Beirut, Lebanon, which had happened earlier that day. On the following day, October 24, Reagan attended a previously scheduled press meeting with representatives from regional broadcasters (not the normal Washington correspondents). He used this forum to make the statement presented here and to answer questions.

In this short prepared statement, Reagan reaffirmed the American interest in having a stable and vital Lebanese nation. As on the previous day, he stated that those responsible for the bombing, and the bombing at the French barracks, would be held accountable. For Reagan, strengthening the democratic government of Lebanon was a step toward creating not only a more stable Middle East, but a more stable world. In the question-and-answer session following his statement, Reagan attempted to show how the presence of the Marines in Lebanon was in line with previous policies, in addition to giving further information regarding the immediate future for US troops in Lebanon.

Defining Moment

On the morning of October 23, 1983, a truck carrying about 2,000 pounds of explosives was driven into a building near the Beirut airport which the Marine Corps had been using as a barracks. The resulting explosion killed 241 members of the US military, 220 of them Marines. (This was the largest loss of life for the Marine Corps since the closing battles of World War II.) As part of President Reagan's efforts to communicate with the American people, he occasionally scheduled gatherings with individuals representing local or regional news organizations, not the normal Washington press corps. Making use of this luncheon/press conference, Reagan gave a fuller explanation of the mission which the Marines had been serving. For the first time, he also provided information about the commandant of the Marine Corps traveling to Beirut and gathering information to be used as the basis for recommendation of future actions.

The death of so many individuals from one act of terrorism was traumatic for the nation. Most Americans could not understand how this could have happened. Reagan did not comment on the specifics of the bombing, other than that it happened and the death toll; rather, he tried to make clear the importance of the mission in which the Marines had been engaged. The deployment of Marines to Lebanon, in 1981, had been as part of a multilateral force which was to strengthen the Lebanese government. Also wielding power in the country, however, were various Islamic and Christian militias, many of which were allied with

The U.S. embassy in Beirut after being bombed.

Syria or Iraq, traditional enemies of the United States. After that initial task of stabilization had been accomplished, most of the multilateral forces were withdrawn, including the American forces. However, the country was not completely stable, and in 1982 the United States sent in the Marines to protect Palestinian refugees, in response to hundreds of Palestinian civilians being killed by non-Palestinian militias. This US force was more symbolic than active, with some of the sentries not even carrying loaded weapons.

As a result of the bombing, which intelligence information indicated had been planned and carried out by Hezbollah (a hardline Islamist group aligned with Iran and Syria), the relationship between Iran and the United States deteriorated even further. (The 1979 capture of the US Embassy in Tehran, by Iranian militants was the beginning of enmity between the two nations.) As the principal state sponsor of Hezbollah, Iran had some of its assets seized and these ultimately given to the families of those killed in the attack.

Author Biography

Ronald Wilson Reagan (1911-2004) was the fortieth president of the United States, serving from 1981 to 1989. Raised in Illinois, he was a 1932 graduate of Eureka College. He worked in radio prior to moving to Hollywood and becoming an actor. In the 1950s, he became well known from his television work, during which time he served two terms as the president of the Screen Actors Guild. Becoming a staunch conservative Republican, in the early 1960s he was elected governor of California, serving from 1967 to 1975, He was elected president in 1980, and served two terms. He was a strong anti-Communist, and the military build-up during his administration played a role in moving the Soviet Union to toward a peaceful dissolution. Just after he left office, Reagan was diagnosed with Alzheimer's which limited his post-presidential activity.

Major news organizations assign individuals to cover events in the White House and other governmental activities in Washington, D.C. The Regional Editors and Broadcasters, to whom Reagan spoke on this occasion, were individuals sent by local radio/television stations to take part in this special luncheon/press conference. Reagan's idea was that these individuals would ask questions on issues which concerned the "average citizen" not the "out-of-touch journalist."

HISTORICAL DOCUMENT: *Remarks on the Attack in Beirut*

Good afternoon. And given what has happened in Lebanon, I've put aside the remarks that I was prepared to give here today and I'd like to read you this statement.

Yesterday's acts of terrorism in Beirut, which killed so many young American and French servicemen, were a horrifying reminder of the type of enemy that we face in many critical areas of the world today—vicious, cowardly and ruthless.

Words can never convey the depth of compassion that we feel for those brave men and for their loved ones.

Many Americans are wondering why we must keep our forces in Lebanon.

Well, the reason they must stay there until the situation is under control is quite clear. We have vital interests in Lebanon. And our actions in Lebanon are in the cause of world peace. With our allies, England, France and Italy, we're part of a multinational peacekeeping force seeking a withdrawal of all foreign forces from Lebanon and from the Beirut area while a new Lebanese Government undertakes to restore sovereignty throughout that country.

By promoting peace in Lebanon we strengthen the forces for peace throughout the Middle East. This is not a Republican or a Democratic goal, but one that all Americans share. Peace in Lebanon is key to the region's stability now and in the future.

To the extent that the prospect for future stability is heavily influenced by the presence of our forces, it is central to our credibility on a global scale. We must not allow international criminals and thugs such as these to undermine the peace in Lebanon.

The struggle for peace is indivisible. We cannot pick and choose where we will support freedom. We can only determine how. If it's lost in one place, all of us lose. If others feel confident that they can intimidate us and our allies in Lebanon they will become more bold elsewhere. If Lebanon ends up under the tyranny of forces hostile to the West, not only will our strategic position in the eastern Mediterranean be threatened but also the stability of the entire Middle East including the vast resource areas of the Arabian Peninsula.

In conjunction with our multinational force partners, we're try, taking measures to strengthen the capabilities of our forces to defend themselves. The United States will not be intimidated by terrorists.

We have strong circumstantial evidence linking the perpetrators of this latest atrocity to others that have occurred against us in the recent past, including the bombing of our embassy in Beirut last April.

Every effort will be made to find the criminals responsible for this act of terrorism so this despicable act will not go unpunished.

And now I know you have some questions.

QUESTIONS AND ANSWERS

Q. What are the options? Do you increase the number of the troops in Lebanon? Do you withdraw the troops in Lebanon? What do you consider the options to be?

A. The option that we cannot consider is withdrawing while their mission still remains. And they do have a mission, contrary to what some people have intimated in the last 24 hours or so. And it is tied in with the effort that we launched more than a year ago to try and bring peace to the total area of the Middle East because of its strategic importance to the whole free world, not just the United States.

I couldn't give you a time on this. The options are, well, I have sent, as of this morning, General Kelly, the Commandant of the Marine Corps, is on his way to Lebanon to review again what we can do with regard to improving the defensive measures, the safety measures, for the Marines who are stationed there. And we're looking at every possible option in that regard. But the mission remains and it remains as yet unfulfilled, although there's been tremendous success so far.

I'll take the gentleman and then I'll take you.

Q. Mr. President, Bill Applegate from WLS in Chicago. You have discussed the diplomatic mission. But what specifically is the military mission for the Marines?

A. Well, you have to go back a little bit in memory on the situation there in the Middle East. We know, of course, our country, since 1948, has been pledged to the continued existence and the security of Israel. And we've had these numerous wars between the Arab states and Israel with a number of the Arab states, or virtually all of them, refusing to accept the existence of Israel as a nation. We have, back over the years, as witness more recently—the previous Administration—the Camp David accords. So what we submitted was the idea of us continuing to help

continues on page 236

continued from page 235

as we did at Camp David, in furthering that process, bringing more nations into the kind of peaceful arrangement that occurred between Egypt and Israel, producing more Egypts if you will. At the same time, however, and for a number of years now, Lebanon has been torn, torn with strife. They've had factions. And from just factions and kind of rioting situations, they've developed over the years to where kind of warlords set up with their own military forces.

So we recognized that before we could proceed with the peace plan—remember that when we started this Israel had been forced to cross its own border, was shelling Beirut—the P.L.O. militias inside Beirut were shelling back—the casualties were hundreds of civilians every day, dying and being grievously wounded—so we recognized that what we had to resolve first was this issue. To get Syria, which had crossed from the other border, get Syria, get Israel, get the P.L.O. organization out of Lebanon. And then to have a stabilizing force while a government could be established in Lebanon and their military could then acquire the capability necessary to reinstituting their control over their own borders.

And this was why the multinational force went in. To provide that stability so that when the Lebanese forces moved out as the other forces— the Israelis and the Syrians—left, there could be maintenance of order behind them.

> ***The struggle for peace is indivisible. We cannot pick and choose where we will support freedom. We can only determine how.***

Now that mission remains, except that, and it did have measures of great success, some 5,000 of the organized P.L.O. militias, as you remember, were shipped out of Lebanon. Some of those, we fear, have been infiltrated back in, mainly by way of Syria now. But that was accomplished. A government was established. The, we have helped very definitely with the training of the Lebanese Army and they proved the quality of that training recently in the fighting in the hills and around Suk al Gharb and we've, we think that they have, they don't have the size yet to where they could take over, let's say, the policing of that area and of the airport, and still have enough manpower to go out and restore order as they're supposed to.

So that mission remains. And as of now, they have finally agreed upon a date and a place for a meeting in which the Government of Lebanon is going to try and bring in representatives of the hostile factions within Lebanon to broaden the base of the Government.

So we think that the goal is worthy. And we think that great progress has been made that would not have been made if it were not for the multinational force.

Now I can take you.

Q. Mr. President, Susan Hutchison, KIRO-TV from Seattle. I'm a journalist but I'm also the wife of a US Marine Corps captain. And as such I am personally grieved over the loss of life. I am wondering what message you can give to Americans who are frustrated with the loss of life in a region that historically has not known peace, and, many think, will never know peace, and yet our men are over there as peacekeepers.

A. I wish there were an instant answer here that would resolve all your concerns. You didn't tell me about that one when we were having lunch here. I understand your concern. I understand all Americans' concern and I have to say that I don't know of anything that is worse than the job I have, and having to make the calls that I have made as a result of these snipings that have taken place in the past.

I wish it could be without hazard.

But the alternative is to look at this region, which, as I say, is vital. Our allies in Western Europe; the Japanese; it would be a disaster if a force took over the Middle East, and a force is ready to do that, as witness what has taken place in Yemen, in Ethiopia and now the forces that, some several thousand that are theirs, in Syria. The free world cannot stand by and see that happen.

Yes, this has been an area torn by strife over the centuries. And yet, not too many years ago, before the kind of breakup, Lebanon was a very prosperous, peaceful nation that was kind of known as the gateway to the East. And we believe it can be again. The, probably no one or no country was more at war with Israel than Egypt and yet we've saw Egypt and Israel come to a peace treaty and Israel give up the Sinai and so forth that it conquered in war. We have to believe that this we must strive for. Because the alternative could be disaster for all of our world.

Yes, way back there. I've been staying up front too much.

Q. Mr. President, I'm Ronald Post with KRON in San Francisco. I want to ask you, you've addressed now several times the issue that we cannot get out of the Middle East. But would you address the other argument that if you're not going to get out, then let's just not put Marines back in to replace those who have been killed and wounded to do exactly the same thing in the same place, but if you're going to do a job, go into Lebanon and do it with some real force, which is another argument that's been raised.

A. But, you see, what that entails, and that is the difficult thing, we would then be engaged in the combat. We would be the combat force. We would be fighting against Arab states. And that is not the road to peace. We're still thinking in terms of that long-range peace.

Lebanon must be resolved and resolve within itself its own problems.

Then, and incidentally, not much attention has been paid to the diplomatic process that's been going on for all of this time and before, round the clock. And we

continues on page 238

continued from page 237

now are seeking a replacement for Ambassador McFarlane, who's with us here today, who is now national security adviser, but someone to replace him. But he could tell you, and I used to sit here feeling guilty, hearing his schedule of from Damascus to Beirut to Tel Aviv, back. And hours and hours of meetings. But they have all led to this present cease-fire, to this Government that is now in Lebanon and to the effort to enlarge that Government.

So we're keeping on with that process. But to in, with the present mission of the multinational force, and remember there are four nations involved there, enlarging their forces, if it would help with the mission they're performing, would be one thing.

But to join in to the combat and become a part of the combative force, actually all we would really be doing would be increasing the number of targets. And this is, and risking really the start of overall conflict and world war.

No. Our mission, I think, makes sense. I think it has proven itself so far. The tragedy is coming not really from the warring forces. It is coming from little bands of individuals, literally criminal-minded, who now see in the disorder that's going on an opportunity to do what they want to do. And we are, we're going to make every effort we can to minimize the risk but also to find those responsible.

Q. Lilly Flores-Vella, KIII-TV in Corpus Christi, Tex. I'd like to know what exactly is under way now. What efforts are under way to identify the casualties and those missing and how are the relatives being notified about this?

A. You have touched upon what is a heartbreaking part of this particular incident.

That was the headquarters building. There were more than 200 men sleeping in that building when this occurred. The records—the personnel records—are either destroyed or buried someplace beneath all that rubble. And because they were sleeping, many of the men were not wearing their dog tags. And the delay in notification of the families, it must be a cruel additional punishment for these people who wait in suspense and we have no answers until—we're doing everything, or the Marines are, that they can to identify and, when they can get actual identification, such as bodies that did have dog tags or where comrades can recognize and identify, to notify the individual families. But it's a long and tragic story because of the other, the loss of the records.

Economic Outlook

Q. Mr. President, I'm Ray Rosenblum with WBRJ in Marietta, Ohio, and I want to congratulate you on paying attention to the news media outside of Washington. Regarding the economy, I'd like to ask—if you were an investor, would you invest today in the US stock market and do you think it will continue to grow?

A. Yes, I do and I can't because I have a secret trust on account of I'm not supposed to know what I have anymore. (General laughter.) So I can't buy anything like that. But yes, I think this recovery is solid and I think that it is based on something that we've never had in any of the previous recessions—there have been about eight since World War II. And every one of them prior to this was treated with a quick fix, an artificial stimulant by Government spending and money supply and so forth and if you'll look back at the history of them, every one of them was followed within a matter of two or three years by another one and each time inflation was higher and unemployment was greater than before.

But this one—we have brought inflation, as you've probably been told in the briefings already, down from two years of double-digit and even figures as high as 17 percent, to where for the last 12 months it has been 2.6 percent, which is the lowest 12-month average in 17 years. And I think that what we're seeing there in the stock market, it flurries a little bit, goes up but then every once in a while there's some profit-taking and it drops a few points.

But I think one figure that's been ignored and maybe all of you can treat with it, just a week or so ago, it was announced that we were up now to 70, more than 78 percent of our industrial capacity is now at work. We were way down, far below that to where there was just unused industrial capacity because there wasn't any demand for the product. But this is getting practically up to prosperous times to have that much of our capacity used.

Q. One more question, Mr. President.
A. I can't ignore that, that look. You.

Q. Jean Enerson, KING television in Seattle. You said that General Kelly, who is on his way to the Middle East, will recommend more safety measures. If he recommends more troops be sent in, will you do that? And what if, what other safety measures are you considering?

A. Well, if this were recommended on the basis that their mission, as I say, could be furthered by some difference in the size of the mission, I would certainly take seriously the recommendation of the man who's the Commandant of the entire Marine Corps.

There are a number of other things to look at—options that have been presented. We know, for example, that we have to follow, or find a new headquarters, an operational post for the headquarters, because that was totally destroyed. One of the options being considered is, could part of the support services of that kind be stationed on one of our ships that are offshore there, one of our naval vessels. More improvements in the actual defensive structure. There're any number of options and that's why an expert is going over there to come back and tell us what can be done.

continues on page 240

Final Comments

UNIDENTIFIED: Thank you, Mr. President.

REAGAN: Carna has told me that I can't take any more on account of the time is up. Carna said that that was a, that had, did say that that was the last one wasn't it?

UNIDENTIFIED: I said that was the last one.

REAGAN: And I can give you the best reason in the world why I've got to leave. The President of Togo is due in my office in just about three minutes and I should be there before he gets there to say hello to him. But your remarks about treating with the regional press. Believe me it is a great pleasure and I wish there were, I'm going to tell them that next time they've got to schedule any luncheons like this for about a half an hour extra or give me some free time following it so that I can run over, if I want to, because you do ask questions and I learn as much from your questions as, maybe more, than you learn from my answers. And it's been a great pleasure to have all of you here.

God bless you all and thank you coming.

GLOSSARY

P.L.O.: Palestinian Liberation Organization, at that time designated a terrorist organization by the US government and militant enemy of Israel; it subsequently evolved into the Palestinian Authority ruling the West Bank and Gaza (but more recently losing Gaza to Hamas)

Suk al Gharb: a city to the southeast of Beirut, which became the site of a major battle when Israel withdrew its forces from Lebanon; the Druze militia defeated others in the area, but was blocked from invading Beirut by the Lebanese Army, which went on to occupy Suk al Gharb with the support of shelling from US naval vessels

Document Analysis

As President Reagan made his short statement to members of the regional press, the extent of the tragedy in Beirut was still being processed by many across the nation. While Reagan had probably been prepared to address the major improvements in the economy (the subject of one of the later questions), the events in Beirut had pushed all else to the side. Through his statement and answers to the various questions, Reagan attempted to explain why the troops were in Beirut and what steps were being taken to deal with the devastation. Although Reagan was clear that the Marines had been there as neutral peace keepers (although their support of the Lebanese Army at Suk al Gharb destroyed the "neutral" image for many anti-government groups), given the attack, he was less clear about the role they should play in the future.

Lebanon was created when the Ottoman Empire was dismantled after World War I, but it was not until after World War II that all foreign (French) troops were withdrawn and it was truly independent. Up until 1975, it was a stable nation with a balanced economy, governed under a constitution which mandated shared power among the various religious communities. However, in 1975 this fell apart due to demographic changes and increased pressure from Palestinian refugees in the south. After Israel invaded in 1982, in response to P.L.O. attacks from Lebanese bases, a multilateral force was sent in as a peace-keeping operation and to secure Beirut. Summarized somewhat differently by Reagan, this was nevertheless the reason American troops were initially sent to Lebanon in 1982. Because of the role played by the United States, Reagan affirmed (in response to a question) his desire that Lebanon follow the example of Egypt and sign a peace treaty with Israel. However, in retrospect, the battle "around Suk al Gharb" was seen by many as a major contributing factor leading to the bombing, since the US Navy had assisted the Lebanese Army against the non-government militia.

The extent of the devastation was made clear by Reagan's answer to the question regarding casualties. He let everyone know why it was going to take days, instead of hours, to know exactly who had been killed in the bombing. Knowing that American troops could no longer depend upon the goodwill of the militias, changes would have to be made. Sending in General Kelly, Commandant of the Marines, was a move to try to resolve the military issues which were inherent in having troops based in Beirut. As Reagan stated in response to the fourth question, the desire had been, and still was, that the American forces would not be seen as "combat force(s)" but rather as peace-keepers. He avoided making any statements which would necessitate a major military response by the US, instead saying the bombing was undertaken by "little bands of individuals, literally criminal-minded." Thus, while Reagan wanted to "minimize the risk" for the troops in Lebanon, he understood that some changes were necessary and made it clear that General Kelly was charged with making certain that in the future, Marines in Lebanon would be secure.

Essential Theme

In the mind of President Reagan, and of many other American leaders, Lebanon being a stable and moderate Arab state was a key component in bringing lasting peace to the Middle East. Thus, it was worth the risk of deploying troops to Lebanon in hopes of restoring the government's "sovereignty throughout the country." Even though the history of the region reflected ongoing conflict among various groups, Reagan was optimistic that peace was a possibility. In addition, he believed that ultimately terrorism had to be confronted. Even though it had proven costly, Reagan saw the situation in Lebanon as one in which the interests of peace (and of the United States) could be achieved. Thus, he was not advocating pulling out all the troops in response to the bombing, but rather focusing on the peace-keeping mission while making changes to ensure safety in the future.

Reagan was surely giving his honest views as of that day, yet the future unrolled differently from what was implied in his statements. With no major change in the situation, four months later all American troops were pulled out of Lebanon. (Some Marines did remain in the region, albeit based on naval vessels.) When the United States verified that Hezbollah had been responsible for the bombing, plans for attacking the base from which the bomber had driven the truck were scrapped for fear that a military raid would upset some of the Arab states friendly with the United States. Many years later, Osama bin Laden stated that he began making plans to attack the United States because, in his view, the United States' failure to respond militarily to this bombing, thus showing that it was weak. Although the rhetoric of dedication to mission and the promise of retaliation by Reagan was forceful in this press conference, it was not matched by subsequent actions. In many ways, this compounded the tragedy of needlessly losing so many lives by lack of preparedness.

—Donald A Watt

Bibliography

Evans, Alexandra T., and A. Bradley Potter. "When Do Leaders Change Course? Theories of Success and the American Withdrawal from Beirut, 1983–1984." *Texas National Security Review*, 28 Feb. 2019, tnsr.org/2019/02/when-do-leaders-change-course-theories-of-success-and-the-american-withdrawal-from-beirut-1983-1984/. Accessed 25 Feb. 2020.

Geraghty, Timothy J. *Peacekeepers at War : Beirut 1983-the Marine Commander Tells His Story*. Washington, D.C., Potomac Books, 2009.

Glass, Andrew. "Reagan Condemns Beirut Bombing, Oct. 23, 1983." *POLITICO*, 23 Oct. 2018, www.politico.com/story/2018/10/23/reagan-condemns-beirut-bombing-oct-23-1983-921655. Accessed 25 Feb. 2020.

Sloyan, Patrick J. *When Reagan Sent in the Marines : The Invasion of Lebanon*. New York, Thomas Dunne Books, 2019.

"Transcript of Address by President on Lebanon and Grenada." *The New York Times*, 28 Oct. 1983, www.nytimes.com/1983/10/28/us/transcript-of-address-by-president-on-lebanon-and-grenada.html. Accessed 25 Feb. 2020.

Zenko, Micah. "When Reagan Cut and Run." *Foreign Policy*, Foreign Policy, 7 Feb. 2014, foreignpolicy.com/2014/02/07/when-reagan-cut-and-run/.

Memos Concerning a Meeting between Donald Rumsfeld and Saddam Hussein

Date: December 19, 1983; December 27, 1983
Authors/Participants: Donald Rumsfeld; Tariq Aziz; Saddam Hussein
Genre: Memos, meeting minutes

Summary Overview

In an attempt to establish peace, attain stability in the Middle East, and work towards ending the Iran-Iraq war (1980–88), Donald Rumsfeld was sent as a presidential envoy representing the Reagan administration to meet with Iraq's foreign minister, Tariq Aziz, and its president, Saddam Hussein. In a series of meetings the men outlined their overall goals, which included the prospect of limiting Iran's access to weaponry and generally increasing Iraqi oil exports. Overall, these meetings were viewed as being positive for US-Iraq relations, but within the decade the United States would come to condemn Iraqi actions, leading to two wars between the nations and, ultimately, the imprisonment and execution of Saddam Hussein.

Defining Moment

A war over territorial disputes between Iran and Iraq began in 1980 and would span a total of eight years. Leading up to the war there was significant upheaval in the Middle East at the time and a series of events created extreme tension between the secular, nationalist Iraq and the Iranian Islamic republic. This tension grew and eventually Iraq decided to attack Iran believing it would be an easy victory. Initially, the United States took a neutral position on this conflict. However, with Iran holding its own in the conflict and actively seeking out weapons, and Iraq facing a very critical weapons depletion, the United States grew concerned that there could be a potential Iranian victory—a nation the US government had no diplomatic ties with since 1980. This concern led the Americans to officially support Iraq in the war and to remove Iraq from their list of those supporting international terrorism. Additionally, and perhaps more importantly, the United States provided loans to Iraq, along with intelligence and military support, and began making official visits to meet with Iraqi leaders.

Serving as a presidential envoy for the Reagan administration, Donald Rumsfeld held two official meetings with Foreign Minister Tariq Aziz and Iraqi President Saddam Hussein in December 1983. In the first meeting, Rumsfeld made it clear to Aziz that the United States had a firm goal of establishing peace and stability in the Middle East. Furthermore, Rumsfeld communicated the wishes of the Reagan administration to end the Iran-Iraq war—a task Aziz would go on to specifically ask Western assistance in doing—and to complete a series of other goals specific to the region. During this meeting the focus of the conversation shifted to oil, and Aziz emphasized the importance of stable relationships with customers like the United States. While Rumsfeld assured the foreign minister that the United States was willing to offer help, he did specify that aid would perhaps be limited to discouraging allies from providing weapons

> - How start?
>   - Saddam moves against Kurds in north?
>   - US discovers Saddam connection to Sept. 11 attack or to anthrax attacks?
>   - Dispute over WMD inspections?
>   - Start now thinking about inspection demands.

Excerpt from Donald Rumsfeld memo dated November 27, 2001.

to Iran. While meeting with Iraqi President Saddam Hussein, Rumsfeld reiterated his promise to dampen arms sales to Iran, and once again the discussion shifted focus to oil exports and potential opportunities in the transport of oil. Overall, these meetings were viewed to be successful in terms of US-Iraq relations.

Author Biographies

After attending Princeton University and serving in the Navy, Donald Rumsfeld spent three terms in the House of Representatives from 1962–69. Rumsfeld held various business positions before working in a variety of capacities for US presidents Nixon, Ford, Reagan, and Bush (Jr.). After 9/11, Rumsfeld, who was Secretary of Defense at the time, oversaw the US-led attack on Afghanistan. Rumsfeld was praised early on but resigned in 2006 under scrutiny for his role in the war efforts.

Foreign Minister Tariq Aziz was a foreign minister and deputy premiere for the Iraqi government, and was considered to be a highly visible figure in the government under the Hussein regime. Aziz was eventually accused and found guilty of committing deliberate crimes against humanity and murder. Although Aziz maintained his innocence, he was sentenced to death by hanging in 2010. Before the execution took place, however, Aziz died in a hospital in 2015 due to ill health.

Saddam Hussein served as the Iraqi president for over two decades from the late 1970s until 2003. Under his regime the Iraqi population was divided by those who flourished through connections and access to wealth and those who endured great suffering at the hands of their own government. Military conflicts with the United States led to the eventual capture of Saddam in 2003. After being found guilty of crimes against humanity, he was put to death by hanging in 2006.

HISTORICAL DOCUMENT: Memos Concerning a Meeting between Donald Rumsfeld and Saddam Hussein

1. Document One

Department of State
[?] December 1983
Subject: Rumsfeld's Larger Meeting with Iraqi Deputy PM and FM Tariq Aziz, December 19

SECRET

[...]
3. Rumsfeld opened by noting that while there were differences of view between us, we also see a number of areas of common interest. We both desire regional peace, stability, and correcting regional imbalance. Aziz had talked about "the unnatural imbalance" which can exist at a certain point in history, giving a country more weight than it deserves. The US agreed with this perception. Three principle areas that had been discussed in this regard:
   —ending the Iran-Iraq War in a way that would not feed Iran's ambitions;
   —bringing Egypt back into the Arab world as a counterweight in the Middle East;
   —freeing Lebanon of foreign forces.
He invited Aziz to summarize Iraq's position ...

4. Aziz eloquently and without notes presented overview of Iraqi policies, noting that Iraq had for the last several years been developing its direct high-level exchange with the US in order to clarify positions and remove misunderstandings that had existed between us because of a lack of such contacts...

7. Aziz stated that oil made this [i.e., economic development] possible and that, as an exporter of oil, Iraq needed long-term, stable, and good relations with its customers. The West also benefitted by Iraq's development ...

8. Turning to Iraq's relationship with the US, Aziz noted that Rumsfeld would find Iraq's president a thoughtful man who analyzed situations and learned from experience ... Although there might still be differences between us, we could develop healthy relations and mutual understanding ...

10. Aziz then requested US and Western help in ending the Iran-Iraq War. Acknowledging that US did not have relations with Iran, he asserted that US could contribute more than it has to reducing Iran's ability to continue the war. He said he had been heartened by the line in the president's [i.e., Reagan's] letter that stated, "the Iran-Iraq could post [sic] serious problems for the economic and security interests of the US, it's friends in the region and in the free world." ... Iraq recognized that Iranians had the right to choose their own government, but Iran did not have the right to interfere in the internal affairs of others...

12. Rumsfeld concluded the meeting by returning to the theme of redressing the present regional imbalance. He stated that when he accepted the job of special

continues on page 246

continued from page 245

negotiator he had quickly realized importance of Iraq in the area and necessity of making a visit ... The US could be helpful, to some extent, in ending the war. We would approach our allies in terms of specific instances where they are directly or indirectly providing weapons which enable Iran to continue the war, and would try to foster their strategic understanding of the dangers of focusing on narrow, short-term interests...

2. *Document Two*

Department of State
27 December 1983
Subject: Rumsfeld Mission: December 20 Meeting with Iraqi President Saddam Hussein

SECRET

[...]
2. Summary and Comment: In his 90-minute meeting with Rumsfeld, Saddam Hussein showed obvious pleasure with President's letter and Rumsfeld's visit and in his remarks removed whatever obstacles remained in the way of resuming diplomatic relations, but did not take the decision to do so. He said Arabs should press Syria to leave Lebanon and also that Iraq favored development of positive relations between PLO and Jordan. Rumsfeld told Saddam US and Iraq had shared interests in preventing Iranian and Syrian expansion. He said US was urging other states to curtail arms sales to Iran and believed it had successfully closed off US-controlled exports by third countries to Iran. In response to Rumsfeld's interest in seeing Iraq increase oil exports, including through possible new pipeline across Jordan to Aqaba, Saddam suggested Israeli threat to security of such a line was major concern and US might be able to provide some assurances in this regard. Our initial assessment is that meeting marked positive milestone in development of US-Iraqi realtions [sic] and will prove to be of wider benefit to US posture in the region.

> **R**umsfeld opened by noting that while there were differences of view between us, we also see a number of areas of common interest. We both desire regional peace, stability, and correcting regional imbalance.

END SUMMARY AND COMMENT.

3. … Foreign Minister Tariq Aziz … attended on Iraqi side … Both Iraqi leaders were in military dress with pistols on hips. While security was elaborate, both [men] appeared vigorous and confident. Iraqi TV photographed Saddam's initial greeting of Rumsfeld and presentation of President Reagan's letter. Rumsfeld opened by conveying president's greetings and expressing his pleasure at being in Baghdad and with his interesting and informative exchange with foreign minister previous evening.

GLOSSARY

PLO (Palestine Liberation Organization): organization devoted to the liberation of Palestine; it generally opposes Israel

Document Themes and Analysis

The official goal of these December 1983 meetings from the US perspective, according to the transcripts, appears to be to send a message to the Iraqi government that there is intent to aid it in its conflict with Iran. While some statements are clouded in vagueness, such as the general desire to establish overall stability in the region, other statements are much more specific, particularly when it comes to the discussion of the transport of oil in the area. It is clear that both the United States and Iraq perceive Iran as a credible threat in the war, and both sides agree that Iran's capability of gathering weapons to continue the war efforts needed to be disrupted. It is also clear that the United States and Iraq intended to continue to rely on one another in terms of the buying and selling of oil exports.

What is especially interesting in this context is that in 1983 there were reports issued by Iran accusing Iraq of chemical warfare. Rumsfeld, however, did not mention chemical warfare in the meetings with Aziz or Hussein. While Aziz did make mention of human rights in the meeting with Rumsfeld, the issue regarding whether or not chemical weapons were used on either the Iraqi or the Iranian side was simply not addressed. Nevertheless, by 1983 the United States officially condemned the Iraqi use of chemical weapons, and, in 1988, the United Nations arranged a ceasefire agreement between Iraq and Iran. This was a violent and brutal war resulting in anywhere from 500,000 to 1 million casualties (there are conflicting reports), both military and civilian. While this war raged on for eight full years and caused extreme loss to both Iran and Iraq, there were no reparations and there were no border changes—both of which had been contributing causes to the start of the initial conflict.

Some two decades later—i.e., in the midst of the Iraq War that began in 2003—both Aziz and Hussein were charged and found guilty of committing crimes against humanity and the murder of their own people. Both men were sentenced to death for their crimes, with Aziz dying of poor health prior to execution. Hussein was executed in a public hanging in 2006.

Bitter divisions remain in the region to this day, as violent conflict rages on. There are continuing clashes between the Shia and the Sunni, and between Iran and various Arab nations. Violence and conflict is rampant in Syria, Iraq, and Yemen. Some speculate that the unrest in the Middle East will see no end, regardless of what outside forces may attempt to do for the region.

—Amber R. Dickinson

Bibliography and Additional Reading

Balaghi, Shiva. *Saddam Hussein: a Biography*. Greenwood Press, 2006.

Cockburn, Andrew. *Rumsfeld: His Rise, Fall, and Catastrophic Legacy*. Scribner, 2011.

Doucet, Lyse. "Legacy of Iran-Iraq War Lives On." *BBC News*, BBC, 6 Oct. 2015, www.bbc.com/news/world-middle-east-34444337.

Evans, Michael. "Shaking Hands with Saddam Hussein." *JFK and the Diem Coup: Declassified Records*, nsarchive2.gwu.edu/NSAEBB/NSAEBB82/.

Johnson, Robert. *The Iran-Iraq War*. Palgrave Macmillan, 2011.

Nassiriya, Iraq Agence France-Presse in. "Tariq Aziz, Former Aide to Saddam Hussein, Dies in Iraqi Hospital." *The Guardian*, Guardian News and Media, 5 June 2015, www.theguardian.com/world/2015/jun/05/tariq-aziz-dies-iraq.

The Iran-Contra Affair

Date: March 4, 1987
Author: Ronald Reagan
Genre: Address

Summary Overview

In late 1986, an obscure Lebanese newspaper broke the story that members of President Ronald Reagan's administration had been secretly selling missiles to the Islamic Republic of Iran in exchange for their promised assistance in freeing American hostages held in Lebanon. These revelations were followed by news that profits from these arms sales had been secretly diverted to the Contras, a right-wing group based in Honduras and Costa Rica seeking to topple the leftist Sandinista government in Nicaragua. Congress had banned aid to the Contras in 1984, yet members of Reagan's National Security Council led by Lt. Col. Oliver North had created a secret network to keep them funded and armed. Discovery of the Reagan administration's illegal shadow foreign policy led to three separate investigations—a special commission led by Senator John Tower, televised Congressional hearings, and an Independent Counsel investigation by Lawrence E. Walsh; these resulted in several indictments, convictions, appeals, and presidential pardons over subsequent years. Questions of what Reagan knew about the details of these illegal operations have persisted. Although charges were never brought against Reagan himself, the Iran-Contra Affair resulted in a significant drop in the president's high poll numbers and was considered to be the worst US political scandal since Watergate.

Defining Moment

The Iran-Contra Affair was a scandal arising from the intersection of two parallel covert programs in the mid-1980s. Reagan was committed to rolling back communism globally, and as part of that campaign he had the CIA assemble an anti-Sandinista army in Honduras in order to overthrow the Marxist-led government in Nicaragua. The Nicaraguan rebels came to be called the "Contras" and were largely unknown until 1982. As Congress became more aware of their activities, the Reagan administration argued that their goal was to interdict weapons from the Sandinistas to Marxist guerrillas in El Salvador. After authorizing aid for this narrow purpose, revelations of Contra abuses in Nicaragua led Congress to place more restrictions on US aid, culminating in the passage, in 1984, of the Boland Amendment (after Senator Edward Boland of Massachusetts), which banned further US assistance to them.

Reagan was committed to the Contras, however, whom he referred to as the "moral equivalent of our Founding Fathers." He gave permission for members of his National Security Council to set-up a secret network to arm the Contras. Overseen by Reagan's National Security Advisor Robert McFarlane and his successor Admiral John Poindexter, and spearheaded by Marine Lt. Colonel Oliver North, the covert operation sought secret foreign donations from nations like Saudi Arabia to keep the Contras supplied and fighting. These covert activities were hidden

President Ronald Reagan with Caspar Weinberger, George Shultz, Ed Meese, and Don Regan discussing the President's remarks on the Iran-Contra affair, Oval Office.

from Congress and continued until Congress reauthorized lethal aid in 1986.

During this same time, Iran supported a militia named Islamic Jihad in Lebanon's civil war, which was responsible for kidnapping seven Americans, including a CIA station chief. The United States had declared Iran a state-supporter of terrorism, which made it ineligible for any US weapons. In 1985, a shadowy Iranian named Manucher Ghorbanifar claimed to have connections in the Iranian government who could help free American hostages. Ghorbanifar established secret ties with Israeli arms dealers, who approached Americans about an opening to Iranian "moderates," who promised that in exchange for missiles for use in their war against Iraq they would assist in the release of American hostages. Reagan's team worked with Ghorbanifar and the Israelis to send Iran American TOW and HAWK missiles (eventually totaling 1,500). Despite only one hostage initially being released (two others later), and the murder of the CIA station chief, the operation continued. In early 1986, North put in motion what he described as "a neat idea," the diversion of profits from the illegal Iranian missile sales to the Contras.

It is documented that Reagan knew of the missile sales and illegal Contra funding. Several members of his administration have written that Reagan agonized over the American hostages and also felt their captivity made him look weak. Evidence as to whether Reagan knew of the diversion of Iranian missile sale profits to the Contras is less concrete, although recollections

Oliver North's mugshot, after his arrest.

by participants such as North indicate that Reagan knew of and approved the diversion.

In the fall of 1986, a Lebanese newspaper revealed Reagan's "arms-for-hostages" efforts. Reagan had pledged to never negotiate with terrorists or kidnappers, so these revelations damaged Reagan's hard-line reputation. The majority of the American public told pollsters that they did not believe Reagan's denials.

Public disapproval pressured Reagan to appoint a commission headed by Senator John Tower of Texas to investigate "the Iran-Contra Affair." The Tower Commission issued its report in early 1987 and stated that although it found no evidence of Reagan's involvement, his hands-off approach to governing allowed his subordinates to carry out the illegal activities.

On March 4, Reagan gave an Oval Office address to the nation in which he accepted responsibility for the Iran-Contra affair but portrayed it as one that grew out of good intentions and escalated slowly out of control through negligence, rather than being an organized effort.

Author Biography

Ronald Wilson Reagan was born on February 6, 1911, in Tampico, Illinois. He graduated from Eureka College in 1932 and became a well-known Hollywood actor. Reagan was elected as the president of the Screen Actors' Guild in 1947. In the 1950s his political views moved from liberal to a conservative and he hosted a popular TV show *General Electric Theater* and toured GE plants praising American capitalism. In 1966 Reagan was elected to the first of two terms as governor of California. He was elected fortieth president of the United States as an ardent cold warrior and small-government conservative in 1980 and was re-elected in 1984. Reagan married actor Jane Wyman in 1940 with whom he had two children; they divorced in 1948 and in 1952 Reagan married actor Nancy Davis with whom he had two children. Reagan died on June 5, 2004.

HISTORICAL DOCUMENT: *The Iran-Contra Affair*

My fellow Americans:
I've spoken to you from this historic office on many occasions and about many things. The power of the Presidency is often thought to reside within this Oval Office. Yet it doesn't rest here; it rests in you, the American people, and in your trust. Your trust

continued from page 251

is what gives a President his powers of leadership and his personal strength, and it's what I want to talk to you about this evening.

For the past 3 months, I've been silent on the revelations about Iran. And you must have been thinking: "Well, why doesn't he tell us what's happening? Why doesn't he just speak to us as he has in the past when we've faced troubles or tragedies?" Others of you, I guess, were thinking: "What's he doing hiding out in the White House?" Well, the reason I haven't spoken to you before now is this: You deserve the truth. And as frustrating as the waiting has been, I felt it was improper to come to you with sketchy reports, or possibly even erroneous statements, which would then have to be corrected, creating even more doubt and confusion. There's been enough of that. I've paid a price for my silence in terms of your trust and confidence. But I've had to wait, as you have, for the complete story. That's why I appointed Ambassador David Abshire as my Special Counsellor to help get out the thousands of documents to the various investigations. And I appointed a Special Review Board, the Tower board, which took on the chore of pulling the truth together for me and getting to the bottom of things. It has now issued its findings.

I'm often accused of being an optimist, and it's true I had to hunt pretty hard to find any good news in the Board's report. As you know, it's well-stocked with criticisms, which I'll discuss in a moment; but I was very relieved to read this sentence: ". . . the Board is convinced that the President does indeed want the full story to be told." And that will continue to be my pledge to you as the other investigations go forward. I want to thank the members of the panel: former Senator John Tower, former Secretary of State Edmund Muskie, and former national security adviser Brent Scowcroft. They have done the Nation, as well as me personally, a great service by submitting a report of such integrity and depth. They have my genuine and enduring gratitude.

> *I've studied the Board's report. Its findings are honest, convincing, and highly critical; and I accept them.*

I've studied the Board's report. Its findings are honest, convincing, and highly critical; and I accept them. And tonight I want to share with you my thoughts on these findings and report to you on the actions I'm taking to implement the Board's recommendations. First, let me say I take full responsibility for my own actions and for those of my administration. As angry as I may be about activities undertaken without my knowledge, I am still accountable for those activities. As disappointed as I may be in some who served me, I'm still the one who must answer to the American people for this behavior. And as personally distasteful as I find secret bank accounts and diverted funds—well, as the Navy would say, this happened on my watch.

Let's start with the part that is the most controversial. A few months ago I told the American people I did not trade arms for hostages. My heart and my best intentions still tell me that's true, but the facts and the evidence tell me it is not. As the Tower board reported, what began as a strategic opening to Iran deteriorated, in its implementation, into trading arms for hostages. This runs counter to my own beliefs, to administration policy, and to the original strategy we had in mind. There are reasons why it happened, but no excuses. It was a mistake. I undertook the original Iran initiative in order to develop relations with those who might assume leadership in a post-Khomeini government.

It's clear from the Board's report, however, that I let my personal concern for the hostages spill over into the geopolitical strategy of reaching out to Iran. I asked so many questions about the hostages welfare that I didn't ask enough about the specifics of the total Iran plan. Let me say to the hostage families: We have not given up. We never will. And I promise you we'll use every legitimate means to free your loved ones from captivity. But I must also caution that those Americans who freely remain in such dangerous areas must know that they're responsible for their own safety.

Now, another major aspect of the Board's findings regards the transfer of funds to the Nicaraguan contras. The Tower board wasn't able to find out what happened to this money, so the facts here will be left to the continuing investigations of the court appointed Independent Counsel and the two congressional investigating committees. I'm confident the truth will come out about this matter, as well. As I told the Tower board, I didn't know about any diversion of funds to the contras. But as President, I cannot escape responsibility.

Much has been said about my management style, a style that's worked successfully for me during 8 years as Governor of California and for most of my Presidency. The way I work is to identify the problem, find the right individuals to do the job, and then let them go to it. I've found this invariably brings out the best in people. They seem to rise to their full capability, and in the long run you get more done. When it came to managing the NSC staff, let's face it, my style didn't match its previous track record. I've already begun correcting this. As a start, yesterday I met with the entire professional staff of the National Security Council. I defined for them the values I want to guide the national security policies of this country. I told them that I wanted a policy that was as justifiable and understandable in public as it was in secret. I wanted a policy that reflected the will of the Congress as well as of the White House. And I told them that there'll be no more freelancing by individuals when it comes to our national security.

You've heard a lot about the staff of the National Security Council in recent months. Well, I can tell you, they are good and dedicated government employees, who put in long hours for the Nation's benefit. They are eager and anxious to serve their country. One thing still upsetting me, however, is that no one kept

continues on page 254

continued from page 253

proper records of meetings or decisions. This led to my failure to recollect whether I approved an arms shipment before or after the fact. I did approve it; I just can't say specifically when. Well, rest assured, there's plenty of record-keeping now going on at 1600 Pennsylvania Avenue.

For nearly a week now, I've been studying the Board's report. I want the American people to know that this wrenching ordeal of recent months has not been in vain. I endorse every one of the Tower board's recommendations. In fact, I'm going beyond its recommendations so as to put the house in even better order. I'm taking action in three basic areas: personnel, national security policy, and the process for making sure that the system works.

First, personnel—I've brought in an accomplished and highly respected new team here at the White House. They bring new blood, new energy, and new credibility and experience. Former Senator Howard Baker, my new Chief of Staff, possesses a breadth of legislative and foreign affairs skills that's impossible to match. I'm hopeful that his experience as minority and majority leader of the Senate can help us forge a new partnership with the Congress, especially on foreign and national security policies. I'm genuinely honored that he's given up his own Presidential aspirations to serve the country as my Chief of Staff. Frank Carlucci, my new national security adviser, is respected for his experience in government and trusted for his judgment and counsel. Under him, the NSC staff is being rebuilt with proper management discipline. Already, almost half the NSC professional staff is comprised of new people.

Yesterday I nominated William Webster, a man of sterling reputation, to be Director of the Central Intelligence Agency. Mr. Webster has served as Director of the FBI and as a US District Court judge. He understands the meaning of "rule of law." So that his knowledge of national security matters can be available to me on a continuing basis, I will also appoint John Tower to serve as a member of my Foreign Intelligence Advisory Board. I am considering other changes in personnel, and I'll move more furniture, as I see fit, in the weeks and months ahead.

Second, in the area of national security policy, I have ordered the NSC to begin a comprehensive review of all covert operations. I have also directed that any covert activity be in support of clear policy objectives and in compliance with American values. I expect a covert policy that, if Americans saw it on the front page of their newspaper, they'd say, "That makes sense." I have had issued a directive prohibiting the NSC staff itself from undertaking covert operations—no ifs, ands, or buts. I have asked Vice President Bush to reconvene his task force on terrorism to review our terrorist policy in light of the events that have occurred.

Third, in terms of the process of reaching national security decisions, I am adopting in total the Tower report's model of how the NSC process and staff should work. I am directing Mr. Carlucci to take the necessary steps to make that happen. He will report back to me on further reforms that might be needed. I've created the post of NSC legal adviser to assure a greater sensitivity to matters of law. I am also determined to make the congressional oversight process work. Proper procedures for consultation with the Congress will be followed, not only in letter but in spirit. Before the end of March, I will report to the Congress on all the steps I've taken in line with the Tower board's conclusions.

Now, what should happen when you make a mistake is this: You take your knocks, you learn your lessons, and then you move on. That's the healthiest way to deal with a problem. This in no way diminishes the importance of the other continuing investigations, but the business of our country and our people must proceed. I've gotten this message from Republicans and Democrats in Congress, from allies around the world, and—if we're reading the signals right—even from the Soviets. And of course, I've heard the message from you, the American people. You know, by the time you reach my age, you've made plenty of mistakes. And if you've lived your life properly—so, you learn. You put things in perspective. You pull your energies together. You change. You go forward.

My fellow Americans, I have a great deal that I want to accomplish with you and for you over the next 2 years. And the Lord willing, that's exactly what I intend to do.

Good night, and God bless you.

Document Themes and Analysis

In this address, Reagan breaks several months of silence since his initial denials that any arms were sold to Iran in exchange for the release of hostages. Reagan declares that this was in order for him to ascertain the facts. He is responding to the just released Tower Commission Report (he refers to it as "the Board"), chaired by Senator Tower, former Senator Edmund Muskie, and former National Security Advisor Brent Scowcroft, which concluded that although the president was largely out of the loop on details, he had approved the arms-for-hostages effort. Reagan asserts that the missile sales began as a strategic opening to improve relations with elements of the Iranian government and that this degenerated into an arms-for-hostage-program. Reagan pleads ignorance on any diversion of funds to the Contras. He accepts the Tower Commission's conclusion that his hands-off style of delegating authority to others was to blame. At the time, many shared this view of an out-of-touch president and a run-away National Security staff. Reagan concludes his address with promises to reform his National Security Council and re-earn the trust of the American people. Reagan was known as the "Great Communicator" and was most effective when addressing the American people directly. His speech had some success in this regard, although his critics continued to suspect Reagan was more involved than he admitted.

Many Democrats were skeptical of the denials and in the summer of 1987 joint House-Senate hearings were held. The sensational hearings were televised and most of the major players, except the president, were brought before the Congressional committee to testify. Oliver North was defiant, appearing before the committee in his Marine uniform, coming across to some television viewers as a selfless patriot. The committee issued two reports, a majority Democratic report condemning the Iran-Contra operations as abuses of executive power, and a minority Republican report which portrayed the administration's actions as legal and necessitated by excessive Congressional interference.

More revelations came from the investigation of Independent Counsel Lawrence Walsh, conducted from 1987 through 1992. Walsh charged 14 participants, winning 11 guilty verdicts on charges such as conspiracy, withholding information from Congress, and obstruction of justice. His most high-profile convictions were of North and Poindexter; however, those were overturned on appeal due to their prior testimony to Congress under immunity. Six participants were pardoned by President George H.W. Bush, whom some accused of hiding his own role as vice president in the Iran-Contra operations. Walsh issued his final report in 1993, which like earlier reports did not accuse Reagan of personally breaking the law but of creating an environment in which others acted unlawfully.

Bibliography and Additional Readings

Byrne, Malcolm. *Iran-Contra: Reagan's Scandal and the Unchecked Abuse of Presidential Power*. Lawrence: University of Kansas Press, 2014.

Draper, Theodore. *A Very Thin Line: The Iran-Contra Affairs*. New York: Simon and Schuster, 1992.

Walsh, Lawrence E. Firewall: *The Iran-Contra Conspiracy and Cover-Up*. New York: Norton, 1997.

The Cessation of the Persian Gulf War

Date: March 6, 1991
Author: George H.W. Bush
Genre: Speech

Summary Overview

One week after ordering a halt to military operations in Iraq and Kuwait, President George H.W. Bush made this formal declaration regarding the future of the two nations, as well as the United States. In August 1990, Bush and his coalition partners had set the basic goals of pushing Iraq out of Kuwait and minimizing any future Iraqi military threat. By the end of February, with these goals having seemingly been achieved, Bush made this formal unilateral declaration ending the conflict. (Iraq had few viable military resources left with which to continue fighting.) This also signaled the beginning of diplomatic efforts to ensure Iraq's long-term adherence to the American/Coalition's dictates—i.e., that it live in peace with other nations of the world.

Defining Moment

Borders between ethnic groups and political entities have been fluid throughout the history of the Middle East. The unwieldy modern borders reflected decisions by the European victors in World War I, with the borders outlined for Iraq (drawn in 1932) clearly excluding Kuwait, then a British protectorate. However, in 1990, Saddam Hussein resurrected the idea that Kuwait should have been part of Iraq and proceeded to invade the smaller nation on August 2, 1990. Precipitating Iraq's action at that time were claims that Kuwait was "stealing" Iraqi oil, by slant drilling across the border. Most observers believed that this economic issue was the real reason for the invasion, not any great desire for political reunification or to "free" the Kuwaitis from an oppressive royal family. Within two days, Iraq was firmly in control of Kuwait, and nations around the world were criticizing this occupation/annexation. Saudi Arabia, fearing possible invasion, together with a Kuwaiti government-in-exile requested assistance from the United States and the United Nations. With the support of twelve U.N. Security Council resolutions, the United States organized a military coalition, using Saudi Arabia as its base of operations. From mid-August 1990 to mid-January 1991, Saddam was told to withdraw his forces from Kuwait. Learning of his refusal, on the night of January 16–17, 1991, the US-led coalition initiated an intense air war against Iraqi military forces, followed by an invasion. The coalition totally defeated Iraqi forces within six weeks. Having ordered cessation of hostilities on February 25, 1991, Bush followed up with this speech. In the negotiations to follow, Bush sought only to ensure that Iraq would accept the US/Coalition's two goals—Kuwaiti independence and a less militarily capable Iraq. This limited agenda for postwar accords enabled a quick resolution to the war, although Saddam remaining in power was a major reason for another war a decade later led by Bush's son and the forty-third US president, George W. Bush.

President Bush visiting American troops in Saudi Arabia on Thanksgiving Day, 1990.

Author Biography

George Herbert Walker Bush (born 1924) grew up in New England, in a moderately wealthy family. When he turned eighteen, Bush volunteered to serve in World War II, becoming a naval pilot and earning the Distinguished Flying Cross. He married Barbara Pierce in 1945, and graduated from Yale University in 1948. After working in the oil industry, he served two terms in Congress, as US ambassador to the United Nations, envoy to China, and director of the Central Intelligence Agency. In 1980, he was elected as Ronald Reagan's vice-president.

Bush was elected president in 1988, serving one term. During his time in office, several major international changes occurred, such as the break-up of the Soviet Union. Bush created domestic and international coalitions to support and implement the removal of Saddam Hussein's Iraqi troops from Kuwait. After his presidency, Bush remained active in politics, supporting his son's successful quest for the presidency. After 2000, Bush often joined with former president Bill Clinton to raise funds to assist people harmed by natural disasters. Bush received the Presidential Medal of Freedom in 2011.

F-15Es parked during Operation Desert Shield.

HISTORICAL DOCUMENT: *The Cessation of the Persian Gulf War*

Members of Congress, 5 short weeks ago I came to this House to speak to you about the state of the Union. We met then in time of war. Tonight, we meet in a world blessed by the promise of peace.

From the moment Operation Desert Storm commenced on January 16th until the time the guns fell silent at midnight 1 week ago, this nation has watched its sons and daughters with pride, watched over them with prayer. As Commander in Chief, I can report to you our armed forces fought with honor and valor. And as President, I can report to the Nation aggression is defeated. The war is over.

This is a victory for every country in the coalition, for the United Nations. A victory for unprecedented international cooperation and diplomacy, so well led by our Secretary of State, James Baker. It is a victory for the rule of law and for what is right.

Desert Storm's success belongs to the team that so ably leads our Armed Forces: our Secretary of Defense and our Chairman of the Joint Chiefs, Dick Cheney and Colin Powell. And while you're standing—[laughter]—this military victory also

continued from page 259

belongs to the one the British call the "Man of the Match"—the tower of calm at the eye of Desert Storm—General Norman Schwarzkopf.

And recognizing this was a coalition effort, let us not forget Saudi General Khalid, Britain's General de la Billiere, or General Roquejeoffre of France, and all the others whose leadership played such a vital role. And most importantly, most importantly of all, all those who served in the field.

I thank the Members of this Congress—support here for our troops in battle was overwhelming. And above all, I thank those whose unfailing love and support sustained our courageous men and women: I thank the American people.

Tonight, I come to this House to speak about the world—the world after war. The recent challenge could not have been clearer. Saddam Hussein was the villain; Kuwait, the victim. To the aid of this small country came nations from North America and Europe, from Asia and South America, from Africa and the Arab world, all united against aggression. Our uncommon coalition must now work in common purpose: to forge a future that should never again be held hostage to the darker side of human nature.

Tonight in Iraq, Saddam walks amidst ruin. His war machine is crushed. His ability to threaten mass destruction is itself destroyed. His people have been lied to, denied the truth. And when his defeated legions come home, all Iraqis will see and feel the havoc he has wrought. And this I promise you: For all that Saddam has done to his own people, to the Kuwaitis, and to the entire world, Saddam and those around him are accountable.

> *All of us grieve for the victims of war, for the people of Kuwait and the suffering that scars the soul of that proud nation...for all our fallen soldiers and their families, for all the innocents caught up in this conflict. And, yes, we grieve for the people of Iraq, a people who have never been our enemy.*

All of us grieve for the victims of war, for the people of Kuwait and the suffering that scars the soul of that proud nation. We grieve for all our fallen soldiers and their families, for all the innocents caught up in this conflict. And, yes, we grieve for the people of Iraq, a people who have never been our enemy. My hope is that one day we will once again welcome them as friends into the community of nations. Our commitment to peace in the Middle East does not end with the liberation of Kuwait. So, tonight let me outline four key challenges to be met.

First, we must work together to create shared security arrangements in the region. Our friends and allies in the Middle East recognize that they will bear the bulk of the responsibility for regional security. But we want them to know that just as we stood with them to repel aggression, so now America stands ready to work with them to secure the peace. This does not mean stationing US ground forces in the Arabian Peninsula, but it does mean American participation in joint exercises involving both air and ground forces. It means maintaining a capable US naval presence in the region, just as we have for over 40 years. Let it be clear: Our vital national interests depend on a stable and secure Gulf.

Second, we must act to control the proliferation of weapons of mass destruction and the missiles used to deliver them. It would be tragic if the nations of the Middle East and Persian Gulf were now, in the wake of war, to embark on a new arms race. Iraq requires special vigilance. Until Iraq convinces the world of its peaceful intentions—that its leaders will not use new revenues to rearm and rebuild its menacing war machine—Iraq must not have access to the instruments of war.

And third, we must work to create new opportunities for peace and stability in the Middle East. On the night I announced Operation Desert Storm, I expressed my hope that out of the horrors of war might come new momentum for peace. We've learned in the modern age geography cannot guarantee security, and security does not come from military power alone.

All of us know the depth of bitterness that has made the dispute between Israel and its neighbors so painful and intractable. Yet, in the conflict just concluded, Israel and many of the Arab States have for the first time found themselves confronting the same aggressor. By now, it should be plain to all parties that peacemaking in the Middle East requires compromise. At the same time, peace brings real benefits to everyone. We must do all that we can to close the gap between Israel and the Arab States—and between Israelis and Palestinians. The tactics of terror lead absolutely nowhere. There can be no substitute for diplomacy.

A comprehensive peace must be grounded in United Nations Security Council Resolutions 242 and 338 and the principle of territory for peace. This principle must be elaborated to provide for Israel's security and recognition and at the same time for legitimate Palestinian political rights. Anything else would fail the twin test of fairness and security. The time has come to put an end to Arab-Israeli conflict.

The war with Iraq is over. The quest for solutions to the problems in Lebanon, in the Arab-Israeli dispute, and in the Gulf must go forward with new vigor and determination. And I guarantee you: No one will work harder for a stable peace in the region than we will.

Fourth, we must foster economic development for the sake of peace and progress. The Persian Gulf and Middle East form a region rich in natural resources with a wealth of untapped human potential. Resources once squandered on military might must be redirected to more peaceful ends. We are already addressing the immediate economic consequences of Iraq's aggression. Now, the challenge is to reach higher, to foster economic freedom and prosperity for all the people of the region.

continues on page 262

continued from page 261

By meeting these four challenges we can build a framework for peace. I've asked Secretary of State Baker to go to the Middle East to begin the process. He will go to listen, to probe, to offer suggestions—to advance the search for peace and stability. I've also asked him to raise the plight of the hostages held in Lebanon. We have not forgotten them, and we will not forget them.

To all the challenges that confront this region of the world there is no single solution, no solely American answer. But we can make a difference. America will work tirelessly as a catalyst for positive change.

But we cannot lead a new world abroad if, at home, it's politics as usual on American defense and diplomacy. It's time to turn away from the temptation to protect unneeded weapons systems and obsolete bases. It's time to put an end to micromanagement of foreign and security assistance programs—micromanagement that humiliates our friends and allies and hamstrings our diplomacy. It's time to rise above the parochial and the pork barrel, to do what is necessary, what's right, and what will enable this nation to play the leadership role required of us.

The consequences of the conflict in the Gulf reach far beyond the confines of the Middle East. Twice before in this century, an entire world was convulsed by war. Twice this century, out of the horrors of war hope emerged for enduring peace. Twice before, those hopes proved to be a distant dream, beyond the grasp of man. Until now, the world we've known has been a world divided—a world of barbed wire and concrete block, conflict, and cold war.

Now, we can see a new world coming into view. A world in which there is the very real prospect of a new world order. In the words of Winston Churchill, a world order in which "the principles of justice and fair play protect the weak against the strong. . . ." A world where the United Nations, freed from cold war stalemate, is poised to fulfill the historic vision of its founders. A world in which freedom and respect for human rights find a home among all nations. The Gulf war put this new world to its first test. And my fellow Americans, we passed that test.

For the sake of our principles, for the sake of the Kuwaiti people, we stood our ground. Because the world would not look the other way, Ambassador al-Sabah, tonight Kuwait is free. And we're very happy about that.

Tonight, as our troops begin to come home, let us recognize that the hard work of freedom still calls us forward. We've learned the hard lessons of history. The victory over Iraq was not waged as "a war to end all wars." Even the new world order cannot guarantee an era of perpetual peace. But enduring peace must be our mission. Our success in the Gulf will shape not only the new world order we seek but our mission here at home.

In the war just ended, there were clear-cut objectives—timetables—and, above all, an overriding imperative to achieve results. We must bring that same sense of self-discipline, that same sense of urgency, to the way we meet challenges here at home. In my State of the Union Address and in my budget, I defined a comprehensive agenda to prepare for the next American century.

Our first priority is to get this economy rolling again. The fear and uncertainty caused by the Gulf crisis were understandable. But now that the war is over, oil prices are down, interest rates are down, and confidence is rightly coming back. Americans can move forward to lend, spend, and invest in this, the strongest economy on Earth.

We must also enact the legislation that is key to building a better America. For example, in 1990, we enacted an historic Clean Air Act. And now we've proposed a national energy strategy. We passed a child-care bill that put power in the hands of parents. And today, we're ready to do the same thing with our schools and expand choice in education. We passed a crime bill that made a useful start in fighting crime and drugs. This year, we're sending to Congress our comprehensive crime package to finish the job. We passed the landmark Americans with Disabilities Act. And now we've sent forward our civil rights bill. We also passed the aviation bill. This year, we've sent up our new highway bill. And these are just a few of our pending proposals for reform and renewal.

So, tonight I call on the Congress to move forward aggressively on our domestic front. Let's begin with two initiatives we should be able to agree on quickly: transportation and crime. And then, let's build on success with those and enact the rest of our agenda. If our forces could win the ground war in 100 hours, then surely the Congress can pass this legislation in 100 days. Let that be a promise we make tonight to the American people.

When I spoke in this House about the state of our Union, I asked all of you: If we can selflessly confront evil for the sake of good in a land so far away, then surely we can make this land all that it should be. In the time since then, the brave men and women of Desert Storm accomplished more than even they may realize. They set out to confront an enemy abroad, and in the process, they transformed a nation at home. Think of the way they went about their mission—with confidence and quiet pride. Think about their sense of duty, about all they taught us about our values, about ourselves.

We hear so often about our young people in turmoil—how our children fall short, how our schools fail us, how American products and American workers are second-class. Well, don't you believe it. The America we saw in Desert Storm was first-class talent. And they did it using America's state-of-the-art technology. We saw the excellence embodied in the Patriot missile and the patriots who made it work. And we saw soldiers who know about honor and bravery and duty and country and the world-shaking power of these simple words. There is something noble and majestic about the pride, about the patriotism that we feel tonight.

continues on page 264

continued from page 263

So, to everyone here and everyone watching at home, think about the men and women of Desert Storm. Let us honor them with our gratitude. Let us comfort the families of the fallen and remember each precious life lost.

Let us learn from them as well. Let us honor those who have served us by serving others. Let us honor them as individuals—men and women of every race, all creeds and colors—by setting the face of this nation against discrimination, bigotry, and hate. Eliminate them.

I'm sure that many of you saw on the television the unforgettable scene of four terrified Iraqi soldiers surrendering. They emerged from their bunker broken, tears streaming from their eyes, fearing the worst. And then there was an American soldier. Remember what he said? He said: "It's okay. You're all right now. You're all right now." That scene says a lot about America, a lot about who we are. Americans are a caring people. We are a good people, a generous people. Let us always be caring and good and generous in all we do.

Soon, very soon, our troops will begin the march we've all been waiting for—their march home. And I have directed Secretary Cheney to begin the immediate return of American combat units from the Gulf. Less than 2 hours from now, the first planeload of American soldiers will lift off from Saudi Arabia, headed for the USA. That plane will carry the men and women of the 24th Mechanized Infantry Division bound for Fort Stewart, Georgia. This is just the beginning of a steady flow of American troops coming home. Let their return remind us that all those who have gone before are linked with us in the long line of freedom's march.

Americans have always tried to serve, to sacrifice nobly for what we believe to be right. Tonight, I ask every community in this country to make this coming Fourth of July a day of special celebration for our returning troops. They may have missed Thanksgiving and Christmas, but I can tell you this: For them and for their families, we can make this a holiday they'll never forget.

In a very real sense, this victory belongs to them—to the privates and the pilots, to the sergeants and the supply officers, to the men and women in the machines and the men and women who made them work. It belongs to the regulars, to the reserves, to the National Guard. This victory belongs to the finest fighting force this nation has ever known in its history.

We went halfway around the world to do what is moral and just and right. We fought hard and, with others, we won the war. We lifted the yoke of aggression and tyranny from a small country that many Americans had never even heard of, and we ask nothing in return.

We're coming home now—proud, confident, heads high. There is much that we must do, at home and abroad. And we will do it. We are Americans.

May God bless this great nation, the United States of America. Thank you all very, very much.

GLOSSARY

coalition: group of thirty-nine nations (not all supplied troops) which the United States helped create and organize to militarily oppose the invasion of Kuwait

Desert Storm: code name for the military campaign against Iraq in January, 1991

Resolutions 242 and 338: U.N. resolutions, passed in 1967 and 1973, calling for an end to Arab-Israeli conflicts via a land-for-peace strategy

Document Themes and Analysis

Having a clear understanding of the desired outcomes when initiating warfare, and knowing when these have been reached—these two things are considered key to successful military operations in the modern era. For President George H.W. Bush, the goals of operation Desert Storm were clear: remove Iraqi forces from Kuwait and reduce Iraq's military strength. Having quickly attained these goals, Bush made this speech not only to announce the conclusion of the military campaign, but also to put forward new goals for the United States and the global community. Domestically, Bush advocated an end to using military expenditures for political gain, shifting expenditures to programs addressing "transportation and crime." Internationally, he sought peace in the Middle East through the use of "shared security arrangements" and economic development, as well as an end to the division between Arab states and Israel. While focusing on Iraq, Bush sought to ensure that there would be no "new arms race" in the Middle East.

Regarding the reason for making this speech, Bush is straightforward in stating his appreciation for those who had successfully led, or otherwise participated in, Operation Desert Storm. Although he focuses on Americans who participated in the campaign, he also makes a point of thanking others who participated, and offers condolences to those who suffered loss. It was clear by the time he made this speech that Kuwait was once again free. As for Iraqi military strength, Iraq had suffered major losses of equipment as well as numerous casualties, although more of Iraq's military equipment was operational at the end of the war than had been hoped. (Many Iraqi soldiers fled with their equipment when it was clear that coalition forces were moving into Kuwait.) However, the Iraqi military did suffer large losses and never again exhibited any substantial strength during the rule of Saddam Hussein.

Having relatively easily attained these prewar goals, Bush's desire to advance four other Middle Eastern issues might be seen as his trying to build on recent success. Ultimately, however, these four areas saw only minor progress. Only the first one, "shared security arrangements," was achieved, in that US/Coalition forces remained stationed in the Middle East. (In fact, this resulted in the creation of new grievances by new groups within the Middle East, in part on the basis of having non-Muslim troops stationed in Saudi Arabia.) For nations such as Kuwait, having American forces stationed in the area of the Persian Gulf did gave them greater security. Two of the points made by Bush did not produce changes but rather a continuation of the status quo: new weapons of mass destruction and economic development. There was no breakthrough on relations between Israel and its

US Army soldiers from the 11th Air Defense Artillery Brigade during the Gulf War.

Arab neighbors. Although there were some disputes about whether Iraq had weapons of mass destruction during the next decade, none were found when Iraq was searched during the next war starting in 2003.

The domestic addendum that Bush inserted into the speech was a total failure. During 1991, no new legislation was passed by Congress furthering any of the goals he announced in this speech. While he had hoped to build on his foreign policy success, he was unable to translate this into a success on desired domestic policies.

Overall, the key points of the speech, dealing with the Iraqi invasion of Kuwait and the desire to reduce Iraq's power, reflected the changed situation as of March 1991. Saddam Hussein's ability to annex Kuwait had been destroyed with the military defeat that his forces suffered. Although it was only a little over a decade until the next war pitting the United States against Iraq, that was not the result of any failure to achieve the goal of reducing Iraq's military presence in the Middle East. From the time of Bush's speech until the beginning of the Iraq War (2003–11), Iraq had undertaken only two military actions (one attempt to down Coalition aircraft, and another against separatist Kurds), both within its borders. Thus, it was clear that Saddam's ability to project military power outside his borders had ended, as indicated in this speech. Those who criticized Bush and this speech failed to understand the limited goals that he had sought to, and did, achieve.

—*Donald A. Watt*

Bibliography and Additional Reading

Allison, William Thomas. *The Gulf War, 1990–91.* (Twentieth Century Wars, 2012 edition) New York: Palgrave Macmillan, 2012. Print.

Frontline. "The Gulf War: an in-depth examination of the 1990–191 Persian Gulf Crisis." *Frontline.* Boston: WGBH Educational Foundation, 1996. Web. 29 August 2018.

Greenblatt, Alan. "Twenty Years Later, First Iraq War Still Resonates." *NPR.* Washington: NPR, Inc., 2011. Web. 29 August 2018.

History. "Persian Gulf War." *History.* New York: A&E Television Networks LLC, 2018. Web. 29 August 2018.

Meacham, Jon. *Destiny and Power: The American Odyssey of George Herbert Walker Bush.* New York: Random House, 2015. Print.

The 1993 World Trade Center Bombing: Report and Analysis

Date: February 1993
Author: Anthony L. Fusco
Genre: Report

Summary Overview

This excerpt from a report written by the City of New York Fire Department (FDNY) incident commander outlined much of the damage caused by the 1993 explosion under the World Trade Center (WTC), as well as the FDNY's response. The scope of the operation required in response to the massive explosion is outlined in this document. The author makes clear the extent of human suffering caused by the blast in addition to the massive property damage. Since the author had been on-site and in contact with most emergency responders, his insights, in addition to the factual information, make this a key document for those studying these events. Being written shortly after the event, it benefited from Fusco having the facts clear in his mind.

Defining Moment

As the Cold War came to an end with the dissolution of the Soviet Union, the Arab states and peoples that the USSR had supported had less hope for future economic prosperity or their ability to restrain or diminish their common enemy in the region, Israel. In 1990 the leader of Iraq, Saddam Hussein, ordered his military to invade and annex the neighboring state of Kuwait. Basically, he wanted Kuwait's oil but made a pretense of being motivated by the need to return to pre-World War I borders. Saddam, however, miscalculated regarding the prospect of Saudi Arabia staying out of the war; in fact, the Saudis invited American troops into the kingdom to fight for the preservation of Kuwait. After the brief Persian Gulf War, non-Muslim troops (mainly from the United States) stayed in Saudi Arabia, causing some ultra-conservative Muslims to believe that the nation, which contained the holiest sites of Islam, was being polluted.

Meanwhile, the ongoing civil war in Afghanistan was being won by Islamic forces. That gave the more extreme Islamist conservatives, or jihadists, a base for military training and the receipt of weapons. One result was the formation of an anti-Western—particularly anti-American—terrorist group led by Osama bin Laden. Known as al-Qaeda, this organization undertook terrorist acts as well as training other terrorists operating independently from al-Qaeda's leadership. The 1993 bombing of the WTC, at that time the tallest building in the world and a symbol of American capitalism, was a direct result of these perceived grievances and training.

Author Biography

Anthony L. Fusco was Chief of Department and a 33-year veteran of the City of New York Fire Department at the time he wrote this report. (Chief of Department was the highest ranking

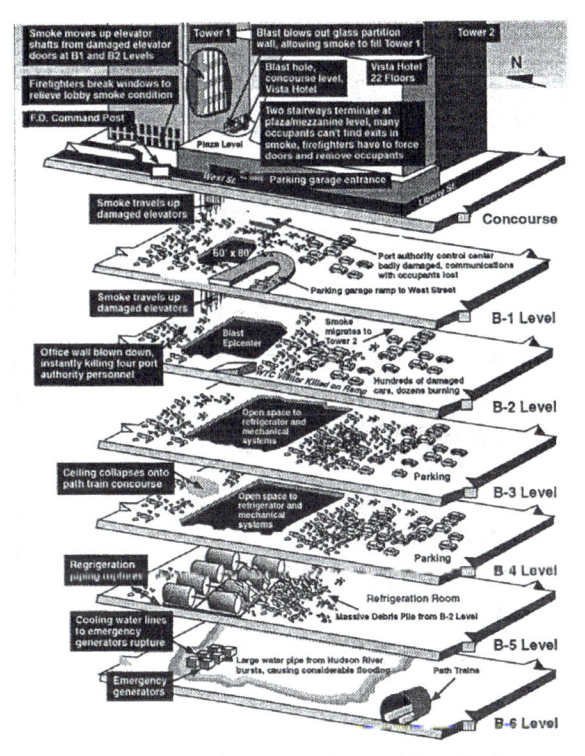

Depiction of blast damage at the World Trade Center.

uniformed member of the FDNY, overseeing all training and emergency services, which included fire prevention, suppression, and emergency medical services.) Fusco served as the incident commander for the World Trade Center bombing. About a year later, after the election of Mayor Rudolf Giuliani and his appointment of a new Fire Commissioner, Fusco retired from the FDNY, at the age of fifty-seven, due to an unspecified "condition." After the 9/11 attacks, commissions investigating the fire department's response questioned Fusco about how his 1993 communications problems were related to problems the FDNY encountered in 2001.

HISTORICAL DOCUMENT: The 1993 World Trade Center Bombing: Report and Analysis

The 1993 World Trade Center Bombing: Report and Analysis

Report from Chief of Department
by Anthony L. Fusco

The City of New York Fire Department has responded hundreds of times to the World Trade Center (WTC) since it was first occupied in 1970. These responses normally consist of minor fires or false alarms but have included major fires such as the one that occurred on February 13, 1975. None of these experiences could have prepared us for what was to occur on February 26, 1993.

The bombing of the WTC was an event of immense proportions, the largest—incident ever handled in the City of New York Fire Department's 128-year history—so complex that it was effectively several major multiple-alarm fires combined into

continued from page 269

one. In terms of the number of fire department units that responded, it was the equivalent of a 16-alarm fire.

As the incident commander, I can attest to the fact that it was the firefighters' tremendous efforts and courage that brought this incident to a successful conclusion.

The statistics are staggering: Six people died and 1,042 were injured. Of those injured, 15 received traumatic injuries from the blast itself. Nearly 20 people complained of cardiac problems, and nearly 30 pregnant women were rescued. Eighty-eight firefighters (one requiring hospitalization), 35 police officers, and one EMS worker sustained injuries.

It is estimated that approximately 50,000 people were evacuated from the WTC complex, including nearly 25,000 from each of the two towers. Fire alarm dispatchers received more than 1,000 phone calls, most reporting victims trapped on the upper floors of the towers. Search and evacuation of the towers finally were completed some 11 hours after the incident began.

A nitrourea bomb, in excess of 1,000 pounds, with hydrogen cylinders to add impact, was detonated in the now-infamous yellow Ryder Econoline van on the B-2 level of the parking garage, causing massive destruction that spanned seven levels, six below grade. The L-shaped blast crater on B-2 at its maximum measured 130 feet wide by 150 feet long. The blast's epicenter was under the northeast corner of the Vista Hotel.

FDNY ultimately responded to the incident with 84 engine companies, 60 truck companies, 28 battalion chiefs, nine deputy chiefs, and five rescue companies and 26 other special units (representing nearly 45 percent of the on-duty staff of FDNY). The fire department units maintained a presence at the scene for 28 days.

> *A nitrourea bomb, in excess of 1,000 pounds, with hydrogen cylinders to add impact, was detonated in the now-infamous yellow Ryder Econoline van on the B-2 level of the parking garage, causing massive destruction that spanned seven levels, six below grade.*

FEBRUARY 26, 1993

Snow was falling in lower Manhattan during the noon lunch hour on February 26. Temperatures hovered in the mid-20s. At 1218 hours, an explosion rocked the WTC complex...

From all indications, the explosion and resultant fire appeared to be located under the Vista Hotel. Chief Casey assumed command and established his command post in front of the hotel on West Street. Almost immediately after his arrival, he received reports that the Tower 1 lobby was filling with smoke and that people here trapped below grade. He transmitted a second alarm for Box 69 at 12:27 p.m. (due to problems developing in the Vista Hotel) and a third alarm for Box 69 (problems developing in Tower 1) at 12:30 p.m...

My pager began beeping incessantly for each additional alarm—this was "The Big One." I responded from headquarters in Brooklyn, as did several other staff officers.

By now, the battalion and deputy chiefs at the scene began to comprehend the magnitude of the incident. A major fire was burning below grade. People were injured and trapped by the explosion. Communications were lost in the WTC complex. Smoke was contaminating Tower 1 and the Vista Hotel. A major extinguishment and rescue scenario was unfolding.

Deputy Assistant Chief Cerreta was receiving numerous reports of smoke problems in Tower 1 and dispatched a fire company to investigate this specific problem. They reported a heavy smoke condition in the lobby and contamination of vertical shafts, including the stairways and elevators. Occupants were self-evacuating, and some were breaking windows on the upper floors. Assistant Chief Donald Burns, chief of operations, arrived shortly after from Fire Department Headquarters and went directly to Tower 1, establishing a sector command post at that location.

I arrived at the command post at 12:48 hours. I could see smoke pouring out of the parking garage doors of the Vista Hotel. I also noted that the lobby windows of Tower 1 were blackened with smoke.

Cerreta briefed me on what information was known. He, Beier, and I discussed their size-up. Reports of a transformer explosion had been given over the department radio, but this had not yet been confirmed. The only known facts were that an explosion had occurred, people were injured, fire was burning on a lower level (or levels), and voluminous amounts of smoke were being produced, with three very large buildings affected...

A major detriment to our ability to strengthen control of the incident was fire department on-scene communications. Communications were a serious problem from the outset. With 156 units and 31 chiefs operating at the height of this incident, try to imagine how difficult it was to gain control of the portable-radio operations frequency. Two command channels and one tactical channel were used. In many cases, runners were sent by a sector commander to communicate with the incident commander. Generally, the problem...

continues on page 272

continued from page 271

OPERATIONS

Within one hour of my arrival on the scene, the rescue of Firefighter Shea was completed and the fires in the below-grade area were being brought under control. Our focus narrowed to primary search of the below-grade levels (we had reports of still-missing occupants); primary search and evacuation of the towers and the hotel; and an assessment of the damage and stability of the below-grade areas, such as it would impact the safety of personnel still operating there.

Damage/hazard assessment.

Lights were brought into the below-grade areas. Damage from the blast was extensive. The B-2 level surrounding ground zero was completely destroyed. Piping and conduit were snapped like twigs. Masonry walls and steel-reinforced concrete flooring were blown apart. Cars were strewn about like toys. Steel columns were shocked but held.

A chief was directed to secure and define the stability of the collapse area. He was to accomplish the assessment with Port Authority engineers. The explosion severed four of the seven operating electrical feeders. This had the effect of disrupting all fire protection systems and also causing sporadic power loss throughout the complex. For reasons too numerous to mention, power shutoff by the FDNY command post was never requested. All train traffic in the area vas stopped, and the gas to the complex was shut down. Members were advised to operate cautiously at all below-grade areas. For reasons unknown to me, power was completely removed from the complex at around 1:30 p.m.

It was determined that operations below grade could continue within reasonable safety limits, but the potential for secondary collapse was ever present.

Below grade.

With such extensive damage to the below-grade levels—debris was piled several feet high about the blast area—primary and secondary searches were very difficult and dangerous. Chief Cerreta supervised the search effort. Searches were conducted under the protection of charged hoselines.

Port Authority personnel assisted by establishing a probable victim location in occupied work areas on the B-2 level under the Vista Hotel and Tower 1. The blast destroyed a dividing wall between the garage and this work area (demolished, it was later found, by a steel support beam hurled through it with the unimaginable force created by the blast). A search first was concentrated in this area, and four fatalities were located and removed by FDNY to a temporary morgue established in the Vista

Hotel. Five of the six fatalities in this incident were removed within the first two hours. (One victim was found by FDNY on a driveway ramp early in the incident.) The sixth victim was located in rubble by police personnel during their investigation 17 days later.

Members removed 16 civilians trapped under the debris in a locker room near the epicenter of the blast; located and rescued civilians from a demolished room suspended precariously over the crater; rescued victims who fell into the crater; and conducted very thorough, exhausting primary and secondary searches of the blast area, removing scores of injured.

In total, 71 companies were utilized for extinguishment, rescue, primary and secondary searches, recoveries, and logistics support on the below-grade levels...

Above grade.

... As challenging as stairway evacuation and floor search were, the most difficult part of this operation from the standpoint of strategy and tactics was locating and searching the 99 elevators in each of the towers and the 12 in the Vista Hotel. Many elevators were in blind shafts and between floors. Identification of car location was difficult and time-consuming. Many walls had to be breached to gain entry into elevator cars. Literally hundreds of people were trapped in elevators when the power went down. In one case, 10 elevator occupants in Tower 1 were found unconscious, lying on the car floor—they were resuscitated and safely turned over to EMS personnel. In another case, 72 schoolchildren in Tower 2 were rescued from a car stuck in a blind shaft.

Once outside the building, victims had to contend with falling glass broken by a few occupants on upper floors. This was a real problem over which the fire department had no control. Some of this glass breaking was due to erroneous information disseminated by the media, encouraging people in the towers to take such action.

An unusual aspect of this incident was that a large elevator company has offices within the WTC towers. This company had several maintenance technicians working within the building at the time of the explosion. Knowing that people were trapped in the elevators, these technicians early in the incident began the process of manually moving the stalled cabs to the tower lobbies, but not all of their well-intentioned efforts were communicated to FDNY, at least initially. Had better interagency communications existed, elevator searches could have been better coordinated with the fire department.

More than eight million square feet of space were searched in Tower 1, Tower 2, and the Vista Hotel. Tower 1 required the largest commitment of above-grade resources. When other sectors began reducing units, they were told to report to the

continues on page 274

command post. We would reassign them as necessary unless the members were fatigued, in which case they would be relieved. During the entire course of the incident, 55 companies operated in Tower 1, 27 in Tower 2, and 20 in the Vista Hotel.

Operations continued well into the night. At 11:45 p.m., the last elevator was located and the people removed. They had been in the elevator for more than 11 hours.

Change of tour relief would be handled by the transmission of additional alarms. Some members, due to the fact that they had climbed to the upper floors of the towers, could not be relieved. It took hours to reach the upper floors of the two 110- story buildings, and of necessity, these members would keep working until they could make their way down the buildings, performing secondary searches as they did so…

GLOSSARY

blind shaft: elevators with access to only a limited number of floors, not all floors

nitrourea bomb: a bomb based on a derivative of urine with the addition of a nitrogen compound—a type of "fertilizer" bomb

Document Themes and Analysis

Fusco's account was one of several "chapters" in the larger report. It shows Fusco in the dual position, as chief, of both receiving reports from the various fire and emergency service units attempting to deal with the results of the bombing, and being present at the scene. Clearly, he experienced the physical conditions (fire, smoke and other dangers) at the complex and understood the challenges confronting the first responders. In his account, Fusco attempts to communicate his initial assessment of the extent of the damages as compared with any previous New York City fire. He then deals with areas in which chance or the sheer scope of the problem made it difficult to get optimal results. Included in this excerpt is a diagram illustrating the damage done to the basement levels of the WTC complex.

The 1993 WTC bombing was the "largest incident ever handled" by the FDNY up to that time. The 84 engine companies, whose main task was getting hoses in place and operating, and the 60 truck companies, charged with ensuring access to the fire location, meant that nearly half of New York's fire equipment was assigned to this emergency. The expenditure of such an amount of resources at one location was due to the size of the structures and the extent of the damage. As shown in the diagram, of the seven buildings in the WTC complex, two tall towers of the WTC and the Vista Hotel were directly affected. Above ground, smoke and disruption of the power supply were the main threats to public health and safety.

In the portion of Fusco's description excerpted here, it is clear that once the firefighters were able to get close to the fire, they did not have great difficulty with it. However, since all basement levels were affected by the blast, safely getting near the fire was difficult. As he described the situation, with the fire limited to the basement levels, above ground the main task was rescuing people from the ninety-nine elevators and assisting those on upper floors down the stairs to the exits. As he reported, numerous injuries but no deaths occurred above ground level. Because electrical service was cut partway through the evacuation, and the radios/frequencies in use were not always reliable, rescue was made more difficult. Also, rescue efforts by civilians were not coordinated with the fire department, causing some delays. Since Tower 1 was more directly over the blast, it had the most damage, smoke, and injuries. Thus, he assigned twice as many fire companies to work in Tower 1 as in Tower 2. (Even though directly over the blast, the hotel being much shorter did not require as many companies as either tower.) Having all but one person rescued within eleven hours was a major accomplishment.

Although the actual number of casualties was nowhere near what the terrorists had hoped for, since the remaining supports under the hotel and Tower 1 held up those buildings, this account of the rescue efforts by the FDNY outlined the tremendous efforts undertaken to keep those numbers low. It was clear from the diagram that the main force of the blast was directed downward, rather than up toward the buildings. If the terrorists had constructed the bomb differently, they may have been able to succeed in their goal of toppling at least one tower in the WTC complex. As a result of this blast, New York officials had warnings not only about the WTC being a target for terrorists, but about the difficulties that a major terrorist event would cause. As Fusco testified almost a decade later, after the 9/11 events, the radio/communications problem was not adequately addressed. The other major problem, the time and energy it took to get personnel to the upper floors, also persisted, but that was based on the limitations of the human body. Overall, as Fusco could honestly report, the FDNY performed well in this unprecedented incident.

—Donald A. Watt

Bibliography and Additional Reading

Fusco, Anthony L., author, William A. Manning, ed. "The World Trade Center Bombing: Report and Analysis." *US Fire Administration/Technical Report Series—Report 076*. Washington: Homeland Security, 1993. Web. 30 August 30, 2018.

Parachini, John V. "The World Trade Center Bombers (1993)." *James Martin Center for Nonproliferation Studies, Middlebury Institute of International Studies at Monterey*. Cambridge: MIT Press, 2000. Web. 30 August 2018.

Precht, Robert E. *Defending Mohammad: Justice on Trial*. Ithaca NY: Cornell University Press, 2003. Print.

Stewart, Scott. "A Look Back at the 1993 World Trade Center Bombing." *Stratfor Worldview*. Austin: Stratfor Enterprises LLC, 2015. Web. 30 August 2018.

Oslo Accords

Date: September 13, 1993 (Oslo I); September 24, 1995 (Oslo II)
Authors: signed by Yasser Arafat and Yitzhak Rabin; written by many different parties.
Genre: Treaty

Summary Overview

The Oslo Accords represent an important pair of documents in that for the first time the Palestinian Authority and Israel recognized one another's right to exist. In many ways, this was the land-for-peace deal that had been suggested many times over the years but rejected by one side or the other. The process of developing the document (which can be thought of as a single treaty) seemed to prove what had been known for years: that progress was better reached in secret, outside of the limelight of external scrutiny. The authors here show how much had changed in the process, as Yitzhak Rabin and Yasser Arafat had been enemies for years—both personally and as representatives of their people or nations. Rabin, for instance, had ordered a brutal repression of the First Intifada (uprising) in the late 1980s, and Arafat had launched attacks on Israel from Lebanon. Both, however, ultimately switched tactics and went from war to negotiation to acceptance of the other's claim. Such acceptance is shown here in the two accords and in an exchange of letters that occurred right before the first accord (Oslo I). Arafat sent a letter to Rabin that recognized Israel and promised no more violence, and Rabin sent one in return that recognized the Palestine Liberation Organization (PLO). Observers had for years assumed that neither would ever happen. The Oslo Accords, then, were in some way the high-water mark for the Palestinian-Israeli peace process, for it has since become bogged down, and Rabin was assassinated shortly after Oslo II by an Israeli opposed to the peace process.

Defining Moment

The Oslo Accords signified the first time that the PLO and Israel had mutually signed a peace treaty. There had been treaties before between Israel and Egypt (notably, 1979), and one was made between Israel and Jordan (1994) in the period between Oslo I and Oslo II, but this—Oslo I, specifically—was the first treaty between the PLO and Israel, which heretofore had largely sought to destroy one another. (Israel had succeeded in forcing the PLO out of the country but not in eliminating it). The agreement is also significant in that it shows the acceptance by both parties of a two-state (or two-entity) solution. Israel had for a time wanted to wipe out the PLO and toyed with the idea of sticking with a single-state solution, while the PLO had called for the eradication of Israel and the return of all lands to Palestinian control.

Thus, while Oslo may have been the high-water mark, its success did not last long. The peace process began to stall soon afterward, Rabin being killed in 1995 and Arafat dying in 2004—after being detained by the Israelis for much of his last two years. Israeli opinion

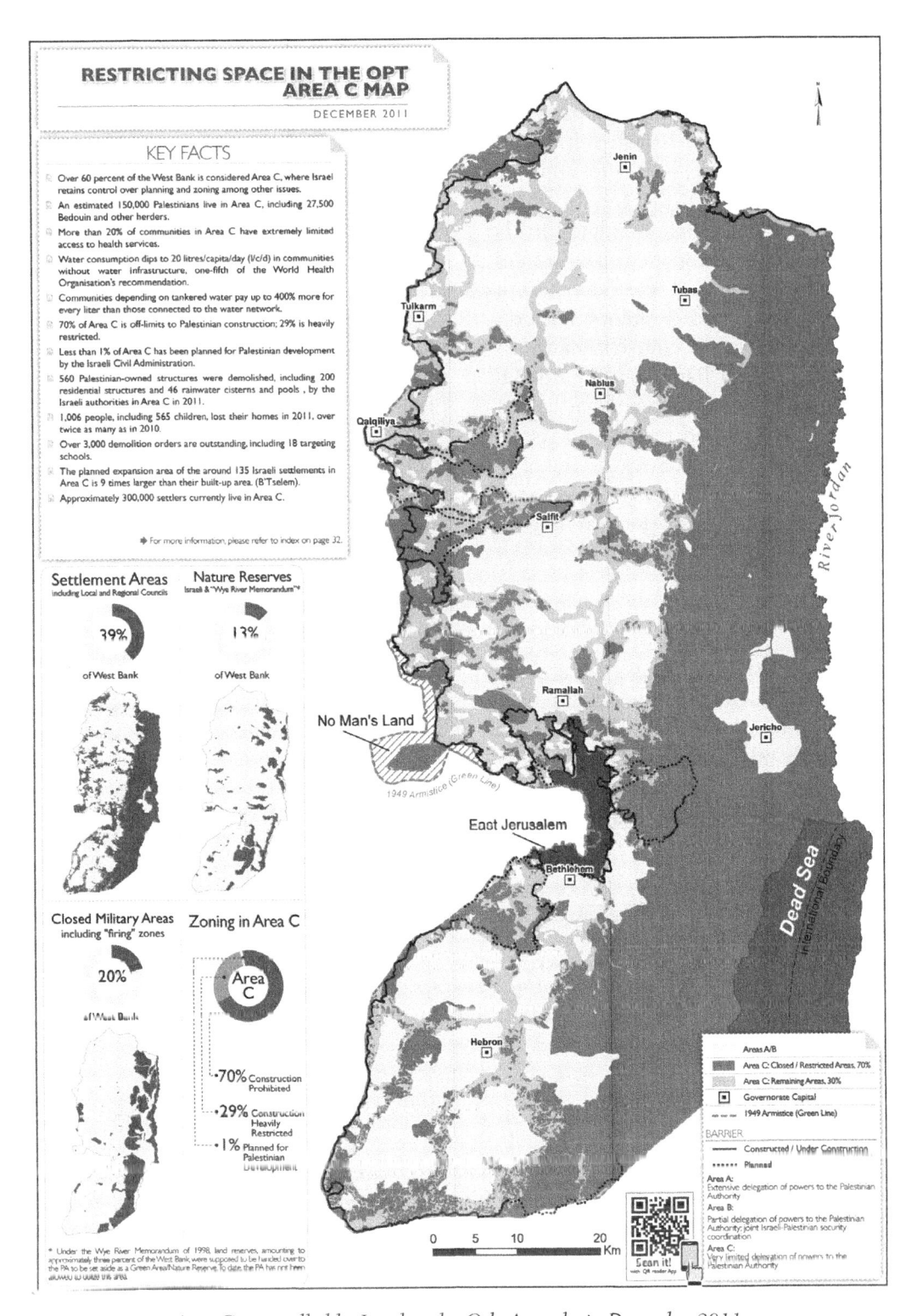

Area C, controlled by Israel under Oslo Accords, in December 2011.

of the peace process did not improve in the interim. The Palestinians, too, started to favor the more radical Hamas organization/party over the Palestinian Authority (existing government), which in turn caused increased repression from the Israelis. In many ways, this trend came to a head in 2006, when violence erupted in the Hamas-controlled Gaza Strip area on both sides, and, in the West Bank region, the Fatah government, which had succeeded Arafat's authority, continued pursuing its own course somewhat.

Since 2006, the West Bank has continued to operate under Fatah leadership and has continued to deal with Israel and the issue of Israeli settlements there. The Gaza Strip, on the other hand, has become more of an occupied state with a closed border and Israel controlling the sea and airspace around it as well.

Author Biography

Yasser Arafat was born in Egypt in 1929 and was educated as a civil engineer. After World War II, he joined the fight against Israel, siding with the Muslim Brotherhood faction. He was one of the founders of Fatah, which aimed to attack Israel. In the late 1960s, Arafat joined the Palestinian Liberation Organization (PLO) and moved up in its ranks to become leader. After being in Jordan for a time, he relocated to Lebanon and from there attacked Israel. Being driven to Tunisia by 1983, he then aimed to negotiate a solution and eventually become involved in the Oslo peace talks. In the early 2000s, the Israeli army confined him to his house in Ramallah and it was there that he died in 2004.

Yitzhak Rabin was born in Jerusalem in 1922 and grew up there. In 1941 he joined the Haganah (the Jewish paramilitary) and trained secretly while the British still controlled Palestine. Following World War II, he opposed Britain's continued occupation and, in 1948, fought against Egypt in the war following Israel's creation. He remained in the Israeli Defense Force until 1967 and became chief of staff. He was prime minister from 1974 to 1977 and then served as minister of defense in the 1980s. In 1993, he became prime minister again and negotiated a peace treaty with Jordan in addition to the two Oslo accords. He, along with Arafat and Shimon Peres (another Israeli leader) were jointly awarded the Nobel Peace Prize in 1994. In 1995, Rabin was assassinated by a right-wing Israeli opposed to the Oslo Accords.

HISTORICAL DOCUMENT: *Oslo Accords*

Declaration of Principles on Interim Self-Government Arrangements (Oslo I)

September 13, 1993

The Government of the State of Israel and the P.L.O. team (in the Jordanian-Palestinian delegation to the Middle East Peace Conference) (the "Palestinian Delegation"), representing the Palestinian people, agree that it is time to put an end to decades of confrontation and conflict, recognize their mutual legitimate and political rights, and strive to live in peaceful coexistence and mutual dignity and security and achieve a just, lasting and comprehensive peace settlement and historic reconciliation through the agreed political process. Accordingly, the two sides agree to the following principles:

Article I: Aim of the Negotiations

The aim of the Israeli-Palestinian negotiations within the current Middle East peace process is, among other things, to establish a Palestinian Interim Self-Government Authority, the elected Council (the "Council"), for the Palestinian people in the West Bank and the Gaza Strip, for a transitional period not exceeding five years, leading to a permanent settlement based on Security Council Resolutions 242 and 338.

It is understood that the interim arrangements are an integral part of the whole peace process and that the negotiations on the permanent status will lead to the implementation of Security Council Resolutions 242 and 338.

Article II: Framework for the Interim Period

The agreed framework for the interim period is set forth in this Declaration of Principles.

Article III: Elections

1. In order that the Palestinian people in the West Bank and Gaza Strip may govern themselves according to democratic principles, direct, free and general political elections will be held for the Council under agreed supervision and international observation, while the Palestinian police will ensure public order.

2. An agreement will be concluded on the exact mode and conditions of the elections in accordance with the protocol attached as Annex I, with the goal of holding the elections not later than nine months after the entry into force of this Declaration of Principles.

3. These elections will constitute a significant interim preparatory step toward the realization of the legitimate rights of the Palestinian people and their just requirements.

Article IV: Jurisdiction

Jurisdiction of the Council will cover West Bank and Gaza Strip territory, except for issues that will be negotiated in the permanent status negotiations. The two sides view the West Bank and the Gaza Strip as a single territorial unit, whose integrity will be preserved during the interim period.

Article V: Transitional Period and Permanent Status Negotiations

1. The five-year transitional period will begin upon the withdrawal from the Gaza Strip and Jericho area.

2. Permanent status negotiations will commence as soon as possible, but not later than the beginning of the third year of the interim period, between the Government of Israel and the Palestinian people representatives.

continues on page 280

continued from page 279

3. It is understood that these negotiations shall cover remaining issues, including: Jerusalem, refugees, settlements, security arrangements, borders, relations and cooperation with other neighbors, and other issues of common interest.
4. The two parties agree that the outcome of the permanent status negotiations should not be prejudiced or preempted by agreements reached for the interim period.

Article VI: Preparatory Transfer of Powers and Responsibilities

1. Upon the entry into force of this Declaration of Principles and the withdrawal from the Gaza Strip and the Jericho area, a transfer of authority from the Israeli military government and its Civil Administration to the authorised Palestinians for this task, as detailed herein, will commence. This transfer of authority will be of a preparatory nature until the inauguration of the Council.
2. Immediately after the entry into force of this Declaration of Principles and the withdrawal from the Gaza Strip and Jericho area, with the view to promoting economic development in the West Bank and Gaza Strip, authority will be transferred to the Palestinians on the following spheres: education and culture, health, social welfare, direct taxation, and tourism. The Palestinian side will commence in building the Palestinian police force, as agreed upon. Pending the inauguration of the Council, the two parties may negotiate the transfer of additional powers and responsibilities, as agreed upon.

> *The Government of the State of Israel and the P.L.O. team (in the Jordanian-Palestinian delegation to the Middle East Peace Conference) (the "Palestinian Delegation"), representing the Palestinian people, agree that it is time to put an end to decades of confrontation and conflict*

Article VII: Interim Agreement

1. The Israeli and Palestinian delegations will negotiate an agreement on the interim period (the "Interim Agreement")
2. The Interim Agreement shall specify, among other things, the structure of the Council, the number of its members, and the transfer of powers and responsibilities from the Israeli military government and its Civil Administration to the Council. The Interim Agreement shall also specify the Council's executive authority, legislative authority in accordance with Article IX below, and the independent Palestinian judicial organs.

3. The Interim Agreement shall include arrangements, to be implemented upon the inauguration of the Council, for the assumption by the Council of all of the powers and responsibilities transferred previously in accordance with Article VI above.

4. In order to enable the Council to promote economic growth, upon its inauguration, the Council will establish, among other things, a Palestinian Electricity Authority, a Gaza Sea Port Authority, a Palestinian Development Bank, a Palestinian Export Promotion Board, a Palestinian Environmental Authority, a Palestinian Land Authority and a Palestinian Water Administration Authority, and any other Authorities agreed upon, in accordance with the Interim Agreement that will specify their powers and responsibilities.

5. After the inauguration of the Council, the Civil Administration will be dissolved, and the Israeli military government will be withdrawn.

Article VIII: Public Order and Security

In order to guarantee public order and internal security for the Palestinians of the West Bank and the Gaza Strip, the Council will establish a strong police force, while Israel will continue to carry the responsibility for defending against external threats, as well as the responsibility for overall security of Israelis for the purpose of safeguarding their internal security and public order.

Article IX: Laws and Military Orders

1. The Council will be empowered to legislate, in accordance with the Interim Agreement, within all authorities transferred to it.

2. Both parties will review jointly laws and military orders presently in force in remaining spheres.

Article X; Joint Israeli-Palestinian Liaison Committee

In order to provide for a smooth implementation of this Declaration of Principles and any subsequent agreements pertaining to the interim period, upon the entry into force of this Declaration of Principles, a Joint Israeli-Palestinian Liaison Committee will be established in order to deal with issues requiring coordination, other issues of common interest, and disputes.

Article XI: Israeli-Palestinian Cooperation in Economic Fields

Recognizing the mutual benefit of cooperation in promoting the development of the West Bank, the Gaza Strip and Israel, upon the entry into force of this Declaration of Principles, an Israeli-Palestinian Economic Cooperation Committee will be established in order to develop and implement in a cooperative manner the programs identified in the protocols attached as Annex III and Annex IV.

continues on page 282

continued from page 281

Article XII: Liaison and Cooperation with Jordan and Egypt

The two parties will invite the Governments of Jordan and Egypt to participate in establishing further liaison and cooperation arrangements between the Government of Israel and the Palestinian representatives, on the one hand, and the Governments of Jordan and Egypt, on the other hand, to promote cooperation between them. These arrangements will include the constitution of a Continuing Committee that will decide by agreement on the modalities of admission of persons displaced from the West Bank and Gaza Strip in 1967, together with necessary measures to prevent disruption and disorder. Other matters of common concern will be dealt with by this Committee.

Article XIII: Redeployment of Israeli Forces

1. After the entry into force of this Declaration of Principles, and not later than the eve of elections for the Council, a redeployment of Israeli military forces in the West Bank and the Gaza Strip will take place, in addition to withdrawal of Israeli forces carried out in accordance with Article XIV.
2. In redeploying its military forces, Israel will be guided by the principle that its military forces should be redeployed outside populated areas.
3. Further redeployments to specified locations will be gradually implemented commensurate with the assumption of responsibility for public order and internal security by the Palestinian police force pursuant to Article VIII above.

Article XIV: Israeli Withdrawal from the Gaza Strip and Jericho Area

Israel will withdraw from the Gaza Strip and Jericho area, as detailed in the protocol attached as Annex II.

Article XV: Resolution of Disputes

1. Disputes arising out of the application or interpretation of this Declaration of Principles. or any subsequent agreements pertaining to the interim period, shall be resolved by negotiations through the Joint Liaison Committee to be established pursuant to Article X above.
2. Disputes which cannot be settled by negotiations may be resolved by a mechanism of conciliation to be agreed upon by the parties.
3. The parties may agree to submit to arbitration disputes relating to the interim period, which cannot be settled through conciliation. To this end, upon the agreement of both parties, the parties will establish an Arbitration Committee.

Article XVI: Israeli-Palestinian Cooperation Concerning Regional Programs

Both parties view the multilateral working groups as an appropriate instrument for promoting a "Marshall Plan", the regional programs and other programs, including special programs for the West Bank and Gaza Strip, as indicated in the protocol attached as Annex IV.

Article XVII: Miscellaneous Provisions

1. This Declaration of Principles will enter into force one month after its signing.
2. All protocols annexed to this Declaration of Principles and Agreed Minutes pertaining thereto shall be regarded as an integral part hereof.

Done at Washington, DC, this thirteenth day of September, 1993.

Annexes

Annex I: Protocol on the Mode and Conditions of Elections

1. Palestinians of Jerusalem who live there will have the right to participate in the election process, according to an agreement between the two sides.
2. In addition, the election agreement should cover, among other things, the following issues:
   a. the system of elections;
   b. the mode of the agreed supervision and international observation and their personal composition; and
   c. rules and regulations regarding election campaign, including agreed arrangements for the organizing of mass media, and the possibility of licensing a broadcasting and TV station.
3. The future status of displaced Palestinians who were registered on 4th June 1967 will not be prejudiced because they are unable to participate in the election process due to practical reasons.

Annex II: Protocol on Withdrawal of Israeli Forces from the Gaza Strip and Jericho Area

1. The two sides will conclude and sign within two months from the date of entry into force of this Declaration of Principles, an agreement on the withdrawal of Israeli military forces from the Gaza Strip and Jericho area. This agreement will include comprehensive arrangements to apply in the Gaza Strip and the Jericho area subsequent to the Israeli withdrawal.

continues on page 284

continued from page 283

2. Israel will implement an accelerated and scheduled withdrawal of Israeli military forces from the Gaza Strip and Jericho area, beginning immediately with the signing of the agreement on the Gaza Strip and Jericho area and to be completed within a period not exceeding four months after the signing of this agreement.

3. The above agreement will include, among other things:

    a. Arrangements for a smooth and peaceful transfer of authority from the Israeli military government and its Civil Administration to the Palestinian representatives.

    b. Structure, powers and responsibilities of the Palestinian authority in these areas, except: external security, settlements, Israelis, foreign relations, and other mutually agreed matters.

    c. Arrangements for the assumption of internal security and public order by the Palestinian police force consisting of police officers recruited locally and from abroad holding Jordanian passports and Palestinian documents issued by Egypt). Those who will participate in the Palestinian police force coming from abroad should be trained as police and police officers.

    d. A temporary international or foreign presence, as agreed upon.

    e. Establishment of a joint Palestinian-Israeli Coordination and Cooperation Committee for mutual security purposes.

    f. An economic development and stabilization program, including the establishment of an Emergency Fund, to encourage foreign investment, and financial and economic support. Both sides will coordinate and cooperate jointly and unilaterally with regional and international parties to support these aims.

    g. Arrangements for a safe passage for persons and transportation between the Gaza Strip and Jericho area.

4. The above agreement will include arrangements for coordination between both parties regarding passages:

    a. Gaza–Egypt; and

    b. Jericho–Jordan.

5. The offices responsible for carrying out the powers and responsibilities of the Palestinian authority under this Annex II and Article VI of the Declaration of Principles will be located in the Gaza Strip and in the Jericho area pending the inauguration of the Council.

6. Other than these agreed arrangements, the status of the Gaza Strip and Jericho area will continue to be an integral part of the West Bank and Gaza Strip, and will not be changed in the interim period.

Annex III: Protocol on Israeli-Palestinian Cooperation in Economic and Development Programs

The two sides agree to establish an Israeli-Palestinian continuing Committee for Economic Cooperation, focusing, among other things, on the following:

1. Cooperation in the field of water, including a Water Development Program prepared by experts from both sides, which will also specify the mode of cooperation in the management of water resources in the West Bank and Gaza Strip, and will include proposals for studies and plans on water rights of each party, as well as on the equitable utilization of joint water resources for implementation in and beyond the interim period.
2. Cooperation in the field of electricity, including an Electricity Development Program, which will also specify the mode of cooperation for the production, maintenance, purchase and sale of electricity resources.
3. Cooperation in the field of energy, including an Energy Development Program, which will provide for the exploitation of oil and gas for industrial purposes, particularly in the Gaza Strip and in the Negev, and will encourage further joint exploitation of other energy resources. This Program may also provide for the construction of a Petrochemical industrial complex in the Gaza Strip and the construction of oil and gas pipelines.
4. Cooperation in the field of finance, including a Financial Development and Action Program for the encouragement of international investment in the West Bank and the Gaza Strip, and in Israel, as well as the establishment of a Palestinian Development Bank.
5. Cooperation in the field of transport and communications, including a Program, which will define guidelines for the establishment of a Gaza Sea Port Area, and will provide for the establishing of transport and communications lines to and from the West Bank and the Gaza Strip to Israel and to other countries. In addition, this Program will provide for carrying out the necessary construction of roads, railways, communications lines, etc.
6. Cooperation in the field of trade, including studies, and Trade Promotion Programs, which will encourage local, regional and inter-regional trade, as well as a feasibility study of creating free trade zones in the Gaza Strip and in Israel, mutual access to these zones, and cooperation in other areas related to trade and commerce.
7. Cooperation in the field of industry, including Industrial Development Programs, which will provide for the establishment of joint Israeli-Palestinian Industrial Research and Development Centers, will promote Palestinian-Israeli joint ventures, and provide guidelines for cooperation in the textile, food, pharmaceutical, electronics, diamonds, computer and science-based industries.
8. A program for cooperation in, and regulation of, labor relations and cooperation in social welfare issues.

continues on page 286

continued from page 285

9. A Human Resources Development and Cooperation Plan, providing for joint Israeli-Palestinian workshops and seminars, and for the establishment of joint vocational training centers, research institutes and data banks.

10. An Environmental Protection Plan, providing for joint and/or coordinated measures in this sphere.

11. A program for developing coordination and cooperation in the field of communication and media.

12. Any other programs of mutual interest.

Annex IV: Protocol on Israeli-Palestinian Cooperation Concerning Regional Development Programs

1. The two sides will cooperate in the context of the multilateral peace efforts in promoting a Development Program for the region, including the West Bank and the Gaza Strip, to be initiated by the G-7. The parties will request the G-7 to seek the participation in this program of other interested states, such as members of the Organisation for Economic Cooperation and Development, regional Arab states and institutions, as well as members of the private sector.

2. The Development Program will consist of two elements:

    a. an Economic Development Program for the West Bank and the Gaza Strip.

    b. a Regional Economic Development Program:

        A. The Economic Development Program for the West Bank and the Gaza strip will consist of the following elements:

            1. A Social Rehabilitation Program, including a Housing and Construction Program.
            2. A Small and Medium Business Development Plan.
            3. An Infrastructure Development Program (water, electricity, transportation and communications, etc.)
            4. A Human Resources Plan.
            5. Other programs.

        B. The Regional Economic Development Program may consist of the following elements:

            1. The establishment of a Middle East Development Fund, as a first step, and a Middle East Development Bank, as a second step.
            2. The development of a joint Israeli-Palestinian-Jordanian Plan for coordinated exploitation of the Dead Sea area.
            3. The Mediterranean Sea (Gaza)–Dead Sea Canal.

4. Regional Desalinization and other water development projects.
   5. A regional plan for agricultural development, including a coordinated regional effort for the prevention of desertification.
   6. Interconnection of electricity grids.
   7. Regional cooperation for the transfer, distribution and industrial exploitation of gas, oil and other energy resources.
   8. A Regional Tourism, Transportation and Telecommunications Development Plan.
   9. Regional cooperation in other spheres.
3. The two sides will encourage the multilateral working groups, and will coordinate towards their success. The two parties will encourage intersessional activities, as well as pre-feasibility and feasibility studies, within the various multilateral working groups.

Agreed Minutes to the Declaration of Principles on Interim Self-Government Arrangements

A. General Understandings and Agreements

Any powers and responsibilities transferred to the Palestinians pursuant to the Declaration of Principles prior to the inauguration of the Council will be subject to the same principles pertaining to Article IV, as set out in these Agreed Minutes below.

B. Specific Understandings and Agreements

Article IV
It is understood that:

1. Jurisdiction of the Council will cover West Bank and Gaza Strip territory, except for issues that will be negotiated in the permanent status negotiations: Jerusalem, settlements, military locations, and Israelis.
2. The Council's jurisdiction will apply with regard to the agreed powers, responsibilities, spheres and authorities transferred to it.

Article VI (2)
It is agreed that the transfer of authority will be as follows:

1. The Palestinian side will inform the Israeli side of the names of the authorised Palestinians who will assume the powers, authorities and responsibilities that will be transferred to the Palestinians according to the Declaration of Principles in the

continues on page 288

continued from page 287

following fields: education and culture, health, social welfare, direct taxation, tourism, and any other authorities agreed upon.
2. It is understood that the rights and obligations of these offices will not be affected.
3. Each of the spheres described above will continue to enjoy existing budgetary allocations in accordance with arrangements to be mutually agreed upon. These arrangements also will provide for the necessary adjustments required in order to take into account the taxes collected by the direct taxation office.
4. Upon the execution of the Declaration of Principles, the Israeli and Palestinian delegations will immediately commence negotiations on a detailed plan for the transfer of authority on the above offices in accordance with the above understandings.

Article VII (2)
The Interim Agreement will also include arrangements for coordination and cooperation.

Article VII (5)
The withdrawal of the military government will not prevent Israel from exercising the powers and responsibilities not transferred to the Council.

Article VIII
It is understood that the Interim Agreement will include arrangements for cooperation and coordination between the two parties in this regard. It is also agreed that the transfer of powers and responsibilities to the Palestinian police will be accomplished in a phased manner, as agreed in the Interim Agreement.

Article X
It is agreed that, upon the entry into force of the Declaration of Principles, the Israeli and Palestinian delegations will exchange the names of the individuals designated by them as members of the Joint Israeli-Palestinian Liaison Committee.

It is further agreed that each side will have an equal number of members in the Joint Committee. The Joint Committee will reach decisions by agreement. The Joint Committee may add other technicians and experts, as necessary. The Joint Committee will decide on the frequency and place or places of its meetings.

Annex II
It is understood that, subsequent to the Israeli withdrawal, Israel will continue to be responsible for external security, and for internal security and public order of settlements and Israelis. Israeli military forces and civilians may continue to use roads freely within the Gaza Strip and the Jericho area.

GLOSSARY

Al Waqf land: land that belonged to the religious foundations

Basic Law: a code of law that was supposed to be created by the governing authority to replace the Israeli law

Marshall Plan: the US effort after World War II to rebuild Europe

permanent status: the achievement of independent statehood

Ra'ees: a chief or leader, used to signify those who lead the Executive Authority

Document Analysis

Oslo I, in 1993, started the process toward creation of an independent Palestinian state (or was supposed to have). This is essentially what was hailed as the Oslo Accords, with less attention being paid to the second installment of agreements two years later. The first part of the first agreement notes that both parties wish to work toward peace and the implementation of U.N. Resolutions 242 and 338 (both of which sought a withdrawal of Israeli forces from territories occupied in 1967). The second part of Oslo I notes that there is supposed to be a five-year interim period during which both parties work toward implementation of the Oslo accords and iron out other details. The agreement also held that the Gaza Strip and West Bank, which are not physically connected, were to be one state for Palestinians. It goes on to identify the areas of government that would immediately be transferred, such as education, and those that would await transfer, such as a police force, even as the Palestinians begin preparing for such transfers (as by training a police force). The next part notes how the interim agreement is to start at once and how the Palestinians are expected to maintain a strong police force in order to establish order. The agreement then looks at liaisons that are planned to take place. Withdrawal of forces and resolutions of disputes complete the agreement. There is also, however, a six page annex that notes a number of points concerning cooperation.

The second agreement starts out with a preamble and thus is a bit more formal than the first. It notes that powers are to be transferred first to the Palestinian Authority and then to an elected council, and that only the powers specified are to be so transferred. After the council is established, the Israelis will be expected to withdraw. The second part of the second agreement deals with elections and notes that the people in Jerusalem are to be allowed to vote. It should be noted that the agreement treats Jerusalem as a separate area distinct from the West Bank, which partly surrounds it.

The agreement then notes that the council will be both legislative and executive in nature, thus resembling a parliamentary system in which the winning candidate picks members of the executive. The council would serve five years. Once an executive is picked, that executive could name up to sixteen people to serve on the council. The council would have open meetings, generally, would allow judicial review of its decisions, and could have committees. The council is given no power in the area of foreign relations other than in cultural affairs. The council is specifically banned from having embassies or making agreements with foreign powers—those things were left for future negotiations. The agreement specifies that Israeli military forces would be redeployed outside the areas covered by the agreement, and notes that such redeployment is to be accomplished within 18 months. The issue of land is noted, with the land being divided up into three parts—"A" "B" and "C"—with power in areas A and B being given first to the Palestinians along with limited power over area C. In the areas of police and security, the Israelis are supposed to be given power outside of the West Bank and Gaza Strip, with the Palestinian police being given power inside. The agreement describes the Palestinian police force that needs to be created as a "strong" one. One difference between areas A and B is that, in area A, police forces are to be allowed early on while in area B it would be delayed somewhat. The agreement also notes that confidence-building measures should be undertaken to ensure success. It describes how the council is to be given general powers over the area, except in the area C parts, which would be transferred generally. The agreement includes a set of articles noting how the Israelis and Palestinians are to work together to handle disagreements. It closes with a series of notes, including one about permanent status negotiation to begin in early 1996.

Essential Themes

The main theme here is that of peace and compromise after a period of extended conflict. The Oslo Accords essentially sought to exchange land (occupied by Israel) for peace. They gave the Palestinians some level of control over their land, particularly the Gaza Strip and parts of the West Bank, and expected the Palestinians to cease hostilities against Israel. However, over time, the people of both sides seem largely to have moved away from the agreements. Israel has dragged its feet on implementing the Oslo Accords, while the Palestinian Authority has been slow to oppose terrorism. More fatal to the agreement has been the rising power of Hamas among the Palestinians; for Hamas never agreed to the accords in the place. In 2006 Hamas gained power in the Gaza Strip, leading to retaliation and hostilities on both sides. For their part, voters in Israel have been unwilling to push the peace process forward, leading to administrations that are unwilling to expend effort in that direction and more inclined, in fact, to follow a hard line.

In Gaza, for example, a buffer zone has been imposed by Israel, which takes up much of Gaza's land (Gaza is only 141 square miles, about 25 miles long, and 6 miles wide). Israel's main concern here is stopping attacks from the region. Its main concern regarding the West Bank, in contrast, is land, where it has allowed Jewish settlers to take up residence. A sizable portion of what is now the West Bank has either already been taken up by Jewish settlements or eyed for future Jewish settlements. The question persists as to what is to be done regarding those areas. Some have suggested swapping land in the West Bank currently set up as Jewish settlements with land in Israel, but the details of that arrangement remain hazy and no concrete action has been taken. As for the Gaza Strip, the problem for Israel is how to force Hamas, which controls the area, to cease attacks. Israel continues to retaliate against such attacks, but that has not proved effective in any lasting way so far. Most recently, the US president, Donald Trump, has stated that the American Embassy is to be moved to West Jerusalem, a move that bolsters the hardliners inside Israel. Some observers have remarked that, as a result, the two-state solution is more threatened than it ever has been.

—*Scott A. Merriman*

Bibliography and Additional Reading

Brown, Nathan J. *Palestinian Politics after the Oslo Accords: Resuming Arab Palestine.* Berkeley: University of California Press, 2003.

Rosler, Nimrod. "Leadership and Peacemaking: Yitzhak Rabin and the Oslo Accords." *International Journal of Intercultural Relations*, vol. 54, 01 Sept. 2016, pp. 55–67.

Somdeep Sen, author. "'It's Nakba, Not a Party': Re-Stating the (Continued) Legacy of the Oslo Accords." *Arab Studies Quarterly*, no. 2, 2015, p. 161.

Watson, Geoffrey R. *The Oslo Accords: International Law and the Israeli-Palestinian Peace Agreements.* New York: Oxford University Press, 2000.

Yitzhak Rabin Speaks at Signing of the Oslo Accords (1993) Ca. 1993. [Place of publication not identified]: WPA Film Library, [1993], 2008. EBSCOhost